Beyond Sovereignty

An Inter-American Dialogue Book

Beyond Sovereignty

Collectively Defending Democracy in the Americas

Edited by Tom Farer

The Johns Hopkins University Press
Baltimore and London

© 1996 The Johns Hopkins University Press
All rights reserved. Published 1996
Printed in the United States of America on acid-free paper
05 04 03 02 01 00 99 98 97 96   5 4 3 2 1

The Johns Hopkins University Press
2715 North Charles Street
Baltimore, Maryland 21218-4319
The Johns Hopkins Press Ltd., London

Library of Congress Cataloging-in-Publication Data will be found
at the end of this book.
A catalog record for this book is available from the British Library.

ISBN 0-8018-5165-3
ISBN 0-8018-5166-1 (pbk.)

To Sandy Lomax, Marilyn Burrows,
Don Harville, and Phillip Martinez,
for One Reason Only: Friendship

Contents

Foreword

In June 1991, the General Assembly of the Organization of American States (OAS) approved Resolution 1080, which required the OAS to respond to violations of democratic process. Shortly thereafter the Inter-American Dialogue undertook to explore the intellectual and political tensions between the new hemispheric commitment to the collective defense of democracy and traditional notions of sovereignty. Tom Farer and Heraldo Muñoz were invited by the Dialogue to prepare a paper for our plenary meeting in early 1992 and then to pursue the issues by organizing a conference and commissioning the chapters in this volume. The volume is a mix of country case studies and detailed analyses of crosscutting issues. Together, they review the legal justifications for international action to defend democracy and human rights, to analyze the effectiveness of alternative approaches, and to assess their significance as precedents for future initiatives.

The authors of the volume offer several important conclusions. They agree that external actors can contribute significantly to the defense and enhancement of democracy, although they also emphasize that internal events are invariably more important and that the likelihood that external action will succeed is greatly enhanced by strong national institutions. It is also clear that support for international action to defend democracy and human rights—from electoral observation to economic embargoes—has increased dramatically, overriding the traditional claim that sovereignty shields domestic political processes from any external appraisal (much less action). The tolerance for external action dwindles in the case of unilateral action with a coercive character, however.

This volume is part of a continuing Dialogue effort to foster multilateral cooperation and democratic advance throughout the hemisphere. In early December 1993, the Inter-American Dialogue convened a working group specifically to explore the role of the OAS in advancing democracy and human rights and to identify ways that that capacity could be enhanced. This initiative resulted in the Dialogue publication, *Advancing Democracy and Human Rights in the Americas: What Role for the OAS?* (Washington, D.C.: May 1994). Starting with the same fundamental question that shaped the December conference, the Dialogue organized a commission to study and prepare a report of practical recommendations on how the OAS could most effectively advance human rights, democracy, and the rule of law in the Americas. The ten-member commission issued a report containing specific proposals for the OAS and its member states to consider: *The Organization of American States: Advancing Democracy, Human Rights, and the Rule of Law* (Washington, D.C.: Sept. 1994).

Overall, the Inter-American Dialogue's research and publications are designed to improve the quality of public debate and decision on key issues in Western Hemisphere affairs. The Dialogue is both a forum for sustained exchange among leaders and an independent, nonpartisan center for policy analysis on U.S.–Latin American economic and political relations. The Dialogue's hundred members—from the United States, Canada, Latin America, and the Caribbean—include former presidents and prominent political, business, labor, academic, media, military, and religious leaders. At periodic plenary sessions, members analyze key hemispheric issues and formulate recommendations for policy and action. The Dialogue presents its findings in comprehensive reports circulated throughout the Americas. Its research agenda focuses on four broad themes: democratic governance, inter-American cooperation, economic integration, and social equity.

The Inter-American Dialogue wishes to express its gratitude to the Arca Foundation and the United States Institute of Peace for their contribution to the preparation of this volume. We also are pleased to acknowledge the broader support that the Dialogue has obtained from the Ford, A. W. Mellon, and William and Flora Hewlett foundations and the Carnegie Corporation of New York. We are particularly grateful to Joan Caivano of the Inter-American Dialogue for her skilled management of this project.

Peter Hakim
President
Inter-American Dialogue

Acknowledgments

I am sensible of an unusually extensive intellectual and institutional indebtedness. This book culminates a project that began with an idea in the fertile mind of Richard Feinberg, then president of the Inter-American Dialogue—and now, one hopes, able to translate ideas into policy as senior director of Inter-American Affairs on the National Security Council.

Richard asked me and the eminent Chilean scholar-diplomat Heraldo Muñoz to collaborate on a working paper for a meeting of the Inter-American Dialogue. Richard and I believed that the issues identified in the Farer-Muñoz paper, issues that members of the Dialogue illuminated and refined in a lively discussion, could be explored adequately only though a collective effort, drawing on some of the best talent in the hemispheric community of scholars. Happily, we found that the scholars we contacted concurred with us on the policy relevance and intellectual virtue of the project. So we had no difficulty in assembling the team that produced this volume.

The volume is a collaborative effort, not only in the superficial sense of a plurality of authors but also in the deeper sense that we came together to review each other's drafts and to assist both in their enhancement and in their tight organization around the overarching question of how external actors can contribute to the promotion, consolidation, and defense of democratic regimes.

All of the authors are *distinguidos* in their respective fields, with ample grounds for well-developed egos. Yet I have rarely found a group of writers so open to suggestion from each other, from members of the Dialogue and staff who contributed formal and informal comments, and from this editor, whose stream of advice could readily have been seen as giving enlarged meaning to the word *copious*. Some were friends from the beginning. More surprisingly, perhaps, all were friends when we finished. Thanks to them, in spite of all the work involved, this project was also zestful intellectual play. I am very much in their debt both for making work a pleasure and for providing essays that are penetrating, enlightening, and original.

As I indicated above, the authors and I benefited greatly from the comments of Dialogue members and other interested persons. At the intimidating risk of omitting any of them, I would like to mention Mariclaire Acosta, Robert Pastor, Elliot Richardson, Viron P. Vaky, Richard Bloomfield, John

Graham, Carl Kaysen, William LeoGrande, Abraham Lowenthal, Ellen Lutz, Johanna Mendelson, Juan Méndez, Charles Nelson, Guillermo O'Donnell, Laura Reed, and Janet Shenk. Richard Feinberg's successor as president of the Dialogue, Peter Hakim, shared Richard's enthusiasm for the effort and maintained the strong institutional support needed to bring our work to a successful conclusion.

Projects of this size need financial as well as intellectual nourishment. There is no rhetorical excess in the statement that without the assistance of the Arca Foundation and the United States Institute of Peace this book could not have been completed.

After the project was on its way, Michael Shifter joined the Dialogue staff and became another enthusiastic supporter and adviser. His fertile mind and joie de vivre helped move us lightly over the occasional obstacle. Jorge Domínguez, one of our authors, also contributed more generally as a Dialogue member and, during a key period in our work, as the Dialogue's Visiting Fellow. He has very few peers in acuteness of perception, and I feel myself a fortunate beneficiary of his suggestions, including those about my introductory essay.

Two people whose friendship and wisdom I value greatly were in at the beginning but were deflected by the demands of their official positions from being with us at the end. I refer to Heraldo Muñoz, my original collaborator, and Luis Solís, former director of the Arias Foundation and now Costa Rica's special envoy to Central America. Luis was our choice to write the El Salvador chapter but was unable to complete it because of his appointment to the Foreign Ministry. We were, nevertheless, the beneficiaries of his profound understanding of how Central America—with the aid of various people, above all Oscar Arias, former President of Costa Rica—found its way from fratricidal war to the beginnings of what we all hope will be a permanent peace.

It is conventional to make reference to your most profound debt at the end of the Acknowledgments. In this respect, I choose to be conventional. From the inception of the project, Joan Caivano was my full partner in converting Richard Feinberg's idea into this volume. Anyone who has edited a volume knows that it represents a considerable challenge in logistics and intellectual coordination. The challenge is greater when your ambition is to achieve the degree of cohesion native to a single-authored volume and when you are attempting to produce a work that adds something valuable to the corpus of scholarship and, at the same time, contributes to the policy discourse of governments and other consequential actors. If we, the authors, have in some measure realized that ambition, Joan is preeminently responsible. I cannot thank her sufficiently. I can only express my admiration for her energy, her serenity, and her lucid intellect—and my thanks for her friendship.

Beyond Sovereignty

1 Collectively Defending Democracy in the Western Hemisphere

Introduction and Overview

Tom Farer

With almost all the countries of Latin America enjoying elected governments, it is easy to forget that, as recently as the early 1980s, such governments appeared to be an endangered species. Generals reigned not only in such a traditional purlieu of authoritarian rule as Guatemala but also in Chile and Uruguay, which had for decades been Latin paragons of elected regimes, and in Argentina and Brazil, which had long oscillated between elected civilian and putschist governments. Where men in uniform did not themselves rule, as in Duvalier's Haiti, they often served as the guarantors of thugs in suits.

It was not simply the ubiquity of authoritarian government that flattened the hopes of democrats throughout the hemisphere. Beyond ubiquity, there was the appearance of longevity. Previously during the twentieth century military interventions, particularly in the hemisphere's more economically developed countries, had been heralded as brief interruptions in constitutional government induced by an emergency beyond the coping capacity of elected officials. The intervenors of the 1960s and 1970s adopted a very different stance. They had come, they seemed to say, not to rescue but to suspend indefinitely both elected regimes and the frequent companions of such regimes, freedom of speech and freedom of association. Uninhibited by the dysfunctional constraints of electoral and constitutional government, they would proceed methodically to heal a feverish national society by cauterizing its leftist infections and enclosing it in a new political economy. This was, the officers implied, a project of indefinite duration. Organized, disciplined, and determined, supported by their own arms and key segments of the middle and upper classes, they would not be hurried. They had come to stay.

Social scientists labeled this phenomenon "bureaucratic authoritarianism."[1] They sought through this rubric to capture the mass and heft, the novelty, and the apparent durability of this new way of governing Latin states. For just as it was not the transient interruption of constitutional government familiar to some Latin polities, neither was it a dressed-up version of the parasitic military dictatorships without ideas (government as looting) that had been an equally familiar feature of the Latin political scene since independence. No, this was government by a military institution staffed by a comparatively well-educated generation of officers and imbued with the economic ideas of Milton Friedman and, in many cases—ironically—with the social ideas of the antimodernist popes.[2] These military regimes were backed by important elements of the middle and upper classes, which had lost whatever faith they had ever had in other political and economic nostrums. Certain social scientists contributed unwillingly to this impression of a stolid, faceless, irresistible force occupying Latin America by discovering its source in a kind of iron law of development for capitalist states on the periphery of the global economy.[3]

The Democratic Renaissance in Latin America

Rarely have scholars so enjoyed a demonstration of their fallibility: their predicted long night of bureaucratic military rule has turned out to be simply an eclipse. Civilian governments, chosen through sometimes flawed but not fraudulent electoral processes, have moved in fifteen years from anomaly to norm. As David Scott Palmer notes in this volume in his chapter on Peru (chap. 11), between 1978 and 1991, "no fewer than fifteen of the twenty countries returned to or established elected civilian government after experiencing one form or another of authoritarian rule." In addition, during this period, the Latin countries were the site of fewer *golpes de estado* than in any previous decade since the wars of independence, and of the total of seven (in just four countries), four were carried out by military forces "to open up the political process to democratic elections." Finally, and most vividly underscoring the unprecedented depth of the democratic wave, of the thirty-plus national elections held between 1978 and 1992 in the fifteen countries that had been under authoritarian rule, eleven were the second consecutive presidential election and five were the third or fourth; approximately three-fourths of these second, third, or fourth elections were won by opposition parties.

That is the good news. The bad news is that, as Larry Diamond points out in chapter 3 of this volume, while the citizens of almost every Latin country now enjoy the experience of rule by elected governments, the inhabitants of only about half of those countries concomitantly enjoy the experience of living in a democracy. Democracy, to be sure, is a matter of definition, and even within any widely accepted definition, democracy is a matter of degree. But these days, virtually no one claims that holding periodic elections for a head of state and a legislative assembly suffices to earn the name. There is, on the contrary, broad agreement among partisans of the democratic cause that, as Diamond points out, we must look beyond formal constitutional structure to ask questions such as the following:

> Are elections truly free, fair, and competitive? Does the opposition have a realistic chance of increasing its support and eventually gaining power? Is power effectively exercised by elected officials and their appointees, or do democratically unaccountable officials—the military, local bosses, and landed elites—constrain, veto, and undermine the constitutional flows of power and the rule of law? Do citizens have the ability to elect their own leaders at the local and regional level? Are basic freedoms of expression, organization, assembly, movement, conscience, and due process well respected in practice? Do citizens have the freedom to criticize, oppose, and mobilize around their interests and beliefs without fear of punishment, either by the state or powerful private interests?

Consistent with these interrogations, Diamond, together with Juan Linz and Seymour Martin Lipset, urges a distinction between democracies and "semidemocracies," the latter being regimes in which "the effective power of elected officials is so limited, or political party competition is so restricted, or the freedom and fairness of elections so compromised that electoral outcomes, while competitive, still deviate significantly from popular preferences; and/or where civil and political liberties are so limited that some political orientations and interests are unable to organize and express themselves."[4]

Conceding that "there has been tremendous democratic progress in Latin America and the Caribbean over the past decade," Diamond nevertheless concludes that only eleven of the twenty-two Latin countries fall within the democratic category, and of the eleven, as many as six are much closer in character to semidemocracies than to the fully institutionalized democracies of North America and Western Europe. While other analysts might be more generous in their labeling, virtually all serious observers of Latin American political systems recognize that, with very few exceptions, Latin America's formal democracies fail in significant measure (1) to deliver a high level of protection for civil liberties, (2) to guarantee the rule of law, and (3) to provide all sectors of the society a reasonable opportunity to participate in the formation and implementation of public policy. Inevitably feeding on themselves, chronic performance failures underscore (and help to explain) the fragility of the 1980s democratic trend.

This Study

Concern over democracy's uncertain prospects inspired the project that culminates in this volume. Two assumptions shaped the collective effort of its contributors: one, that external actors can contribute to the defense and enhancement of democracy, and two, that tolerance for such external action has increased dramatically—even measures that would once have been widely condemned as impermissible intervention are acquiring a remarkable aura of legitimacy. An increase in tolerance is least marked, however, for unilateral action of a coercive nature, which in the Western Hemisphere usually means action that the United States has taken on its own initiative.

To reflect that fact, along with the increasing reluctance on the part of the United States to act alone, this volume concentrates on initiatives by institutions other than national governments, although it does contain diagnoses and prescriptions relevant to the policy choices of governments. It is a closely integrated, collective effort to record (and thereby to consolidate and reinforce) precedents for the defense of democracy, but primarily it is an effort to ascertain what measures are most likely to work under different sets of conditions.

The central part of the book falls into two sections. The first reviews the past efforts and the present capacity of various external actors—the United Nations, the Organization of American States, the international financial institutions, and the transnational networks of nongovernmental organizations—to contribute to the defense and deepening of democracy. The second section consists of case studies. Four case studies (of Chile, El Salvador, Haiti, and Peru) are in large measure retrospective, focusing on the role external actors played or might have played in advancing or failing to advance democratic development. Case studies of Cuba and Mexico look to the future, illustrating how we might apply lessons drawn from the cases and from institutional studies to influence prospective transitions: in the case of Mexico, from semidemocracy to full democracy; in the case of Cuba, from a disintegrating totalitarian regime to an incipiently democratic regime.

The premise is that, although external action is not often decisive, the credible threat of externally imposed economic or military sanctions can give an incipient democracy breathing space or can facilitate its restoration after a coup.[5] And external action can protect deeply rooted democracies from blows orchestrated by hostile foreign leaders even if delivered in part by indigenous hands. Haiti and possibly one or two Central American states fall into the first category. Within the hemisphere, perhaps only the small Anglophonic Caribbean island states fall into the second category. Such local factors as adroit and enlightened national leadership, societal collective learning, the capacity of local elites to imagine means other than repression for protecting their interests, and changes in social structures and in the way the national economy links with the international economy are important proximate causes of democratic consolidation and deepening. Their incidence, in turn, is doubtless related to global economic opportunity and other contextual variables that even the most powerful states find difficult to influence, much less to control.

That said, nothing in the case studies subverts the conviction all of us began with—that external action wisely conceived and sensitively executed can do much to advance the democratic agenda. The possibility of effective external action has been widened by a growing tolerance for measures, from electoral observation to economic embargoes, that would once have been indicted by key Latin elites on grounds of principle, if no other. This widened tolerance, if not active enthusiasm, for collective action represents a new and very great retreat from the original and intrinsically flawed idea of sovereignty as unbounded national will, a retreat made inevitable by the contradictory interests of the governing elites, who irrespective of their will form a loose but still recognizable regional political system.

The Shrinking of Sovereignty's Prerogatives

From its beginning in the seventeenth century, the claim of territorial sovereigns to a plenary, unreviewable discretion collided with the reality of interaction and interdependence. The reduced cost of transportation, the printing press, the spread of literacy and learning, the growing administrative capacity of governments and the consequent spread of public order, the development of markets and banking, the increase in the division of labor all conspired to accelerate the movement of people, property, and ideas across frontiers. Since a sovereign unit included not only the land but also the people who normally inhabited and identified with it,[6] and since protection of people was the reciprocal for their loyalty, states (at least those—

primarily European—states who were then the principal architects of international law) gradually conceded to each other a right of protection over "nationals" traveling, living, or doing business abroad. The Law of State Responsibility, as the incrementally elaborated norms of fair treatment came to be called, was a formal limitation on the supposed plenary discretion of sovereigns, one made inevitable by the location of these independent political units in a system in which the actions of one within its territory became increasingly consequential for the interests of others.[7]

While the practical necessities of interdependence eroded sovereignty from one side, the reality of power differentials hammered it from the other. Yes, all sovereign units enjoyed an equal discretion to formulate, implement, and determine the circumference of public policy. But among the matters with respect to which they could exercise a discretionary judgment was the use of force.[8] And so one formally equal sovereign could decide, free of legal stigma, to plunder, truncate, or wholly absorb another sovereign. Each being free to terminate wholly the life, and hence the sovereignty, of all others, a sovereign's theoretically free will was in practice constrained by the imperative of survival.

In condemning the leaders of Nazi Germany for the crime of aggressive war and rejecting their defense that each state was the only judge of its strategic necessities, the Nuremberg tribunal declared a formal end to this ancient de facto limitation on sovereignty, a limitation, however, intrinsic to the conception of sovereignty in a universe of multiple sovereigns.[9] In other words, the determination that a state was not free to use force or the threat thereof to promote its interests or vindicate its rights (including its legal rights) was itself a limitation on sovereignty.

The two postwar charters appeared to confirm this result. Article 2 (4) of the 1945 United Nations Charter prohibited the threat or use of force against the political independence or territorial integrity of any state or for any other purpose inconsistent with the principles of the charter; Article 51 recognized a single exception for "individual or collective self-defense" against an armed attack. In Chapter VII the drafters provided a mechanism for collective response to acts of aggression.

Article 9 of the Organization of American States Charter announces that states "enjoy equal rights and equal capacity to exercise these rights" and that the "rights of each State depend not upon its power to ensure the exercise thereof, but upon the mere fact of its existence as a person under international law." Article 20 declares that the territory of a state "may not be the object, even temporarily, of military occupation or of other measures of force taken by another State, directly or indirectly, on any grounds whatever." In Articles 18 and 19, the OAS Charter purports to go further still in outlawing the use of power differentials by one sovereign to constrain the discretion of another:

> No state or group of States has the right to intervene, directly or indirectly, for any reason whatever, in the internal affairs of any other State. The foregoing principle prohibits not only armed force but also any other form of interference or attempted threat against the personality of the State or against its political, economic, and cultural elements. (Art. 18)

> No State may use or encourage the use of coercive measures of an economic or political character in order to force the sovereign will of another State and obtain from it advantages of any kind. (Art. 19)

While attempting, through the charters, to eliminate one traditional restraint on their discretion (thereby, as noted above, accepting its obverse), national governments coincidentally narrowed the range of issues on which an unfettered discretion could be exercised. They narrowed their discretion by means of obligations respecting human rights possessing an organic capacity for growth. In so doing, they were once again generalizing the mandate of the Nuremberg tribunal. Aggressive war was only one of three declared international crimes at the tribunal. "Crimes against humanity" was included so that the Nazis could be punished for crimes against their own nationals as well as the nationals of the countries they had occupied. Gross abuse of the citizens of occupied territories had previously been proscribed by the humanitarian law of war, but until World War II, the right of each equal sovereign to be monstrous to his or her own nationals was only occasionally questioned.[10]

Nuremberg thus marked a revolution in international jurisprudence. Previously in international law, individuals were regarded only as symbolic representatives or capital assets of their states. The Nuremberg tribunal transformed individuals from mere objects of the state to subjects having rights they could assert against their own states. Those states (and the individuals who acted on their behalf) bore corresponding obligations.

In this respect as well, the charters confirmed the Nuremberg mandate. The members of the united Nations "pledge themselves" in Articles 55 and 56 of the charter to take "joint and separate action in co-operation with the OAS for the achievement of . . . universal respect for . . . human rights and fundamental freedoms for all." Despite their apprehensions about intervention, states of the Americas "reaffirm" in the OAS Charter's opening statement of principles that "social justice and social security are bases of lasting peace" and "proclaim the fundamental rights of the individual without distinction as to race, nationality, creed, or sex."

The chapters by Fernando Tesón and Domingo Acevedo and Claudio

Grossman (chaps. 2 and 5) document a gathering Western Hemisphere consensus supporting international action to safeguard the effective exercise of popular will.[11] This consensus, which overwhelms the traditional claim that sovereignty shields domestic political processes from any external appraisal (much less action), constitutes accepting in practice a link between hemispheric peace and democratic government that was long ago declared in theory. In the preamble to the charter, which was adopted at the close of World War II, OAS member states recognize the right to participation as the linchpin of inter-American relations: "The obligation of mutual assistance and common defense of the American Republics is essentially related to their democratic ideals."

Democracy and Hemispheric Security

On balance, recent studies tend to reinforce the intuition that informed at least the most influential founders of the OAS, namely that the mutual possession of authentically democratic political orders reduces the security dilemmas of states and correspondingly enhances their capacity for cooperation.[12] Some scholars conclude on the basis of their reading of the historical record that authentic democracies have never fought each other. Others, perhaps employing slightly different definitions of democracy (or of fighting), demur from that sweeping generalization while agreeing that armed conflict between democratically elected regimes is exceptional.

To be sure, the sample is very small by historic standards. Democratic government did not become the norm even in Western Europe and the Western Hemisphere until very recently. As late as 1914, two of the five Great Powers in Europe were autocracies. A third, Germany, was at best only partially democratic. While Germany had an elected parliament with authority to reject budgets, executive power lay in the hands of the Kaiser and his ministers, who required only the confidence of the Kaiser to remain in office.[13] Being independent of Parliament, ministers could and did conduct foreign policy without need or inclination to consult the electorate's representatives. The very limited scope of their power to influence, much less to determine, the policy of the German state, particularly in matters involving foreign policy, leaves the Kaiser's Germany outside the scope of all but the most whimsical definition of democracy. What was true of Central and Western Europe until 1945, namely a mixture of authoritarian and democratic regimes, with several of the latter under pressure from an opposition disloyal to the democratic ideal, was true of Latin America until the mid-1980s.

The limited opportunity to test the Kantian hypothesis about relations among democratic states is only one weakness of the empirical case for its truth. The other is the availability of alternative explanations for the examples of sustained peaceful relations. For instance, the post–World War II peace between France and Great Britain, on the one hand, and Germany, on the other, can be plausibly explained by reference both to the intimidating power of nuclear weapons and the logic of bipolarity in the globe's political structure.[14] The coincident existence of democratic government in all the West European states may be exactly that: coincidence.

But while the empirical evidence is inconclusive, the theoretical case is fairly persuasive. By their nature, democracies are incomparably more transparent than autocracies. They can observe each other's budgets, industrial practices, political debates, and popular sentiments. Claims of building and deploying forces for purely defensive purposes are therefore subject to substantial verification. Authentic democracies, moreover, have political institutions that are undergirded by legitimacy and that are shaped to accommodate the competing demands of diverse social forces. Hence, democracies normally have fewer incentives than authoritarian regimes to promote a belligerent hypernationalism and to demonize other states, measures employed by some authoritarian governments to deflect internal pressures for change and to increase their legitimacy.[15] In addition, governments experience ideological constraints on aggressive impulses when they confront other democracies, because democracies owe their legitimacy to the principle of popular self-determination. Hence, when one attempts to impose its will upon the other, the aggressor violates the very principle on which his own claim to govern rests.

Thus there is a plausible basis for claiming that the overthrow of a democratic government threatens regional peace and security. To be sure, the threat may not become concrete for some time. But even in the short term, it can compel neighboring democracies to shift a slice of government revenue into nonproductive military expenditures, with consequent aggravation of social tensions. Moreover, as the United States can attest from its experience with the claims of Haitians to refugee status, the overthrow of an elected government and the effort to rule without electoral legitimacy can send people spilling across national frontiers in search of safety and hope. This process, however, can sometimes impair their neighbors' "security," in the wider sense that term has acquired over the past several decades.[16]

Sovereignty and Democracy during the Cold War

By rooting their alliance in a supposedly shared democratic ideology and linking democracy with mutual security, the founding governments of the

OAS committed themselves to a profound ambivalence, for they included in their ranks authoritarian regimes (for instance, that of the Somoza family in Nicaragua, of the Institutional Revolution Party in Mexico, and of Juan Perón in Argentina) for whom elections were a transparent facade. The ambivalence would have been less severe if the founders had acted with a cynical wink and nod to each other—if, in other words, everyone had understood that the reference to democracy was entirely cosmetic, a bone for liberals generally and the U.S. public in particular. But in fact all of Latin America has a republican tradition. And while that tradition has not possessed the ideological hegemony among all classes all of the time that the idea of representative government has had in the United States, in almost all countries it has been strong enough to make dictatorial governments appear aberrational.[17] The regular schedule of elections most of these countries attempted to maintain testifies to that strength.

Ambivalence stemmed as well from the history of U.S. intervention in Latin states in the name of promoting democratic values. Linking democracy and security threatened to provide the hemispheric superpower with a normative fig leaf for the pursuit of parochial ends by essentially unilateral means. Latin governments had to wager that providing the United States with a multilateral alternative would enable them simultaneously to soften the thrust of U.S. power and to harness it for the shared ends of collective security and economic development.[18]

In navigating during the World War II era between the claims of nonintervention, on the one hand, and human rights and democracy, on the other, hemispheric leaders were obviously affected by the current of the Cold War. Sometimes it pushed them off course to the point of undermining rather than reinforcing democratic regimes. Perhaps the most glaring case was Guatemala in 1954, where, operating under the normative cloak of an OAS resolution declaring Marxist regimes a threat to peace and security, the United States orchestrated the overthrow of that country's democratically elected government.[19]

Five years later, however, the OAS aligned practice with text by moving against one of the hemisphere's most enduring and vicious dictators, Rafael Trujillo in the Dominican Republic. Responding to evidence of Trujillo's involvement in a plot against the government of Venezuela, the OAS General Assembly called for an economic boycott.[20] The boycott, strongly supported by the United States, may have helped to splinter Trujillo's regime. In any event, a group of his officers, allegedly with the encouragement of the United States, succeeded in assassinating him.

During the next two decades precedents for collective action in defense of democracy and human rights were few. On the whole, the effects of collective action were problematic, with one exception, namely the establishment in 1959 of the Inter-American Commission on Human Rights. In the early 1970s, as authoritarian regimes began sprouting like poisonous mushrooms all over the hemisphere, the commission moved slowly at first then with gathering speed to expose and publicize human rights delinquencies. Enumerating in vivid detail the terrorist methods of many governments, the commission regularly reaffirmed the founding liberal democratic premises of the OAS at a time when they seemed at odds with the convictions, hardly less than the practices, of many member state governments.[21]

Generally, states sought to conceal violations, but this tactic could hardly suffice when they were charged with failure to honor the right to political participation. By repeatedly urging, albeit in general terms, that target states comply with commission recommendations, the OAS General Assembly in 1977 and 1978 implicitly endorsed the commission's insistence that the right requires states to hold periodic and fair elections.[22] Implicit endorsement came as well from some of the culprits. Rather than consistently challenging the commission's jurisdiction, they often claimed either that the failure to hold elections was a temporary and constitutionally legitimate expedient adopted to cope with a national emergency or that they were in the process of constructing an authentic democracy in place of a merely formal one.[23]

Aside from providing the commission with funds and rhetorical endorsement, the political organs of the OAS watched the struggle for democratic governance (and human rights, generally) from the sidelines until 1979, when there erupted a revolutionary struggle to unseat the hemisphere's longest running family dictatorship, the Somozas of Nicaragua.[24] Then, as Acevedo and Grossman describe in chapter 5, the OAS accepted for the first time outside the Cold War context the full operational implications of the charter's linking of democracy with security by calling for the end of autocratic rule and the installation of a democratic government.

Somoza's defeat did not, of course, end Nicaragua's unhappy role as a catalyst for collective action in defense of democracy. The breakup of the anti-Somoza coalition and the repolarization of society, the Reagan administration's organization of the contras and the consequent escalation of tension between Nicaragua and its immediate neighbors, and the Contadora group's effort to restrain U.S. intervention, all these events are sufficiently fresh that they need not be elaborately recalled here.[25] To sketch the changing normative landscape of international action in defense of democracy, it suffices to revisit the endgame.

Retrospection only heightens the singular profile of a plan for tranquilliz-ing the isthmus that was urged on Central American heads of state (and on more distant actors) by Oscar Arias, president of Costa Rica. In the spirit of the old orthodoxy, Arias could have called for the policing of the several countries' borders by an international force, which would thus contain any civil conflict within its national envelope. The genius of the Arias plan consisted of three central propositions. First, the plan recognized that peace and security in Central America were inseparable from peace and security within the isthmus's national units. Second, it acknowledged that democratic government and human rights were the necessary conditions of domestic peace. Finally, the plan emphasized that collective, extraregional involvement was essential to the establishment of national and regional peace. In the mid-twentieth century, these propositions would doubtless have seemed incompatible with the prerogatives of sovereignty; in the late twentieth century, however, they were seen as merely statements of fact. By translating the plan into the Esquipulas Agreement, the nations of Central America drew the necessary legal conclusions.[26]

The agreement, itself a very important legal precedent, was powerfully reinforced by the steps taken to put flesh on its verbal bones, steps that also foreshadowed some of the practical means to facilitate the transition to— or the consolidation of—democracy. While discussions between govern-ments and their opponents began more or less simultaneously in all the concerned states, Nicaragua was the first venue for the behavioral transla-tion of the Esquipulas principles. The United Nations and the Organiza-tion of American States, collaborating in peacemaking for the first time, mediated an agreement on cease-fire and on the conditions for a general election in which all opposition elements could compete with the Sandi-nista government. With that government's approval, the OAS's truce and election monitors spread throughout the country to encourage compli-ance. The government also facilitated the presence and active involvement of various nongovernmental organizations, most notably the Council of Freely Elected Heads of Government chaired by Jimmy Carter.[27]

The initial result was a remarkable, peaceful transition from a tough leftist-nationalist regime to one of the center-right, a change that brought to a close large-scale violence within Nicaragua, ended the tension be-tween it and its neighbors, reduced the polarization of political forces in Honduras, and helped propel a movement toward peace within El Sal-vador. The end result? Well, of course, history goes on; a country with Nicaragua's sad history of class, regional and family division, and foreign intervention and its legacy of public and private poverty cannot easily enter the paradise of liberal democracy. Diamond ranks it as a restrictive semi-democracy. However much remains to be done, Nicaragua nevertheless exemplifies the crucial role the UN and the OAS can play in the resolution of internal conflicts by bridging the communications gap between belligerents, by presenting ideas for settlement (so the antagonists can avoid appearing weak by, themselves, proposing ways of ending the conflict), and by providing an impartial executor and monitor for the settlement agreement.

Substantial though it was, international participation in the Nicaraguan settlement seems slight against the backdrop of the Salvadoran accords adopted by the Salvadoran government and the Farabundo Martí Liberation Front (FMLN) over the period July 1991 to January of 1992.[28] Having served as broker in the long, intense negotiations that finally produced this remarkable agreement, the United Nations has accepted an integral responsibility for its execution. Acting pursuant to Security Council authorization, the secretary-general deployed personnel throughout the country to monitor and facilitate compliance with the terms of a settlement that calls for the radical reconstruction of the society's political and bureaucratic institutions. In addition to verification, the UN Observer Mission in El Salvador, ONUSAL, was granted extraordinary operational authority. For instance, armed forces and FMLN troop movement outside areas of concentration designated in the accords required prior ONUSAL consent.

Diamond, using the Freedom House scoring system, which integrates separate scores for political rights and civil liberties, labels the result a competitive semidemocracy, a category one step higher than the one El Salvador achieved in 1987 and in which he now places Nicaragua. It remains to be seen whether El Salvador will continue on its meliorative trajectory in the wake of the March 1994 elections and the withdrawal of UN observers scheduled for 1995. Sporadic death squad assaults on former guerrilla leaders, primarily in the period preceding the election, are among the reasons why optimism is restrained.

In terms of the evolution of a hemispheric consensus favoring international action for the defense and promotion of democracy, Panama is another signpost, albeit not an entirely unambiguous one. Whatever pressures drove the Nicaraguan and Salvadoran governments to solicit international involvement in their domestic dramas, the solicitation was still voluntary—as that term is employed in the practice of states. (Pressure is, after all, an endemic feature of statecraft, even among states whose fundamental relationship is cooperative.) Hence, if not peacekeeping in conventional United Nations parlance, the UN and OAS roles in those two countries are closely analogous.[29]

By contrast, the OAS responded to Manuel Noriega's de facto nullification of the internationally monitored election of 1989 by means of a formal condemnation.[30] The condemnation of Noriega came close to licensing at least some form of coercion but finally flinched at the threshold of force. A majority of member states no doubt feared U.S. intervention if the OAS declared Noriega's continuance in power to be a threat to the peace and security of the hemisphere. Sensing that the United States would press for authorization to use force, the member states did not want to give the United States an opening to construe the jurisdictional finding as authorization enough. The irony, of course, is that, by rejecting collective action, they lost an opportunity to dictate the timing, the dimensions, and the goals of the intervention and to more deeply enmesh the United States in collective decisionmaking.[31] There is no reason to doubt that the United States, having sought collective action, would have paid this price to obtain it.

The Santiago Declaration

Even though U.S. troops quickly transferred power to the previously elected government and withdrew, a large OAS majority condemned the intervention.[32] The states comprising that majority might have regarded Panama as a sign of the way collective efforts to defend democracy could spin out of control and therefore have demanded a halt in the movement toward collectively defending democracy. Instead, at the twenty-first regular session of the OAS General Assembly held in Santiago in June 1991, they joined the United States in codifying the multiplying precedents for international action on behalf of democracy and human rights and in translating a rhetorical preference for democracy into a commitment to act on its behalf.[33]

Stating the rationale for their decision to meet immediately and consider concrete countermeasures in the event of any suspension of the democratic political process, the member states invoked the preamble to the charter as establishing the premise "that representative democracy is an indispensable condition for the stability, peace, and development of the region" and affirmed the necessity, in light of "the widespread existence of democratic governments in the hemisphere," to make the charter premise "operative."

Why did the OAS countries take this major initiative for the protection of representative democracy? Surely, as suggested earlier, it had something to do with the end of the Cold War, which sharply reduced the risk that resolutions endorsing hemispheric action on behalf of democracy would be treated as licenses for the pursuit of political ends related only loosely (if at all) to the consolidation and preservation of representative government. In addition, almost all of the governments endorsing the Santiago Declaration were the product of competitive elections, and a substantial number of them presided over states in which more-or-less democratic governments had for years been alternating with authoritarian ones. Relatively confident about their own legitimacy, these member states shared a powerful interest in building barriers against another reversal of democratic fortunes. Would that interest carry them beyond the threshold where they had halted in the face of Manuel Noriega's obduracy?

If, following the Declaration of Santiago, the OAS foreign ministers had sought the ideal case for demonstrating the seriousness of their commitment to democracy, they could have found the following scenario not far away:

—A weak, incompetent, unpopular, and marvelously brutal military institution overthrows and attempts to murder a president who had received two-thirds of the popular vote in an election certified as fair by official monitors of the OAS, the UN, and reliable nongovernmental institutions, a man who according to informed observers continues to enjoy overwhelming popularity.

—The president escapes and appeals to the OAS for assistance in restoring democratic rule.

—Meanwhile, the armed forces engage in an orgy of violence against supporters of the president.

—To escape the pitiless repression and the worsening conditions of life generally, large numbers of people attempt to flee the country.

—The surge of emigrants threatens to aggravate economic strains and social tensions in the state they attempt to enter, so the coup has external consequences that are material as well as psychological.

They would, in other words, have found Haiti.[34]

If it was not clear at the outset of the OAS effort, it was clear soon enough that the porous sanctions adopted (and possibly any sanctions short of a blockade by land and sea) would fail to restore the status quo. The tougher sanctions subsequently imposed by the UN as enforcement measures under Chapter VII also failed predictably.[35] Certain things were clear from the very outset of this drama: that a U.S.-led force, operating under OAS aegis, could brush aside the Haitian military if it chose to resist but that sanctions would immediately increase the country's misery index;[36] and that even if the Haitian military ever agreed to the return of Aristide, he would rule under constant threat of assassination or coup unless that military institution were disarmed and disbanded or at least reduced and subordinated to the control of a patently superior military force. In short, it was clear that armed intervention was by far the most likely way to give democracy a fighting chance in Haiti and that not only were all alternatives likely to fail but, in the process of failing, they would extract a frightful toll from the Haitian people.

Looking back now on an exercise in collective diplomacy that, up to the very eve of the U.S. intervention under UN auspices, fused farce and failure, it is clear that support had been thin in Washington and the rest of the United States and absent in most Latin states for the use of force even to restore democracy—even where its overthrow was followed by gross violation of fundamental human rights and conspicuous disdain for the pleas of the OAS.

What Is to Be Done?

The Use of Force

Haiti no doubt distorted the use-of-force issue, making the prolonged refusal to threaten, much less employ, force appear more consequential for the protection of democracy than it is, even if opposition to its use softens. Let us suppose that the OAS formally resolved that, in the event of a threat to, or an actual interruption of, constitutional government, member states would consult about appropriate measures up to and including the use of force. Despite the ultimate decision of a U.S. president—incrementally committed by rhetoric and inertia—to dispatch troops to Haiti, such a general OAS resolution would not, I am confident, induce high expectations that force would in fact be employed, other than in the event of a sanguinary coup by a tiny force in a Caribbean island state—if then. Force is likely to be an option only where the United States is prepared to assume the main burden of employing it.

In Haiti, where the refugee problem and the sympathy of African American political leaders for President Aristide provided significant domestic incentives for action, even a Democratic administration reached the decision to invade only after the logic of events and prior positions overwhelmed a patent reluctance to act. And, if the administration is to be taken at its word, it would not have acted without UN Security Council authorization, authorization that will remain dependent on U.S. relations with Russia and China. So it is hard to see Haiti as an augury of future U.S.

action if intervention were proposed for any sizable Latin country, where, unlike Haiti, putschists in the armed forces could mount serious resistance.

The prospect of immediate armed resistance is, of course, only one element in the calculus of costs. The prospective duration of the intervention is another. Now that more-or-less free elections have become a criterion of legitimacy even among those previously uncommitted or hostile to democracy, a successful coup is likely to reflect deep social pathologies or grave sins of omission or commission by top elected officials. Under those circumstances, the beleaguered or displaced government may well require for its survival a sustained international presence. Not only may such an intervention generate costs far greater than those incurred on initial entry, the intervening force, by shielding the regime, may encourage it to persist in the behavior that eroded its electoral mandate.

The authors in this volume who address the question agree that the depth, authenticity, and solidity of any democracy is largely a function of the vitality of its civil society and the extent to which its procedures have been internalized by, and become routine for, political actors. Such deepening obviously occurs through means and in forms peculiar to each polity, and not necessarily in a straight line. Armed intervention can resolve a crisis, but it cannot substitute for the gradual processes of maturation and self-education that most entrenched democracies have experienced. And even as it helps a democratizing country over one hurdle, intervention can have problematical effects on the country's ability to leap the many hurdles ahead. Moreover, because intervention temporarily cushions the impact but normally does not resolve (and could even aggravate) internal tensions, and because it may function as a shield for a government that is barely democratic, it will often lack the moral allure required to generate popular support among the electorates of the intervening states.

But there are exceptions. In Haiti a parasitic armed force in alliance with a tiny upper class and the lumpen elements at large in every society sought to abort an incipient democratic process. El Salvador and Guatemala may yet prove to be cases of democracy continuously thwarted by a small minority of incorrigible opponents who violently arrest the process whenever it begins to build. Intervention would be most appropriate—and least subject to the difficulties suggested above—in the case of threats to the well-developed democracies of the Anglophonic Caribbean, whether that threat is from their small constabularies, indigenous adventurers, or multinational criminal gangs, possibly working through local criminals or corrupt officials.

From the evidence to date, it appears that the Latin states of the OAS reject the use of force even after *golpistas* have deposed an elected government. What remains uncertain is how they would react in the event of an appeal by an endangered government for a deterrent show of force. In the nineteenth and early twentieth centuries, before self-determination and human rights became legal norms and when the Westphalian system was at its apogee, the logic of sovereignty seemed to endow governments with an uninhibited right to invite foreign troops into the national territory for any purpose.[37] To be sure, not all scholars accepted that logic. The great English jurisprude, William Hall, argued that a government would assume the risk of licensing foreign troops to assist in maintaining order only if the alternative were defeat. In that event, Hall concluded, the government had already effectively lost the mandate to speak for the state, and therefore its license was invalid.[38] This however, seems to have been a minority view.

In my scenario, the point of terminal desperation has not been reached. Assuming that any member state can respond to the invitation, a fortiori, the whole community can. If the force is to signal community concern and discourage violence, collective intervention (perhaps we should simply say "presence," in this case) could be seen as a variant of peacekeeping.[39] In UN practice, it would be merely a Chapter VI operation, one not requiring an immediate threat to the peace.[40]

Presumably, opponents of the use of force to restore democracy would be somewhat less resistant to prophylactic measures involving the dispatch of troops under the auspices of the OAS or the UN. By virtue of the appeal from a sitting government, the logic of traditional notions of sovereignty, to which many small states still lean, no less than the vested interests and insecurities that explain their inclination, will make such measures seem benign compared to restoration attempts.

But, as elites inclined to flinch from violent enforcement measures will doubtless note, the line between preservation and restoration is permeable. What if deterrence fails? What if, overnight, the armed forces or some paramilitary group seize all the levers of power and, in the worst case, appear to enjoy a good deal of popular support? The deposed government may, for instance, have itself begun using constitutional shortcuts to deal with fiscal or public order emergencies. Thus a large part of the electorate may see the coupists as saviors rather than betrayers of legal order.

Perhaps it was these considerations, as well as a reflexive hostility to foreign intervention, that led a small group of Latin states (led by Columbia) to successfully oppose an affirmative response by the UN to a request from the post-Duvalier interim government of Haiti for *armed* election observers. Their behavior in that instance presages opposition to deterrent, no less than to post facto, interventions.

The Use of Economic Sanctions

Since the Santiago Declaration in June 1991, the commitment to protect democracy announced therein has been tested by the armed forces of Haiti and by the elected presidents of Peru and Guatemala. The response of Western Hemisphere states to all three coups has assumed the form of denunciation, diplomacy, and economic pressure. Economic measures against Haiti succeeded only in deepening the misery of the Haitian masses and enriching those military and police officers who controlled the black market trade in embargoed goods.[41] The initial economic measures merely recommended by the OAS and conspicuously lacking authorization for a blockade to enforce them were ignored not only by extrahemispheric states but also by OAS members.[42] Until very late in the game, no effort was made to target the bank accounts and visas of the uniformed delinquents and their financial supporters. The subsequent mandatory UN sanctions reduced conspicuous indifference to community demands; but embargoed goods continued to sift through the Dominican Republic's cheesecloth border control into putschist hands.[43]

With its semisubsistence economy, impoverished civil society, and isolated, inward-looking, deeply threatened, parasitic elite, Haiti may be the hemisphere's worst case for demonstrating the potency of economic sanctions. When one considers the half-hearted way in which they were adopted and enforced, it is impossible to claim that their often-claimed impotence in all cases has been definitively confirmed. Haiti aside, the several authors in this volume who have examined the other post–Santiago Declaration cases conclude that economic measures can influence the balance of domestic political forces and the choices of would-be coupmasters. Sanctions were tested first against Peruvian President Alberto Fujimori when, in April 1992, he suddenly closed down the Congress, arrested the leaders of opposition parties, suspended freedom of speech, press, and association, initiated legislation by decree, and placed the courts under his direct control.[44] While the OAS Permanent Council met to "deplore the events . . . in Peru," urged the authorities "to immediately reinstate democratic institutions and full respect for human rights under the rule of law," and convoked "an ad hoc meeting of Ministers of Foreign Affairs,"[45] the United States was influencing the international financial community and the dozen countries in the Peru support group to suspend $2 billion in bridge loans, a $420 million Inter-American Development Bank loan, and several hundred million dollars in the support group assistance package (see chap. 11).

Within a week, the OAS foreign ministers convened, added the word "strongly" to the council's "deplore," called for the reestablishment of democratic institutions, urged the release of political leaders, and demanded the restoration of civil liberties. They also proposed that the chair of the ministers' meeting go to Peru, together with whatever ministers he might choose, along with the OAS's secretary-general. This delegation was formed to facilitate a dialogue between Fujimori and his political opponents to the end of restoring democracy and respect for human rights and the rule of law. The ministers also hinted of sanctions if Fujimori failed to respond positively.

The net result of their effort (and, presumably, of behind-the-scenes negotiations, bilateral as well as multilateral) was the release of most detainees and a commitment from Fujimori to hold elections for an assembly whose main function would be constitutional revision. While the electoral campaign proceeded, Fujimori continued running the country by decree and set about purging the judiciary.[46] Finally, the elections were held, essentially legitimized by a team of OAS monitors.[47] The ongoing ad hoc meeting of ministers, after declaring "that the election of the Democratic Constitutional Congress on 22 November 1992 and its forthcoming installation formalize an important step in the process of restoring democratic institutional order in Peru," and after asking Fujimori to keep the Permanent Council informed about the further "evolution of the process of restoration," declared itself closed.[48]

The result was considerably less than a restoration of the status quo ante. Fujimori succeeded, through unconstitutional means but with popular as well as military support, in tightening his grip on power. Arguably, the collective response succeeded in making that grip lighter than it would otherwise have been and in preventing the autocoup from evolving toward a closed dictatorial regime, which might then have moved against the remarkably autonomous, creative, and resilient grassroots organizations that have begun to provide the impoverished popular classes with means for self-help and effective political action.

In Guatemala, when President Jorge Serrano bid for autocratic power by purporting to close Congress and suspend the judiciary, the U.S. threat to suspend trade benefits under the general system of preferences and the Caribbean Basin Initiative is believed to have pushed key business leaders to ally with labor, popular organizations, and other civic groups in the effort to block the president's autocoup, then to prevent the military from installing Serrano's vice president, and finally to install as president the former attorney general for human rights, Ramiro de Leon Carpio.

The formation of the alliance and its success in attaining its immediate objectives testifies to the power even modest sanctions can have. But the aftermath suggests the limits of negative external measures. As the official advocate of human rights responsible for investigating and denouncing violations, Carpio had displayed noteworthy zeal for a man of the political center, a European ethnic, and a member of the country's prosperous classes. He had condemned at least some instances of endemically abusive behavior by the military in the countryside and had drawn the opposition of the military establishment and the paramilitary right. So his selection appeared to be a major move toward a rule-of-law regime.

For those who so viewed it, Carpio's accession has been a grave disappointment, albeit consistent with the dashed expectations that accompanied the election of an earlier president with liberal credentials, Vinicio Cerezo. Carpio has refused to challenge the main source of quotidian rights violations, that is, army rule over the countryside through rural civil patrols, and has apparently failed to protect even the occasional judge willing to investigate allegations against armed forces members and their accomplices.[49] One must therefore conclude either that the presidential palace contains a contagious antidemocratic virus, which its occupants contract on entering, or that presidents are quickly made to realize that their survival in office depends on their truckling to the deeper preferences of the armed forces. Carpio's kowtow implies that one reason civic resistance to the autocoup (which initially appeared to have armed forces support) succeeded was that success did not threaten the grip of the military establishment (which is historically allied, albeit uneasily, with the land- and industry-owning class) on the real levers of power and policy.

Still, the ability to resist even the tertiary preferences of antidemocratic forces in Guatemala was a considerable achievement within the straitened confines of the country's political possibilities. It revealed, as Kathryn Sikkink argues in chapter 6, the growth of a more vibrant and less categorically segmented civil society. For all its disappointments, "the return of electoral politics in 1985 . . . opened space for the growth of . . . NGOs, parties, and grassroots social movements." This growth also allowed "the Congress and the judiciary . . . to gain some independent life."

The collective commitment to democratic consolidation in the Western Hemisphere is most consistently and effectively expressed through efforts to expand the space for civil society (particularly where it has traditionally been cramped) and to foster within that space institutions for aggregating and advocating the preferences of all social groups. If the thrust of the studies in this volume could be summed up in one sentence, that would be it. The foregoing does not imply, however, that coercive measures can be abandoned. Civil society does not thrive when participants are threatened with pain and mutilation. Hence, protecting it requires a continuing emphasis on the documentation and denunciation, by public and private human rights organs, of torture, disappearance, extrajudicial executions, and arbitrary detention. While in the hemisphere as a whole these practices have diminished, their incidence continues to limit civic activism. The prosperity of civil society also requires a strong response to restraints on press freedom and the organization of traditionally disadvantaged groups, particularly peasants and workers.

The Use of Other Measures

In a hemisphere where human rights and democratic governance are more strongly privileged than ever before, exposure itself can have positive effect. So can other measures intended to embarrass and to reduce a regime's aura of legitimacy within its own political system, measures like the recall of ambassadors or suspension from participation in the OAS, a symbolic sanction previously applied only to Fidel Castro's regime. OAS member states are now resolved to deny participation to governments that subvert constitutional governments. They should be prepared to take the same step if an elected regime persistently violates fundamental human rights.

The efficacy of exposure and political sanctions is enhanced when they augur material ones. While generally skeptical about attaching non-economic conditions to the lending activities of the international financial institutions, Joan Nelson and Stephanie Eglinton concede in chapter 7 that conditionality may be appropriate in certain situations, especially related to narrowly defined human rights abuse, and they cite the detention of political opponents and regulations that restrict freedom of press or the formation of unions as possible targets of conditionality.

For the influential business elites of many Latin countries, certainly in all of Central America, the most intimidating threat is denial of access to the U.S. market. It is, however, one that the United States has been traditionally reluctant to apply except in the case of communist governments. In many circumstances that reluctance is entirely appropriate. But a flat refusal to use import embargoes against either military officers who seize power by force or elected governments that violate human rights would much reduce the prospects for democratic consolidation.

If their commitment to promoting democracy is real, OAS member states can deter assaults on democratic governance by taking steps to facilitate the effective application of economic sanctions in the event deterrence failed. The OAS political organs should, for instance, call on the Unit for Democracy in the Secretariat to prepare model legislation that would empower each member country's executive authority to comply with an

OAS recommendation for sanctions by cutting off all commercial contact with the target state. The model legislation would also specify minimum penal sanctions for violations. Member states would commit themselves to introducing the model with only minor adaptations required by their respective constitutional systems. The members might also agree to develop a multinational cadre of sanctions monitors, trained national officials who would be seconded to the OAS, organized into teams, and dispatched to member states to evaluate compliance and report to the meeting of foreign ministers, the organization's apex political organ. To equalize the burden of compliance, members should agree to compensate any state peculiarly disadvantaged by the interruption of commercial relationships with the target country.

Whenever OAS ministers adopted a resolution calling for suspension of loan disbursements by international financial institutions, member states could instruct their representatives on the boards of these institutions to vote for such suspension. Yet another way for the OAS to communicate firmness of purpose, and coincidentally to enhance the prospective impact of economic sanctions, would be to press the European Economic Community (EEC) and Japan to agree to force their own nationals to comply with OAS-recommended sanctions.

Sanctions are bound to be episodic responses to particularly flagrant bouts of abuse. Hence, the quotidian security of civil society in unconsolidated democracies is strongly dependent on the capacity of the respective national systems of justice to enforce the rights formally guaranteed by every national constitution, as well as international agreements. Where the courts are sluggish and inept or cringingly deferential to public and private power, civic life will be correspondingly diminished. This reality calls for a several-pronged approach by external actors. In the first place, national justice systems need to be periodically monitored and appraised by both nongovernmental organizations (NGOs) and the Inter-American Commission on Human Rights. Since monitoring the performance of the judicial process requires sophisticated and sustained scrutiny, the commission requires additional resources and the leverage to extract governmental permission for the conduct of prolonged on-site reviews. Member states should be urged to provide the additional resources, to declare that periodic monitoring would be appropriate, and to provide the commission with the necessary permission.

Where the deficiencies of the justice system are more a function of traditional neglect and overstrained national budgets than the malign preferences of national leaders, they can be usefully addressed with technical and financial assistance. The United States, Canada, and the rich states that maintain observer status at the OAS—principally Japan and most members of the EEC—should take the lead. Each of the developed countries might assume responsibility for a particular system. The World Bank and the Inter-American Development Bank should be prepared to cooperate in such an effort, both because of their belated discovery of a connection between the quality of governance (in particular, the rule of law) and development and because the community of democratic states demand it (if they do).[50]

While free elections are not sufficient to establish democracy, all agree that they are necessary. Through its Unit for Democracy, the OAS has become an increasingly frequent monitor of national elections. But monitoring still is not routinized. To that end, the OAS General Assembly should call for the official monitoring of all national elections and should declare that a state's failure to permit OAS monitors to enter or, after they have entered, to provide them with necessary assistance creates a presumption that its elections failed to meet minimum standards of fairness. Such failure would therefore be deemed grounds for suspension of the nominally elected government from all organs of the OAS, pending new elections. In carrying out such a mandate, the OAS should formalize cooperation with national and international NGOs that have experience in monitoring and have demonstrated their objectivity.

In chapter 13, Karen Remmer writes: "From a historical perspective, what stands out about the contemporary situation is less the conditioning impact of domestic forces [in their stunning diversity] than the extraordinary capacity of outside actors to shift the political momentum in the direction of democratic options." That capacity, she argues, was greater in the 1980s than in preceding decades. Increased capacity coincided with increased will, not least among the makers of U.S. foreign policy. For, as she notes, the end of the Cold War "removed a major source of policy ambivalence and inconsistency on the part of the United States." The marked reduction (if not quite disappearance) of that ambivalence has been a salient feature of an environment singularly encouraging to democratic projects.[51]

What the end of the Cold War has not done is alter—indeed, it probably has materially strengthened—the hegemonic position of the United States in the Western Hemisphere. Further adding to potential U.S. influence is the growing integration of Latin American economic systems with those of the developed countries; access to the U.S. consumer and capital markets is essential for the economic health of most Latin states. Still positioned to apply powerful leverage on behalf of the democratic project, the United States should be more prepared now than it was during the Cold War to

Beyond Sovereignty

accept the results as well as to celebrate the theory of popular sovereignty. But though it remains the world's strongest state and is free of the particular moral distortions occasioned by competition with the Soviet Union, the United States shows signs of becoming more self-absorbed now than at any time since the 1930s. And to the extent that it is concerned with the rest of the world other than Mexico, it is Europe, the Middle East, and Asia that engage most of its attention.

The initiatives for consolidating democracy sketched here and elaborated in the ensuing chapters will not occur spontaneously. They will occur if the U.S. government invests the requisite time, energy, and resources—if, in other words, it has the will to seize the democratic moment in Latin America. Seizing the moment does not imply unilateral initiatives. The Latin states have never been more receptive to a genuinely collective effort. And as their economies become more intertwined and their politics more compatible, their influence over each other is enhanced. So a collective effort is more feasible than ever and can provide parallel unilateral measures with operational coherence and a normative framework that enhances their impact.

Despite its action in Haiti and its frequent rhetorical celebrations of concern for human rights and participatory governance throughout the world, the Clinton administration's real priorities remain blurred. An occasion for clarification would arise if the government of El Salvador were to renege on the commitments that brought that country's civil war to an end. And another would present itself if Guatemala sought access to an enlarged North American free trade area while grimly continuing to deny civil rights to the majority of its population.

Those who believe that Washington's use of its economic leverage would be bad for business or free trade or would constitute unwarranted interference in the political process of sovereign states will hope to witness flaccidity of will in the White House whenever representative government and other human rights are at issue. That they will be disappointed is the converse hope of those who sense a remarkable and possibly transient moment in our region's history, a moment that offers the United States a chance to lead the hemisphere in the task of collectively defending democracy.

I   Theory

Sovereignty and Democracy in the 1990s

2 Changing Perceptions of Domestic Jurisdiction and Intervention

Fernando R. Tesón

The Charter of the United Nations prohibits the organization from intervening "in matters which are essentially within the domestic jurisdiction of any state."[1] This limitation does not apply to the enforcement measures taken by the UN Security Council under Chapter VII of the charter. The prohibition in Article 2 (7) is but one instance of a broader duty of international organizations and states not to intervene in matters that fall within the domestic jurisdiction of sovereign states.[2] Yet the principles and policies that govern unilateral intervention differ substantially from those that govern collective intervention, especially intervention authorized by international organizations such as the United Nations and the Organization of American States.[3]

In this chapter, I discuss collective intervention authorized by the UN Security Council, with a special emphasis on the concept of exclusive domestic jurisdiction, first examining the different meanings of the notoriously ambiguous word *intervention*. Because the legitimacy of collective intervention depends in part on whether the matter falls within the domestic jurisdiction of the target state, I then discuss contemporary views of domestic jurisdiction. Finally, I discuss collective humanitarian intervention under the principles of the UN Charter and examine the practice of the Security Council since the end of the Cold War.

My conclusion is that international law today recognizes, as a matter of practice, the legitimacy of collective forcible humanitarian intervention, that is, of military measures authorized by the Security Council for the purpose of remedying serious human rights violations. While traditionally the only grounds for collective military action has been the need to respond to breaches of the peace (especially aggression), the international community has accepted a norm that allows collective humanitarian intervention as a response to serious human rights abuses.

Soft, Hard, and Forcible Intervention

In international law, *prohibited intervention* is defined as "dictatorial interference . . . in the affairs of another state for the purpose of maintaining or altering the actual condition of things."[4] It involves, therefore, some kind of coercive action. The International Court of Justice, confirming this definition, has held that acts of prohibited intervention must be coercive and be aimed at thwarting choices by the target state that, under international law, must remain free.[5] Thus the means of the intervention must be coercive (although not necessarily forcible) and the ends of the intervention must be to influence another state (by effect of the coercion exercised) on a matter falling under the state's domestic jurisdiction.[6] Both requirements must be met for an action to be prohibited intervention, in this traditional sense.

Yet obviously the word *intervene* in Article 2 (7) cannot possibly be limited to this meaning, since it prohibits any UN organ from even discussing, examining, or issuing recommendations on matters that fall within a state's domestic jurisdiction.[7] The prohibition in Article 2 (7) thus covers noncoercive action by the United Nations, using the word *intervene* in its ordinary, nontechnical sense, not as a legal term of art. This is confirmed by the fact that Article 2 (7) expressly exempts from the prohibition those cases where the United Nations is entitled to take coercive enforcement measures under Chapter VII of its charter. Thus, in the context of UN law, we need to ask two questions. First, what is the present scope of domestic jurisdiction removed from the scrutiny of the United Nations under Article 2 (7)? Second, can the United Nations validly adopt coercive measures (including force) against a state to remedy a situation other than a breach of the peace or an act of aggression?

As a preliminary matter, it is necessary to distinguish between three different meanings of *intervention,* according to the degree of coercion utilized in the attempts to influence other states. The first is the sense in which the word is used in Article 2 (7): *intervention,* here, means simply discussion, examination, and recommendatory action. This I call *soft* intervention. The second meaning refers to the adoption of measures that (unlike soft intervention) are coercive but do not involve the use of force, such as economic and other kinds of sanctions. This I refer to as *hard* intervention. And finally, *intervention* often refers to acts involving the use of force (as in *humanitarian intervention*). This I call *forcible* intervention. The important issue regarding forcible intervention is that the use of force is subject to independent legal constraints. Therefore, a situation that could qualify for collective soft or hard intervention may nevertheless not be appropriate for collective forcible action.

The distinction between forms of intervention according to their degree of coercion leaves intact a common requirement: prohibited intervention is action aimed at influencing a government on an issue where the target state has legal discretion. This is plain in the case of soft intervention, where the only issue is an issue of ends, not of means, since the means (discussion, recommendation) are perfectly permitted in principle. But the same is true in cases of hard and forcible intervention. If State A violates, say, a fishing treaty with State B, and B adopts economic sanctions in retaliation, B's action will not be deemed intervention, because A was not legally free to violate the treaty; that matter did not fall within A's exclusive jurisdiction. The legality of B's retaliation will be determined by the law of countermeasures, in particular by the principle of proportionality. If, however, State A decides, say, to nationalize certain natural resources, and B responds by declaring an economic embargo against A, this action amounts to prohibited hard intervention, because B's action is coercive (although not forcible) and the question of nationalization of natural resources is one over which A has, in principle and absent an international commitment, exclusive jurisdiction. In this example, B has no right to coerce A into reversing the nationalizations.

The same analysis holds for forcible intervention. Applying the general requirements that define unlawful intervention, prohibited forcible intervention will occur when two conditions are met: first, the action by the intervenor can be described as use (indirect or direct) of force, and second, the choices that the intervenor attempts to influence should remain free for the target state; that is, the choices have to fall under its exclusive jurisdiction.[8] Here again, the two requirements must be met. If a state violates a trade agreement with another state and the latter retaliates with a limited forcible measure, this is a violation of the prohibition on the use of force (since treaty breaches of this kind do not justify the use of force) but not a violation of the principle of nonintervention, because actions concerning a treaty are not within the legal discretion of the target state.[9] The need to determine whether or not a matter falls within the domestic jurisdiction of a state arises, therefore, in the assessment of all three forms of intervention.

Exclusive Domestic Jurisdiction

The concept of exclusive domestic jurisdiction has been the subject of controversy both during the life of the League of Nations and in the United Nations era. Two schools of thought competed. According to the first one, there are matters that necessarily fall within the domestic jurisdiction of states. For this view, the essence of sovereignty requires that certain matters, in particular matters broadly referred to as domestic policy, be outside the reach of international law.[10] In particular, such matters ought not be subject to action by international organizations. In this view, the concept of domestic jurisdiction does not depend on the development of international law; it is not relative, but fixed, at least as long as we continue to live in a world of sovereign states. The essential attributes of the sovereign state require that certain matters be left to the state's own sovereign judgment. There are, therefore, matters that fall essentially within the domestic jurisdiction of states—just as the language of Article 2 (7) suggests. Those who defend the essentialist view give various versions of the content and scope of domestic jurisdiction, but the common theme is that matters pertaining to exclusive domestic jurisdiction are closely related to the sovereignty of the state.[11]

The second position is the legalist view of domestic jurisdiction. For this view, whether a matter falls within the state's *domaine reservé* cannot be determined by appealing to the notion of sovereignty. This is, instead, a relative matter, which depends on the state of international law at any given time in history.[12] Thus, to cite the most notorious example of such evolution, human rights were a matter of exclusive domestic jurisdiction before 1945, but this is no longer the case today. Where a rule of international law regulates an issue, it automatically ceases to be a matter of exclusive domestic jurisdiction for the states formally bound by the rule.[13]

There are problems with both positions. The essentialist view can be defended only by appealing to an abstract and autonomous normative conception of state sovereignty. The gist of the essentialist argument is that certain matters ought not be regulated by international law, come what may. But this cannot be defended without providing a justification of state sovereignty in the first place; otherwise, the argument becomes circular (exclusive domestic jurisdiction derives from the attributes of sovereignty, and sovereignty consists of matters that are within the state's exclusive domestic jurisdiction). So the essentialist view is less a theoretical explication of domestic jurisdiction than a moral injunction to international actors not to intervene in matters that are closely bound with the sovereignty of the state.[14]

At first blush, the legalist position seems closer to the truth. Indeed, international law defines the boundaries of state sovereignty. Yet the problem with the legalist position is that, without more, it is tautological. It simply says that domestic jurisdiction ends where international jurisdiction begins. This is true, but trivial: where exactly does international jurisdiction take over? At least the essentialist view had some (perhaps unattractive) suggestions about substance. Legalism needs to provide a criterion to decide which matters fall within the state's exclusive domestic jurisdiction, and the answer will depend on the operational definition of international law. On a strictly positivist view of international law, only custom and treaty count. In contrast, on a more teleological view of international law, moral principles, purposes, and policies count as well. Domestic jurisdiction then swells or shrinks accordingly.[15]

I do not attempt to solve here this jurisprudential controversy, except to say that the substantial international effects policy seems today outmoded. To buttress this conclusion, I review a number of areas where the concept of domestic jurisdiction has undergone spectacular transformations in recent years. Areas traditionally claimed by states as falling within their *domaine reservé* are now unequivocally subject to review by international bodies— in particular, to soft and hard intervention by international organizations.

Human Rights

Human rights have long been subtracted from the exclusive domestic jurisdiction of states, notwithstanding the fact that they seem to constitute the paradigm of an essentially domestic matter, since they define the relationship between a government and its subjects. In early discussions of the concept of domestic jurisdiction in the UN Charter, writers reached this conclusion, citing not only the well-known provisions of the UN Charter but also a number of human rights cases that had been addressed by the various organs of the United Nations.[16]

The proposition that human rights are no longer a matter of exclusive domestic jurisdiction is indisputable.[17] This is so, independent of the legal grounds for the obligation of states to respect human rights and independent, too, of whether or not the human rights violations produce international effects.[18] Governments very rarely claim that discussion of their human rights problems is a violation of Article 2 (7) of the UN Charter. The only question, therefore, is whether or not human rights violations can lawfully trigger coercive or forcible measures by the United Nations. I address this question (humanitarian intervention) below.

Form of Government: Democracy

Many who accept the premise that observance of human rights, in the sense of the treatment by a government of its own citizens, is an appropriate subject for international scrutiny draw, nonetheless, the line on the question of the legitimacy of the government itself. They argue that this is a question of domestic jurisdiction, if there ever was one. In the absence of widespread human rights violations, the international community should not be in the business of passing judgment on the legitimacy of the origin of a government.[19] The question of internal political legitimacy, in this view, falls under the exclusive jurisdiction of the state and is thus exempt from even soft intervention by international organizations or the international community.

But there are a priori reasons to doubt that international law should not be concerned with democratic legitimacy. First and fundamental is the question of agency: if international law is largely created by nation-states, then the international community needs some criterion to determine when some official actually represents the state. Traditional international law proposes the criterion of effectiveness. A government internationally represents a people living in a territory if that government has effective political control over that people.[20] Traditional international law is indifferent to how that political control has been acquired. Whether political power has been consensually granted to the government or whether usurpers rule, instead, through fear and terror is of little interest to supporters of the traditional doctrine of effectiveness. Such a view is indefensible: if the international system is going to be the result of what the peoples of the United Nations want it to be, then it makes sense to require that governments that participate in the creation of international law be the real representatives of the people who reside within the boundaries of the state.[21] A rule requiring democratic legitimacy in the form of free adult universal suffrage seems the best approximation to actual political consent and true representativeness.

Second, there are strong reasons to believe that democratic rule is a necessary condition for enjoying other human rights. While it is always possible to imagine a society where human rights are respected by an enlightened despot, this has never occurred in practice. This is why the right to political participation is included in the major human rights conventions.[22] The right to participate in government is a very important human right in itself. It is also crucially instrumental to the enjoyment of other rights. Its violation should therefore trigger appropriate international scrutiny.

The third reason for requiring democratic rule is the one indicated by Kant: democracies are more peaceful, and therefore a rule requiring democratic rule is consonant with the ideal of a lasting world peace, in a way that the rule of effectiveness or pure political power, which countenances tyrannies, is not.[23] This is so because tyrannies tend to be more aggressive and because the difference in regimes is a major cause of conflict. Democracies have built-in mechanisms that cause them to avoid war with one another. The reason that democracies are sometimes belligerent is that they often perceive threats by illiberal regimes to their democratic institutions. These threats are sometimes real and sometimes imaginary, which is why democracies also get involved in unjustified wars. But these wars are always against illiberal regimes. So if the aim of international law is to secure a lasting peace, where the benefits of international cooperation can be reaped by all, then it has to require democratic legitimacy.

But even if none of this were true, even if there were no correlation between democracy and peace, international law should require democratic rule simply because that is the right thing to do. I do not need a complicated philosophical defense of democracy: a simple comparison with the traditional rule of effectiveness will suffice. Traditional international law authorizes tyranny. It gives carte blanche to anyone who wishes to bypass popular will and seize and maintain power by sheer political force. This is delicately described by pertinent international materials as a state's right to "choose" its political system.[24] Such a state-centric view suffers from acute moral and conceptual poverty. Both ordinary common sense morality and the structure of international law, which presupposes agency and representation, require that governments be recognized and accepted in the international community only if they genuinely represent their people.

These arguments suffice, I believe, to demonstrate why international law must recognize an individual and collective right to democratic rule. It has become abundantly clear, moreover, that the principle is supported by contemporary state practice. Thomas Franck's findings are well known, and I am content to rest on them here.[25] There can be little doubt that a principle of democratic rule is today part of international law. While in a universal context the recognition of the principle has had, perhaps, only the effect of subtracting the question of democratic rule from the exclusive jurisdiction of states, the nations in Europe and the Americas have elevated the principle of democracy to the category of a rule that is fully enforceable through appropriate regional collective mechanisms.[26]

Collective Humanitarian Intervention

General Principles

International lawyers have been engaged in recent years in a debate about the legitimacy of the use of force to remedy serious human rights violations, also known as humanitarian intervention.[27] Some writers reject the legitimacy of humanitarian intervention altogether, collective or unilateral.[28] Undeniably, the anti-interventionist position has the support of traditional state-centric conceptions of international law and relations.[29] It is also informed by the commendable moral purpose of reducing the permissible instances of war, of containing armed conflict.

Yet this extreme position, highly protective of despotic regimes, cannot be maintained today. The content and purpose of state sovereignty have undergone, since 1945, and more dramatically since 1989, profound changes. Human beings have claims against their own states and governments that the international community cannot simply ignore. While of course war ought to be the remedy of last resort to redress human rights violations, there are some, admittedly rare, serious cases of human rights deprivations where a strong case can be made for forcible intervention authorized by the international community and even by individual states. Whether these cases are to be seen as extreme instances of "moral catastrophe," and thus outside the law, or whether they are instead genuine exceptions to the legal prohibition is a jurisprudential preference to which little weight ought to be attached. I cannot see much consequence to the proposition that an act is illegal but morally permitted (or obligatory), as contrasted with the proposition that the act is legally permitted (or obligatory) in those rare instances.[30] This is so because moral reasons are overriding. If anti-interventionists can agree on the kind of cases where the international community can or must intervene, their protestations that this is nevertheless illegal does not carry much credibility.

That states have a right to intervene in other states, even by force, to put an end to serious human rights violations is demonstrated, among other things, by state practice since 1945.[31] Yet here I wish to concentrate exclusively on collective humanitarian intervention. In more technical terms, the question is whether or not the UN Security Council may authorize Article 42 measures to put an end to serious, or extreme, human rights violations. Some writers who are hostile to the legitimacy of unilateral action concede that the legal situation changes when the humanitarian intervention is authorized by the United Nations or an appropriate regional body.[32] This support for multilateral action may be prompted by the feeling that, if a coercive action is authorized by some kind of formal international *process* (such as voting in the Security Council), then it acquires a legality that it would lack were the decision to intervene to be left to national governments acting unilaterally. Or they may think that collective humanitarian intervention is more likely to curb the danger of abuse posed by unilateral intervention.[33]

More technically, some may argue that the Security Council, unlike

Beyond Sovereignty

individual states, has absolute discretion in deciding when to authorize the use of force. In this view, under Article 39 of the UN Charter, the Security Council *determines* the existence of a breach of the peace, a threat to the peace, or an act of aggression. Therefore, if the Security Council authorizes enforcement measures in a case of serious human rights deprivations, it has determined that such a situation qualifies under Article 39 as the kind of situation that is a breach of the peace.[34]

Anti-interventionists disagree. They argue that under Article 39, the Security Council can authorize collective forcible action only in cases of threats to the peace, breaches of the peace, and acts of aggression.[35] Serious human rights violations do not, if contained within state borders, constitute aggression or threat or breach of (international) peace. In addition, anti-interventionists deny absolute discretion to the Security Council in this regard. For them, the Security Council is subject to standards imposed by the UN Charter and cannot lawfully overstep those constraints.[36] Unless a violation of human rights threatens international peace, the Security Council does not have the power to authorize forcible action. The Security Council, they argue, can at most criticize the dictatorial government and demand peremptorily that the violations cease. Such a demand is legally binding under Article 25. The Security Council can even authorize *hard* intervention, such as economic or other sanctions, by members against the outlaw state.[37] But the Security Council may not authorize the use of force.

The first question is whether the Security Council has complete discretion to interpret Article 39 and thus to authorize the use of force, without being formally constrained by the language of that article. As we saw, those who respond in the affirmative say that whatever the Security Council says is a breach of the peace is legally a breach of the peace. This position, however, must be rejected. The Security Council, like any other UN organ, is bound by the principles, rules, and standards set forth in the UN Charter. Its actions, therefore, are subject to legal scrutiny, both substantively and procedurally.[38] Those who vindicate the absolute discretion of the Security Council confuse two different meanings of the term *discretion*.[39]

One meaning of *discretion* arises when an official's decision, authorized by law, is not subject to review by a higher body. This is a weak meaning of the word, because it does not presuppose that the law lacks standards to guide the official's decision. That decision is perhaps nonreviewable, but it may not be lawless; it is controlled by substantive legal standards. The second meaning of *discretion* is that the official's decision is not guided by any standards, that he has absolute power to decide one way or the other, unconstrained by law (except, of course, by the rule of competence that empowered him as the legitimate authority). This is *discretion* in a strong sense, because it conceives of the official as deciding the case anew, as creating fresh law.

The difference between the two definitions is very important. In the first case, the official's decision is vulnerable to the criticism that he applied the law incorrectly, that the decision is legally wrong. In the second case, however, the official is not open to the criticism that he misapplied the law, because the official's decision is not substantively constrained. He is deemed to be authorized to create fresh law for the case.

It is reasonable to suppose that the Security Council under the UN Charter enjoys, at most, discretion in the first, weak, sense. Under the charter, neither the General Assembly nor the International Court of Justice have original or plenary jurisdiction to review the decisions of the Security Council (although, as the Lockerbie case demonstrates, the International Court of Justice may, in appropriate cases, be called upon to decide the legality of the Security Council's actions).[40] But the Security Council has no discretion in the strong sense: its decisions *are* constrained by international law, in particular by the UN Charter, and thus are subject to the judgment of legality by governments and international lawyers generally, even if its decisions are not formally subject to review. Anti-interventionists are right, therefore, in rejecting the view that the Security Council can decree a collective intervention for any reason. There is a substantive law of collective use of force, and the Security Council is bound to comply with it, just as anybody else is.

Nor is it possible (to respond to anti-interventionists) simply to echo, as some do, the uncontroversial proposition that human rights are no longer part of the exclusive domestic jurisdiction of states.[41] Anti-interventionists rightly respond that this affects only soft (and perhaps even hard) intervention. They happily concede that UN organs, including the Security Council, may address human rights issues, even condemn states for their human rights abuses, *as long as no use of force is involved*. They correctly point out that the collective use of force is subject to independent constraints, which are to be found in Chapter VII. Thus, Article 39, not the chameleon Article 2 (7), is the right place to look when evaluating the legitimacy of collective forcible intervention.[42]

A complete answer to the anti-interventionist view draws from text, morality, history, and practice. The legitimacy of collective humanitarian intervention to remedy gross human rights violations, irrespective of international effects, finds some textual support in the charter.[43] The Preamble declares that armed force should not be used "save in the common interest," and there is no reason to assume that common interest excludes the interest in upholding human rights, particularly since in the Preamble itself the "Peoples of the United Nations" reaffirm "faith in fundamental human rights [and] in the dignity and worth of the human person."[44] The Preamble also states the UN determination "to establish conditions under which justice . . . can be maintained." It would be a very narrow definition of justice, indeed, that did not include human rights in any context, let alone in this one, where human rights are one of the pillars of the organization.

In addition, the anti-interventionist's reading of Article 39 and Chapter VII is just too narrow and is not supported by UN and state practice, as we shall see. Subsequent practice under the charter, if unchallenged on the whole, may determine the more precise meaning of the words in the charter.[45]

The legitimacy of collective humanitarian intervention in appropriate cases flows from an interpretation of the UN Charter that looks beyond the letter, to the purposes and principles that animate, shape, and define legitimacy in the international community today. I am not suggesting playing verbal games; indeed, as we saw, it is always possible to define serious human rights violations as a breach of peace and to thus trigger enforcement action under Article 39. Instead, I am suggesting that the substantive law of the charter has evolved to include human rights as a centerpiece of international order and serious human rights violations as one of the situations that may warrant collective enforcement action. The principle of respect for human rights may be enforced, in rare cases and as a matter of last resort, by the Security Council, acting on behalf of the international community.

There is, of course, a case where even anti-interventionists would agree that serious violations of human rights can trigger enforcement action: that is, where those violations do constitute a "threat to peace."[46] This will be the case quite often, as it was for apartheid in South Africa and for Iraq's treatment of the Kurds (discussed below). It is possible to argue, as a consequence, that the basis for collective humanitarian intervention is the threat to peace, not the gravity of the human rights violations. In this view, only when the human rights deprivations cause international effects will the United Nations have a right to intervene.[47] Presumably, genocidal action that is purely internal—that is, contained within a state's borders—is beyond the reach of Security Council action.

The crucial question, however, is what the Security Council does, not what it says. Suppose there is a massive human rights violation, and the Security Council decides to intervene. When doing so, it uses the "threat or breach of the peace" language of Article 39. This, let us suppose, becomes an institutional habit. It is intolerably formalistic to cling to the view, on such facts, that the Security Council is not authorizing humanitarian intervention, when a commonsense reading of the situation by any unprejudiced observer will indicate that that is precisely what the Security Council is doing. The better interpretation is that, regardless of the language in which it cloaks its decision, the Security Council authorizes the use of force in two instances: to counter aggression and restore peace, and to remedy serious human rights abuses. In both situations, the Security Council will authorize the use of force only in rare and extreme cases, where everything else has proved ineffective or unavailable.

Moreover, the anti-inerventionist position is peculiarly blind to history. The United Nations was created as a response to the horrors caused by one of the most tyrannical regimes in modern history. World War II was in great part (although not only) a humanitarian effort. It is therefore surprising to be told that the very crimes that prompted the massive, cruel, and costly struggle from which the United Nations was born are now immune from action undertaken by the organ entrusted to preserving the fruits of the peace so hardly won. An undiscriminating anti-interventionist position thus not only rewards tyrants; it betrays the purposes of the very international order that they claim to protect.

The reasons of political philosophy that support the legitimacy of humanitarian intervention are many and complex, and I have discussed them elsewhere at length.[48] The central point is that states derive their legitimacy, their sovereignty, from popular consent and the protection of basic human rights. The purpose of states is to protect human rights in the first place. Therefore, governments forfeit their legitimacy in the international arena when they turn against their citizens and betray the ethical end that justifies their existence. In some cases, therefore, forcible humanitarian intervention is morally permitted, subject to several constraints. These reasons gain in strength when the intervention is collective, for in that case a number of concerns about intervention are assuaged—in particular the concern about the dangers of unilateral abuse.[49]

Iraq and the Kurds, 1991

These textual, historical, and moral arguments are validated by recent practice. In the case of the Kurds, the first stage of the UN action against Iraq is well known, and I will not discuss it here.[50] That case can be properly addressed within the traditional interpretation of the principles set forth in Article 39, 41, and 42 of the charter. In the second phase of the case, after the defeat of the Iraqi army, the Security Council, faced with mounting atrocities committed by the Iraqi government against the Kurds

Beyond Sovereignty

and others, adopted Resolution 688.[51] In that document, the Security Council first condemned "the repression of the Iraqi civilian population in many parts of Iraq" and demanded that "Iraq . . . immediately end this repression." The Security Council further urged Iraq to "allow immediate access by international humanitarian organizations" and appealed to "all member States . . . to contribute to these humanitarian relief efforts."[52] The Security Council also demanded that Iraq cooperate with the secretary-general to these ends.

The Security Council added several provisos linking the resolution to the language of Article 39, perhaps to make sure that its action was consistent with its powers under the charter. In particular, the resolution stated that these human rights violations threatened international peace and security in the region" and characterized the requested Iraqi compliance with its human rights demands as "a contribution to international peace and security in the region." Also, Resolution 688 contains in the Preamble a rare reference to Article 2 (7). It is therefore easy for anti-interventionists to claim that Resolution 688 was a lawful Security Council action in response to a "threat to the peace" and, thus, well within the traditional paradigm of aggression. Again, this is excessively formalistic. The relevant issue is not whether the Security Council can do anything it wants, as long as it styles it "threat to the peace"; the issue is that this is a human rights issue concerning Iraq's treatment of its own citizens. A reasonable interpretation of Resolution 688 is that the Security Council was centrally concerned with the human rights violations themselves and that the reference to the threat to peace and security was added for good measure.

Anti-interventionists retort that the Security Council did not authorize forcible measures in the Kurdish crisis but only nonforcible humanitarian relief.[53] Once more, this is just blind adherence to words on paper. While apparently referring to nonforcible intervention, the context of this resolution reveals that the UN effort relied upon a number of factors that demonstrate that actual or potential forcible action was contemplated. As David Scheffer shows, those factors were (1) allied military intervention in northern Iraq to create a security zone, (2) allied threats to respond to any Iraqi operations, (3) the deployment of a UN force to protect humanitarian relief efforts; and (4) an agreement with Iraq that contemplated the possible use of force in case of noncompliance.[54] In the light of these facts, it is hard to avoid the conclusion that this was a genuine case of collective humanitarian intervention.

Another strategy to justify Resolution 688 within the old paradigm of aggression (that is, without introducing the concept of humanitarian intervention) is to claim that Resolution 688 was adopted in the context of the series of Security Council resolutions aimed at countering Iraqi aggression. In this view, the action authorized by the Security Council to protect the Kurds was simply an extension of the enforcement measures authorized to counter aggression.[55] Resolution 688 would thus be analogous to Resolution 687, which authorized a sweeping range of measures on matters that normally would fall under the exclusive jurisdiction of Iraq (mainly regarding the disarming and denuclearization of that state). The argument is that the intervention to protect the Kurds was justified because it was a sequel to Chapter VII action, itself justified as a response to Iraqi aggression.

Once again, this interpretation is highly contrived. The Iraqi government perpetrated at least two distinct violations of international law: the attack against Kuwait (a violation of Article 2 (4), which triggers Security Council action under Chapter VII), and a massive violation of the human rights of individuals in Iraq, most notably the Kurds.[56] Resolution 688, by its very terms, was addressed to the latter. Not only did the resolution peremptorily demand Iraq to stop the repression, it authorized, as we saw, nonconsensual relief measures. Moreover, from the fact that the Security Council decreed mandatory disarmament of the defeated aggressor (thus instituting coercive measures on matters that would normally fall within the exclusive jurisdiction of Iraq), it does not follow that the Security Council has authority to institute coercive measures on any matter that would normally fall within Iraq's exclusive jurisdiction. In other words, while Resolution 687 does follow logically from the previous resolutions of the Security Council (especially from Resolution 678, authorizing the use of force as a response to Iraq's refusal to withdraw from Kuwait), we need the humanitarian intervention standard, in addition to the "breach of the peace" standard, to justify Resolution 688.

Somalia, 1992–1993

On 4 December 1992, the Security Council adopted Resolution 794, which authorized forcible intervention to provide relief to people caught in a chaotic and cruel civil war in Somalia.[57] The Somali crisis was touched off by the power vacuum created when the country's longtime dictator, President Mohammed Siad Barre, fled Mogadishu in January 1991.[58] Barre's absence split the opposition. Troops under the command of General Mohammed Farah Aideed gave chase to Siad Barre, while those under the control of Ali Mahdi Mohammed remained in the capital and declared themselves the new government.

From then on, Somalia did not have a functioning government. As the various clan militias turned on one another, the country was effectively divided into twelve zones of control. By November 1991, the struggle between the warring factions had escalated to a full-scale civil war. The collapse of all governmental authority, combined with drought and the continuation of traditional clan and subclan warfare and growing chaos, led to mass starvation. Although the United States supplied food aid through the international Committee of the Red Cross (ICRC) and private voluntary relief organizations, the majority of the food was confiscated by clan groups. By September 1992, the ICRC estimated that 1.5 million Somalis faced imminent starvation and that three times that number were already dependent on external food assistance.

Unlike the case of Iraq, here there was not even the possibility of appealing to the catchall language of Article 39 to justify this humanitarian mission. The civil war in Somalia did not pose any serious danger of breach of international peace. The main reason that prompted enforcement action by the Security Council was the extreme situation of famine, death, and disease caused by the civil war, by the breach of *humanitarian* law by the warring factions, and by the general situation of anarchy. The resolution referred to "the magnitude of the human tragedy caused by the conflict" and to "the deterioration of the humanitarian situation."[59] Most significantly, the Security Council mentioned the reports of "widespread violations of international humanitarian law" in Somalia, including violence against personnel participating in humanitarian relief there. The Security Council summarized the situation as "intolerable," adding that it had become necessary to review "the basic premises and principles of the UN effort" in Somalia. This was, of course, a reference to the distinction between peacekeeping action (which, among other things, is based on consent by the territorial state) and enforcement action based on Chapter VII of the charter.[60]

After demanding a cease-fire in the civil conflict, the Security Council, "acting under Chapter VII," authorized the secretary-general and member states to use "all necessary means to establish as soon as possible a secure environment for humanitarian relief operations in Somalia."[61] Of course, "all necessary means" includes the use of force; this had been established in the Gulf War precedent but was specifically recognized in Resolution 794 when the Security Council endorsed the recommendation of the secretary-general to that effect. The import of Resolution 794 is thus not difficult to glean: the Security Council authorized member states to stop, by force if necessary, the egregious violations of humanitarian law that were occurring in Somalia. The Security Council expressly reaffirmed that it was not its task to dictate a solution to internal differences: the Somali people "bear ultimate responsibility for the reconstruction of their own country." But the message of Resolution 794 was that, in deciding their own political fate, political groups may not violate the constraints imposed by humanitarian law. This is, therefore, a pristine case of collective, forcible intervention to put an end to a civil war in the course of which warring factions became guilty of serious violations of human rights. The reference in the resolution to the "call by Somalia" underscored that the goal was to rescue the Somali people from the horrors of the war.

Some may challenge the validity of this precedent for humanitarian intervention on the grounds that this is not an action to overthrow a tyrannical government, which is the traditional (and contested) paradigm of humanitarian intervention. They may emphasize that there is not even a government in Somalia. Therefore, this is an intervention that, unlike the cases that supporters of humanitarian intervention cite, does not aim at stopping government-directed human rights violations. Therefore Resolution 794, it is argued, is not a valid precedent for the legitimacy of collective humanitarian intervention.

This argument is not convincing. For one thing, the fact that there is no government does not mean that there is no state. No one denies that Somalia is a state or that Somalians have a right to their own state; indeed, this point is expressly underscored by the Security Council. The intervention, however, punctures the sovereignty of Somalia as a state. In addition, this is a case of civil war, which for the traditional doctrine is a typical domestic situation in which foreign intervention is banned.[62] And finally, it is important to underscore that what is called "humanitarian law" is no more than the body of human rights principles that must be respected by all parties in an armed conflict.[63] Therefore, an intervention to put an end to violations of humanitarian law is an intervention to uphold human rights—the human rights that parties in a war, civil or international, ought to honor. Resolution 794 goes further, in that it demands not merely respect for the laws of war but an end to the civil conflict itself. And the reason it goes that far is because the "human tragedy" has been caused by the war. Human suffering thus has taken precedence over state sovereignty, which is precisely the policy that undergirds humanitarian intervention.

Here again, anti-interventionists will call attention to the language in the preamble of Resolution 794. There the Security Council determined "that the magnitude of the human tragedy caused by the conflict in Somalia" constituted "a threat to international peace and security."[64] Thus this is a case, the argument goes, that falls squarely within the terms of Article 39, which defines the powers of the Security Council only in terms of breach of international peace or threat thereof. The answer is the same I gave before: this view wrongly focuses on what the Security Council says and not on what it does.

The Security Council's decisions are governed by international law. The Security Council, therefore, runs afoul of the UN Charter if it determines that a situation is a threat to the peace when in reality it is not. The council does not have discretion (in the strong sense of creating fresh law) to authorize enforcement measures to address any situation as long as it invokes, like a catchall, the language of Article 39. Hence, a defense of Resolution 794 requires postulating a preexisting legal principle that justifies that resolution, a principle that the international community could invoke as grounds for the action in Somalia. That principle can only be the power of the Security Council to authorize forcible measures in extreme situations of human rights violations.

Anti-interventionists would be on surer footing if they would flatly challenge the legality of Resolution 794 because it falls outside Article 39 standards, rather than claiming that the resolution is really about restoring international peace and not about protecting human rights. In fact, if they take the latter position, their anti-interventionism becomes empty: the Security Council can do as it pleases, provided it pays lip service to the language of Article 39.

Nor is it a bar to the language in Resolution 794 to the effect that the situation in Somalia had a "unique character" of a "deteriorating, complex, and extraordinary nature."[65] That the situation was unique and extraordinary is obviously true, in the sense that only these kinds of extreme situations warrant the collective use of force. This is perfectly consistent with the doctrine of humanitarian intervention. The doctrine does not recommend the use of force to remedy any human rights problem, any more than the doctrine of self-defense recommends using force to repel any unlawful act. Only serious human rights violations that cannot be remedied by any other means warrant proportionate collective forcible intervention for the purpose of restoring human rights, provided further that the victims themselves welcome the intervention (as was the case in Somalia). Thus for example, the Security Council would be exceeding its powers if it installed one of the leaders of the warring factions in power, because that would be inconsistent with the humanitarian character of the intervention.

That the situation is "unique" thus cannot mean that this is the only one case, the only exception where intervention in the domestic affairs of a state will ever be authorized, for that would mean that the Security Council did not act on principle. The reference to the uniqueness of the situation in

Resolution 794 means, instead, that this is an extraordinary case covered by a principle that authorizes intervention only in this class of extraordinary cases, and that the resolution should not therefore be construed as a precedent for a broad power of the Security Council to authorize intervention in less egregious cases. This interpretation of the "uniqueness" language was confirmed by the Haitian case.

Haiti, 1994

The case of Haiti is the most important precedent supporting the legitimacy both of an international principle of democratic rule and of collective humanitarian intervention. In 1987 the Organization of American States urged Haiti to resume the democratic process through free elections.[66] The UN General Assembly took up the Haitian case in 1991, relying on the action that had previously been taken by the Organization of American States. The General Assembly went further than ever before: it strongly condemned the "illegal replacement of the constitutional President of Haiti" and affirmed as "unacceptable any entity resulting from that illegal situation."[67] There was no mention of Haiti's "right" to "choose its political system" nor any reference to Haiti's sovereignty of self-determination.

After the refusal of the military dictators to reinstate the democratically elected government, the matter went to the Security Council. Acting under Chapter VII of the charter, the Security Council imposed a mandatory embargo on Haiti.[68] This binding resolution expressly affirmed that the solution to the crisis in Haiti "should take into account the above-mentioned resolutions of the Organization of American States and of the General Assembly of the United Nations," that is, the restoration of democracy in the country.[69]

After the Haitian junta refused to yield power to the first democratically elected government in Haiti's history, on 31 July 1994 the UN Security Council adopted Resolution 940. This resolution in its operative part authorized member states "to form a multinational force and . . . to use all necessary means to facilitate the departure from Haiti of the military leadership."[70] Acting under this mandate, U.S. envoys persuaded the recalcitrant junta to step down, which they did at the last minute under threat of invasion by a multinational force led by the United States. Immediately thereafter, Haiti was virtually occupied by the invasion force.[71]

An analysis of the resolution and of subsequent events confirms the conclusions reached in the cases of Iraq and Somalia. The resolution determined that "the illegal de facto regime" in Haiti had failed to comply with previous resolutions of the Security Council. The council expressed its concern with the "significant further deterioration of the humanitarian situation," in particular with the regime's "systematic violation of civil liberties." Thus the Security Council invoked human rights abuses as well as the illegitimacy of the regime as the operative reasons for authorizing military action.

Unlike the Somalia case, in this resolution the Security Council did not determine that the situation in Haiti constituted a threat to international peace and security, while at the same time asserting that it was acting under Chapter VII of the charter. Thus, this case strengthens the interpretation of the charter suggested in this chapter: that the practice of states has been to accept serious violations of human rights as grounds for action by the Security Council, under Chapter VII. Resolution 940 refers to the "unique character of the present situation in Haiti and its deteriorating, complex, and extraordinary nature, requiring an exceptional response." That the Security Council considered Haiti another "unique situation" confirms the interpretation of this language suggested in the discussion of the events in Somalia, above, namely, that Somalia was not strictly "unique" but was certainly "extraordinary" and that subsequent, equally extraordinary, cases can occur—as shown by the fact that there have been now two such "unique" cases.

What are the possible arguments against treating the Haitian case as a genuine precedent for collective humanitarian intervention? Anti-interventionists may argue, again, that in fact the Security Council found a threat to the peace and thus authorized the military action under the classic terms of Article 39. To the reply that Resolution 940 does not even try to characterize the situation in Haiti as a threat to the peace, they may rejoin that Resolution 940 refers to previous Security Council resolutions on Haiti and that, in those resolutions, the council did determine that there was a threat to international peace and security in the region.[72] And again, the answer is that this is stubborn adherence to the anti-interventionsts thesis, even when it flies in the face of the facts. No one can seriously claim that the Haitian situation posed a threat to international peace and security in the region. A more accurate reading of Resolution 940 is that the previous reference to threat to peace in the region, in Resolution 841, was unpersuasive because it reflected neither the facts nor the normative context of the Haitian situation. For that reason the council, in Resolution 940, sensibly abandoned the reference to the language of Article 39.

Another strategy could be to say that the United States really acted out of pure selfish motives, not humanitarian ones, either to stop the influx of refugees or to get rid of a problem in its backyard. First, as I argue elsewhere, this view confuses psychological motivation with legal justification.[73] Second, the view is inconsistent with the wording of Resolution 940—the legal grounds for the U.S.-led intervention. Anti-interventionists would have to say that the Security Council simply lied when it mentioned human rights abuses and the restoration of democracy in the resolution.

More important, the humanitarian justification of the intervention was given by President Clinton in his address of 15 September 1994.[74] There, the U.S. president referred repeatedly to the atrocities committed by the Haitian dictators (not just to the fact that they interrupted the democratic process in Haiti). The president did stress that such atrocities affected U.S. interests, but that begs the question of what is the legitimate U.S. national interest. If one asks why the atrocities affected U.S. interests, a plausible answer is that the national interest (defined in a broader sense, not just in terms of pure national egoism) was affected precisely because the atrocities were morally intolerable.[75]

One could reply that U.S. interests were affected because of the flow of Haitian refugees into U.S. territory, a justification cited, in fact, by President Clinton. But that only means that the United States had a self-regarding motive (stopping the influx of refugees) *in addition to* the humanitarian motives. The United States receives a huge influx of illegal immigrants from Mexico every year, and no one would suggest that it would justify armed, or even unarmed action against Mexico. The "refugee problem" in Haiti is best defined as "the refugee exodus caused by oppression" and not as "the refugee exodus" *tout court*. Finally, there is no reason why the existence of mixed motives (and in the Haitian case the humanitarian motive is overwhelmingly predominant) should blight an otherwise justified intervention.

Another possible argument here is that the action by the multinational force is not a case of humanitarian forcible intervention, because the U.S.-led forces occupied the country either with the consent of the junta, that is, of the effective government as required by traditional international law, or alternatively, with the consent of the legitimate government, President Aristide, as required by modern international law. Thus this is, so the argument goes, a mere case of peacekeeping and not of enforcement action. But this position cannot be seriously maintained. The position that the junta's consent validates the intervention is deficient for two reasons. First, it begs the question of the junta as the legitimate government of Haiti and, thus, as the valid consenting agent.[76] But second, no one can say, on these facts, that the junta validly consented to the occupation. Their "consent" was exacted by the U.S. envoys led by former president Jimmy Carter under the threat of military invasion.[77] A cursory reading of the Vienna Conven-

Beyond Sovereignty

tion on the Law of Treaties will suffice to dismiss such agreement as internationally binding.[78]

The correct legal position is that the overthrow of the junta was achieved by the threat of force, which would be prohibited by the UN Charter but for such a justification as humanitarian intervention.[79] And because the language of Resolution 940 ("all necessary means") includes the use of force, a fortiori, it includes the threat of force. The method followed by the United States is, in addition, in compliance with the requirements of necessity and proportionality, since it was the least intrusive action necessary to achieve the result mandated by Resolution 940.[80] And from a moral and political standpoint, the U.S. government must be commended for having achieved the desired result (restoration of human rights in Haiti) without having to resort to open combat.

The argument that President Aristide consented to the intervention fares better, yet it is questionable on several grounds. First, it is not clear that such consent was actually given.[81] Second, the position contradicts one of the most cherished of the anti-interventionists' dogmas—the principle that the internationally legitimate government is the one that has effective control. (This is of course not fatal to anti-interventionists, because they may reject the principle of effective control and endorse, instead, the right to democratic governance, while still opposing the legitimacy of forcible humanitarian intervention.) Third, a fair reading of Resolution 940 and the statements of President Clinton and others show that the legitimacy of forcible action did not depend on the position that Aristide is the legitimate government. Because the situation in Haiti was much more serious than the mere illegitimacy of origin of the government, a denial of consent by Aristide would not have sufficed to foreclose the legality of the collective action, nor was such consent required by Resolution 940. And finally, even if the consent by Aristide is considered valid, that would only mean that the intervention was, here again, overdetermined, that is, justified under more than one principle.

The only argument denying the validity of this precedent consistent with the facts (and internally consistent) is simply to take the position that the whole incident was a huge violation of international law, in which the Security Council, under undue political pressure from the United States, overstepped its powers under the UN Charter. This position certainly bites the bullet. It would presumably also deny the legality of the current practices of the Security Council in the other cases discussed here.

This argument has the merit of avoiding verbal sophistry but faces, instead, a formidable challenge: it is not possible to maintain this view and simultaneously adhere to a positivist conception of international law, where state and UN practice are the yardstick of legitimacy. The anti-interventionist making this argument must supply policy and moral reasons why this practice is illegitimate, notwithstanding the fact that it seems to satisfy the requirements of right process (to use Professor Franck's words.)[82] For example, noninterventionists might argue, along the lines suggested by Michael Walzer, that the Security Council ignored Haiti's communal integrity, that is, the right of Haitians to resolve their political differences among themselves, and that therefore Resolution 940 must be seen as a violation of Article 39 of the charter (interpreted in the light of Walzer's principle), not as an extension of the permissible grounds for collective action.[83]

I have elsewhere responded at length to this argument.[84] States exist primarily to protect human rights. A government such as the Haitian junta, which seizes power by force and turns against its own citizens, betrays its very raison d'être and therefore cannot be treated as legitimate. The view that describes governmental murder, rape, and torture as "a process of self-determination" is simply grotesque and may be dismissed without regrets.[85]

Summary and Conclusion

The domain reserved to the exclusive jurisdiction of the state is now quite small; international law has evolved to the point that matters that would have been unthinkable for states to have relinquished only twenty or so years ago are now subject to international scrutiny. The most recent and exciting development in this field is the principle of democratic legitimacy. And the principle that the international community has a right to intervene to uphold basic human rights is supported by the recent practice of the United Nations, in particular in Iraq, Somalia, Rwanda, and Haiti.

The end of the Cold War has impelled historians, politicians, political scientists, lawyers, and philosophers to attempt to make sense of what happened and why. but surely at least one thing is clear: there would have been no end of the Cold War without the moral defeat of tyranny, without the resolve of the liberal alliance to resist the internal and external pressures of the various enemies of freedom. As Kant rightly argued, not only are democracy and human rights the only morally defensible foundation of international law. Internal freedom, respect for democracy, and human rights make states less aggressive, not the other way around. It is a mistake to believe that once states become peaceful they will then become democratic. On the contrary, only democratic states have a chance to maintain a peaceful and stable international system for a long period of time. The rise of collective humanitarian intervention and the shrinking of traditional conceptions of sovereignty and domestic jurisdiction are essential for the preservation of peace in the new international order.

Conversely, if we lose the battle for democracy and human rights, we necessarily lose the battle for peace and security. The lesson is, perhaps, that the gradual dilution of state sovereignty is not just one more historic phenomenon, one more stage in the unfolding of the blind laws of history over which we lack control. It is, rather, a moral imperative.

3   Democracy in Latin America

Degrees, Illusions, and Directions for Consolidation

Larry Diamond

One of the functions of comparative politics is to help us see a spectrum where before we saw only two colors.

—Francisco Weffort

It is now commonly accepted in policy and journalistic circles that, save for Haiti, Cuba, and Mexico (and the possible temporary exception of Peru), the entire Western Hemisphere can be classified as democratic in its forms of governance. "Senior officials of the Bush administration liked to claim that '96 percent of Latin Americans now live in democracy' and that the Americas are becoming 'the first completely democratic hemisphere in human history.'"[1] In justifying prospective American military action to restore President Aristide to power in Haiti, President Clinton remarked: "Today 33 of the 35 countries in the Americas have democratically elected leaders."[2]

Increasingly, the member states of the hemisphere are presenting themselves as a single democratic community, committed to safeguarding and consolidating democratic regimes throughout the region. Such commitment and collective self-conception have been evolving over several decades but were given historic codification in the June 1991 Santiago Declaration, signed by foreign ministers of the OAS member states, and in the simultaneously adopted Resolution 1080, which created mechanisms for an automatic OAS response to any illegal interruption or overthrow of democracy in the hemisphere.[3]

While gratifying, this conception of a now nearly universal community of democracies in the Americas is illusory in several respects. There are, of course, the obvious anomalies. Cuba remains a communist dictatorship, though one that looks increasingly vulnerable to collapse. Haiti experienced brutal dictatorship and a human rights disaster after the overthrow of President Aristide in September 1991, and even with his restoration to power three years later, profound obstacles to effective democracy remained. But even beyond these, President Clinton's more limited statement above is wrong. At the time of his speech, the leaders of at least two countries, Mexico and the Dominican Republic (Presidents Salinas de Gortari and Balaguer), had come to power via elections that were not free and fair; a third, in Peru, seized unconstitutional powers, failed to restore democracy, and subsequently organized tainted elections for a constituent assembly and a constitutional referendum.[4]

One of the sharpest anomalies is that Mexico, the second most populous Latin American country and the first to be offered a free trade agreement with the United States, remains a one-party hegemonic state with some very authoritarian features. Although Mexico made historic progress in its August 1994 presidential election—probably the cleanest and most competitive since the ruling PRI came to power—and some other political reforms have occurred, it remains to be seen whether Ernesto Zedillo can achieve what President Salinas never seriously attempted, to transform the Mexican party-state into a true democracy. Until then, Mexico will remain a semidemocracy, where opposition can be costly and the human rights landscape is "marred by cases of torture; election-related violence, including extrajudicial killings; limitations on the right of assembly of workers, peasants, and indigenous peoples; attacks on journalists; and impunity for those responsible for all these acts."[5]

Beyond these transparent anomalies lies a great deal of ambiguity and variation in actual regime forms, as I explore below. If we look beyond formal constitutional structure, it could be argued that more than half the major states of the region (with populations over one million) fail to qualify as democracies. Several of those that do qualify suffer serious lapses in human rights and vary considerably in the nature and the quality—and progress toward the consolidation—of their democracies.

Rather than viewing democracy as merely present or absent (a sterile perspective, now that most countries of the region have transited from authoritarian rule, at least in their formal, constitutional frameworks), it is more fruitful to view democracy as a spectrum, with a range of variation in degree and form. Only by doing so can we comprehend the prospects of, and requirements for, consolidating democracy in Latin America. The experience of Latin America testifies to a simple but powerful thesis, which I argue throughout this chapter: the stability of democracy is intimately related to its quality and authenticity; democracy cannot be consolidated in the region unless it is deepened and made more genuine for all of its citizens, and this requires prominently political institutionalization.

While the transition to democracy is incomplete (or yet to begin) in Mexico, Haiti, Peru, and Cuba, the two central imperatives in the region today are the *consolidation* and *deepening* of democracy. Consolidation is the process by which democracy becomes so broadly and profoundly legitimate among its citizens that it is unlikely to break down. It involves behavioral and institutional changes that normalize democratic politics and narrow its uncertainty (even to the point of rendering it rather boring). Put differently (though not inconsistently with the above), the consolidation process transforms "the accidental arrangements, prudential norms, and contingent solutions that have emerged during the transition into relations of cooperation and competition that are reliably known, regularly practiced, and voluntarily accepted by . . . politicians and citizens."[6] Thus, while they may experience frequent alternation in party control of government, consolidated democracies are so stable in their rules and existence that their future existence can be (and too often is) taken for granted.

Democratic deepening improves the quality, depth, and authenticity of democracy in several dimensions: fairer, freer, more vigorous, and more extensive political competition; broader, more autonomous, and more inclusive participation and representation; more comprehensively and rigorously protected civil liberties; and more systematic and transparent accountability. In most recently established democracies in Latin America (and in all of the crisis-ridden ones), deepening is essential for generating the broad, intrinsic political legitimacy that is the sine qua non of consolidation.

Yet there is often a paradoxical, even dialectical, relationship between deepening and consolidation. A quarter century ago, Samuel Huntington argued that modernity generates political stability but that the *process* of modernization often breeds instability.[7] Similarly, the *process* of deepening democracy—democratizing political parties and local governments, strengthening the legislative and judicial branches, developing grassroots civic movements, empowering the poor, punishing corruption and human rights abuses, and subjecting the military to civilian control—typically involves heightened conflict. Such conflict may be creative for democracy, but it is also destabilizing.[8] As I argue below with respect to establishing democratic civil-military relations, democratic leaders must have a shrewd sense of political vision, strategy, and tactics if they are to find the pace and sequencing of reforms to deepen democracy without igniting a dangerous and polarizing conflict (or what Juan Linz calls "disloyal" reactions on the part of key power groups).[9]

The ideal pace and sequence of reform will differ from country to country and across time. The relationship between democratic deepening and stability is curvilinear: that is, some degree and speed of reform will do more to consolidate democracy than to destabilize it, but beyond a certain pace and scope the risks to short-term democratic stability will exceed the stabilizing gains for democratic consolidation. As with economic reform, however, there are sometimes historic moments (often at the start of a presidential term) when political leaders have peak amounts of political capital that they can draw on to launch new initiatives and achieve dramatic gains.

Conceptualizing Democracy

Features, Forms, and Degrees

Even while accepting that there is great variation in regime forms, it is possible to identify criteria that distinguish those regimes that can broadly be classified as democratic from those that do not quite—or do not at all—meet the performance standards of a democracy. In our multicountry study of democracy in developing countries, Juan Linz, Seymour Martin Lipset, and I define democracy in terms just slightly reformulating those of Robert Dahl for *polyarchy:*

> Democracy denotes . . . a system of government that meets three essential conditions: meaningful and extensive *competition* among individuals and groups (especially political parties) for all effective positions of government power, at regular intervals and excluding the use of force; a highly inclusive level of *political participation* in the selection of leaders and policies, at least through regular and fair elections, such that no major (adult) social group is excluded; and a level of *civil and political liberties*—freedom of expression, freedom of the press, freedom to form and join organizations—sufficient to ensure the integrity of political competition and participation.[10]

Implicit in this definition are the notions that rulers will be held accountable for their actions in the public realm by citizens and their representatives and that there exist multiple channels for representation of citizen interests beyond the formal political frameworks of parties, parliaments, and elections.[11]

These features of democracy are closely (though not perfectly) captured by Freedom House's annual ratings of political rights and civil liberties. Political rights enable the individual to participate freely in the making of policies and the selection of "authoritative policy makers"; they include the right of all adults to vote and compete for public office, through free and fair elections and alternative political parties, and the ability of elected representatives to have a decisive vote on policies. "Civil liberties are the freedoms to develop views, institutions, and personal autonomy apart from the state"; they include freedoms of conscience, religion, expression, information, assembly, and organization, as well as freedom from torture and terror and due process and equality under the law.[12] Every country is rated from 1 to 7 on each of these two measures, with 1 being the most free and 7 the most authoritarian. These two related measures are then combined (for the purpose of categorizing countries) into a total score, which ranges from 2 to 14 (and then summarizes the much more detailed raw point scores).[13] The combined score is used to aggregate countries into three broad categories: *free, partly free,* and *not free.* Any country with a combined freedom score of 5 or lower is rated *free.*

This combined score represents the most precise annual measure available of a regime's democraticness, and that is how I use it in this chapter. My usage differs from that of Freedom House, which counts countries as democratic on formal structural criteria, independent of its empirical ratings.[14] Instead, I consider the *free* category the best empirical indicator for the concept of democracy as defined above. Thus, throughout this chapter, I consider as *democratic* only those countries rated *free* by Freedom House. However, Freedom House's category *partly free* encompasses much more than *semidemocratic,* and my classification of Latin American regimes, based on the Freedom House data (see table 1), uses a much finer typology.

It is of particular importance for Latin America that we make a distinction between *democracy* and *semidemocracy,* defining *semidemocracy* as a regime in which "the effective power of elected officials is so limited, or political party competition is so restricted, or the freedom and fairness of elections so compromised that electoral outcomes, while competitive, still deviate significantly from popular preferences; and/or where civil and political liberties are so limited that some political orientations and interests are unable to organize and express themselves."[15] Semidemocracy has often been the empirical reality in countries whose *formal* constitutional structures look quite democratic.

With Mexico particularly in mind, my colleagues and I distinguished a more restrictive form of semidemocracy, which we termed (after Giovanni Sartori) a *hegemonic party system,* "in which opposition parties are legal but denied—through pervasive electoral malpractices and frequent state coercion—any real chance to compete for power." And, urging close attention to the actual behavior of regimes, we further identified a subclass of authoritarian regimes, which we called *pseudodemocracies,* in that "the existence of formally democratic political institutions, such as multiparty electoral competition, masks (often, in part, to legitimate) the reality of authoritarian domination."

While these few categories render the classification more rigorous and

Table 1. The Democratic Status of Latin American Countries, 1987 and 1994

Regime Type and Combined Freedom Score	Countries and Freedom Scores for Political Rights and Civil Liberties[a]	
	1987	1994
Liberal democracy, 2	Costa Rica (1, 1) Trinidad and Tobago (1, 1)⇑	
Democracy, 3–4	Argentina (2, 1) Uruguay (2, 2) Jamaica (2, 2)⇑ Dominican Republic (1, 3) Brazil (2, 2) Venezuela (1, 2)	Costa Rica (1, 2)# Trinidad and Tobago (1, 2)⇓ Uruguay (2, 2)# Chile (2, 2)
Partially illiberal democracy, 5	Colombia (2, 3) Bolivia (2, 3) Ecuador (2, 3) Peru (2, 3) Honduras (2, 3)	Argentina (2, 3) ↓ Bolivia (2, 3) ↓ Ecuador (2, 3) ↓ Jamaica (2, 3)⇓ Panama (2, 3)⇑
Near democracy, 6	Guatemala (3, 3)	Brazil (2, 4)⇑ El Salvador (3, 3) Honduras (3, 3)# Venezuela (3, 3) ↓
Semidemocracy, 7	El Salvador (3, 4)	Colombia (3, 4)⇓ Dominican Republic (4, 3)⇓ Paraguay (4, 3)⇓
Semicompetitive authoritarian, 8–9	Mexico (4, 4)	Mexico (4, 4)⇓ Nicaragua (4, 5)⇓ Guatemala (4, 5) ↓ Peru (5, 4)
Authoritarian, 10–12	Chile (6, 5) Haiti (5, 6)⇓ Nicaragua (5, 5)⇑ Panama (5, 5)⇓ Paraguay (5, 6)	Haiti (5, 5)⇑
State hegemonic closed, 13–14	Cuba (6, 6)	Cuba (7, 7)

Source: Freedom House, *Freedom in the World: Political Rights and Civil Liberties, 1987–1988* (New York: Freedom House, 1988); and *Freedom Review* (Jan.–Feb. 1995).

Note: The table excludes countries with less than 1 million population. The figures in parentheses are the Freedom House scores for individual countries (political rights and civil liberties, respectively). Each scale ranges from 1 to 7, with 1 being most free. The following symbols apply to the last year of change in either 1993 or 1994: ⇑ Indicates a shift upward in the freedom score from the previous year; # Indicates that the rating was changed for purely methodological reasons; ⇓ Indicates a shift downward; ↓ Indicates a downward trend in the level of democracy but not significant enough to have changed the freedom rating.

[a]Political rights are those of contestation, opposition, and participation; civil liberties are those of expression, information, organization, due process, etc.

meaningful, the term *democracy* encompasses even more degrees of variation (as the Freedom House ratings demonstrate). In the formal terms of social science, *democracy* is a continuous rather than categorical variable, so the more categories we employ, the more sensitively we will capture its range of variation. (At the same time, if we use too many categories, we lose the ability to group countries in ways that can be useful both for theory and policy.) For purposes of classifying contemporary Latin American regimes, table 1 uses eight categories, three above the threshold of democracy and five below it. The theoretically important category of *competitive semi-democracy*, whose performance in terms of electoral fairness, political accountability, political violence, individual liberties, and so on places them just below the threshold of democracy, might be called *near democracy* and is, essentially, comparable to the category of *near polyarchies* identified by Robert Dahl.[16]

There are many possible schemes for regime classification, and my purpose is not to appeal for the superiority of my own but to underscore the importance of making careful, empirical distinctions between actual levels of democracy. This requires looking beyond the formal constitutional structure to ask questions such as the following: Are elections free, fair, and competitive? Does the opposition have a realistic chance of increasing its support and eventually gaining power? Is power effectively exercised by elected officials and their appointees, or do democratically unaccountable officials—the military, local bosses, and landed elites—constrain, veto, and undermine the constitutional flow of power and rule of law? Can citizens elect their own leaders at the local and regional level? Are basic freedoms of expression, organization, assembly, movement, conscience, and due process respected in practice? Do citizens have the freedom to criticize, to oppose, or to mobilize around their interests and beliefs without fear of punishment, either by the state or powerful private interests?[17]

Types of Democracy and Degrees of Institutionalization

We need to think seriously as well about the types of democracy that are emerging in this "third wave" of global democratization.[18] There are two senses in which type of democracy is highly salient: in the formal institutional structures and in the informal patterns in which power is exercised. Formally, there are two striking (and unfortunate) commonalities in the constitutional structures of Latin America's democracies. They are all presidential rather than parliamentary, and almost all elect their national legislatures on the basis of proportional representation (PR) rather than single-member districts. As a result, most of them have multiparty systems. In fact, they are virtually the only countries in the world that combine presidentialism with PR elections, an institutional arrangement highly prone to instability, as we will see below. Historically, these governments have tended to be heavily centralized, with power, resources, and representation devolving to localities only recently in some countries.

In institutional practice, one finds important variations. The few countries with relatively deep democratic roots—Chile, Uruguay, Costa Rica, and (decreasingly in recent years) Venezuela and Colombia—have enjoyed a relatively settled and institutionalized political party system. Most countries, such as Brazil, Peru, Bolivia, Nicaragua, and Panama, have no tradition of strong, institutionalized parties to draw upon and have suffered from it in the performance of their party systems.

This lack of institutionalization is a critical feature in a related dimension of variation, marked by a particular type of democracy, a "new species"–which Guillermo O'Donnell calls "delegative democracy."[19] The terms *low-intensity democracy, democracy by default, poor democracy,* and *empty democracy* have also been used to describe the institutionally weak and substantively superficial nature of Latin America's new democracies.[20] However, these conceptions are not as precisely circumscribed, theoretically, as O'Donnell's, which hinges critically on the relative absence of "horizontal accountability" between the elected president and the other two branches of government.

Although delegative democracies have the formal constitutional structures of democracy—and may even meet the empirical standards articulated here, as Argentina seems to do—they tend to be institutionally hollow and fragile. Voters are mobilized by clientelistic ties and populist, personalistic (rather than programmatic) appeals; parties and independent interest groups are weak and fragmented. Instead of producing an effective means of ongoing representation of popular interests, elections delegate sweeping (and largely unaccountable) authority to whoever wins the presidential election. For his or her term of office, the (democratically) elected president can then govern by decree and even whim, claiming to embody the will of the nation, while invoking an authority based more on personal charisma and the backing of a popular movement than on a political party or institution.

In such plebiscitary systems, O'Donnell argues, change (including economic reform) can be implemented swiftly and decisively precisely because so much power is delegated to a single office. However, policy is also more likely to be erratic and unsustainable, because the very swiftness and lack of consultation generate "a higher likelihood of gross mistakes," because election campaigns do not produce any clear programmatic and policy commitments that subsequently constrain leaders and because no effort is made after the election to build a broad and informed coalition of support for the new policies.[21] The only real platform of the elected president is, as Argentine President Carlos Menem said in his election campaign, *siganme* (follow me).[22]

For those concerned to see the consolidation of democracy in the region, delegative democracies thus present a number of problems. While truly representative systems also delegate authority from the people, they do so in ways that check and separate powers and establish accountability—not only vertically and at election time but horizontally and continuously, in the play between independent branches of government.[23] Because they rest on well-developed political institutions—parties, legislatures, courts, local governments, and so on—and are much more inclined to engage organized forces in civil society (and thus to provide more continuous vertical accountability), representative democracies, in O'Donnell's scheme, are not only more likely to check the abuse of power, they are also more likely to produce stable, sustainable, and broadly acceptable policies (though ones perhaps less capable of "miracles"). They are thus more likely to avoid repeated crisis and to attenuate rather than swell popular cynicism. For all these reasons, democracies are more likely to become consolidated the more they are representative rather than delegative.

Democracy in Latin America Today

Progress and Illusion

Around the world, democracy has expanded dramatically since 1974. The number of states that qualify empirically as democracies (i.e., that are rated as *free* in the Freedom House annual survey) has grown steadily, from forty-two in 1972 (the first year of the survey) to fifty-two in 1980, and seventy-six in 1994. During this period, the proportion of the world's regimes that are democratic increased from 29 percent in 1972 to roughly 40 percent in 1994.[24]

Tracing the movements since 1980 among the regime categories in table 1 shows even more dramatic progress than is revealed by the movement between the categories of *free, partly free,* and *not free.* The most extreme, authoritarian, state hegemonic regimes remained stable in number between 1980 and 1989 but declined sharply between 1989 and 1991 (from 41 percent to 30 percent of all states). There were also many fewer moderately authoritarian regimes and more semidemocracies. Most encouragingly, in the three most democratic categories, the biggest increase was in the most democratic regime type (stable, liberal democracies), which increased from eighteen to twenty-nine between 1980 and 1991. During 1993, however, this progress began to ebb, as the number of highly authoritarian (not free) regimes increased dramatically from thirty-eight to fifty-five.

How does Latin America and the Caribbean compare with this overall global democratic trend? As the Inter-American Dialogue observes, "the 1980s were a period of extraordinary political renewal in Latin America. . . . In 1979, elected leaders governed in only two of ten South American countries—Venezuela and Colombia—and in just one of the six republics of Central America and Panama—Costa Rica. A dozen years later, popularly elected presidents held office in every Central and South American nation, and democratic rule remained strong in most of the Commonwealth Caribbean."[25] Of the twenty-two countries in the region with populations over one million, only seven met the empirical standard of democracy in 1980. By 1987, as shown in table 1, thirteen did so. Moreover, several of these countries were recording historic firsts in democratic persistence. In Bolivia in 1985, the presidency passed from one party to another through competitive elections for the first time ever. One democratically elected president succeeded another for the first time ever in Peru in 1985, and for the first time in six decades in Argentina in 1989.[26]

However, the existence of a popularly elected president does not necessarily signify democracy. And since 1987, despite commonplace North American perceptions to the contrary, Latin America has not made significant net progress toward greater democracy. Rather, while the level of democracy has improved in some countries (and in some aspects in a number of countries), it has generally declined in the region. At the end of 1992, only eleven of the twenty-two countries stood within the conceptual threshold of democracy, and six of these had the least democratic score (5) of the four overall freedom scores qualifying as democratic (2, 3, 4, and 5). Two years later, as indicated in table 1, the region was even less democratic, and by a significant margin: only nine of the countries were democracies; another four were near democracies. Three countries improved their level of democracy during 1993 and 1994, but seven declined, and in another five countries whose sum score on political rights and civil liberties did not change, Freedom House noted an overall downward trend in level of freedom. (By sharp contrast, nine of the eleven Latin American and Caribbean countries with populations of less than one million were democracies in 1994, and seven of them—all former British colonies—had combined freedom scores of 2 or 3.)[27]

To be sure, at the end of 1994 there were fewer authoritarian regimes (Cuba, Haiti, and Peru) than there were in 1987 (when there were six). And the regimes in Mexico, Nicaragua, Panama, and Paraguay have become more competitive and liberal. But Nicaragua has slipped back considerably, and election malpractices and bias remain a barrier to full democracy in several countries (including, in addition to those mentioned earlier, Paraguay).[28] Electoral participation increased significantly in several new democracies during the 1980s, and various political and social pacts reflected a new emphasis on moderation and consensus.[29] Most significantly, Chile has returned to democracy.

However, these positive trends have been counterbalanced by a number of negative developments:

—Venezuela and Colombia, second only to Costa Rica in the number of years of continuous democracy, slipped to semidemocratic status amid growing signs of institutional decay and popular alienation.

—Peru suffered an *autogolpe* in April 1992 at the hands of an elected, civilian president, Alberto Fujimori, who has governed in authoritarian fashion.

—Guatemala deteriorated from a near democracy to a less competitive and more repressive regime and then suffered an attempted *autogolpe* in early 1993, from which it has yet to recover institutionally.

—Haiti's brief, tentative, elected government was overthrown by a military coup in September 1991, after less than a year in power; it was restored only through armed intervention and is in need of sweeping social and institutional reforms.

—Argentina remained democratic but with a lower level of civil liberties and governmental accountability.

—Even before the crisis-ridden May 1994 presidential elections, in which President Balaguer fraudulently won reelection to a third term, the Dominican Republic had slipped below the threshold of democracy "because of the continuing erosion of public and political institutions and unchecked official corruption."[30]

—Brazil fell to semidemocratic status due to the stunning corruption and inefficacy of its political institutions, the consequent increasing influence of the military in politics, and the sharp deterioration of civil liberties amid "a growing climate of lawlessness" and "a breakdown of police discipline."[31]

In short, if we take the definition and actual performance of democracy seriously, it is impossible to claim that the Americas are overwhelmingly democratic today, or that the broad political trend has been democratic in recent years. In 1994, a dozen of the principal countries with democratic constitutions fell short of this standard. In both recently established systems, from Brazil to Panama and Nicaragua, and in such long-standing ones as Colombia and Venezuela, formally democratic regimes suffer from a number of common afflictions: weak or decaying political institutions; unwieldy institutional designs; crippling political divisions and personal rivalries that fragment coalitions and undermine governability; escalating criminal and political violence, drug trafficking, and human rights abuses; weak, intimidated, and ineffective judiciaries; persistent and even increasing high levels of unemployment, inflation, and poverty; massive inequalities; and endemic corruption. Certainly these problems are not unique to democracy, but they may be uniquely corrosive of it.

A closer look at some individual countries illustrates the democratically debilitating consequences of these problems and belies the assumption that Latin America has now entered "a distinctive historical phase" of more authentic and durable democracy.[32]

The most serious blow to the regional advance of democracy was dealt by the Fujimori coup in Peru. Even more striking than President Fujimori's seizure of unconstitutional powers and closure of Congress and the judiciary in Peru was the widespread domestic support for (and less than forceful regional response to) his actions. Public opinion polls showed more than three-quarters of a desperate and despairing Peruvian public approved his authoritarian steps, even while almost the same proportion still expressed a preference for democracy in principle.[33] Throughout 1992, Fujimori's public approval rating never dipped below 60 percent.[34] The majority of business and military leaders also supported the coup, and despite the resistance of opposition parties, the "new caudillo" had little difficulty in imposing his plan for reshaping the political system to his liking, beginning with constituent assembly elections in November 1992.

With extensive manipulation of the electoral rules and timetable, those elections gave Fujimori an outright legislative majority for the first time but with less than 40 percent of the vote for his coalition. Further doubt about his level of public support was cast by the October 1993 referendum for a new constitution to legitimate and facilitate his rule, which Fujimori officially won with 52 percent of the votes but with evidence of fraud that some impartial observers believe provided the margin of victory.[35] Fujimori did win reelection to a second term, in April 1995, in a massive first-ballot victory, but the pursuit of effective redemocratization is bedeviled by the systematic desecration of independent institutions, the steady expansion of the military's political role, and the dramatic aggrandizement of presidential power in the new constitution (including provisions for an immediate reelection, the dissolution of Congress, and greater authority by decree).[36]

The superficiality of public democratic commitment (evidenced in the majority view that the postcoup Fujimori government was democratic) and the country's willingness to abide authoritarian measures stemmed from two factors in Peruvian life: (1) the steady erosion and discrediting of democratic institutions since their inauguration in 1980 (reflected in its declining annual freedom ratings in the years before 1992) and (2) the relentless growth of terrorist political violence and economic decay. During the 1980s the real minimum wage declined by 77 percent, by far the steepest drop in Latin America, and by 1991 about half the population was living in "critical poverty."[37] Traditional political parties fragmented and became the object of wide public disdain; torture, disappearances, and other human rights abuses soared; governance became increasingly militarized (with over half the country under army control); drug trafficking mushroomed, nevertheless; and terrorist violence (principally by Sendero Luminoso) claimed more and more lives with ever greater impunity, while the judiciary became paralyzed by fear and corruption.[38] Plainly, democracy had become a very shallow reality in Peru well before Fujimori suspended it altogether and reified the country's status as "one of the most tormented countries of Latin America."[39]

The Peruvian example is important theoretically, not only because it manifests all the afflictions of democracy in Latin America today but also because, as a particularly glaring example of O'Donnell's "delegative democracy," it suggests the greater vulnerability to breakdown of this type of regime. It may thus signal the direction in which other centralized, personalistic, corrupt, clientelistic, fragmented, and weakly institutionalized democracies are headed if significant improvements are not forthcoming. Some see this future already visible in the failed *autogolpe* of President Jorge Serrano in Guatemala in 1993 and the two coup attempts in Venezuela during 1992.

Guatemala evinced many classic signs of a hollow, stalemated, delegative democracy. In the absence of strong parties, Serrano, like Fujimori, surged virtually from nowhere to a dramatic runoff victory by casting himself as an antipolitician. Like Fujimori, he lacked a base of support in Congress and ruled with contempt for Congress. Tired of having to bribe the members shamelessly for every vote he wanted, fearful (like Fujimori) of exposure for his own personal corruption, apparently waiting (like Fujimori) for the authoritarian moment from the very start of his presidency, and no doubt encouraged by Fujimori's own success (and the lack of a forceful international response), Serrano decided to stage his own self-coup.

Serrano's failure owed not to any greater institutional resilience in

Guatemala than in Peru but to much quicker and more determined opposition from civil society and from the United States and the inter-American community.[40] But while those forceful responses defeated the coup and helped usher the respected human rights ombudsman, Ramiro de Leon Carpio, into the vacant presidency, they have not changed the underlying reality of military domination. Ever since the restoration of formally constitutional government with the inauguration of President Vinicio Cerezo in 1985, the military has continued to wield the greatest share of real power in the country, blocking a negotiated settlement of the decades-long guerrilla war, controlling the countryside through a vast paramilitary apparatus, while murdering, bombing, torturing and terrorizing leftist politicians, civic organizers, human rights activists, and journalists with impunity. As a result, even before Serrano's attempt to suspend the constitution, Freedom House gave Guatemala the worst freedom rating in the hemisphere, after Cuba, Haiti, and Peru. The democratically minded de Leon Carpio has proved powerless to effect real political reform.[41]

The repeated coup attempts in Venezuela were even more shocking because Venezuela had long been regarded as a pillar of democracy in Latin America, with a stable two-party system that had operated thirty-five years without interruption (and nearly three decades without a coup attempt). President Carlos Andrés Pérez's surprise announcement of economic austerity measures, shortly after his inauguration in February 1989, triggered massive, bloody rioting. The coup attempts then came on the heels of a rather spectacular (if possibly cyclical) recovery from the punishing economic decline of the 1980s.

Venezuela's democratic stability had obviously been built on the quicksand of an unsustainable political economy. The profligate distribution of state petroleum revenues (and when these dwindled, foreign debt), through lavish patronage and corruption, high profits, high wages, and the lowest taxes on the continent (as well as the extreme protectionism characteristic of other countries on the continent), eventually produced a fiscal crisis and adjustment imperatives for which the country, politically and psychologically, was totally unprepared.[42]

Moreover, closer examination might have gleaned from the 1989 *caracazo* (explosion) in Caracas (which may have claimed as much as eight times the official death toll of 277) the warning sign "that no institutions existed to channel Venezuelans' discontent."[43] Mounting intraparty factionalism and personal rivalry and the steady erosion of the spirit of cooperation and compromise "had weakened beyond recognition" the distinctive pattern of democratic pragmatism, collaboration, and incorporation initiated by the Pact of Punto Fijo with the rebirth of democracy in 1958.[44]

The two strong, dominant parties increasingly appeared to constitute a venal, self-interested *partidocracia,* which, in its extreme internal centralization and pervasive reach, monopolized power, limited accountability to the voters, and "blocked channels for representation outside the parties, within the parties, and among the parties."[45]

Yet recent Venezuelan experience also reflects the emergence of a reformist countertrend in Latin America. The Commission for the Reform of the State appointed by President Jaime Lusinchi in 1984 proposed "thorough and wide-ranging reforms to improve accountability," and many of these have been gradually adopted over the ensuing decade, including (1) the direct election of mayors and governors, (2) some devolution of resources and authority to states and localities, (3) midterm elections for municipal and state-level officials, (4) the recall of city council members, and (5) primary elections within the two largest parties.[46] Although the leader of the 1992 coups became instantly popular, the Venezuelan public continued to manifest overwhelming support (up to 97%) for democracy, as opposed to military rule.[47] Pressure was also relieved by the impeachment and removal on corruption charges of President Pérez in May 1993 and the election by Congress in June of a successor (Senator Ramón José Valásquez) to serve the remaining months of Peréz's term.

In one sense, the outcome of the December 1993 presidential election reflected political decay: a decisive rejection of the two main parties (AD and COPEI), which together captured the lowest share of the vote since competitive politics was restored in 1958, and a skimpy plurality of 31 percent for aging former president Rafael Caldera, a founder of COPEI who ran as a populist (some charged demagogic) independent, supported by a patchwork of leftist and right-wing groups. Yet the election may also signal the weakening of *partidocracia* and the invigoration of political competition. This may be an instance where democratic deepening or renewal interacts with stability in complex, dialectical, and delayed fashion; where the positive benefits of institutional reform are realized only gradually and cumulatively; and therefore where democrats must not only have the energy to deepen reforms but also the patience to let them work.[48]

The vast majority of Panamanians (80%) also still express a preference for democracy as a form of government. But when people become widely disillusioned with the way that democracy is actually working in their country, as they have become in Panama, the system becomes vulnerable. The pervasive, paralyzing, political infighting and utter disintegration of President Guillermo Endara's broad, post-Noriega coalition, his consequent loss of control over the National Assembly and even over his own party, and the mounting corruption, crime, and violence (especially associated with the flourishing drug trade) stripped political support not only from Endara (who fell to 9% approval in the polls) but from most the other politicians as well.

As elsewhere in Latin America where democracy is in crisis, the political vacuum in Panama interacts with a social and economic reality that leaves broad swaths of the population (most explosively, urban youth) poor, marginalized, unemployed, and profoundly disillusioned.[49] It remains to be seen whether the election of a new president in May 1994—businessman Ernesto Pérez Balladares—will lead to political and social reform. His small electoral plurality (33% of the vote), his party's past association with General Noriega, and most of all, the country's disdain for politicians are handicaps. But the peaceful transfer of power to an opposing party, through an election made cleaner by reforms that established an independent electoral commission, was an important step forward.

The Dominican Republic appeared for many years to be a paradigmatic case of democratic persistence (since 1978) without consolidation or effective governance. But by 1993 corruption and misgovernance had undermined the regime's status as a democracy, and that decline was decisively reflected in the May 1994 presidential elections, when electoral fraud appeared to provide the narrow margin of victory in reelecting the country's dominant political figure of three decades, the blind, eighty-seven-year-old President Joaquín Balaguer. The election results were "widely disbelieved by vast sectors of the population and by international actors" and "helped to demonstrate the continuing fragility of the Dominican political regime and the low legitimacy of state institutions and basic political processes."[50]

Plagued by a legacy of venal, patrimonial politics, the Dominican Republic failed to improve its weak political institutions since the return of democracy; in fact, the party system has become even more fragmented of late. The centrality of the state sector in economic and social life, the strongly presidential system (manifesting many features of delegative democracy), and the extreme underdevelopment of structures for accountability all generate enormous electoral stakes and high incentives for fraud and misconduct.[51] Absent an effective party system and governmental reforms to increase participation, decentralize power, insulate and depoliticize the electoral administration, and address enduring problems of poverty, statism, corruption, and waste, the best the Dominican Republic can hope for is to stumble on with a fragile near-democracy, unresponsive to deepening public cynicism and disillusionment.[52]

Perhaps the archetypical delegative democracy is the regime in Argentina, where President Carlos Menem has made impressive progress in implementing economic reform, while ruling primarily by decree and with considerable contempt for democratic institutions. By September 1993, Menem had issued 244 decrees, an amazing 91 percent of all Argentine presidential decrees under emergency laws since 1853.[53] "Under Menem . . . the judicial system has been made into a political instrument of the president,"[54] who packed the Supreme Court and then used it the following year to uphold his executive orders removing officials mandated to probe political corruption. In 1993, he forced some of the judges he appointed in 1990 to resign as part of a package deal with former President Raúl Alfonsín (still leader of the opposition Radical Party). In exchange for that and certain other political concessions and spoils, Alfonsín agreed to provide the additional legislative support Menem needed for a constitutional amendment to permit presidential reelection.

Meanwhile, journalists have come under increasing pressure and assault as they have investigated and exposed massive government corruption (producing twenty major scandals and some two dozen senior government resignations in the first four and a half years of Menem's administration), as well as criminal activity by Menem's Peronist Party. In the period before the October 1993 Chamber of Deputies elections (which failed to give Menem's Peronist Party the two-thirds majority it needed to amend the constitution unilaterally), "Peronists were implicated in a series of death threats and physical attacks against prominent journalists critical of Menem," and Menem himself has sought to intimidate and demoralize critical journalists with an assault of expensive lawsuits.[55]

While Brazil may be seen as a classic instance of delegative democracy, many discerned a new accountability and institutional vigor arising from the process that forced the resignation of President Fernando Collor de Mello on 29 December 1992. When Collor resigned, the Senate was just about to begin his impeachment trial, voted by the Chamber of Deputies in September, in which he was charged with bribery and influence peddling. The Senate's overwhelming vote of conviction the next day, barring Collor from political office for eight years, the smooth succession of Vice President Itamar Franco as acting president on 2 October (and then president after the resignation), the sustained and vigorous independence of the press and the courts, the resolute neutrality of the military, and the responsible behavior of the country's "usually undisciplined" political parties all appeared as "proof of the vitality of Brazilian democratic institutions."[56]

However, the dramatic victory for constitutionalism was short-lived and did not alter the more fundamental vulnerabilities of Brazilian democracy:

—Massive social inequalities (falling heavily along racial lines), which give the country one of the most unequal income distributions in the world, with more than a fifth of its population living in hunger[57]

—Persistent high inflation, which by July 1993 was robbing the cruzeiro of 1 percent of its value every thirty-six hours, and the absence of any national consensus on a course of economic reform

—Young, weak, fragmented, and fleeting political parties without durable bases of mass support

—A profoundly contradictory blend of plebiscitarian and consociational institutions that presses toward a distinctive type of ungovernability, what Bolivar Lamounier calls "hyperactive paralysis"[58]

—Systemic political corruption, which continued to cripple government functioning in 1993, as dozens of legislators, cabinet ministers, governors, and industrialists became enmeshed in scandal

—A continuing penchant for embracing colorful and corrupt politicians at the polls (as in the election of Paulo Maluf as mayor of São Paulo during Collor's impeachment in November 1992)

Nor did the impeachment crisis, to which the personalistic nature of presidential rule in Brazil clearly contributed, lead the country to seize the opportunity for fundamental institutional change. In a long-scheduled referendum the following April, Brazilians voted solidly to reject parliamentarism and retain the presidential system. The election to the presidency in October 1994 of Fernando Henrique Cardoso, a highly respected centrist and proven coalition builder, and the success of the stabilization plan he had launched earlier in the year (as finance minister) in controlling inflation, offered hope of progress toward democratic consolidation. But the combined weight of Brazil's problems has produced a "crisis of confidence in representative institutions" that has further eroded governability[59] and opened the door to expansion of the military's political role and prerogatives.[60]

The Brazilian situation may be an extreme case. Francisco Weffort, however, suggests that it is reflective of the institutional weaknesses that beset the "new democracies" of Latin America:

> We have personalistic rather than national leaders; we have political groups . . . rather than political parties; we have ideological trends and intellectual proposals that make for a democratic atmosphere, rather than debate about a new national project. We have a fragmented, dispersed agglomeration of leaders loosely unified by support for democracy within public opinion and by democratic competition itself. Yet we do not have a political class (or political elite) imbued with a general consciousness of its

role in the process of democratic consolidation or in the building of a new state (or, more precisely, a democratic state).[61]

Among the recently restored democracies of Latin America, only Uruguay and Chile depart clearly from this pattern. There, democratic values and political parties have deep (though not unblemished) historic roots, and posttransition governments have been able to mobilize some degree of national vision and consensus while rising above narrow partisan and factional divisions. The first posttransition presidents, Julio María Sanguinetti in Uruguay and Patricio Aylwin in Chile, governed in a style notably different from the *personalismo* and *decretismo* of delegative democracies. Rather than bypassing representative institutions and imposing personal policies, they sought to mobilize and maintain broad consensual support. The capacity of seventeen center-left parties to hold together in Chile's Concertación de Partidos por la Democracia has been particularly impressive and resulted in a decisive victory for the coalition in the December 1993 presidential election, when Eduardo Frei won with 58 percent of the vote (to 24% for his principal right-wing rival). Chile was also advantaged by the surprising degree of economic policy consensus that emerged with the booming success of Pinochet's economic liberalization policies late in his rule.

Ironically enough, however, while Chile's economic dynamism (10% GDP growth in 1992), strong parties, broad political cooperation, and moderate, accommodating political leadership reflect democratic maturity and potential, it confronts significant obstacles to the consolidation of full democracy. As Alicia Frohmann shows in this volume (see chap. 10), these obstacles heavily derive from the ability of General Pinochet, the armed forces as an institution, and their right-wing political allies to set the boundaries of the current constitutional system and then to block democratizing reforms by using the political power they had guaranteed themselves (through such measures as nine military-appointed senators, military appointment of commanders-in-chief, and perpetuation of the Pinochet-dominated courts).[62]

Nevertheless, virtually alone among the new democracies of the region, time may be on the side of the democrats in Chile. Under the 1980 constitution, General Pinochet will depart as commander of the army in 1997, at which time the eight-year term of the appointed senators will expire (and they will be either changed or abolished). And there has been incremental progress toward further democratization, including (1) the military's acceptance of direct elections for municipal governments, successfully conducted in June 1992 (when the parties of the concertación reestablished their claim to majority support), (2) the impeachment in January 1993 of a right-wing Supreme Court justice (over military opposition), (3) Aylwin's deft (and popular) rebuff of Pinochet's attempts to pressure his government, and (4) the November 1993 convictions in a civil court of two former military officers for the 1976 murder in the United States of Salvador Allende's ambassador to Washington, Orlando Letelier.

However, for the time being at least, political stalemate persists on a variety of fundamental issues, such as reforming the judiciary and punishing those responsible for grave human rights abuses under Pinochet.[63] Not only in Chile, but also in Uruguay, Argentina, Brazil, El Salvador, and perhaps Haiti as well, the pursuit of a rule of law, so essential to democratic consolidation, remains haunted, first, by the Faustian bargain— democracy in exchange for amnesty—that civilian leaders have had to strike with the military and, second, by the apparently growing cooperation by South American security services in shielding one another from prosecution.[64]

Democracy and Human Rights

Democracy encompasses more than competitive elections and a universal franchise. Citizens must have the ability to decide who will exercise *effective* power, not just formal authority, in their country. They must be able to hold their rulers accountable under the constitution and the law and to voice and lobby for their interests between elections. No contemporary democracy meets these standards perfectly, but no polity that violates them systematically can be considered democratic. In Latin America, and throughout the new (and in such cases as India, Sri Lanka, and Colombia, longstanding) democracies of the "third wave," the status of democracy is closely linked to the protection of human rights: individual rights of conscience, expression, organization, and peaceful demonstration; freedom from torture and arbitrary detention and violence; due process under a rule of law; equality of treatment for women and ethnic minorities; and the right of minorities to practice their cultures and organize for their interests. In fact, this linkage is by definition, in that these rights essentially comprise the civil liberties without which democracy cannot be liberal, or even adequately competitive and inclusive.

No aspect of politics and governance so seriously challenges the image of sustained democratic progress in Latin America as the persistence of grave human rights abuses throughout the region. While these abuses are most serious, systematic, and immune to legal accountability in countries where democracy is absent or in suspension, like Cuba and Peru, they exist to troubling degrees in many countries with civilian, constitutional rule, including some that Freedom House continues to recognize (just barely, perhaps) as free. The democratic wave of the 1980s and early 90s has brought a much freer, more vigorous, and more pluralistic civil society in Latin America, including mass media and human rights organizations that are prepared to monitor human rights conditions and inclined to expose abuses (see Kathryn Sikkink, chap. 6). Nevertheless,

> periodic elections and transfers of power have not automatically led to an improvement in the quality of democracy experienced on a daily basis by the majority of citizens. Impunity for serious human rights violations committed by state agents is still appallingly pervasive; for the most part, military and police forces are accountable to courts and to civilian authorities on paper only. The courts fail miserably in providing citizens with a fair and impartial forum for the resolution of private disputes, and even more miserably in protecting them from abuse at the hands of the state, or in redressing those abuses.[65]

Even in countries where ongoing abuse of human rights has been substantially contained, the inability to establish accountability for past crimes violates what the Inter-American Commission on Human Rights identifies, in a report critical of the amnesty laws in Uruguay and Argentina, as the intrinsic right of victims to justice. The commission found that the laws were incompatible with these countries' obligations under the American Convention on Human Rights, a ruling that prompted Argentina and Uruguay to seek to limit the commission's jurisdiction to de facto violations.[66]

We need to question what we mean by *democracy* when situations like the following prevail in Latin American countries commonly regarded as constitutional democracies:

> —Widespread police violence, including torture and even murder, by police in Brazil and Argentina against suspected common criminals (and an estimated seven to ten million Brazilian street children) in impoverished, crime-ridden barrios[67]

> —Violence, murder, and forced labor inflicted on landless peasants and rural activists in Brazil and Central America by the private armies of powerful landlords, in complicity with local or regional authorities or even elements of the security forces[68]

> —Political assassinations and indiscriminate attacks on civilian populations by guerrilla armies in Peru, Colombia, and Guatemala, countered by equally indiscriminate aerial bombing and ground attacks and forced displacement of rural populations by security forces, as well as "dirty war" tactics (murder, torture, disappearance) by military and paramilitary forces

Beyond Sovereignty

—Massive violence, corruption, and terror, including the murder of judges, prosecutors, journalists, and politicians, by drug cartels in Colombia and throughout the Andes (often allied with insurgents), countered by special courts and procedures (violating basic tenets of due process)

—Shifting alliances among drug traffickers, guerrilla armies, large land-owners, and the military and police, spawning and condoning further violence against community activists, trade union and leftist political leaders, peasant and indigenous leaders, and human rights activists

—Discriminatory and often violent conscription into the army of young Paraguayans from poor families, who are then forced to work for the private gain of military leaders

—Pervasive absence or inefficacy throughout the region of civilian-led procedures for independently scrutinizing and punishing the murderous misconduct of military, police, intelligence, and prison authorities, as well as army and police officials operating off duty as death squads[69]

—The subversion, politicization, corruption, and intimidation of judges and courts, to the point where the judicial system becomes, as in Guatemala, "dysfunctional, a virtual black hole for any legal or human rights complaints"[70]

—A resurgence of political murders and right-wing death squads in El Salvador, claiming the lives of two key leaders of the former guerilla front (among others), in the approach to the March 1994 elections, and continued impunity for these and other human rights violations, most of which "continue to be left without investigation," according to UN human rights monitors.[71]

Respect for human rights constitutes a continuum, and different observers are bound to disagree about how far a country can fall short and still be considered democratic. Of the twenty-two principal Latin American countries, ten have a civil liberties rating of three on the seven-point scale (table 1). Five of these just qualify as democracies because they rate a two on political rights, but all ten have levels of human rights abuse that are incompatible with the consolidation of democracy.

The illiberal nature of "democracy" in Latin America today is cause for concern for several reasons. First, civil liberties are an intrinsic concern for those who value freedom and democracy, and only four of the twenty-two major countries in Latin America and the Caribbean perform well on this dimension (with a rating of 2 or 1). Second, civil liberties have significantly deteriorated in recent years in Brazil, Argentina, Venezuela, Colombia, and Guatemala (not to mention Peru and Haiti).[72] Third, when it is steep and prolonged, such deterioration renders a country more susceptible to the complete breakdown of the regime. Fujimori's *autogolpe* in Peru was preceded by four years of declining freedom ratings by Freedom House, from a 2 and 3 (political rights and civil liberties) in 1980 through 1987 to a 2 and 4 in 1988, a 3 and 4 in 1990, and a 3 and 5 in 1991. The attempted coups in Venezuela and Guatemala also followed steady declines in political rights and civil liberties. "Civilian inability to control paramilitary death squads or sanction human rights violations has seriously diminished regime legitimacy by baring the limits of the rule of law and demonstrating the inability of governments to protect their own citizens."[73] Improved protection for civil liberties and minority rights are thus an essential condition for the consolidation or reequilibration of democracy.

This returns us again to the principal thesis of this chapter, the intimate connection between the deepening and consolidation of democracy. Democratic regimes will not be stable and secure until they are considered legitimate by all major sections of their populations. For at least three reasons, this is highly unlikely to happen with the levels of human rights abuse now prevalent. First, the peoples of Latin America seek more than economic growth and economic security. They also value political liberty and freedom from terror, violence, and disorder. Regimes that cannot rein in systemic criminal and terrorist violence and subject the police and the military to accountability before the law are unlikely to garner the legitimacy that is the hallmark of consolidation. In such systems, only the rich and the powerful can feel secure—and then only behind very high walls.

Second, where the military is not accountable to civilian oversight and justice, civilian democratic authority can never be considered secure. One critical realm of power—official violence—lies beyond the effective control of citizens and their representatives and can be turned against them at any time. The very threat of this intimidates and diminishes democracy.

Third, human rights victims are usually not randomly distributed. They are disproportionately poor, landless, powerless, and members of racial and cultural minorities. So long as discrete groups in society are more or less excluded from the promise and protection of democracy, the regime will be unable to achieve the comprehensive inclusion necessary for broad legitimation among both elites and masses. Even if the regime achieves the "consensually unified elite" that signifies, for one theoretical school, the consolidation of democracy,[74] there will eventually arise from the excluded sector, as there has in Colombia and Venezuela, a counterelite that challenges the existing political settlement and demands inclusion. These demands may eventually exact a high price in blood and fear and in rapidly escalating human rights violations, as they have during insurgencies in Central America, Peru, and Colombia (and in a different way, criminal violence in Brazil).

Legitimate force has a role to play in combating these armed challenges, but serious insurgencies cannot be quashed by force alone. Only through negotiation and inclusion can peace (and thus an enabling environment for human rights) be secured.[75] Only by incorporating marginalized groups into the political system, with access to decision making and a chance to win a share of power, can fear be ended and democracy made stable. And only by improving protection for the rights of all citizens can these groups become safely, and thus effectively, involved in the democratic game.

Consolidating Democracy in Latin America

Facilitating and Obstructing Factors

In the original formulation of his thesis, O'Donnell argued that, while delegative democracies "are neither consolidated nor institutionalized democracies . . . they may be *enduring*."[76] By contrast, I argue here that precisely because they are institutionally weak *and* democratically incomplete, they are significantly less stable and more vulnerable to complete breakdown. The crucial intervening variable here is regime legitimacy: the more shallow, exclusive, abusive, and ineffective the regime, the greater the probability of broad popular disillusionment with it over time, and thus the lower the costs will become for either an elected president or the military (or as in Peru, the two institutions collaborating) to overthrow the system.

It has become more conventional for political scientists and analysts to argue that the absence of viable alternatives to democracy that have domestic and international legitimacy, and the intensity of international and regional pressures to become and remain democratic, make the formal abandonment of democracy very costly and unlikely. As Karen Remmer shows, Latin American publics have responded to the protracted economic crises of their countries (and especially to bad economic performance in the short and medium term) during the 1980s and early 1990s by voting out incumbent governments, just as citizens in the industrialized democracies do, rather than mobilizing behind extremist, antisystem political alternatives.[77] This response was as apparent in the newer democracies as in the older ones and was mediated not by the age of democracies but by the party system structure (which diminished electoral volatility in two-party systems).

It is tempting for political scientists to view the repeated electoral turnover of government as the hallmark of democratic consolidation.[78] But in Latin America (and many third-wave democracies elsewhere), this response still has much of the flavor of democracy by default. Electoral turnover masks glaring deficiencies in other dimensions of democracy and reflects a limited time frame of no more than a decade or so in most cases. Further, it begs the question of what will happen in the longer run if all political parties and alternatives fail to deal with persistent and agonizing social and economic problems, as they failed in Peru when Fujimori suspended democracy to popular acclaim. As Juan Carlos Torre observes, "If alternation in office comes to mean a parade of weak and short-lived governments, there is a danger that most or all of the leading politicians and parties may become tainted, with discontent shifting to the regime itself."[79] In a number of Latin American countries today, that shift is under way: in Brazil, where opinion polls show a nostalgia for military rule; in Ecuador and Panama, where the credibility of the legislative, judicial, and executive institutions of democracy is eroding; in Nicaragua, where unofficial power sharing between the Chamorro government and the Sandinistas (who control the military) has led to resurgent political corruption and violence; in Venezuela, where a February 1992 military coup attempt almost succeeded and where "trust in the political system has been in steep decline since the 1980s."[80]

A critical imperative in thinking about democracy in Latin America in the 1990s is not to confuse its persistence with the genuine stability that flows from consolidation. Equally, we should not confuse the absence of regime breakdown with the healthy persistence of democracy. As the evidence above shows, corruption, human rights abuses, and institutional decay and inefficacy have already pushed a number of regimes below the threshold of democracy, and prolonged economic decay has played no small role in this.[81]

In light of longer and wider experience, two hypotheses may be advanced. First, "democracy by default" is inherently vulnerable. Stability requires not a passive acceptance of the system, because there is no better alternative at the moment, but a positive belief in the moral value of democracy in principle and an assessment that democracy as embodied by the particular regime is right and proper for the country. This does not mean that new democracies are inherently and automatically vulnerable, however. To the extent that they begin with or accrue legitimacy from other factors (such as previous experience with authoritarianism, the regional and international context, shifts in political culture induced by broad patterns of social and economic change, and the performance of the new regime in delivering valued political goods, such as order and political freedom, constitutionalism, and choice), new democracies may become consolidated and stable rather quickly, even in the context of seriously disappointing economic performance. Such was the case with Spain during the mid-1970s to the mid-1980s, when unemployment rose and economic growth declined dramatically, yet the legitimacy of democracy as a system increased.[82]

Several of the newly restored democracies of Latin America (Brazil, Uruguay, Argentina, and Chile) experienced, "as a result of the massive and unprecedented abuses of state power by the bureaucratic-authoritarian regimes in these states . . . the increased valorization of democracy as an important end that needed to be protected in and for itself."[83] Certainly, as Juan Linz and Alfred Stepan note, legitimation under such circumstances benefits from the broad perception that all feasible alternative regimes would be worse.[84] But if this comparative assessment is based on only negative experience, it may give "postauthoritarian elites" nothing more than "a cushion of precious time . . . to improve democratic governance."[85] Consolidating democracy amid adverse economic and social circumstances requires what Linz and Stepan term the "political processing of adversity"—the ability of political parties and leaders to forge viable coalitions and new policies while governing democratically and with respect for the rule of law. These political conditions are crucial to preventing the perception of government failure from being generalized into "system blame."[86] Uruguay and Chile, like Spain and Portugal, have had that type of effective governance and responsible politics since their transitions. Brazil has not, and that is why its democracy has been so much more embattled and imperiled.

A second hypothesis is that, even though perceptions of regime legitimacy may be independent of its recent economic performance, there is a strong relationship between these two variables over time. As Seymour Martin Lipset argues, the development of a broad and intrinsic (rather than instrumental) belief in the legitimacy of democracy often derives from sustained success in addressing the country's social and economic problems.[87] Support for this thesis can be found in the historic experience of a number of Latin American democracies, such as Chile, Uruguay, Costa Rica, and Venezuela.[88] Once such intrinsic legitimacy has accumulated, it provides a substantial fund of political capital on which the regime may draw in times of temporary crisis, as Costa Rica did in weathering prolonged economic difficulties in the late 1970s and 1980s with little evidence of damage to its democratic values or stability.[89] Where democratic breakdown occurs after such a long period of successful democratic performance, it is typically after a prolonged period of regime malfunctioning (over successive administrations) and "is not solely the product of economic crises, but, perhaps even more preeminently, of political polarization and decay brought on by disastrous leadership and deeply flawed political institutions."[90]

Political Institutionalization

We return, then, to the importance of political institutions and their linkage to the quality and the consolidation of democracy. The more articulated and coherent are a country's political institutions (not just executive structures of power but legislatures, judicial systems, local and state or regional governments, and political parties), the more progress it will make toward consolidation, for several reasons.

First, because institutions structure behavior into stable, predictable, and recurrent patterns, institutionalized systems are less volatile and more enduring, and so are institutionalized democracies. Where the political institutions of democracy are well established and effective, political interests and preferences are aggregated and articulated by a settled array of strategic political actors, and the rules of political competition and conflict are known and accepted by those actors. Acting within these institutional settings, individuals and groups confine themselves to legal and constitutional methods that eschew the use or threat of force. The outcomes of electoral and other conflicts remain uncertain, but that uncertainty is bounded by rules that protect basic interests, and it is also eased by the knowledge that these institutionalized interactions will continue indefinitely, generating a long-term view that induces moderation, bargaining, accommodation, and trust among competing actors.[91]

Second, regardless of how they perform economically, democracies with more coherent and effective political institutions will be more likely to perform well politically in maintaining not only political order but a rule of law, ensuring civil liberties, checking the abuse of power, and providing meaningful representation, competition, choice, and accountability. In other words, well-institutionalized democracies produce a higher quality and intensity of democracy.

Third, democracies with more coherent political institutions are more likely to produce, over the long run, workable, sustainable, and effective economic and social policies, because they have more effective and stable structures for representing interests and because they are more likely to produce working congressional majorities or coalitions that can adopt and sustain policies. The institutionalization of the party system is especially important here, because it facilitates governability and effective macroeconomic management even in the face of the prolonged economic crisis Latin American democracies have experienced over the late 1970s and early 1980s.[92] More generally, political parties remain "the most important mediating institutions between the citizenry and the state," indispensable not only for forming government but also for constituting effective opposition. Thus, "a crucial condition for a stable democracy is that major parties exist which have an almost permanent significant base of support."[93]

Finally, and owing in large measure to the above factors, democracies with capable, coherent, democratic institutions are better able to limit military involvement in politics and assert civilian control over the military. The political power of the military expands where civilian political institutions are feeble and fragmented, and "weak political institutions are particularly dangerous in countries where the armed forces have achieved a high degree of organizational and technical development."[94]

All of these factors, in turn, contribute to the deep, broad, and enduring legitimation of democracy as a system of government.

Parties and Party Systems

Substantial evidence for these generalizations may be found in the recent and earlier experiences of Latin America. Most striking, perhaps, is the relationship between the institutionalization of the party system and the strength and durability of democracy. Institutionalized party systems have strong, coherent, autonomous, well-organized, and enduring parties, with relatively stable bases of electoral support.

Those countries that have experienced the longest periods of democratic rule in Latin America—Chile and Uruguay until their breakdowns in the early 1970s, Costa Rica since 1948, Colombia and Venezuela since 1958—have also had the most institutionalized party systems.[95] While the persistence of democracy helped provide the parties time to mature institutionally, strong, relatively coherent parties with mass support were evident from the beginning of the present constitutional systems in Colombia and Venezuela and had much to do with their coming into being.[96] In all five countries, strong, competitive parties, reaching down to the grass roots and adapting with social change to incorporate new groups, were the primary vehicles for organizing political participation, representation, and conflict. It is not coincidental that four of these five systems were or are two-party dominant systems, raising a crucial issue of institutional design we will consider shortly.

The positive contribution of party system strength is not negated by the breakdowns in Chile and Uruguay or the recent democratic deterioration in Colombia and Venezuela. The Chilean system was made vulnerable by poor institutional design, as we will see. Such was also the case for

Uruguay, with its double simultaneous vote, which encouraged factionalism and clientelism within parties and a politics of outbidding, which undermined party coherence and the ability of successive governments to formulate and implement policies to confront the deepening economic crisis in the two decades before 1973.[97] The deterioration and crises of democracy in Venezuela and Colombia were caused by the increasing rigidity, arrogance, and unresponsiveness of political parties, whose power-sharing arrangements had become increasingly corrupt, domineering, and exclusive of newly emergent political actors.[98]

Democratic instability and failure in Latin America have long been closely associated with frailty and instability in the party system. Brazil's democratic breakdown in 1964 owed much to the "deinstitutionalization" of the party system that began in the mid-1950s, fragmenting or dividing each of the major parties, diminishing their capacity to implement needed socioeconomic reforms, and subjecting the system overall to "increasing radicalization."[99] Similarly, in Peru, the volatile nature of the party system historically made it difficult for democratic regimes to implement policies to reduce socioeconomic inequality,[100] and the weakness, fragmentation, internal divisions, and general public discredit of all the traditional political parties ripened the conditions for the recent democratic breakdown.[101] The fragile and penetrated character of political parties generally, relative to powerful and politicized interest groups, and the extraordinary incoherence of the Peronist Party in particular, has been a major factor in the historic instability of competitive politics in Argentina since 1930.[102] Similar causal connections between weak parties, volatile party systems, and unstable democracies could be noted for Bolivia, Ecuador, the Dominican Republic, and Panama. In general, Diamond and Linz "find that weak parties, lacking in structural depth and excessively dependent on personalities, have made for weak democracy."[103] Volatility in party systems (producing wide swings in party votes from one election to the next) also contributes to regime instability by making "frequent fundamental changes in the rules of the game."[104]

Despite the rising power of interest groups and social movements, party systems continue to be the most important institutional factor in shaping political conflict over distributive issues during periods of economic crisis and adjustment. A key variable is the sheer number of parties. Fragmented party systems give rise to bidding wars, trade union militancy, ideological polarization, and weak and unstable coalitions governments held together mainly by "extensive, and costly, sidepayments," thus producing "perverse incentives that are detrimental not only to macroeconomic stability but to democratic governance as well."[105] By contrast, aggregative party systems, in which one or two broadly based and centrist parties can consistently obtain electoral majorities or near majorities, are better positioned to resist "class or narrow sectoral interests," maintain policy continuity across administrations, and diminish the influence of political extremes.[106] Multiparty systems might also be able to implement and sustain economic reform if they could produce stable center-right or center-left coalitions, but the political conditions for such coalitional stability are lacking in most of Latin America (though less so today in Chile).[107]

Party system institutionalization is reflected not only in the internal coherence and organizational depth and resourcefulness of political parties. An important dimension of institutionalization, and a condition for the persistence of institutions through time, is adaptability.[108] A major weakness in the literature on consociational democracy and elite settlements is its failure to recognize the way in which these institutional foundations of democratic stability can erode and unravel because of failure to adapt to social change and incorporate new groups.[109] Unfortunately, adaptability and incorporation are fostered by features of internal organization, such as decentralization and openness, that may undermine coherence. The ability of central party leaders to choose closed lists of legislative candidates in proportional representation (PR) elections promotes party coherence and control but may undermine the ability of parties to incorporate and appeal to new social forces. Switching to open lists or party "primary elections" to elect party slates would promote adaptability, incorporation, and responsiveness but would undermine party coherence (especially in presidential systems, which are otherwise prone to extremely weak party discipline).

Latin American political parties will therefore need to chart careful courses of political reform that bring political parties closer to the people, make them more responsive and accountable, while preserving (or generating) mechanisms to foster discipline and coherence. As I argue below, the most effective reform (for this and many other reasons) would be to switch to a parliamentary form of government, which, by inducing party discipline in order to retain control of government, could permit a softening of the internal party inducements to coherence (especially, centralized control over nominations and other party matters by small circles of party bosses). Governmental decentralization (see below) can also help; in this context, parties can be required to choose their candidates for state governor by primary election; to devolve the choice of other state and local candidates down to the state and local branches of the party; and to open up all internal party elections to supervision by an independent electoral tribunal, while still retaining proportional representation and closed lists.

Legislatures and Courts

It should by now be apparent that many features of delegative democracy in Latin America have deep historical roots. Personalism, clientelism, populism, and plebiscitarianism, reflecting the shallowness of institutions, are long-standing traditions in the politics of most Latin American countries. A major manifestation of both the historical phenomenon and its contemporary expression is the exalted status of the presidency in relation to weak and heavily manipulated legislative and judicial branches. In Latin America, the executive's responsibility for writing implementing legislation and his or her control over a vast and patronage-rich state bureaucracy are "supplemented by far-reaching decree powers that are rarely checked by Congress or courts, even if they are of questionable constitutionality."[110]

In the balance of powers, as in so many other aspects of democracy, we encounter a paradox or contradiction. Presidential systems require for effectiveness reliable congressional majorities. At the same time, they require some independence on the part of the legislature in order to scrutinize the executive branch, check its excesses, and impose what O'Donnell calls "horizontal accountability." If they are to perform and balance these roles effectively, legislatures not only must be based upon a relatively consolidated party system (which in at least some countries, like Brazil, would seem to require change in the electoral system), they must also have autonomous capacities to gather and process information, as through a congressional research service and a professionally staffed committee structure. And they must themselves be held accountable through politically autonomous mechanisms to detect and punish the bribery and extortion that reduce too many Latin American legislatures to "a labyrinthian racket for the self-aggrandizement of its members."[111] All of this seems a distant prospect, however, unless legislatures come to be composed of stronger, more disciplined, and more purposeful political parties.

As the above review of human rights conditions indicates, most Latin America judicial systems are feeble and ineffective, crippled by chronic corruption, intimidation, politicization, and lack of resources and training. Increasingly, these conditions afflict not only the new "democracies" but such long-standing constitutional systems as Venezuela's and Colombia's. And increasingly, they share a common leading cause: the breathtaking illicit wealth, extortion, and violence associated with the drug trade. The international drug trade is a rapidly spreading cancer on the democratic body politic in Latin America. Yet military-style efforts to combat it, with U.S. assistance, have achieved little, if anything. As in so many other areas that cry out for reform, progress can probably be no more than incremental, but here it would seem to require much greater emphasis on demand reduction and treatment (not only in the United States but among increasingly addicted Latin American populations as well).

Unfortunately, the region is caught in a vicious circle of causation: drug lords cannot be reined in without an effective judicial system, but the system cannot become effective in the face of such overwhelming criminal money and violence. Part of the answer lies in reforms (like those recently adopted in Costa Rica, Colombia, and Ecuador) to professionalize, depoliticize, insulate, and decentralize the judicial system. In addition, judges, prosecutors, and investigators need more training and resources, higher pay to deter temptation, and more effective and honest police to protect them from criminal retribution and to attack organized crime more aggressively.

Stronger and more autonomous institutions, including government auditing agencies and the means to monitor the personal assets of public officials, are also needed specifically to combat corruption. The judicial system can hardly remain chaste when the rest of the political system is saturated with corruption. A serious assault on political corruption would, in most of Latin America, amount to radical change, and politicians will hardly pursue that willingly. The impetus for reform can come only from outside the political system, from a civil society that organizes vigorously to reclaim and reform democracy. Where there is such vigorous civic and political pressure for reform, resources can make a difference, and U.S. aid would be better spent on strengthening the judiciary and police (and the state more generally) than on military efforts to eradicate drug production.

State and Local Government

Until the 1980s, virtually all governance in Latin America (even under democracy) was highly centralized. Even at the state and local level, fiscal resources, bureaucracies, police, and human services were all tightly controlled from the center. Mayors and governors were appointed from the center. Such centralization has reduced the quality and legitimacy of democracy as experienced at levels closest to the people in Latin America. It has inhibited local participation and shielded long-standing authoritarian enclaves from grassroots mobilization to dismantle coercive, violently abusive, and clientelistic practices. In particular, it has entrenched the exclusion of the poor from effective political participation and redress. The aggregate impact of such exclusionary and unaccountable practices at the local level has been to diminish democracy at the national level as well in countries such as Brazil, Peru, Guatemala, Colombia, and Venezuela (among others).[112]

Local democratization serves democratic consolidation by removing barriers to participation, enhancing the responsiveness and accountability of government, testing innovations in governance, enabling better targeting of antipoverty programs, diminishing the winner-take-all character of politics, and giving newer political parties and social forces a chance to learn how to govern and how to establish political credibility and responsibility by developing experience first at lower levels of power.[113] In the early 1990s, Latin American countries have implemented a number of reforms to decentralize government and democratize power at the local level. Colombia, Venezuela, Chile, Nicaragua, Panama, and Paraguay instituted direct elections for mayors and other municipal officials; Colombia and Venezuela also instituted elections for state governors.[114]

Political Reform

Broad efforts at institutional reform and renewal are also under way in Latin America. Like Venezuela, Colombia has been engaged in an effort that has also encompassed legal and constitutional reform. Venezuela's party system has become much more competitive and at least somewhat more decentralized and accessible. Panama's new electoral code also provides for an independent electoral commission. Costa Rica has instituted new campaign laws to make party financing more transparent and created an ombudsman to receive human rights complaints. Furthermore, judicial reforms have a significant potential to deepen democracy, improve accountability, and widen popular participation and influence. They represent at least some currents of democratic progress and hope, but they have generally been outweighed by the larger trends of erosion and decay. And they have not yet touched one of the most vexing problems for Latin American democracy, its structural proclivity to political deadlock and inefficacy.

Institutional Design

Latin American democracies are virtually unique in the world for combining presidentialism with an electoral system—proportional representation—that tends to give rise to multiparty systems. As Scott Mainwaring argues, this combination is especially inimical to stable democracy, because it is much more prone to ideological polarization and immobilizing deadlock between the executive and legislative branches, and because the multiparty coalitions necessary to govern where no party has anywhere near an outright legislative majority are much more difficult to assemble under presidentialism, which is a winner-take-all system.[115] Where presidents do not have majority support in the Congress, "a perverse logic sets in early as opposition forces soon perceive that their own political futures can best be assured with the political failure of the incumbent."[116] Executive-legislative deadlock (without the means for resolving it quickly through a new election, which parliamentary systems provide) in turn tempts both presidents and oppositions into high-handed and extra-constitutional tactics.[117]

Given also the plebiscitary nature of presidentialism, inducing elected heads of state to view themselves as the embodiment of the popular will (however narrow their electoral support); given the fixed, inflexible nature of the presidential term (and the bar on immediate reelection in many countries), creating a sense of political urgency for the president and a lame-duck situation as the end of term approaches; and given the extraordinary difficulty of removing a president before the end of his term, it is not surprising that power tends to be heavily personalized (and easily abused) in presidential systems.[118] Thus, presidentialism must be seen as an important contributor not only to the ills of delegative democracy but also to the quest for self-serving constitutional reform sought by Menem in Argentina and (with more blatantly authoritarian means) by Fujimori in Peru.

The lack of fit between a highly polarized and competitive multi-party system (necessitating bargaining and coalition building) and a presidential system of centralized authority, zero-sum outcomes, and fixed terms helped create the conditions for democratic breakdown in Chile in 1973.[119] Governmental deadlock and other ills of presidentialism played a prominent role in at least several other democratic breakdowns in Latin America before the 1980s.[120] Since about 1980, presidentialism has been no small partner to the travails of democracy in Latin America. "Of the 33 presidents elected in Latin America in the current phase of redemocratization . . . less than half—14 to be exact—obtained absolute electoral majorities," and only six presidents (in only four countries) enjoyed majority congressional support throughout their terms.[121] This problem figured prominently in the recent crises and erosion of democracy in Peru, Guatemala, and Brazil. In Ecuador, President Sixto Duran Ballen's economic modernization plan was obstructed by a Chamber of Deputies in which his party won only thirteen of seventy-seven seats.

Given the lack of fit between presidentialism and PR, the health of democracy would seem to require (particularly where PR has given rise to a fragmented and polarized multiparty system) change in one of these two structures. Electoral systems are extremely difficult to change once established, and the exclusion of minorities through a majoritarian (first past the post) system would in any case create serious legitimacy problems. Modest reforms of executive structure (such as runoff presidential elections, simultaneous presidential and congressional elections, and French-style semi-presidentialism) may not sufficiently reduce the prospect of stalemate. A switch to parliamentary government would seem to offer many (if not most) Latin American countries significantly better prospects for governability and democratic consolidation.[122] Yet, as the referendum in Brazil suggests, "the idea of a president is so strongly rooted in the political culture that any system that lacked a president probably would be considered alien."[123] Is there, then, any path away from deadlock?

An avenue with some promise is partial reform of the electoral system to reduce fragmentation and polarization and (in some cases) increase party coherence within legislatures. Raising the electoral threshold would weed out some smaller and more extreme parties; so would switching to moderately sized multimember districts (where representatives would also have to develop bonds of accountability to specific constituencies). A particular imperative in Brazil (which has one of the most fractionalized and paralyzed party systems) is to raise the electoral threshold for the Federal Chamber of Deputies (which now requires a party to win only a single seat from a state list), and to switch from the present system of selecting a single candidate from the list to closed or partially closed lists.[124] More specifically, Lamounier proposes (inter alia) a 5 percent threshold for entry into the Chamber and the consideration of another crucial feature of the German model, the mixed system of PR-list and single-member districts, within a system that is proportional in its overall allocation of seats.[125]

Despite the strong cultural and historic resistance, democratic reformers should not abandon the case for parliamentary democracy. Deep cultural patterns may change only glacially, but they can and do change. Big reforms take a long time to gather support, but protracted malfunctioning can lead new generations to consider new options. In the meantime, modest reforms, such as allowing immediate presidential reelection for a second term, might offer modest scope to reduce stalemate and improve accountability.[126]

Civil-Military Relations

The 1992 military coup attempts in Venezuela are a sobering warning to democrats throughout the region. The lessons, however, should be carefully read. It was only in the context of widespread political corruption, institutional decay, and popular disaffection that Venezuelan military officers tried to seize power. While grievances related to the corporate interests of the military and the personal ambitions of its officers may play a role, coups against democracy generally do not succeed (or even progress very far) in the absence of political polarization or crisis and a fairly widespread perception of systemic failings on the part of the civilian regime.[127] Thus, the single most important requirement for keeping the military at bay is to make democracy work, to develop its institutional frameworks and problem-solving capacities so that it accrues broad and unquestioned legitimacy.

In most of Latin America, however, this alone will not roll back the significant autonomous power and prerogatives that the military has already acquired, and that limits—and in some countries (such as Guatemala, Honduras, El Salvador, Nicaragua, and Paraguay) severely constrains—the quality and extent of democracy. Most new democratic regimes in Latin America have managed to co-exist with powerful militaries by making a strategic decision not to challenge their institutional power and prerogatives.[128] Even in the more democratic Southern Cone countries (Chile, Argentina, and Uruguay), the intimidating power of the military has prevented the pursuit of legal accountability for past human rights violations and constitutes an important obstacle to democratic consolidation. Indeed, in Chile, where General Pinochet has embedded military autonomy into the constitution, it may constitute the main obstacle. Thus, even though a "new doctrine of national security" in Latin America pragmatically recognizes the need for democracy to "guarantee long-term stability and governability,"[129] older obsessions with internal threats to national security persist. This results in formal and often quite conditional "adherence to the constitutional regime mixed with assertions of the military's traditional role as political guardians."[130] Hence a long agenda for reform of civil-military relations remains.

A common imperative for virtually all of the new and recently restored democracies in Latin America is to strengthen, or to begin to develop, civilian control over the military while constraining the military more and more strictly to the core national security functions appropriate for it to perform in a democracy: the defense of external boundaries and sea lanes; the combating of armed threats to the civilian constitutional order from terrorism, insurgency, and the drug trade; a readiness to provide emergency relief in case of natural disasters; and participation in international peacekeeping.[131] Civilian control requires reducing military influence over nonmilitary issues and eliminating military ownership or control over nonmilitary institutions. Ultimately, it also means that, even on issues directly related to the military and national security, such as strategy, deployment, and expenditures, military decision making must be subjected to civilian scrutiny and control, hopefully enabling a reduction in the size and budget of the armed forces. Finally, it requires that the right of the military to regulate or intervene in politics and civil society (even informally) be eliminated. In Alfred Stepan's terms, the institutional prerogatives of the military should be circumscribed to purely military functions and subordinated to civilian control.[132]

These changes are going to be difficult to achieve; already, powerful military establishments have tenaciously resisted even modest steps in this direction.[133] But the experience of Uruguay, which cut military budgets and then (under President Lacalle) appointed a civilian minister of defense, suggests that reform is more possible when democratic parties and governmental institutions demonstrate some coherence and effectiveness.[134] As democracy takes hold, autonomous military power often gradually diminishes: stronger civilian political institutions enable elected leaders to deal more confidently with the military, and socioeconomic development tends to erode the basis for military domination of society (especially rural society) by enhancing pluralism, political consciousness, grassroots political skills, and democratic values. Greater cultural and economic integration with the United States and other industrialized democracies will also tend to socialize civilians and officers alike to more democratic models of the military role in society, as has the integration of Spain into NATO.

However, democrats in Latin America cannot afford to wait a generation for these changes to emerge. Democratic consolidation demands an active strategy of "civilian empowerment," through which civilian scholars and policy specialists acquire credible expertise in military and intelligence affairs, legislatures develop the capacity to monitor military and intelligence systems routinely and responsibly, and democratic state leaders implement "a well conceived, *politically led* strategy toward the military" that "narrows their involvement in state regulation of conflict, builds effective procedures for civilian control, seeks to increase military professional capacities, and lessens the risks—for the polity and for the military—of further military intervention."[135] Given the extent of military domination in much of Latin America, such a reform strategy must be incremental and long-term, gradually prying away military prerogatives while offering other incentives for cooperation.

The Elements of a Reform Strategy

Expanding civilian, democratic control over the military involves circumscribing military prerogatives while reducing or minimizing civil-military conflict. Unfortunately, these two goals conflict, if one assumes that the military will normally fight to keep its power and privileges. Stepan thus rightly cautions that reduction of military prerogatives must be gradual, relying on bargaining, engagement, dialogue, and consensus building rather than on blunt confrontation. Since change is more likely to be tolerated if it is piecemeal, civilian leaders should have in mind a sequence of steps something like the following (with some overlapping in time):[136]

1. Purge "all potentially disloyal officers" quickly after inaugurating the new democracy[137] and replace them with officers respected by their peers but less associated with the previous military rule.

2. Remove the military from surveillance, policing, mediation, and intimidation of domestic political and social life. Transfer intelligence functions relating to domestic activity to civilian criminal investigative agencies. Separate the national police force entirely from the military structure (as is now being done under the terms of the 1992 peace accords in El Salvador). This should be an early imperative for any new democracy. And as this is done, new democracies must take steps to establish effective civilian control over the police as well.[138]

3. Terminate military control over corporations and mass media. This can be done within a broader context of privatization of state-owned enterprises.

4. Roll back explicit and institutionalized military involvement in government to only those matters affecting national defense and regional or international security. Remove the military from policy roles in other areas. Transfer military involvement in local development to purely civilian agencies. Restrict military involvement in economic development to purely technical and short-term projects, such as using the army corp of engineers to build roads and bridges where civilian capacities may not be adequate.

5. Gradually subordinate military decision making in national security to civilian oversight and authority. Appoint a civilian defense minister, impose civilian authority over top military promotions and assignments, establish procedures for civilian executive and legislative oversight over military and intelligence budgets, and reorient the military mission around external defense and international security. Among the first steps in this process should be the clear identification of the civilian head of government as commander in chief of the military and the redeployment of army troops from in and around the capital to locations along the frontiers more salient to the mission of external defense.

6. Reduce the size of the armed forces to a level commensurate with real national security needs, while modernizing weaponry, equipment, and defense capabilities. The money saved in the former (pruning in particular the commonly bloated officer corps) can make possible significant improvements in the latter that will refocus the officers on military rather than political concerns and can also finance improvements in pay and benefits (see also below).

7. Modify the curriculum of military officer training programs to reflect a depoliticized, professional role conception and the supremacy of the constitution and civilian authority. This too may need to be done in stages but should be initiated as soon as possible.

8. When the military has been defeated, disorganized, and discredited and no significant external threat exists, seize the opportunity to eliminate it altogether. These conditions clearly exist in Haiti in the wake of President Aristide's restoration to power, and his plan to do just that would clearly advance the country's democratic prospects.

At each point along this path of reform, disgruntled military officers will weigh the costs and benefits of accepting these changes against the costs and benefits of resisting them, ultimately through staging a coup. As a society becomes increasingly democratic and integrated into the world economy, the costs of a coup rise considerably. They will further rise as more officers internalize democratic norms, so that the unity of the military in resisting civilian reforms cannot be relied upon. But civilian leaders also need to pursue deliberate measures to increase the attractions of reform and reduce the perceived costs.

Cost-Reducing Strategies

1. Always accord the military a position of high status, honor, and income. Civil-military conflict over reforms can be reduced if military officers and soldiers are treated with respect, praised and honored for their service to the nation, and otherwise assured a prestigious social status and appealing lifestyle. Officers' incomes and pensions should be competitive with management positions in the private sector, offering comfort and economic security without resort to corruption.

2. Never use the military as a power resource, broker, or referee in domestic political conflict. All parties must agree to keep the military out of politics, not to "knock on the barracks door" in a time of crisis. This should also apply to the resolution and management of political conflict in the streets. The army should not have to be used to quell domestic political disturbances or control rioting (as it was in the Feb. 1989 riots in Caracas, at great cost in human life). Democratic regimes should therefore be able to call on an intermediate force, a national guard or paramilitary police, to restore order when civil disturbances go beyond the capacity of the police to control.

3. Avoid political interference in the process of routine military promotions and discipline. Top promotions and appointments should be subject to civilian approval, but military promotions and assignments should otherwise be given on strictly professional criteria.

4. As a temporary concession, it may be necessary to concede to higher levels of military spending than seem warranted. Civilian politicians have to

weigh their political strength and pick their fights. The early imperative is to get the military permanently out of politics and economic life. In some cases, high defense spending may need to be offered as an inducement to accept a narrowing of roles around national defense and international security functions. And some new spending may in fact be warranted. In particular, civilians should ensure that the military has the equipment and weaponry it needs to perform its core national security functions effectively.

5. In exchange for military withdrawal from power (including military willingness to cede informal power), it may be necessary to offer amnesty for human rights violations and crimes of corruption. Unfortunately, new democracies often face painful conflicts between moral and political imperatives, between "the ethics of conviction and the ethics of responsibility." The highest moral obligation for democratic leaders, argues former Uruguayan President Julio María Sanguinetti, is to choose responsibility, to "always strive to ensure that your actions do not produce consequences which contradict your good intentions."[139] For his judgment that that responsibility required a general amnesty for past crimes, Sanguinetti was bitterly criticized by human rights groups, as were political leaders in Chile, Argentina, and Brazil. However, it is difficult to argue with his political judgment, which did avoid another military coup. Forgiving should not mean forgetting but, rather, should be part of a strategy for reorganizing civil-military relations and for documenting and denouncing these crimes to ensure that they happen "never again."

The many posttransition experiences of third-wave democracies in dealing with past human rights abuses indicate that "justice [is] a function of political power"; prosecution is politically feasible only when the authoritarian regime collapses, and then only when the new government pursues justice quickly and decisively (within a year of coming to power).[140] As Raúl Alfonsín has argued, "punishment is one instrument, but not the sole or even the most important one, for forming the collective moral conscience."[141] Exorcising "the ghosts of a dark past" can also be achieved through the systematic discovery and reporting of the truth by an independent and impartial government commission, as has been done in Chile and Argentina, or even a nongovernmental commission working with official records, as with the report of the Archdiocese of São Paulo.[142]

Civil Society

Civil society is the realm of organized social life that is voluntary, self-generating, largely self-supporting, and independent of state and political parties. It encompasses independent interest groups, civic organizations, churches, social movements, mass media, and cultural and intellectual networks acting in the public sphere to express their ideas and interests, achieve collective goals, make demands on the state, and hold state officials accountable.[143] With political parties everywhere losing their absolute preeminence in the representation of social interests, such social groups and movements figure to become increasingly important to the functioning and consolidation of democracy.[144] Yet, while an increasingly vibrant and self-organized civil society can supplement the contributions of effective party and governmental institutions, it cannot sustain democracy in the absence of them, as Peru's experience demonstrates.

Historically, in Latin America, there appears to be "a strong correlation between the strength and autonomy of associational life and the presence and vitality of democracy."[145] In Costa Rica, Venezuela, and Uruguay, for example, an array of vibrant, autonomous associations played important roles in developing participatory orientations and political awareness, reinforcing democratic norms and practices, recruiting new political leaders, and preempting the state corporatist patterns of popular mobilization that obstructed democracy in Mexico and Argentina. Similar (if more tentative) evidence also suggests a link between democracy and the vigor and independence of the mass media.

To be sure, strong civil societies can also create certain problems for democratic consolidation. A strong, autonomous trade union movement, for example, may constitute a powerful obstacle to the implementation of necessary economic reform policies. More generally, the demands of various highly mobilized social groups may overwhelm the ability of a relatively weak democratic state to satisfy them without throwing the economy into severe stress. Yet independent think tanks and civic groups in Latin America, like the Institute for Liberty and Democracy in Peru, have also been playing a new and critical role in educating politicians and citizens alike about the need for economic reform and in mobilizing research, information, and constituencies in support of the reform process.

On balance, the growth of civil society is clearly serving the cause of democracy in Latin America, as indicated by the broad popular mobilization against the May 1993 attempted *autogolpe* in Guatemala. The rapid coalescence of civic, professional, academic, popular, and business organizations into the Instancia Nacional de Consenso not only played a critical role in turning the tide against authoritarianism but also facilitated a renewed (if fleeting) dialogue between long-polarized social forces, such as business and labor.[146] Although the international response to the *autogolpe* was more forceful in Guatemala than in Peru, it is likely that the most important difference in the two outcomes was the effective mobilization of domestic opposition in Guatemala.[147]

Beyond Sovereignty

Civic education groups like Conciencia, which began in Argentina but has since spread to fourteen other countries, are doing much to develop the culture of democracy at the grass roots, particularly among women, who traditionally have been excluded from power and influence in Latin America. Conciencia has worked not only to educate citizens about the specific elements of the constitutional and electoral systems (and to sponsor unprecedented, face-to-face debates between candidates) but also to develop more general and subtle features of democratic participation and association: the need for tolerance and respect for the views of others, the dynamics of reaching consensus within a group, the means by which people can cooperate to solve the problems of their communities. Beyond these educational programs, targeted on women and young people, Conciencia has sponsored wider campaigns in the mass media, catalyzed neighborhood improvement efforts, and sponsored programs to nurture and train associational leaders.[148]

Civil society is also beginning to challenge entrenched patterns of corruption. Again, an Argentine civic organization, Poder Ciudadano, has played a particularly prominent reformist role in a country where corruption has long been a political way of life but has mushroomed to even more brazen proportions under the Menem administration. In Argentina, Brazil, Venezuela, Peru, Colombia, Guatemala, and Mexico, the mass media have also played a critical and increasingly aggressive role in exposing wrongdoing and strengthening democratic accountability.[149] Also very encouraging has been the impressive growth in number and sophistication of human rights organizations, as Kathryn Sikkink discusses in chapter 6 in this volume.

Further invigorating the quality of public debate and of democracy itself has been the growth of popular, alternative media that provide a public voice and communication network for traditionally marginalized groups, such as women, youth, campesinos, and Indians. Though more financially hard-pressed now than when they began to emerge in the dark days of dictatorship, the popular media are also adapting. Through various partnerships with established media, they are working to open the mainstream press to a wider range of views. And they are greatly expanding their reach through electronic technologies—such as radio, video cassettes, fax machines, satellite connections, and electronic mail—that "decentralize access to information and accelerate the pace of news delivery."[150]

Assistance to independent organizations in civil society from private and public organizations in the United States and Europe is a major way in which the international community is now helping to deepen and consolidate democracy in Latin America. The independent but congressionally

funded U.S. National Endowment for Democracy, for example, is supporting a variety of youth, women's, and other associations (including several
Conciencia affiliates) engaged in civic education, legal and human rights
defense and education, leadership training, and public opinion polling.
The programs of these associations are aimed at strengthening independent trade unions and mass media. Private institutes and foundations analyze and advise Congress on economic reform issues in Argentina, Brazil,
Ecuador, El Salvador, Nicaragua, Paraguay, and Uruguay. They promote
discussion of constitutional reform (in Bolivia) and political reconciliation
(in El Salvador, Guatemala, and Peru); they train local government leaders
(in Chile and Paraguay); they monitor the electoral process (in Mexico);
and they improve civilian oversight of the military (in Nicaragua and
Peru).[151]

Economic Reform

Throughout this chapter, I argue that consolidating (or in some cases,
reconsolidating) democracy in Latin America will require deepening, extending, improving, redesigning, and institutionalizing democratic structures and processes. All of these changes point in the direction of greater
accountability, transparency, participation, and responsiveness. They involve a shift from delegative to representative democracy and, ideally, from
presidential, closed, top-down styles of politics and governance to forms
that emphasize the construction of broad coalitions, the decentralization
of power and policy making, and the generation of broad and relatively
stable bases of partisan support. In many countries, they require a progressive reduction in the autonomous power of the military, the broad enhancement of the rule of law, and a strengthening of civil society.

To these political challenges of consolidation must be added the awe-
some economic challenges of stabilizing chronically inflationary and debt-
ridden economies, reforming their statist and uncompetitive structures,
and reducing inequalities that are some of the ugliest and most severe in the
world. Economic reform is necessary not only to create the foundations for
broad-based and sustainable economic growth so important to enduring
legitimation but also to alter the rent-seeking, exclusionary, crisis-ridden
political dynamics of petrostatism in Venezuela and autarkic industrialization in the Southern Cone and elsewhere.[152]

However, the new conventional wisdom suggests that these political
and economic dimensions of consolidation cannot be pursued simultaneously; that "authoritarian governments are better positioned than
democratic governments to promote economic liberalization," and thus

that economic reform should ideally come first; and that even under the formal structures of democracy, power must be concentrated (not further checked, decentralized, and democratized) in order to achieve economic stabilization and liberalization.[153] Is there a contradiction? Must Latin America's new democracies choose between the economic and political foundations of democratic consolidation?

Much evidence and analysis suggests the necessity for such a choice. The paradigmatic case of economic reform in Latin America, in Chile under Pinochet, was achieved under an authoritarian regime that was able to implement painful and dislocating economic liberalization measures precisely because it had forcibly excluded most of society, including organized labor and uncompetitive industrialists, from influence over policy.[154] As in Chile, but with less raw repression, economic reform has been imposed unilaterally from the top down in Mexico, where President Carlos Salinas de Gortari has used the monolithic powers of the presidency and his tight control over the hegemonic ruling party and the corporatist labor unions to implement far-reaching privatization and trade liberalization measures. Tensions between economic and political liberalization have been resolved by sacrificing the latter for the former,[155] and President Salinas has frankly conceded that he deferred political democratization because "he needed the immense power he had in the Mexican political system in order to put through . . . economic reforms."[156] President Fujimori justified his seizure of authoritarian power in Peru in large measure by his proclaimed need to overcome congressional obstruction of his economic reform measures.

Economic stabilization and reform have been achieved under democratic auspices, but where they have proceeded the furthest—in Bolivia, Argentina, and Venezuela—they were implemented mainly through presidential directives or decrees and, in the case of Bolivia in the late 1980s, during a state of siege that imprisoned hundreds of union leaders.[157] Seeking to alter expectations suddenly and massively, economic "shock" stabilization programs in particular "took the form of presidential directives planned in secret by technocratic cabinets insulated from social and political pressures."[158] In the context of democracy, it is now widely and compellingly argued that considerable policy insulation and delegation to state technocratic elites is necessary to achieve reform (and doubts remain about the degree to which democracy can accommodate this state autonomy).[159]

On several grounds, however, the thesis of a fundamental contradiction between economic reform and the political consolidation of democracy may be challenged. First, the recent experiences of Argentina and Bolivia, not to mention Poland, Hungary, and the Czech Republic (among other former communist states), show that authoritarianism per se is not a prerequisite for the implementation of economic stabilization and reform policies. In fact, on the whole, authoritarian leaders are no more and perhaps even less likely than democratic ones to want to liberalize their economies or to be immune from antireform pressures and interests.[160] Moreover, distinctive social and political factors—as well as international tolerance for dictatorship—made repression feasible for implementing economic restructuring in Korea, Taiwan, and Chile, and those conditions are not likely to prevail in the 1990s.[161]

Second, the unilateral approach to decision making, while "necessary to avert economic collapse and initiate needed structural adjustment," becomes less politically effective and more problematic over time, bringing "diminishing returns."[162] In contrast to the initiation of reform, which is more likely when politicians and their technocratic allies are insulated from political and interest group pressures, the consolidation of reform ("stabilizing expectations around a new set of incentives") requires extensive political communication to construct "relatively stable coalitions of political support" and to gain at least the acquiescence of potential opposing forces.[163]

Cavalier disregard for the need to build congressional and societal support eventually boomerangs into increasingly intense opposition, and more and more presidential *decretismo* is needed to sustain the process. Authoritarian tendencies in the presidency may swell, as is now happening in Argentina. Or congressional opposition may obstruct reform or even find grounds (not often lacking in the strictest legal terms) to lash back at the president and impeach him, as happened in Venezuela, where Carlos Andrés Pérez was abandoned even by his own party. Or, sensing the breadth and passion of popular anger, the military may seek to overthrow the president and the constitutional system along with him, as it twice nearly did in Venezuela in 1992. Or a budding caudillo, fed up with having to deal with congressional objections, may simply seize all power, as Fujimori did in Peru. Whatever the outcome, the failure to educate the public about the necessity for reform, and to build a broad political and societal consensus behind it, leaves policy contested and the new rules of the economic game unconsolidated. In a political system where the government could be turned out at the next election and policy direction suddenly reversed, this undermines the credibility necessary to induce capital to invest in long-term, wealth-creating activities.[164]

Third, there are some respects in which the two processes are, theoretically, compatible rather than contradictory. Both economic reform and democratic consolidation encompass the creation of stable expectations and rules about behavior, to guarantee the security of capital when it takes risks to invest and to guarantee mutual security among contending political forces. Both forms of security are best entrenched by a strong rule of law and constitutional order, protected by an independent judiciary. Similarly, "both democratic consolidation and progress against inflation rest on a common foundation: the reinforcement of stabilizing expectations."[165] While cumulative fiscal indiscipline and incompetence may create such conditions of hyperinflation as to require, initially, the imposition of a shock treatment from above, generation of a policy consensus on the need for fiscal discipline to enforce relative price stability can simultaneously serve the cause of democratic consolidation and economic stabilization.

Fourth, when politicians who embrace reform lose public support, we should not necessarily assume a cause-and-effect relationship, especially when discontent increases even as economic conditions improve. The Venezuelan case suggests that riots, demonstrations, plummeting poll ratings, and—ultimately—attempted coups may represent the explosion of a long-brewing "sense of outrage toward politicians and public officials," in their duplicity and corruption, rather than hostility toward reform itself.[166] And defeat at the polls may also owe as much or more to issues other than economic reform.[167]

A fifth reason to question the supposed contradiction between economic reform and political consolidation inheres in the dubious nature of the assumption that, if there is tension between the two objectives, it must be resolved by a country completely choosing one or the other and that rapid and comprehensive economic reform should take precedence over the political dimensions of democratic consolidation. In itself, successful economic reform figures to enhance the long-term prospects for democracy by generating economic stability and growth. But if the process of achieving reform hollows out political institutions and intensifies social polarization, that may be a costly victory or, in the end, one that is never quite realizable. Economic reforms may be less far-reaching but more politically sustainable—and less destructive to political institution building—when they are pursued through consultation and negotiation with diverse interest groups, which has the possibility of producing strategies for buffering the pain, compensating the losers, and introducing the reforms at a more politically acceptable pace.

Indeed, the very processes of educating and mobilizing constituencies for reform and of reducing opposition through compensation (most especially, programs targeted at the poor) may help to develop bases of party support and the practice of conciliation and compromise, which undergird a stable democracy.[168] These processes may also serve the long-term cause of economic reform by gradually lowering societal expectations and neutralizing populist appeals for more extravagant and unrealistic distribution. In fact, when mass publics appreciate the reality of an economic crisis, understand the need for strong policies to restore stability and growth, and develop confidence in their governments' reform plans, competence, and resolve (and believe that they will share in the benefits of such reform), they are less likely to mount the large-scale protests that undermine political stability or to turn against the government at the polls.[169] Such mass understanding is much more likely to result from open dialogue, education, and popular participation than from secretive planning and executive imposition.[170]

In the final analysis, both economic liberalization and democratic consolidation figure to be protracted processes in Latin America. Rapid, even shocking, economic liberalization is preferred from the standpoint of economic theory and, in some cases (especially the former communist countries), may be essential to break decisively political and economic structures that are antithetical to democracy and the market. But once stabilization and some initial liberalization is achieved, a protracted period of further liberalization and state building must follow, and these reform efforts cannot be sustained without the construction of political coalitions and the mobilization of broad support.[171] Steady but sustainable progress is preferable to alternation between radical policy alternatives and to the desecration of democratic institutions in the pursuit of "good" policies. As Laurence Whitehead wisely observes: "Beyond immediate tactical considerations, strategic objectives that may take a decade or more to achieve must be kept in view. Economic and political objectives should not be separated into watertight compartments, since a single policy stance can act powerfully in both areas, each of which may interact strongly with the other."[172]

International and bilateral donors may thus need to allow Latin American democracies greater political realism and negotiation, longer time perspectives, and more flexibility in the pursuit of economic reforms—whose ultimate objectives, nevertheless, remain well defined. Indeed, continued firm conditionality with respect to broad policy directions, combined with greater flexibility about the tactics and pace for achieving them, may help to foster precisely the types of democratic coalitions and compromises that can simultaneously advance both economic reform and democratic consolidation.

Inequality and Social Justice

Latin America has some of the worst income distributions in the world. Of the forty-five lower- and middle-income countries for which the World

Bank presents recent data, Brazil shows the worst income distribution: the lowest percentage of household income earned by the bottom 20 percent of the population (2.1%; only Panama, at 2.0%, is worse) and the highest share earned by the top 20 percent (67.5%). Income concentrations in Guatemala, Panama, and Honduras are almost as extreme; those in Chile, Mexico, Colombia, Peru, and the Dominican Republic only slightly better.[173] Although such income distribution data suffer from notorious problems of reliability and comparability across nations, these figures do lend support to more impressionistic perceptions that Latin America harbors the most severe economic inequality of any region in the world.

The Inter-American Dialogue estimates that two of every five Latin Americans (180 million people) live in poverty, about half of them in such abject poverty they do not have enough to eat, and that in many countries (including Brazil, Peru, Bolivia, Honduras, Nicaragua) "a substantial majority of the population" is impoverished.[174] The number of people in poverty increased by some fifty million since 1980,[175] as the economic crises of that decade extracted a cruel toll. From 1982 to 1990, per capita income fell for the region as a whole by 10 percent, and by 25 percent or more for Peru, Argentina, and Nicaragua. Real wage levels plunged to half or lower in some countries.[176]

Reducing these levels of poverty and inequality is one of the paramount imperatives for democratic consolidation in Latin America.[177] As the Inter-American Dialogue trenchantly observes, "economic exclusion is everywhere the handmaiden of political exclusion."[178] Such exclusion and alienation (often so degrading in its social treatment of the very poor as to amount to virtual dehumanization) give rise to violent insurgencies like those in Peru and Central America, explosions of frustration in urban riots ("like those in Los Angeles, Caracas, Buenos Aires, and São Paulo"), broad disaffection with established parties and politicians, heightened receptivity to radical, demagogic, and irresponsible populist appeals, labor instability, and consequent political polarization and fragmentation.[179] All of this undermines the legitimacy and stability of democratic politics and increases the chances of regime breakdown.

On the face of it, economic stabilization and liberalization measures would figure to worsen poverty and inequality. Macroeconomic discipline requires reining in state spending, and social welfare programs have been costly and often wasteful. Privatization and trade liberalization mean the closure of uncompetitive industries and, at least initially, significant increases in unemployment. Reducing the state role in the economy means also reducing its capacity to help and protect the poor and lower classes. Or does it, necessarily?

Economic liberalization need not ravage efforts to address poverty and inequality and may even improve them in some respects. Liberalization measures seek to eliminate subsidies, economic controls and regulations, and protectionist measures that have benefited most the rich and middle classes (and the favored sectors of urban labor) rather than the poor. "Adjustment measures that seek to reduce those controls and reorient services and subsidies therefore do not threaten [the poor] and may indeed help them." Moreover, some forms of nutritional and health assistance for the poor are relatively inexpensive.[180] Depending on how they are constructed and implemented, reform measures may instead compel the state to rationalize its revenue collection and expenditure programs in ways that reduce inequality. The simplification and enforcement of tax laws to ensure that the wealthy actually pay could not only increase revenue but reduce the anger of the poor, and especially the urban formal sector and middle strata, who are likely to suffer the steepest relative losses from economic liberalization and are especially prone to resentment over unfairness. User fees for state services can raise further revenue from middle-class consumers able to pay, while exempting the poor.[181]

Increased country experience and interest on the part of international donors make possible new policies to reduce poverty and inequity. These policies would be targeted on the needy, would be consistent with reform and sound macroeconomic management, and would make better use of funds states are already spending. These changes include improvements in the quality and levels of state investments in education, health, and nutrition; a redirection in educational expenditures from university and secondary education to primary and early childhood education, and from hospitals to preventive health services; a redirection of income transfers and food subsidies to the neediest and most vulnerable groups; expanded state programs for family planning, rural development, and small business assistance; rationalized tax collection and reduced military expenditures to generate the needed revenues; externally financed emergency relief and employment programs; and greater involvement of local governments, community groups, and business and professional associations in the planning and management of education and other social services.[182]

Such new policies, including better designed social safety net programs, would not only enhance social justice, they also would strengthen and in some ways further democratize the necessary functions of the state while fostering institutional development at the local level, improving delivery of essential services, and enhancing regime legitimacy.[183] Moreover, such policies would not contradict the logic of reform. Rather, they would carry it forward into other dimensions of state activity and increase its political sustainability.

As Joan Nelson observes, "ordinary people must be able to see some positive returns from adjustment, if they are to convert what is at best initial skepticism into more durable grumbling acquiescence."[184] Unfortunately, measures to buffer the costs of adjustment for the most politically strategic strata of these "ordinary people," urban formal sector workers and middle classes, are the most expensive and the most likely to involve the old illiberal state subsidies and controls. This underscores the imperatives of (1) good governance, to effect visible sharing of sacrifice at all levels of society and to reduce and control political corruption and profiteering from liberalization measures such as privatization, (2) democratic decentralization, to increase the political power of the poor, and (3) smart politics, to communicate the long-term nature and eventual positive benefits of reform and to generate new partisan attachments that mobilize the poor as an electorally active constituency for reform.

Conclusion: Can the International Community Help?

I have emphasized here the domestic challenges to and directions for democratic consolidation in Latin America. Partly I have done so to provide a balance to the other thematic chapters in this volume, which are focused on the regional and international community. However, it is also the case that the requirements for consolidating democracy in Latin America—political institutionalization; institutional, economic, and social reform; and the coalition building and statecraft needed to bring them about—fall overwhelmingly on the shoulders of domestic political actors. In the 1980s, support from the United States, Europe, and other Latin American democracies "played an important role in deterring potential coups in Bolivia, Ecuador, El Salvador, Honduras, and Peru. In each case, however, international support for democracy *reinforced* domestic groups and sectors of the military opposed to military intervention."[185]

The United States, the OAS, and the international community can deter, punish, and even help to reverse blatant overthrows of the democratic process, as they did in Guatemala in 1993, through vigorous diplomacy and, if necessary, the imposition of sanctions. But usually, when democracies reach this state they are in very poor health. Such emergency rescues do no more than keep the formal structures of democracy alive; they are no substitute for the nurturance to health through active consolidation. Can other countries help with this more fundamental democratic challenge in Latin America?

I believe they can. Even though domestic factors remain paramount, the international community can aid in a number of ways. Political assistance measures, bilaterally and through the OAS, can help to (1) strengthen democratic legislatures, judicial systems, local governments, and political parties, (2) improve civilian mechanisms for oversight and control of the military and intelligence services, (3) train new political leaders, (4) enhance the integrity of the electoral process, and (5) enrich resources, policy knowledge, and political and organizational skills in the increasingly crucial arena of civil society.[186]

However, in this and other respects, the United States must exercise caution. The U.S. record in promoting democracy in the hemisphere has been mixed at best, and much policy has been promulgated "in the name of democracy" that in fact has weakened, undermined, or failed to strengthen it.[187] The checkered U.S. experience in the region, the inconsistency of past U.S. policy, and the considerable persistence of Latin American suspicion about U.S. motives and intentions argue for a cautious and low-profile approach, in which political assistance (especially for groups in civil society) is channeled as much as possible through nongovernmental organizations like the National Endowment for Democracy and through the multilateral frameworks of the OAS. Most of all, the United States needs to craft a prodemocracy policy that has the coherent backing of all foreign policy branches of the government and bipartisan support that can be sustained across administrations. It must then take care to provide "unambiguous and consistent signals" about the high priority it attaches to the maintenance of democracy and human rights.[188] The concern for human rights (codified in aid conditionality) must be vigorously pressed with formally democratic regimes no less than with undemocratic ones.[189]

A particular point of caution for the United States involves relations with Latin American militaries. It should by now be clear that the mere training of Latin American officers in U.S. military schools or traditions may do little to ensure democratic commitments and restraints. The saga of Manuel Noriega is vivid testimony to that. In addition, large-scale U.S. military assistance, of the kind rendered to El Salvador, Guatemala, and Honduras during the 1980s, may only strengthen the military's dominant position vis-à-vis democratic forces in government, politics, and civil society, unless such assistance is explicitly conditioned (which it was not during the 1980s) on respect for human rights and clear submission to civilian authority.[190] Even then, it is not clear what constructive purpose large-scale assistance serves, particularly in the post–Cold War era. It would be tragic if, in the name of fighting the drug trade or building democracy, the United States were to repeat its previous mistakes of aggrandizing Latin American militaries at the expense of democracy.[191]

Probably the most important way the United States and other international actors can help to consolidate democracy in Latin America is economic. In unprecedented fashion, Latin American governments, even of the moderate left, are moving to dismantle statist obstacles to economic growth and open up their economies to international competition. Such liberalizing economic reforms are likely to pay very substantial long-term dividends, as they have already done in Chile and are beginning to do in Mexico, Argentina, and Bolivia, but they impose severe short-term costs, especially when they must be preceded by painful stabilization measures. New aid and concessional lending can make a critical difference to these reform programs by helping to fund the social safety nets and poverty relief programs that seek to alleviate the social distress and injustice associated with reforms and thus make them considerably more viable politically. Additional debt relief can free up scarce foreign exchange for investment to create jobs and improve productivity. And the reduction of trade barriers by the United States and other developed countries figures to stimulate economic growth and reinforce economic openings.

In this regard, the passage of the North American Free Trade Agreement in November 1993 represents a historic advance, not only in providing for the eventual elimination of trade barriers among Mexico, the United States, and Canada, but also in its prospect for eventually incorporating in that free trade community other Latin American regimes that maintain democracy and follow economic reform policies. With growing trade will come a growing cultural connectedness, as CNN and other U.S. cable television networks become available in Spanish throughout the hemisphere, while fax and electronic mail communications, along with business, cultural, educational, and organizational ties, between north and south increase exponentially.[192] Perhaps it is not too much to hope that from these proliferating ties will eventually emerge a community of American nations no less bound than the European Union by a common commitment to democracy and human rights.

Today, however, that remains a distant dream. A decade ago, "when democracy seemed to be in full flower" in many Latin American countries, President Jimmy Carter and Robert Pastor initiated the first conference of the Carter Center with a vital question: Could the historic swings of the pendulum between authoritarian and democratic rule in the region finally be stopped at the point of democracy?[193] This third swing of the pendulum toward democracy in Latin America has lasted longer (twenty years) than either previous one, but there is growing evidence that it is now swinging back—and insidiously, through processes of institutional decay, erosion of freedom, and delegitimation, processes that do not grab the headlines the way a coup would. The decay is not irreversible, and the multiple efforts at reform, however limited, provide real cause for hope. What is least warranted now, however, is apathy—not to mention self-congratulation.

In the near term, what the United States can do to assist the consolidation of democracy in Latin American appears limited and on the margin, but when political and social forces are finely balanced, as they seem to be at this possible turning point in Latin American history, actions on the margin may help to tip the balance.

II Practice and Policy

The Role of Nonstate Actors

4   *The United Nations, Democracy, and the Americas*

David P. Forsythe

The United Nations had apparently little direct linkage with a wave of democratization that swept the Americas and indeed the world from the mid-1970s to the early 1990s. Yet, toward the end of the twentieth century, the UN did contribute to democracy, in the Americas as elsewhere, especially in Central America. As shown by developments in El Salvador, the office of the secretary-general, when backed by the Security Council and General Assembly, can contribute to the strengthening of national political and judicial institutions in order to limit military influence. If the other parts of the UN system, as driven by state foreign policies, could emphasize socioeconomic programs and improve their linkage to democracy, the UN might make an even greater contribution to the creation and consolidation of democracy.

Democracy and the Americas

There have been many definitions of democracy, but an institutional test is central.[1] To have democracy, one must have a broad franchise, free and fair elections, genuine competition among candidates, with the outcome proving decisive in determining who actually governs. Especially when dealing with the Americas, one should recall that apparent freedom of opinion and contested elections do not produce democracy if the military continues to make key decisions unrestrained by the executive and legislative winners.[2] There can be no statistically final determination of democracy; there must always be a judgment as to who actually governs. If the military reserves to itself a veto over important public policies, democracy does not fully exist. (A good example of the problem was found in Chile in the early 1990s; an elected president and Congress were severely restrained by the continuation in military office of the former dictator, Augusto Pinochet, whose supremacy over certain policies was codified in the constitution.)

Liberalization is not democracy. At times in the past, various parties in the Americas concentrated on liberalization—either its creation or consolidation—rather than democracy. The violation of some of the most fundamental human rights, such as to life and to freedom from torture, had been so gross and systematic in places under military rule like Brazil, Chile, Argentina, Uruguay, El Salvador, and Guatemala, inter alia, that those concerned had focused on those abuses. Democracy had seemed a remote possibility. Not all human rights relate directly to democracy, and sometimes in the Americas efforts on behalf of some civil rights overshadowed interest in democratic rights.

The creation of democracy is not the same as the consolidation of democracy. In 1993 almost all states in the Americas had democratic or partially democratic government. Not counting the supposedly temporary suspension of the Peruvian constitution, only Cuba—and for a time Haiti—had a clearly authoritarian government. Other states, like Chile, El Salvador, and Guatemala, had mostly democratic governing arrangements, but the military still significantly restrained executive, legislative, and judicial authority.[3] The primary issue, places like El Salvador aside, is not how to repeatedly have free and fair elections but how to consolidate democracy: how to institutionalize the rule of law, an independent judiciary, electoral supremacy over the military, and a political system supported broadly because its opportunities and benefits are broadly shared. Consolidation is a synonym for stability and maturation.

As for the question of what are the requisites for either democracy or its consolidation, much scholarship leads to a seemingly vague conclusion but with a provocative core thought. Samuel Huntington summarizes the literature on the requisites of democracy this way:

The causes of democratization differ substantially from one place to another and from one time to another. . . . The multiplicity of theories and the diversity of experience suggest the probable validity of the following propositions:

(1) No single factor is sufficient to explain the development of democracy in all countries or in a single country.

(2) No single factor is necessary to the development of democracy in all countries.

Beyond Sovereignty

(3) Democratization in each country is the result of a combination of causes.

(4) The combination of causes producing democracy varies from country to country.

(5) The combination of causes generally responsible for one wave of democratization differs from that responsible for other waves.

(6) The causes responsible for the initial regime changes in a democratization wave are likely to differ from those responsible for later regime changes in that wave.[4]

From this broad and synthetic approach, Huntington eventually extracts two primary factors as crucial for the creation and consolidation of democracy: political leadership and economics.[5] By political leadership he means a commitment to democracy by political elites in the face of various oppositions. By economics he means economic development. The two factors combine when there is commitment by ruling elites not just to democracy but also to economic growth with equitable distribution. A growing literature supports the proposition that democracy is not easily sustained in a context of either broad and extreme poverty or perceived gross inequities between rich and poor.[6]

Democracy is not foreign to the Americas. From the earliest declarations of state independence, the new elites of not just North America but Central and South America as well endorsed democratic principles.[7] But as is well known, Central and South America have oscillated between democratic and military rule. Huntington finds three global waves of democracy, with the first two waves being followed by waves of reversal.[8] His global view encompasses Latin America reasonably well.

I have elsewhere explained the failure to consolidate democracy—and more broadly, to protect human rights—in Latin America by explicating a regional political culture.[9] In this view, Latin America manifests a conflicted political culture. There is an abstract commitment to human rights, including democratic political participation, periodic leadership supportive of these values by small states and the Inter-American Commission on Human Rights, and spasmodic attention to these values by the most powerful hemispheric state, the United States. On the other hand, there has been consistent neglect of the actual rights of the lower classes and most especially indigenous Indians; a lack of effective international cooperation for rights and democracy because of emphasis on state sovereignty; and U.S. preoccupation with opposing extraregional powers rather than systematically supporting political and socioeconomic reform beneficial to a broad citizenry.

One manifestation of this conflicted political culture is a complicated human rights regime association with the OAS, but one that has been mostly ineffectual either in liberalizing authoritarian governments or in creating and consolidating democracy. Democracy is regularly endorsed and just as regularly bypassed. When Brazil, Argentina, and Uruguay regained democracy in the 1970s and 1980s, they did not do so primarily because of the OAS (or the UN, for that matter) but because of other, mostly national, factors.[10]

Against this background, one can well raise the question of whether a third wave of democratization, globally and in the Americas, will not be followed again by reversal. In many parts of Central and South America the re-creation of democracy coexists with a strong military that resists electoral supremacy over its traditional vetos. Moreover, there are major impediments to sustained economic growth (e.g., a large debt burden and inflationary problems) along with great disparities between the very rich and the very poor.

It is in this contemporary as well as historic context that we address the question of whether the UN can help consolidate fragile democracy in the Americas.

The United Nations and Democracy, Historically

The UN has been part of a legal and diplomatic revolution in international relations centering on human rights. Especially since 1945, human rights —including the right to participation in governing arrangements—has been internationalized.[11] The relationship between persons and states is no longer exclusively a matter of domestic jurisdiction, falling under the rubric of state sovereignty. There are now more than two dozen international agreements codifying internationally recognized human rights, which states are expected, in theory at least, to respect. These agreements have been widely endorsed, which of course is not the same as being applied.

The human rights situation of any given state may be discussed at the UN and made the subject of a resolution. Prior to about 1970 such UN diplomacy would have been widely regarded as at least interference, if not intervention, in a state's domestic affairs. Other steps may also be taken at the UN to try to secure the actual practice of internationally recognized human rights within a state. Rapporteurs, special experts, special representatives, and working groups may be appointed. The diplomatic spotlight can be shone on states through these various of diplomatic steps, all in an effort to embarrass states into conforming to UN rights standards. Beyond diplomatic pressure, an economic embargo was applied to a white minority government in Rhodesia, and an arms embargo was applied to a white minority government in South Africa.

This is not to say that the UN has always or even systematically acted to protect human rights. Certainly prior to 1989–91 and the end of the Cold War, the prevailing opinion was that the legal and diplomatic revolution in human rights had not been matched by a real revolution in political behavior beyond UN meeting rooms. One scholar summarizes UN human rights developments thus: they constituted more than a whimper but less than a roar.[12] Another says that the UN constructed strong promotional human rights regimes but weak protective ones.[13] I have, earlier, described the UN as not really in the business of protecting rights in the short run but in nudging or socializing states into accepting the practices of rights over time.[14]

Democracy has always been part of the UN's focus on human rights, but interestingly enough, democracy was not really emphasized through the UN during its first forty years. The Universal Declaration of Human Rights, adopted as a General Assembly resolution in 1948, declares (Article 21) that "everyone has the right to take part in the government of his country, directly or through freely chosen representatives. . . . The will of the people shall be the basis of the authority of government; this will shall be expressed in periodic and genuine elections which shall be by universal and equal suffrage and shall be held by secret vote." Essentially the same basic rule is found (Article 25) in the UN Covenant on Civil and Political Rights, now formally accepted by more than 125 states, including all the major states in the world and all states in the Americas except Cuba. (The United States finally became a full party to this treaty in 1992, albeit with reservations, declarations, and understandings—not to mention a refusal to accept the right of U.S. citizens to petition the UN Human Rights Committee, which monitors application of the convention.)

Because of the number of authoritarian states in the world during the UN's first forty years, whether one speaks of developing or socialist countries, neither democracy per se nor those civil rights associated with democracy—freedom of opinion, speech, association, and assembly received systematic emphasis. Even democratic states had to observe that under international law any number of human rights, such as freedom of speech, could be suspended during times of national emergency threatening the life of the nation. Moreover, some democratic states like the United States gave priority to containment of Soviet-led communism rather than support for elected governments; indeed, the United States overthrew, or tried to, a number of elected governments in developing states.[15] Primarily because of state policies, which are the primary determinants of what UN bodies attempt to do, the UN came to focus on a series of civil rights not directly necessary for the existence of democracy.

Beyond the International Bill of Rights (the Universal Declaration of Human Rights and the covenants on civil-political and socioeconomic rights), supplemental treaties were approved and widely accepted on a series of civil rights: freedom from racial discrimination, apartheid, torture, genocide, slavery and slave-like practices, and hostage taking. Other civil rights were covered in treaties on the nationality of married women, statelessness, refugees, marriage, rights of the child, and prostitution. The only supplemental treaty on political rights was the convention on the political rights of women.

In the UN Commission on Human Rights—an elected body of now fifty-three states—during the Cold War the emphasis remained primarily on civil rights. The commission organized thematic procedures (either working groups or individuals) to focus on torture, forced disappearances, arbitrary detention, summary execution, religious intolerance, mercenaries, and children. When specific countries were considered, again the focus of the commission was mostly basic civil rights rather than other rights.[16] In the UN Subcommission on Human Rights—a body of elected "experts"—by the early 1990s there were working groups on gross violations, slavery, indigenous populations, and detention. In addition, nineteen special studies dealt mostly with basic civil rights. As in the parent commission, in the subcommission there was some attention to democracy and associated civil rights, but this attention was neither systematic nor emphasized.

While it is true that a fully consolidated or mature democracy would not tolerate violations of basic civil rights on a systematic basis, one can certainly have a democracy with some or many of these violations. The United States from the early nineteenth century until the 1960s knew both extensive democracy and legally sanctioned racial discrimination. Switzerland, until very recent times, manifested extensive democracy but widespread gender discrimination. According to both Asia Watch and Amnesty International, democratic India today manifests torture and arbitrary detention. Peru, even before the suspension of its constitution, showed that a genuinely elected government could be combined with forced disappearances.

While it is true that the General Assembly passed resolutions stating that all internationally recognized human rights were equal and should be dealt with in an integrated fashion, in reality the specific diplomatic focus of the UN was on basic civil rights. Moreover, as noted above, some of these were subject to derogation during times of emergency. The UN did not really stress, through concrete and pragmatic action, social and economic rights, codified in the UN Covenant on Social, Economic, and Cultural Rights, although there was much vague rhetoric in their behalf.[17] Nor did the UN read into the right to self-determination, listed as the first right in the two UN covenants, a right to individual political participation inside countries (as opposed to a collective right of a people to be free from external domination).[18]

It bears stressing that the reason for this slant or bias in UN human rights activity stemmed primarily from national policy and secondarily from the lobbying of Western-based nongovernmental organizations. Nongovernmental organizations (NGOs) like Amnesty International helped elevate certain civil rights, like freedom from arbitrary detention, to a place of priority. Some of this focus on basic civil rights might be justified in the sense that if one does not oppose forced disappearances leading to summary execution, or simply political murder, all other rights become academic. Other parts of this focus are more difficult to justify on moral or logical grounds.

Despite much good work by Amnesty International, especially on the issue of torture, some serious thinkers argue that lobbying for prisoners of conscience should not take precedence over working to end mass malnutrition and starvation. Several rights-protective states, like Denmark, legalize prostitution; why then should prostitution by emphasized at the UN via a supplemental treaty? A number of rights-protective states, including most of the industrialized democracies, do not consider mercenaries a fundamental problem. Is UN attention to mercenaries as a human rights issue anything more than a passing emphasis driven by the foreign policies of developing countries? (The central question here is not what makes for good or bad public policy but what policies are so universally fundamental as to be emphasized as core human rights.)

It also bears noting that UN human rights developments were, for a long time, separated from efforts to promote economic growth—usually referred to as economic development. Theo van Boven, former director of the UN Centre for Human Rights, documents the fact that a concern for human rights was not integrated into the UN Development Program (UNDP) and other socioeconomic programs in the UN system.[19]

The United Nations and Democracy, Post–Cold War

The UN has escalated its attention to human rights in the 1990s. While much of this activity still focuses on rights not directly associated with democracy, there has been growing emphasis on rights involved in political participation as well.

The Security Council has stretched the meaning of threats to, or breaches of, the peace in order to cover human rights, including democratic rights. The key step was taken in the spring of 1991 when the council said that the human rights situation in Iraq, with special attention to repression of the Kurds, constituted a threat to international peace and security.[20] Thus a government's repression of "its own" citizens can lead to enforcement action under Chapter VII of the UN Charter (although in the Iraqi case the council did not explicitly authorize such action).

In Somalia, the council authorized the use of military force to create a secure environment for the delivery of humanitarian relief, also declaring that to block that delivery constituted a war crime.[21] The council thus made clear that, in situations entailing the use of force, persons have a right to humanitarian assistance. Likewise for Bosnia, the council authorized "all necessary means" for the delivery of humanitarian relief to civilians in need; later, the council created a commission to gather information for possible war crimes trials.[22] The council regarded the situation in Haiti, by 1994, as a threat to the peace and authorized all necessary means to bring about a restoration of democratic law and order.

At least sometimes, human suffering has been elevated over the traditional notion of sovereignty, which had provided almost plenary discretion to governments in the treatment of their citizens. As a result of changes in thinking, the UN has taken important action to see that the internationally recognized rights of persons are respected. (At other times, UN resolutions on human rights have not been followed by important action; the resolutions seem to reflect diplomatic bluff more than genuine commitment to stop atrocities. At the time of writing, this seems true of several resolutions pertaining to the situation in the Balkans and the Middle East.) The fact that human rights were being violated materially within a state did not always block important and sometimes decisive action by the international community, operating under UN authorization. Secretary-General Boutros Boutros-Ghali stated that the time of "absolute sovereignty" had passed.[23]

There has also been increased attention to democracy. The General Assembly, in its forty-fifth session, adopted by an overwhelming margin a resolution endorsing the values found in Article 21 of the Universal Declaration and Article 25 of the Civil-Political Covenant.[24] At its forty-sixth session the assembly not only repeated that endorsement of a human right to political participation through free and fair elections but also authorized the secretary-general to create an office for electoral supervision.[25] The stated theory of both resolutions was that political rights were instrumental in the achievement of other rights, whether civil-political or socioeconomic. When an elected government was overthrown in Haiti during September 1991, the assembly by consensus condemned the military coup.[26] In June 1993, the Security Council voted a comprehensive economic embargo on Haiti, and within weeks the military rulers agreed to a UN plan to re-establish democratic government.

There was also some increased attention by the General Assembly to a better linkage between human rights and economic development, including political participation. At a special session of the assembly in 1990, dealing ostensibly with the economic rights and duties of states, Western states in particular stressed not just privatization of markets but also democratic reform.[27] As a result of this approach, the assembly approved the following language: "Economic policies should have as their main objective the betterment of the human condition and the enhancement of the contribution of all persons to development. The full utilization of human resources and the recognition of human rights stimulate creativity, innovation, and initiative."[28] In 1991 the UN Centre for Human Rights held a regional seminar in Santiago called "Human Rights, Democracy, Economic and Social Development."[29]

These developments in the UN General Assembly ran parallel to developments in the Council of Europe, the Conference on Security and Cooperation in Europe, and the OAS. In all these multilateral institutions there was endorsement of democratic government as the only legitimate form of public authority.[30] Likewise, the International Bank for Reconstruction and Development, technically part of the UN system, pushed for economic growth and development through "good government," a component of which was democratic government and increased popular participation in development decisions.[31] Virtually all major donor governments in these multilateral institutions placed increased emphasis on democratic government in their bilateral foreign policies as well. This was clearly true for the United States and Germany, if only marginally true for Japan.[32]

In trying to show that democracy had become the only form of legitimate government under international law, some commentators cited U.S. use of force in Grenada in 1983 and Panama in 1989.[33] It was true that, in both instances, U.S. use of force led to the replacement of an authoritarian government by an elected one. But one should not confuse basic motivation with mixed justification. Nor should one confuse international endorsement of democracy per se with permission for unilateral use of foreign force to end authoritarian government. In Grenada, the United States was primarily interested neither in the rescue of U.S. citizens nor in establishing democratic government but rather in the removal of a government aligned with Cuba and the Soviet Union.[34] The United States had to use its veto to prevent UN Security Council disapproval of its invasion; the General Assembly was not so constrained.[35] In Panama, where U.S. motivations were multiple, Washington's forcible action led to condemnation by both the UN General Assembly and the OAS.[36]

Techniques of application aside, although an important issue, it is very clear that the international community in the post–Cold War world has resurrected an emphasis on democratic government. This does not mean that all elected governments will obtain significant international support. Nor does it mean that authoritarian governments will be barred from UN participation, deprived of various forms of assistance, or otherwise punished. One should be wary about an easy jump from vague language in UN meetings to an enforceable right to democratic government. The UN, having authorized force for the liberation of Kuwait from Iraqi control, then failed to pressure the al-Sabah government to move toward democracy when it was restored to power. Should the Russian Republic find itself with an authoritarian government, it is unlikely it would lose its permanent seat in the Security Council or be otherwise significantly sanctioned by the international community (although Western assistance might well be curtailed).

But on balance there is greater prospect for UN action in support of democracy and human rights than ever before. This means that some governments will take a small and somewhat distasteful decision in order to avoid something they perceive as worse. Guatemala, for example, asked for UN technical assistance in the area of human rights, in an effort to forestall the appointment of a UN rapporteur, who would have generated some public and critical attention to its human rights record.

It should be noted, at least in passing, that the UN does have a technical assistance program in human rights matters, that requests from governments for such assistance increased markedly after about 1988, and that some of these requests relate to such issues as the drafting of democratic constitutions or the dissemination of all human rights, including political ones. Columbia, Guatemala, Paraguay, and Uruguay were among the states requesting various types of human rights assistance.[37]

UN trends in favor of democracy, while not a panacea, do signal that democrats in the Americas and elsewhere may have diplomatically important international allies. And UN trends may mean, but do not yet guarantee, that those same democratic leaders in the Americas may find increased international funding for distributional development programs.

Recent events in the Americas would seem to offer some encourage-

Beyond Sovereignty

ment about UN diplomatic support for democracy, even if the question of economic assistance for equitable development remains less than fully answered.

Recent Actions of the United Nations in the Americas

UN major bodies now have a broad range of options they can consider when contemplating action for democracy and human rights in the Americas. (I do not discuss specialized bodies such as the Human Rights Committee under the UN Covenant on Civil and Political Rights.) General debates and nonbinding resolutions are well known, and while states would just as soon not be so targeted, there is not much evidence that this type of UN action has much impact when a faction is determined to rule in violation of international rights.

The UN can attempt more systematic pressure by creating special representatives (of the secretary-general) or rapporteurs (of the Human Rights Commission), in an effort to keep the diplomatic spotlight turned on a country—and perhaps to engage in some quiet diplomacy before a public report is submitted. The office of the secretary-general can engage in "good offices," or in other words intercede in behalf of rights or mediate between disputing parties. Technical assistance can be provided.

Diplomatic—that is, unarmed—human rights observers can be placed in country both for assistance and deterrence reasons. Elections are supervised and certified in such a process. The UN can be put in charge of registering voters. The UN can even be put in charge of governmental ministries pending a transition to democracy. In places like Cambodia and Namibia the UN was nominally something similar to the government of the country while awaiting the outcome of democratic elections.

In recent years, armed "peacekeeping" personnel have been dispatched under the UN symbol not just to observe and report on military matters but to observe and report on human rights affairs. Similar armed personnel can be deployed in areas of tension to show the international flag in hopes of deterring gross violations of rights.

Increasingly, coercive UN policies for rights fall within the realm of the possible. Historically, there have been some nonforcible sanctions in the name of human rights, as when Southern Rhodesia was made the target of comprehensive economic sanctions (there was also the legal issue of the Unilateral Declaration of Independence from Great Britain), and as when South Africa was made the target of an arms embargo (human rights violations were never explicitly stated by the Security Council as the triggering problem). In the 1990s it is at least possible that more heavily armed enforcement action can be undertaken under Chapter VII of the UN Charter to coerce parties in the desired direction. As noted above, foreign force was used in Iraq after Desert Storm in 1991–92, arguably pursuant to the Security Council resolution in order to protect Iraqi Kurds in the north and the Shia in the south. Events in Somalia, however, demonstrated that use of force by the international community in the name of human rights and eventual democratic governance may not work out as intended. Escalating violence caused the United States to abruptly alter its commitment, leading to protracted negotiations among Somali protagonists rather than to decisive international action for a new national and democratic order under the UN aegis.

In the Americas, the United Nations has tried to help create, consolidate, or restore democracy in a number of interesting ways, with some of the more intriguing cases occurring in Central America and the Caribbean.

El Salvador

The UN has been involved in remarkable ways in the multifaceted transnational effort to bring to an end the hugely destructive civil war in El Salvador. Constructive UN involvement, even though linked to factors not always present in other conflict situations, offers some encouragement about UN support for the creation and consolidation of democracy in the Americas.

The pacification of the internationalized civil war in El Salvador, which started in 1979 and had claimed some 75,000 lives by the early 1990s while uprooting perhaps a million persons, has a complex paternity. By the late 1980s, both the government and rebel sides entertained doubts about their ability to prevail through force of arms.[38] This stalemate on the battlefield was crucial to all that followed. The departure of the Reagan administration from Washington in early 1989 gave further pause to the hard-liners in the Salvadoran military, because the more pragmatic Bush administration saw less reason to give full support to those authoritarian elements in the context of the end of the Cold War. When the U.S. Congress halved U.S. foreign assistance to El Salvador in 1990 because of its inability to curtail and correct continuing atrocities, it became clear that U.S. support for the government side was changing in important ways. The departure of the Sandinista government from Managua in 1990 likewise gave further pause to the rebel side, especially given the shifting policies of the soon-to-be-defunct Soviet Union.

Given this emerging transnational or intermestic distribution of power between the two Salvadoran parties, regional mediation took on enhanced importance. Other Latin American parties, led by Oscar Arias of Costa Rica, had been trying to ameliorate the conflict during the 1980s. As a result of their efforts, the UN—and not the OAS—was invited to verify several regional agreements that were reached in the late 1980s. Specifically, the UN was asked in 1989 to verify free and fair elections in Nicaragua and the prohibition on cross-border support for irregular forces challenging any Central American government. The resulting UN field operation was called ONUCA.

The UN secretary-general, Pérez de Cuéllar at that time, boldly accepted these roles on his own authority, claiming a right to do so based on authority inherent in the office of the secretary-general.[39] His action was somewhat ironic, for he had started his tenure giving deference to states and sacking his top human rights official for irritating the Argentine junta and its U.S. supporters.[40] At the request of all the parties involved, and under the leadership of de Cuéllar, the UN gradually expanded its activity in Central America, frequently sharing duties with the OAS. The secretary-general's involvement was eventually endorsed in clear terms by both the Security Council and the General Assembly, giving the Salvadoran parties notice that international support for the continuation of the war was almost nonexistent. A representative of the secretary-general, Alvaro de Soto, came to take over much of the mediation between Salvadorans, especially during the summer and fall of 1990. By all accounts, de Soto was skillful in the art of mediation, but he had the advantage of an overall climate conducive to progress.

That overall climate did not mean, however, that negotiations went smoothly. Periodically both army and rebel commanders violently tested the movement toward peace. In an effort to avoid a diplomatic collapse brought on by renewed violence, de Soto proposed in July 1990 a human rights accord. This the parties accepted without full agreement on a cease-fire and other "political" issues. As part of that agreement there was to be a large and prolonged UN presence to verify compliance. This was a deep intrusion by an international organization into what governments normally regard as their domestic affairs. De Soto and de Cuéllar had to consider the feasibility of dispatching UN personnel throughout much of El Salvador, both in government-controlled and rebel-controlled areas, to verify an end to night arrests, incommunicado detention, torture, and ill treatment. There was to be verification of rights to habeas corpus, freedom of expression, movement, and association, inter alia. All of this was to be done before a formal end to the fighting. Secretariat officials finally concluded that the job could indeed be done, the Security Council voted its approval, the General Assembly agreed to authorize the money, and in January 1991 ONUSAL (the secretary-general's UN Observer Mission in El Salvador) began a preliminary presence. By late July 1991, ONUSAL was in place, with a budget of over $20 million and a staff of over a hundred persons, most of whom were engaged in human rights observation and reporting.

Despite progress via this novel and complicated human rights agreement, it was still difficult to obtain similar agreement in the larger "political" negotiations. But after the United States and the USSR signaled their strong support for a peace accord, and after de Cuéllar lent his prestige to the process, an overall agreement was struck between September and December 1991, as embodied in papers signed in New York and Costa Rica. The army was to be downsized and purged of gross violators of human rights. The Atlacatl battalion, among others, was to be disbanded since, despite its U.S. training, it had been responsible, inter alia, for the massacre of civilians, including children, at Mazote in 1981 and the killing of internationally known Jesuits in 1989. In return, inter alia, the fighters of the Frente Farabundo Martí were to turn in their weapons to UN personnel and disband. They were to be integrated into a new police force, while their leaders were to be allowed to participate in politics under the new constitution, revised in April 1991.

There was also some agreement on land tenure and land reform. Salvadoran support for this new democratic order came from President Cristiani and at least part of his ARENA party (despite its previous and active support for right-wing death squads), most of the rebel leadership, the Catholic church, and most other politically active sectors. Authoritarian elements in the military were mostly isolated but not totally quiescent. The same was true of the far right wing of ARENA.

The rebels insisted on UN verification of the implementation of this overall agreement. No doubt the rebels also relied on U.S. promises to condition future assistance to the military on good faith implementation. ONUSAL began a more general verification process in early 1992, with the emphasis switching from human rights observation to supervision of the cease-fire and rebel demobilization. UN officials helped with the training of the new police force. There was also a new national agency, COPAZ, to monitor progress under the peace accords, on which the UN was represented as a observer. And the UN secretary-general would supervise the purge of human rights violators in the Salvadoran army.

UN mediation and verification were widely described as creative and crucial to the democratic peace of El Salvador. But just as crucial was continued pressure and support from outsiders. The U.S. Congress continued to threaten reduced support to the Salvadoran military, showing that it could proceed, whatever the position of the Bush administration. The Bush administration, aware of its weakened position vis-à-vis the Congress, made clear its support for the emerging accord. The United States promised sizable sums of bilateral foreign assistance for the new El Salvador, along with enhanced funding via the Inter-American Development Bank.[41] The European Community likewise made financial promises to sweeten the deal. Gorbachev made clear that leftist groups in Central America had low priority for the Soviet Union, given its other problems. The Security Council and General Assembly endorsed constructive developments. On the other hand, the UN Human Rights Commission and the General Assembly continued to direct criticism at the human rights situation under the old order. A support group known as Friends of the Secretary-General, consisting of Colombia, Mexico, Spain, and Venezuela, lobbied for progressive change.

During 1992 and early 1993, periodic problems arose. Key army elements resisted being purged. Rebel elements were charged with hiding weapons rather than turning them in to UN personnel, and some rebel forces delayed in disbanding. Various deadlines went unmet and were extended. The rebel side seemed to progressively move toward compliance with the peace accords. But army personnel who heretofore had not shown the slightest interest in due process now claimed that being named as a human rights violator by a panel of three independent Salvadorans, without a hearing and demonstration of evidence, violated their right to due process. President Cristiani continued with the purge in general, while making significant "adjustments."

At one point it appeared that Cristiani and most of the rebel leaders agreed that it was politically necessary not to purge the defense minister, Rene Emilio Ponce, in order to keep the larger purge going without military obstructionism or coup. It also appeared that Secretary-General Boutros-Ghali sent the president a letter saying that Cristiani was not in compliance with the peace accord by such an "adjustment." It was reasonably clear that the secretary-general was trying to support civilian supremacy over the military in endorsing the original accord and subsequent list of gross violators; whether his timing and tactics were helpful was a matter of debate. Other top military leaders, such as Deputy Defense Minister Juan Orlando Zepeda, did not take kindly to being on the list of those to be purged. Zepeda charged that UN offices dealing with Latin America were in the hands of communists, who had arranged the peace accords to further rebel plans.[42]

By the summer of 1993, Cristiani had finally removed the top fifteen military officials implicated in major human rights abuses. His actions were behind schedule but nevertheless in keeping with the original accord of national reconciliation. Both UN and U.S. officials had kept the pressure on Cristiani, the latter withholding bilateral foreign assistance as long as Emilio Ponce and Orlando Zepeda, inter alia, remained in office.[43] Rightist elements also tried to block progressive reforms concerning the police, indicating further opposition to national reconciliation.

Finally in the spring of 1994 the long-awaited nationwide elections occurred, supervised by the UN, along with other observers. Despite the fact that the UN, and most other observers, judged the two rounds of voting relatively free and fair, numerous problems transpired. One result was that the leftist parties, although admitting defeat in the presidential race, felt intense dissatisfaction with the overall process. They felt cheated out of gains in the parliamentary and local races. Any number of analysts concluded that, given the broad concern with a fair election, there was little excuse for the number of irregularities that occurred during the balloting. The allegation that the rightist victor, Armando Calderon Sol of the ARENA party, apparently had previous ties with extreme, antidemocratic elements did not provide full confidence in the future of Salvadoran democratic stability.

Overall, in El Salvador in the late 1980s, and early 1990s, we find the UN becoming involved on the side of a democratic peace. The key UN role was support by the office of the secretary-general for those politicians and military leaders oriented toward reconciliation and a new order. The UN intermediary role, played mostly with astuteness by both de Cuéllar and Boutros-Ghali, and their representatives like de Soto and later Marrack Goulding, was made possible by military stalemate within El Salvador. Successful mediation was also made possible by support from key outsiders, such as Oscar Arias and other Spanish-speaking parties, the Democratic-led U.S. Congress, the pragmatic Republicans in the Bush administration, Gorbachev for the USSR, and the European Community.

Whether this UN diplomatic support for democratic political leaders in El Salvador will be followed by significant economic assistance for economic growth with equitable distribution remained to be seen. Various outside parties pledged sums of assistance that were relatively large given these countries' small size. The U.S. promised $250 million, the Inter-American Development Bank $120 million, the European Community $55 million.

But the UNDP remained small and its linkage to democratic development problematical. It, too, was involved under the peace accords and helped to mediate an early disagreement over economic planning between the Cristiani government and Frente leaders.[44] The right wing of the ARENA party was still opposed to some aspects of land reform.

Yet the overall drift of events from 1987 on was moderately encouraging. Led by the secretary-general's office, the UN had made an important contribution through first its mediation and then its intrusive verification efforts concerning both human rights and broader political accords. While the UN's characterization of the first round of 1994 voting as fair and free was probably generous, the process was, on balance, an improvement on the past.

Whether this process should be termed the creation of democracy or the consolidation of democracy is a question that generated spirited if somewhat academic debate. True, in 1983 Christian Democrat José Napoleon Duarte had been elected in internationally supervised elections, as later had been Cristiani for the further right ARENA party. But the United States had so affected those elections—in 1983, with almost $2 million in mostly covert financing—that real questions could be raised about the integrity of the electoral process. Moreover, after 1983, the top echelon of the army obviously resisted presidential supremacy, as Duarte in particular ruefully noted on a number of occasions before his death. The most important point was that by 1994 there was an enhanced prospect for genuine democracy featuring not only free and fair elections but, also, the rule of law, an independent judiciary, and electoral supremacy. The UN both symbolized international support for democracy and helped advance its prospects by concrete mediation, verification, and electoral assistance.

The UN has been involved in a number of other situations in the Americas in ways related to democracy. None has rivaled El Salvador in complexity, intrusion, and saliency. Mostly, the UN has shared roles with others.

Nicaragua

In 1989, as noted above, the UN was asked to monitor a regional agreement on the termination of cross-border assistance to irregular fighters in Central America. From the Sandinista point of view, the primary issue was the verification of the end of U.S. military support to the contras, which frequently operated out of Honduras against the government of Daniel Ortega. From the U.S. point of view, although Washington was not a signatory to the agreement, the primary issue was the verification of the end of supplying arms to the rebels in neighboring El Salvador. Through ONUCA, the UN thus initially engaged in what is usually called a small peacekeeping operation, entailing lightly armed personnel for observation and reporting.

From this start, the UN came to supervise the 1990 elections that ushered in Violeta Chamorro as president of Nicaragua. This was the first time the UN had supervised elections within a state widely recognized by the international community. ONUVEN was the field operation for this purpose. The prominent American Elliot L. Richardson served as the representative of the secretary-general and the head of ONUVEN. This role of electoral supervision was shared not only with the OAS but also with a variety of other public and private organizations, not to mention perhaps two thousand foreign journalists. ONUVEN raised questions from time to time with the Sandinista government about procedure but eventually pronounced the process reasonably fair and free. When the Sandinistas lost, the Bush administration joined other outsiders in throwing its unqualified support to the electoral system and its outcome.

After the elections, the UN was asked to directly participate in an accord of national reconciliation. This role, preceding as it did ONUSAL next door in El Salvador, represented the first time in the history of the UN that the organization was responsible for the collection of weapons from a rebel side in an internal armed conflict. After the expected charges and counter-charges of bad faith between the two Nicaraguan parties, this process achieved at least some success under UN verification.

Whatever one believes about the correctness of the earlier, 1984 elections in Nicaragua, the UN clearly helped to validate the electoral process in February 1990.[45] And since those who governed were indeed affected by those elections, one can certainly speak of a UN contribution to democracy in Nicaragua at least by 1989–90. The consolidation of democracy there is another matter.

The UN, like the United States, did try to contribute to economic as well as political change. Questions can be raised, however, as to whether international assistance for equitable economic development was either timely or sufficient. The UNDP was managing more than $25 million in programs for infrastructure and agriculture, and other international agencies, including the UN Office of the High Commissioner for Refugees, were contributing more. But Nicaragua had become the second poorest country in the Western Hemisphere (behind only Haiti), inflation was out of control in the early 1990s, there was a heavy debt burden, and economic growth was slow.[46]

Moreover, considerable friction remained between the United Nicaraguan Opposition, the loosely constructed but nominal governing coalition, and the Sandinistas, which remained the largest single party. Violence periodically erupted between their partisans, and ONUCA could only report that new international military support for the two sides was absent. At the time of writing there was some probability of renewed violence on a larger scale, as disbanded contras and decommissioned personnel from the Sandinista army claimed harassment and threatened retaliation. The United States withheld $104 million in foreign assistance until the government devised acceptable policies concerning human rights and land reform, inter alia. The assistance was gradually released under both the Bush and Clinton administrations.

Also, once again the question arose as to whether military elements were beyond the legal control of elected officials. Humberto Ortega, the brother of the former Sandinista president, was retained by President Chamorro as defense minister. But he was charged, partially on evidence collected by the Inter-American Commission on Human Rights, with being responsible for political murder.[47] A broader question was whether the Sandinista-dominated army was fully under control of the Chamorro government.

Thus, whether Nicaragua could advance national reconciliation via equitable economic development and whether the Defense Ministry remained a law unto itself were questions that could not be definitively answered at the time of writing. As difficult as it sometimes is to reach the point of free and fair elections, it is almost always more difficult to move beyond elections to the real consolidation of democracy. This was certainly true in Nicaragua.

Overall, the UN role in Nicaraguan developments had been most important during 1989 in small-scale peacekeeping. This had been made possible primarily by the Bush administration's support for the regional agreements mediated by Arias, which entailed curtailment of military support for the contras. (The U.S. Congress was also important in pressing the Bush team toward this policy.) ONUCA thus symbolized and facilitated new policy directions. The UN also played a prominent role in electoral supervision, but had ONUVEN not been present, the OAS and many private and quasi-private groups would have achieved virtually the same international supervision. (Former President Carter was highly active during the Nicaraguan elections; his electoral supervision group contained both private citizens and a bipartisan group from Congress.) The UN role in the collection of rebel weapons could be seen as a precedent, but that task was only incompletely accomplished, given the continuing suspicions of many Nicaraguan protagonists.

Guatemala

The situation in Guatemala shows the limits of UN observation and mediation when the overall political context is not supportive of difficult changes necessary for an end to internal conflict. The army and other status quo actors remained strong in Guatemala, at least until the summer of 1993, and the rebel side and those seeking an end to gross violations of human rights and democratic change were relatively weak. Thus the situation up to 25 May 1993 was unlike the stalemated situation in Nicaragua and El Salvador in the late 1980s.

The armed rebels, made up mostly of indigenous Indians, were perhaps one-twentieth the size of the regular army and approximately one-fortieth that of the army plus its paramilitary civil patrols.[48] The army, therefore, until the summer of 1993, did not believe that it could be pressured into fundamental changes. The army officially relinquished control of the government only in 1986. During the following years it did not clearly and definitively accept civilian political supremacy in important matters or moderation in its operations. Not only rebel fighters but also over a hundred thousand others who were supportive of human rights and peaceful democratic change were killed, disappeared, and tortured since 1954, when a genuinely elected government was overthrown in an insurrection planned and led by the United States. Until the summer of 1993, U.S. military and economic assistance to Guatemala was virtually nil. The Guatemalan economy, however, depends on trade with the United States for an important part of its GDP, thus providing Washington with some leverage beyond governmental assistance.

Perhaps reflecting regional pressures in support of peace and democracy, talks were opened in 1990 between the government and the rebels. The UN secretary-general was invited to send an observer, which de Cuéllar did. This observer, Francesc Vendrell, became a de facto mediator, along with a representative from the Catholic church. But, given the distribution of power within the country, nothing much emerged from these talks favorable to the military.

In the summer of 1993, surprising events occurred that rearranged at least some aspects of the political situation in Guatemala.[49] The UN was mostly a bystander in these events. The president, Jorge Serrano Elias, tried to arrange an autocoup, an event that had occurred previously in Peru. Serrano Elias, having suspended the constitution, parliament, and the courts, found himself faced with massive popular opposition, not just from students, Indians, and human rights activists but also from many business persons. Important segments of the army, having backed Serrano Elias, then switched their support to the vice president, Gustavo Espina Salguero. But this move failed to pacify the growing number of Guatemalans who demanded a clean break with those supporting the autocoup.

The key to these events was certainly not the UN but, rather, ordinary Guatemalans, who took to the streets, and important business sectors previously aligned with the army, who were fearful that international sanctions would ruin their profits. In this regard, the sanctions applied by the United States and other democratic states were important but not decisive. An almost uniform international reaction against authoritarian moves in Guatemala helped restore democracy, at least temporarily. But without popular resistance, and without a change of heart in the business community, these foreign steps would have been as weak as in the Peruvian case.

The result, at least as of the time of writing, was that Ramiro de León Carpio, head of the official Guatemalan human rights office and one of the leading human rights activists in the country, assumed the presidency. He had long been on the Guatemalan political scene, but he was definitely not a front for military interests. He immediately began to make changes in Guatemala, starting with the top of the military establishment, but it was widely recognized that much of the military was less than enthusiastic about his presidency and resulting policies. As the Guatemalan ambassador to the United States said, the needed changes cannot "be achieved without ruffling the feathers of many fat hens."[50] Over time, de León disappointed many of those interested in human rights and democracy by his compromises with the military establishment. By 1994 continued UN mediation between the government and the Indian-based opposition had led to renewed talks under the aegis of the Catholic church.

The UN role in Guatemalan events was persistent. At first the overall political situation was not conducive to effective mediation, and then events proceeded at a pace too fast for the UN to influence. But after certain authoritarian elements were discredited by the failed autocoup, UN mediation via Jean Arnault, representing the UN secretary-general, at least made some procedural progress. Consolidating democracy and ending the long-standing guerrilla insurgency were certainly formidable objectives.

Haiti

The United Nations found itself deeply involved in Haitian events throughout the 1990s. Its roles ranged from electoral assistance through mediation and human rights monitoring to authorizing forcible and nonforcible sanctions. Yet the basic problem of brutal military government proved resistant to change.

The provisional government of Haiti during 1990 invited the UN to supervise the national presidential elections set for December of that year. The original Haitian request envisioned armed observers, but Colombia and a few other states thought this went too far and managed to alter the UN response. The UN, through the Security Council and the secretary-general, agreed finally to diplomatic observation. ONUVEH carried out that task, along with many other groups, from late 1990 through February 1991, when the last rounds of balloting were completed. This was the first time the UN had supervised elections in a state not characterized by internal armed conflict. Thus, ONUVEH represented electoral supervision as a human rights issue per se, not formally and directly linked to a larger question of internal security.[51]

Following the fair and free elections, the UN sought to increase its socioeconomic programs in Haiti, the poorest state in the hemisphere.[52] But those programs were put on hold when the elected president, Father Jean-Bertrand Aristide, was overthrown by the military in September 1991.

While various UN bodies condemned the coup, it was first through the OAS, not the UN, that the United States and others tried to negotiate an end to military rule and applied a limited and porous economic blockade on the hapless country. Certain individuals thereafter represented both the UN and the OAS in discussions among the protagonists, but developments dragged on, with the military still in power.

During June 1993 the Clinton administration, beset by a periodic influx of Haitians trying to reach U.S. territory to make asylum claims, took the lead in arranging a UN mandatory boycott of the Haitian economy, including oil shipments.[53] The sanctions, while worsening the lot of the Haitian poor and especially the most vulnerable, included the freezing of Haitian elite assets abroad. The original draft resolution also authorized the interception of ships bound for Haiti in order to permit inspections, but Brazil and other Latin states managed to have this section deleted. As a result of this UN-centered pressure, which entailed the full backing of the United States, there was a new agreement, negotiated through Dante Caputo, an Argentine diplomat representing the UN, in which the military accepted the eventual return of Father Aristide as president. As part of this agreement, inter alia, UN human rights monitors were to be stationed throughout the country.

The Haitian military, however, reneged on implementing this agreement and eventually ordered the UN human rights monitors out of the country. The United States, having attempted to tighten the economic sanctions, even with UN-approved patrols by warships, finally turned to the Security Council for authorization of military force to terminate military rule.

Under threat of U.S. invasion, the Haitian military at the last moment agreed to a deal during 1994, brokered by Jimmy Carter, through which Father Aristide returned and assumed the presidency to which he had been elected. Order was maintained by a U.S. military force of some twenty thousand troops, until its responsibilities were handed over to a smaller UN contingent in April 1995. The U.S.-led direct involvement in Haiti went remarkably well. Some observers remained cautious, however, about longer term developments in the wake of events in Somalia. In that East African country, a small UN military presence took over from a larger U.S. one. Subsequent efforts to militarily challenge one of the competing warlords went badly. UN military forces finally withdrew from Somalia in 1995 without having produced a central government reflecting national reconciliation or basic order in the capital of Mogadishu. Likewise, in Haiti, some armed elements of the ancien regime remained in the country and active, and it was not entirely clear that all elements supporting President Aristide were fully committed to tolerance and peaceful political debate.

Haitian developments in the early 1990s show that U.S. leadership was crucial to the success of foreign pressure for democracy in Haiti. Yet even the United States found it advantageous to act via multilateral diplomacy to a great extent. And the UN proved useful in this regard, not only for authorizing a binding embargo and possible military force but also for both mediation and human rights observation within the country. The UN was also useful in relieving the United States of the burdens of a long-term occupation. The OAS once again proved less useful to the United States than the UN, because the regional organization was so limited by its member states' concern for traditional notions of state sovereignty regarding force. This concern was diluted in the UN, and the Security Council was not blocked by Latin vetos.

Conclusions

The increased number of democratic member states of the United Nations, the result of both the collapse of European communism and a broader wave of genuinely elected governments in Latin America and Africa, led to renewed emphasis within the organization on rights to political participation. Moreover, with the end of the Cold War, states that had long been supportive of democracy at home found more room to maneuver for democracy abroad. In this regard, one finds the United States and some other NATO countries.

This increasing emphasis on democratic rights is easily documented by reference especially to General Assembly resolutions. But there are more practical manifestations of this trend. Traditional peacekeeping, meaning the introduction of lightly armed UN personnel for interposition, observation, supervision, and reporting—with the consent of the parties—is now being oriented to human rights, including democratic issues. Mediation on democratic issues, by whatever name (e.g., exercise of good offices) is being carried out by the office of the secretary-general. The UN has created an office of electoral assistance that can be activated by the secretary-general, the Security Council, or the General Assembly. UN technical assistance is being directed to political as well as other rights. As shown by the Haitian case, there could even be enforcement of democratic rights by the UN. When the Security Council links democracy to a threat or breach of the peace, then nonforcible and even forcible sanctions can be undertaken under the UN Charter's Chapter VII.

When the UN becomes involved in questions of democracy in the Americas, almost by definition the organization finds itself deeply involved with matters that used to be referred to as domestic affairs. The primary question becomes, Who is to govern the nation? or, in other verbiage, Who is to speak for the state? As a result, the UN has found itself in roles that are highly intrusive. That this should have occurred in the Americas is somewhat ironic, given the region's emphasis on state sovereignty in reaction to decades of gunboat diplomacy—and sometimes just guns without much diplomacy—by the United States.

While the UN in recent years has worked for democratic peace from Namibia to Cambodia, from Angola to Bosnia, the organization found an expanded program of work in the Americas. The most remarkable diplomatic involvement was in El Salvador, where the overall political situation was conducive to an effective intermediary role of a complicated nature. But other UN efforts are worthy of note in places like Nicaragua and Haiti. On other democratic issues, as in Peru, inter alia, UN involvement has been minimal thus far, with the reasons varying case by case. If a national actor (such as the Guatemalan army, prior to the summer of 1993, or the Peruvian president) believes it can control the situation, it is unlikely to agree to significant involvement by the UN on the fundamental question of who governs.

UN political support for national democrats is only part of the picture however. The issue is not just the creation of a system of free and fair elections. There is the equally important issue of the stabilization or consolidation of democracy. Here, the recent UN record in the Americas is much more hazy, if only because the problems are more daunting than that of moving from military rule to genuine elections. The combined weight of poverty, debt burden, slow growth, and inflation is so great, and the serious efforts to tackle these problems so few, that we really do not know precisely what UN roles might prove useful in creating a supportive economic context for democracy. (The problems are even larger, because economic progress depends to some extent also on social change, such as better education, lower birth rates, etc.)

Since most UN economic resources are borrowed from states, it seems safe to say that only when the United States, the most important hemispheric state, gives serious attention to resource transfer in the Americas will the UN or any other international organization be able to make a significant contribution to democratic consolidation. In this regard, the situation in El Salvador gives grounds for at least some optimism, whereas the lack of significant economic follow-up to the 1990 elections in Nicaragua gives grounds for reasoned pessimism. It remains to be seen whether UN enforcement action for democracy in Haiti will be followed by sustained international attention to the worst poverty in the Americas.

5   The Organization of American States
and the Protection of Democracy

Domingo E. Acevedo and Claudio Grossman

On 3 July 1991, Haiti's first democratically elected president, Jean-Bertrand Aristide, appointed Brigadier General Raoul Cedras as commander in chief of the army. Less than three months later, Cedras showed his appreciation by joining in a military coup that ousted the president.[1] Frantic negotiations on the part of French, Venezuelan, and American diplomats finally succeeded in evacuating Aristide to Venezuela and probably saved his life.[2] The OAS condemned the coup and adopted several coercive measures of a political and economic nature designed to pressure the new military junta and restore President Aristide to office.

In spite of their international isolation, the military remained adamantly opposed to Aristide's return, reneging even on a diplomatic effort signed by Cedras at Governor's Island that would have provided for a negotiated settlement of the Haitian situation. With no other alternative open, the UN Security Council adopted Resolution 940, authorizing the use of "any necessary means" to restore Aristide to power, hoping that the threat to resort to armed force would achieve what economic and political sanctions could not. Again, it was not until U.S. troops left for Haiti that a mission led by President Carter succeeded in forcing the military to surrender power. The coup leaders departed Haiti, and President Aristide returned on 15 October to an emotional welcome by his people after more than three years of brutal dictatorship.

The U.S. action based on a UN decision raises, however, serious questions about the role that the OAS is called to play in promoting and protecting democracy in the Western Hemisphere. For many decades, the OAS has espoused the ideal of representative democracy. Their advocacy of this standard notwithstanding, members of the OAS have traditionally placed a higher premium on the principles of nonintervention and respect for a state-centric notion of sovereignty.[3] Thus, dictatorial regimes with little or no legitimacy among the people they have purported to govern have often been shielded against collective action by a sweeping OAS prohibition against intervention for any reason whatsoever.

Now, however, one can detect an unmistakable shift in the opposite direction. Representative democracy is spreading among the countries of the hemisphere. An increasing number of peoples and governments have, in one form or another, repudiated dictatorial regimes and have sought to reaffirm practices that further pluralism, freedom of expression, free elections, and most importantly, what Thomas Franck refers to as "the craving of governments for validation."[4] Elected presidents have replaced many military rulers, such that every country in Latin America with the exception of Cuba has a governing elected president. In an environment characterized by growing consensus concerning shared values and the need to protect emerging democracies, OAS member states have been willing to redefine their previous antiinterventionist stance.

In June 1991, the General Assembly of the OAS adopted the Santiago Commitment to Democracy and the Renewal of the Inter-American System and an accompanying resolution on representative democracy, wherein the regional organization explicitly ruled that governments shall be held internationally accountable to the regional community for the means by which they have taken and secured power.[5] The interruption of a constitutional or democratic form of government would trigger a process of consultation for the adoption of proper measures. Moreover, through the Protocol of Washington of 1993, the OAS charter was modified, allowing for the suspension of delinquent states.[6]

Many problems remain, however, as the OAS attempts to support the development of democracy.[7] This chapter analyzes some of the questions that, broadly conceptualized, result from the tension between sovereignty and collective action for the purpose of protecting democracy. In particular, can the OAS legitimately use or threaten the use of coercive measures against a de facto government that has come to power by overthrowing an elected government? Do OAS member states have the political will to resort to such measures? What other instruments besides coercion could be used for the promotion and protection of democracy?

The OAS Legal Framework: A Summary

For decades, even before the OAS was formally established in 1948, the countries of the Western Hemisphere repeatedly expressed their allegiance to democracy and to the democratic ideal. At the same time, democratic governments in Latin America were often toppled by coups d'état, and many countries of the region lived for years under a variety of oppressive, authoritarian regimes, some of which held periodic but plainly unfair elections.[8]

The former minister of foreign affairs of Costa Rica, Gonzalo Facio, has noted that "The OAS' traditional failure to act in defense of democracy, which became a characteristic of the decades of the seventies and the eighties, was not the result of an absence of legal authority to act."[9] Indeed, the Declaration of Principles of Inter-American Solidarity and Co-operation, adopted as early as 1936, was the first multilateral recognition of the need for "a common democracy throughout America."[10] In November 1945, the minister of foreign affairs of Uruguay, Eduardo Rodriguez Larreta, sent a note to the governments of the American republics stating that the "parallelism between democracy and peace must constitute a strict rule of action in inter-American policy."[11] He argued that peace was safe only where democratic principles of government prevailed and suggested that, when basic rights were violated in any American republic, other members of the regional community should take collective multilateral action to restore democracy. Acknowledging that his proposal was in direct conflict with the principle of nonintervention, Rodriguez Larreta pointed out that "nonintervention cannot be converted into a right to invoke one principle in order to be able to violate all other principles with impunity."

Predictably, most Latin American states were unalterably opposed to Rodriguez Larreta proposal. In their view, tampering with the prohibition of intervention would legitimize resort to force under a collective umbrella by the only superpower in the region. The precedential nature of such collective action could then be invoked to serve Cold War aims not commonly shared in the region. Given the tension between the issue of democracy and that of nonintervention, it is perhaps ironic that the first reference to democracy in an OAS treaty should appear in the Inter-American Treaty on Reciprocal Assistance (the Rio Treaty) adopted in 1947. Its Preamble states that the "American regional community affirms as a manifest truth that juridical organization is a necessary prerequisite of security and peace, and that peace is founded on justice and moral order and, consequently, on the international recognition and protection of human rights and freedoms, on the indispensable well-being of the people, and on the effectiveness of democracy for the international realization of justice and security."

This paradox is evident when one considers the very broad language of Article 6 of the treaty, which stipulates that the Organ of Consultation would meet and agree on measures to be taken if the inviolability, the territorial integrity, the sovereignty, or the political independence of any American state should be affected by, among other things, any "fact or situation that might endanger the peace of America."

While the states have had considerable latitude to act collectively in defense of the democracy that, according to the treaty, is essential for justice and security, they have never invoked or applied the Rio Treaty to protect democracy per se, despite the succession of democratically elected governments that have been toppled throughout Latin America since the treaty went into force on 3 December 1948.

The failure to apply the Rio Treaty to protect democratically elected governments would suggest that the uppermost concern of the OAS member states was, for most of its history, to protect state sovereignty against external threats rather than to defend democracy. This noninterventionist stance towards the Rio Treaty was strengthened by what many Latin American democratic governments perceived to be an instrumentalization of the treaty as a Cold War mechanism to confront regimes that actually or potentially would side with the Soviet Union.

The OAS Charter and Other Documents

One important difference between the OAS Charter and the UN Charter is that the latter, unlike the former, does not require of its members allegiance to any one system of government.

In the Preamble to the OAS Charter, the member states express their conviction "that representative democracy is an indispensable condition for the stability, peace and development of the region." A more explicit articulation of that principle is included in Article 3 (d), which reads: "The solidarity of the American States and the high aims which are sought through it require the political organization of those States on the basis of the effective exercise of representative democracy." Further, Article 2 (b) proclaims that one of the essential purposes of the OAS is "to promote and consolidate representative democracy, with due respect for the principle of non-intervention." But the charter also provides that the organization "has no powers other than those expressly conferred upon it by the Charter, none of whose provisions authorizes it to intervene in matters that are within the internal jurisdiction of the Member States."[12]

The notion of a democratic government figured even more prominently in the charter after a special session of the OAS General Assembly added a new provision on 14 December 1992. This provision states that a member of the OAS whose "democratically constituted government has been overthrown by force, may be suspended from the exercise of its right to participate in the meetings of the General Assembly" and in the meetings of several other OAS bodies.[13]

Democracy is mentioned in a number of other important OAS documents. For example, the Declaration of Santiago, adopted by the Fifth Meeting of Consultation of Ministers of Foreign Affairs in 1959, states that "harmony among the American Republics can be effective only insofar as human rights and fundamental freedoms and the exercise of representative democracy are a reality within each one of them" and that the "existence of anti-democratic regimes constitutes a violation of the principles on which the Organization of American States is founded, and a danger to united and peaceful relationships in the Hemisphere."[14]

Resolution 3, adopted at the same meeting, requested the Inter-American Council of Jurists to study "the possible juridical relationship between the respect for human rights and the effective exercise of representative democracy."[15] The Fifth Meeting of Consultation also requested the Council of Jurists to prepare a draft convention on the "effective exercise of representative democracy" for submission to the Eleventh Conference of American States.

From 1959 on, several attempts were made to expand and clarify the scope of the democratic commitment of the OAS.[16] More than one, however, was motivated more by the imperative of East-West competition rather than by any real desire to promote and protect democracy.[17] The Eighth Meeting of Consultation, held in 1962 to confront what several members of the OAS perceived as the "communist offensive in America" (and resulting in the exclusion of the present government of Cuba from participating in the inter-American system), noted that under the OAS Charter and the Declaration of Santiago all governments "should result from free elections" and that "freedom to contract obligations is an inseparable part of the principle of self-determination of nations, and consequently a request by one or more countries that such obligations be complied with does not signify."[18]

It is clear from this statement that, as far back as 1962, members of the OAS considered that collective action against illegitimate governments did not constitute a violation of the principle of nonintervention. However, this statement was made in the context of East-West competition, and its reasoning has rarely been invoked again by the OAS members as they remained opposed to expanding the precedent. It was not until the end of the

Cold War that Latin-American countries were prepared to start modifying their noninterventionist stance.

The Santiago Commitment and the OAS Resolution on Representative Democracy

The OAS's commitment to upholding representative democracy appeared to have finally become operational when in 1991, the members approved the Santiago Commitment to Democracy and the Renewal of the Inter-American System and Resolution AG/Res. 1080 (XXI-o/91) on Representative Democracy. The resolution, a brief and simple document, calls for an automatic meeting of the OAS Permanent Council

> in the event of any occurrences giving rise to the sudden or irregular interruption of the democratic political institutional process or of the legitimate exercise of power by the democratically elected government in any of the Organization's member states, in order, within the framework of the Charter, to examine the situation, decide on and convene an ad hoc meeting of the Ministers of Foreign Affairs, or a special session of the General Assembly, all of which must take place within a ten-day period.

It further states that the purpose of either of the latter two meetings should be "to look into the events collectively and adopt any decisions deemed appropriate, in accordance with the Charter and international law." This step had two relatively recent precedents: Nicaragua in 1979 and Panama ten years later.

In the late 1970s, Nicaragua was gripped by civil war. The Sandinista National Liberation Front, bent upon toppling the Somoza dynasty, had won grassroots support. The Carter administration found itself in a dilemma: unwilling to assist a government with such an atrocious human rights record, it was unable to throw its support behind a populist movement whose leaders it believed were Marxists, with Cuban and Soviet ties.[19] The Sandinistas did find support for their cause elsewhere in the hemisphere, through Mexico, Panama, Costa Rica, and the Andean Pact.

On 23 June 1979, the Seventeenth Meeting of Consultation passed a strong resolution condemning the Somoza regime on the basis of its human rights record. The resolution declared that the solution to the problem confronting Nicaragua during the civil strife was "exclusively within the jurisdiction of the people of Nicaragua." With evident inconsistency, however, the same resolution added the following:

> That in the view of the Seventeenth Meeting of Consultation of Ministers of Foreign Affairs this solution should be arrived at on the basis of the following:
>
> i. Immediate and definitive replacement of the Somoza regime.

ii. Installation in Nicaraguan territory of a democratic government, the composition of which should include the principal representative groups which oppose the Somoza regime and which reflect the free will of the people of Nicaragua.

iii. The guarantee of the respect for human rights of all Nicaraguans without exception.

iv. The holding of free elections as soon as possible, that will lead to the establishment of a truly democratic government that guarantees peace, freedom and justice.[20]

The Inter-American Commission on Human Rights commended the resolution, noting that "for the first time in the history of the OAS, and perhaps for the first time in the history of any international organization, the resolution deprived an incumbent government of a member State of the Organization of legitimacy, based on the human rights violations committed by that government against its own population."[21]

While deplorable, Somoza's human rights performance was hardly unique. Extrajudicial executions and systematic torture in other member states were well documented by the Inter-American Commission on Human Rights. Among them were Argentina (where tens of thousands were victims of forced disappearance during the military regime that took power in 1976), Guatemala, and Paraguay (at the time under President Stroessner, the only government apart from Nicaragua to vote against the 1979 OAS resolution).

In that context, the actions against Somoza by the OAS could not be seen as an expression of a consistent policy by the organization against all nondemocratic regimes. However, the regional action opened possibilities for the development of such policy by establishing the legitimacy of regional judgments concerning the political credentials of a member state. This was a major achievement in light of the strong noninterventionist stance that hitherto had characterized the OAS, and it was not until 1989 when it was tested again, in Panama.

Since its creation as a state, Panama has been a relevant topic for the debate on nonintervention and its scope. In the early part of this century, the U.S. government, seizing upon the strategic and commercial importance of the Panama Canal, threw its support behind a rebel movement in the Panamanian isthmus seeking to carve an independent state out of the Colombian Republic. Essentially, the United States traded its military support for control of the Panama Canal. And even though under the Canal Treaties signed in 1977, the United States will cede its rights to the canal by the year 2000, its strategic and economic interest in the canal has remained strong.

That interest has always carried over into Panamanian politics. General Manuel Antonio Noriega, the Panamanian strongman who rose to power following the death of General Omar Torrijos, was in part a creature of the United States' own making. He later entered into direct confrontation with the United States, which was not prepared to tolerate growing independent behavior from a corrupt military dictator. When his candidate of choice lost the presidential election of May 1989 to Guillermo Endara, Noriega canceled the election results, triggering the crisis that would ultimately give the United States a solid justification for invading Panama later that year. The failure of the OAS to deal with and resolve that crisis gave the United States one more rationale for its unilateral action.[22]

In 1989, the Meeting of Consultation—convened to consider the crisis precipitated by the aborted election—passed a resolution criticizing "the abuses by General Manuel Antonio Noriega in the crisis and the electoral process of Panama."[23] The resolution spoke of the Panamanian people's right to freely elect their lawful authorities and noted that one of the essential purposes of the OAS was to promote and consolidate representative democracy. It failed, however, to articulate what the OAS would do, beyond making suggestions, to see that the democratically elected officials were put in office.

The meeting went on to note that an essential purpose of the OAS was "to promote and consolidate representative democracy with due respect for the principle of nonintervention . . . a purpose that is being seriously jeopardized," and concluded that "a transfer of power in the shortest possible time and with full respect for the sovereign will of the Panamanian people" should be effected.

Despite its firm rhetoric, the OAS's overall response implied confusion or ambivalence. As Tom Farer notes, "the Permanent Council of the OAS initially refused to accept the credentials of the ambassador dispatched by Guillermo Endara to represent Panama. So the Noriega regime's ambassador continued to participate and joined in the vote deploring the invasion. Only after the U.S. occupation was secure and Endara had begun to function as head of local administration did the Council relent."[24]

The relatively passive OAS response had two results: first, the continuation of an undemocratic and de facto government, which, despite its questionable legitimacy, managed to hold on to its position, survive, and even thrive against the wishes of the great majority of the Panamanian people; and second, the U.S. invasion of Panama on 20 December 1989.[25] In justifying the invasion, President Bush mentioned the restoration of democracy. The regional community may not have perceived that a more forceful initial response to the elections betrayal and the ensuing repression of anti-Noriega protections would have been in the best interests of the Panamanian people and might have avoided unilateral action by the U.S. As Farer observes, "Latin America lost an opportunity to initiate an authentically multilateral operation from which the United States could not easily have withdrawn."[26]

One point is indisputable: at no time was the Noriega regime subjected to the same form of pressure that the Meeting of Consultation applied in 1979 against President Somoza of Nicaragua. Still, it cannot be said that the OAS was completely supine. It did send a mission to mediate a solution, which involved Noriega's exile. Given its evident purpose, one may fairly conclude, in the words of Robert Pastor, that the single most important outcome of the Panamanian crisis as far as international organizations are concerned was to reaffirm "that International Organizations have a right and responsibility to address internal political issues."[27] The OAS had, of course, established that precedent as early as 1962. With the adoption of the Santiago Commitment to Democracy in 1991, this precedent took an explicit form and, before long, was tested in Peru, Guatemala, and Haiti.

Peru and the Santiago Commitment

On 5 April 1992, democratically elected President Fujimori of Peru unlawfully closed the Peruvian Congress and Supreme Court in a measure that was referred to as an *autogolpe* (what Ambassador Heraldo Muñoz called a self-staged coup).[28] President Fujimori ordered troops to occupy the Congressional Palace and the Palace of Justice and had the presidents of both houses of Congress and other lawmakers placed under house arrest. Political and labor leaders were also arrested, and a number of fundamental rights were suspended. In response to the disruption of institutional democracy in Peru, the OAS Permanent Council convened an ad hoc Meeting of Ministers of Foreign Affairs to consider "the grave events" in that country. The ministers decided "to appeal for the immediate reestablishment of democratic institutional order in Peru, for an end to all actions that impair the observance of human rights, and for abstention from the adoption of any measures that will further aggravate the situation."

As in the Nicaraguan and Panamanian cases, the meeting also decided to send a mission of foreign ministers to Peru, accompanied by the secretary-general, "to promote immediate measures to bring about a dialogue among the Peruvian authorities and the political forces represented in the legislature, with the participation of other democratic sectors, for the purpose of establishing the necessary conditions and securing the commitment of the parties concerned to reinstate the democratic constitutional order, with full respect for the separation of powers, human rights and the rule of law."[29]

Fujimori addressed the subsequent session of the ad hoc meeting and promised to convoke a Constitutional Congress through an election in which the people's right to express their will would be fully guaranteed. The representatives elected to the Constitutional Congress would work on amending the constitution and exercise legislative power until the end of the constitutional term, in July 1995. The elections for representatives to the Democratic Constitutional Congress were held on 22 November 1992. The OAS Foreign Ministers described them as an important step in the process of restoring democratic institutional order in Peru, and with that declared the Meeting of Ministers closed.[30]

The OAS action in Peru has been criticized as not being strong enough against a government that closed its congress and its courts. This criticism has been compounded by accusations of serious human rights violations against Fujimori's government. The actions of the OAS were ambiguous at best, and the organization too quickly declared the matter closed. At the same time, the OAS's almost immediate reaction to the Peruvian situation reinforced the already established precedent that the interruption of the democratic process was not a matter of domestic jurisdiction: the principle of nonintervention did not offer a shield to avoid a discussion of the merits.

The fact that Fujimori promised a series of steps designed to reopen the political system along democratic lines—and participated in the OAS diplomatic game—might have reduced the chances that the OAS would take a stronger approach. Fujimori justified his action on the serious danger created by both the terrorist attacks of the Shining Path and the weakness and corruption of Peruvian political institutions.

Guatemala and the Santiago Commitment

On 25 May 1993, President Jorge Serrano of Guatemala suspended constitutional guarantees and, as President Fujimori of Peru had done a year earlier, dissolved the Congress and the Supreme Court. The OAS reacted swiftly that same day, its Permanent Council convoking an ad hoc Meeting of Ministers of Foreign Affairs. As it had in the cases of Nicaragua, Panama, and Peru, the OAS sent a mission of three foreign ministers to Guatemala, accompanied by the OAS secretary-general. Eight days after his *autogolpe,* Serrano was himself ousted by the military; with strong support from the political parties, the business community, and civic groups. The attorney delegate for human rights in the Serrano administration was installed as Guatemala's new president.

The OAS's swift response was essential to the failure of the *autogolpe*. The presence of the high-level OAS mission in Guatemala dramatized the message that the *autogolpe* would not be recognized. The major players in the Guatemalan political scene realized that Serrano's plan could not work if it faced unified opposition. The OAS action in Guatemala served also to prove another point: that the somehow accommodating reaction in the case of Fujimori could not be taken for granted: if a swift reaction was considered politically possible, the OAS would employ such action.

It is important to consider that in the case of Guatemala—contrary to what had happened with Peru—Serrano's *autogolpe* did not have popular support. As a result, the OAS action had a favorable reception in important segments of the country.

Haiti and the Santiago Commitment

Even by Latin American and Caribbean standards, Haiti has endured from the time it became independent in 1804, a particularly oppressive combination of poverty and de facto authoritarian rulers.[31] Hopes that this impoverished nation might emerge from decades of economic despair were raised on 7 February 1986, when Jean-Claude "Baby Doc" Duvalier fled the country, marking the end of a family dynasty that had ruled Haiti for twenty-nine years. The optimism soon faded, however, as the country drifted through a seemingly unending succession of transitional governments, which at times trod dangerously close to a new dictatorship. Finally, in December 1990, after nearly five years of uncertainty, an internationally monitored election, supervised by the UN, the OAS, and many individual countries and NGOs, produced the first democratically elected leader in Haiti's 186-year history as an independent state.[32]

Touting his credentials as a populist priest representing the downtrodden Haitian masses, the Reverend Jean-Bertrand Aristide garnered a decisive 67 percent of the popular vote, overwhelming Marc Bazin, the conservative candidate with alleged ties to the old Duvalier regime.[33] Aristide was sworn in as Haiti's first democratically elected president on 7 February 1991. He advocated radical reforms in the socioeconomic structure of Haitian society and supported liberation theology.[34] Not surprisingly, Father Aristide's populist approach was viewed as a threat to the entrenched groups that had always represented power, wealth, privilege, and violence in Haiti, particularly the upper classes and the army.

In July, Aristide was overthrown. One of the reasons advanced by the leaders of the coup to justify the overthrow of the elected government was that Aristide had used his position to wage a virulent campaign against the

Beyond Sovereignty

National Assembly and the armed forces.[35] As evidence, they provided copies of Aristide's speeches calling for the demise of politicians and military officers who opposed his programs.[36]

The OAS Permanent Council held an emergency meeting on 30 September and condemned the events in Haiti. The council demanded adherence to the Haitian constitution and respect for the government legitimately established through the free expression of the popular will.[37] The ad hoc Meeting of Ministers of Foreign Affairs convoked by the Permanent Council condemned the disruption of the democratic process in Haiti, which the Meeting of Ministers considered a violation of the Haitian people's right to self-determination. It demanded "full restoration of the rule of law and of the constitutional regime, and the immediate reinstatement of President Jean-Bertrand Aristide in the exercise of his legitimate authority."[38]

In what was undoubtedly the strongest resolution adopted by the OAS against any government of a member state, the Meeting of Ministers also determined that the OAS would recognize as legitimate representatives only those designated by the constitutional government of President Aristide. Further, the Inter-American Commission on Human Rights would immediately take all measures within its competence to protect and defend human rights in Haiti and to report their findings to the Permanent Council. The resolution recommended action to bring about the diplomatic isolation of those who held de facto power in Haiti and called on all member states to suspend their economic, financial, and commercial ties with Haiti.

When the de facto government of Haiti refused to comply with OAS demands that President Aristide be immediately reinstated, the Meeting of Ministers stepped up the pressure by passing another resolution strongly condemning the use of violence, military coercion, and the patently illegal decision to replace the constitutional president of Haiti (with J. Nerette as president and J. J. Honorat as provisional prime minister).[39] The ministers also declared that "no government that may result from this illegal situation will be accepted" and that no representative of such a government would be recognized. They also agreed to President Aristide's request that "a civilian mission be constituted to reestablish and strengthen constitutional democracy in Haiti," to facilitate the reestablishment and strengthening of democratic institutions, "the full force and effect of the Constitution, respect for human rights of all Haitians, and to support the administration of justice and the adequate functioning of all the institutions that will make it possible to achieve these objectives."[40]

Despite these strong resolutions, documents assembled by the General Accounting Office (GAO) of the U.S. government indicate that at least a dozen countries, including some in the hemisphere, had "routinely ignored the embargo." The documents showed, for example, that in the first month of 1992 nearly one million barrels of oil had been shipped to Haiti from France, Portugal, Senegal, and the Netherlands Antilles.[41]

The Meeting of Ministers passed a third resolution on 17 May 1992, which, among other things, urged OAS member states "to adopt whatever actions may be necessary for the greater effectiveness of the measures referred to in resolutions MRE/RES. 1/91 and MRE/RES. 2/91."[42] This new resolution requested member states to "deny access to port facilities to any vessel" that violated the embargo and to monitor compliance with the embargo. The resolution also urged states to deny visas to "perpetrators and supporters of the coup" and to freeze their assets. The ministers stopped short, however, of considering a naval blockade to enforce the embargo or a ban on commercial passenger flights to and from Haiti, that had been urged by some.[43]

In a resolution passed on 13 December 1991, the Meeting of Ministers urged any members of the OAS and the UN that had not done so to take the necessary steps to implement fully the measures agreed upon within the framework of the OAS.[44] Two days prior to passage of this resolution, the UN secretary-general had appointed Dante Caputo, a former minister of foreign affairs of Argentina and former president of the UN General Assembly, as his special representative for Haiti.[45]

Thereafter, the UN, working through Dante Caputo and in coordination with the OAS and the U.S. government, took the lead in working with interested Haitian parties in restoring democracy in that country. This shift to the UN forum was prompted, at least in part, by the prospect of a massive influx of refugees, which drew attention to Haiti's crisis in early January 1993 in both the outgoing Bush administration and the incoming Clinton administration. Reporting in the *New York Times*, Howard French observed that "this attention, coming on top of the recent decision by the United Nations to supplement an ineffective Organization of American States as a broker here, appears to have brought a level of urgency to the situation that for the first time in months has raised hopes for an early solution."[46]

The UN's active involvement helped force Haiti's de facto government to sign the Governor's Island agreement on 3 July 1993, under which President Aristide would have been restored to power by 30 October 1993. It created a brief illusion of success, which quickly vanished: the military dictators soon reneged on their promise. Also, Haitian mobs demonstrated on the docks of Port au Prince to prevent the U.S. ship *Harlan County* from putting ashore police and military training personnel. The ship steamed back to the United States. As these means of pressure proved ineffective, the UN, on 18 July 1994, adopted Resolution 940 under Chapter VII, authorizing "all necessary means" to achieve the restoration of democracy in Haiti. Still, the Haitian dictators did not find the threat of use of force credible until a U.S. military force left the United States bound for Haiti. The Haitian military then prepared to accept Aristide's return.

The Haitian situation shows that (as in Peru and Guatemala) a coup d'état could be placed on the hemispheric agenda. It also shows that the OAS was willing to perform a diplomatic role, to find a political solution acceptable to both President Aristide and his opponents. The OAS was also prepared to adopt political and economic sanctions, isolating the Haitian junta and thus throwing its weight behind the attempts to achieve a political settlement. An OAS and UN civilian mission was deployed in Haiti to report on human rights violations, thus limiting the Haitian military's ability to violate human rights without international knowledge.

The Haitian situation also dramatically reveals the limits of OAS action. The economic boycott was not enforced by all member states, in the absence of hemispheric instruments of supervision. Coercive political and economic measures isolated the military regime and created conditions for adopting stronger, more universal measures, but these measures did not intimidate Haiti's military leaders. Only the imminent use of force solved the Haitian crisis.

If in the case of Panama in 1989 unilateralism was the response to OAS immobility, in the 1990s universalism provided the legal rationale. In the context of the new conditions existing at the UN, its Security Council provided a solid normative collective framework for U.S. action. From a Latin American point of view, UN involvement was a reminder that universal action could legitimately bypass regional hesitation.

From the point of view of the promotion and protection of democracy in the hemisphere, there are other consequences as well. As the Haitian situation proves, there are cases where democracy can be restored only with a credible threat (or use) of physical force. U.S. actions in that regard cannot be taken for granted. In the case of Haiti there were policy considerations that could be considered unique, such as Haiti's proximity to the United States and the problems raised by massive emigration. In that context, a regional inability to pursue "all necessary means" to restore democracy would result in an erosion of the avowed democratic regional goal.

Regional Action: The Institutional and Contextual Limitations of the OAS

Under the Santiago Commitment and Resolution AG/Res. 1080, the illegal replacement of a democratically elected government is no longer considered a matter essentially within the domestic jurisdiction and thus immune from international scrutiny.[47] It is, in effect, becoming more acceptable to consider the denial of a "population's right to participate democratically in the process of governance" as a gross human rights abuse, particularly if international monitoring and supervision of a free electoral process had previously produced a clear indication of the sovereign choice of the people.[48] Both the Santiago Commitment and Resolution AG/Res. 1080 are loaded with a normative, ideological premise that some regard as the emerging "international democratic order." Franck, for example, identifies three subsets or "building blocks" in creating a democratic entitlement: (1) self-determination, which is the historic root from which the democratic entitlement grew, (2) freedom of expression, and (3) defining and overseeing a right to free and open elections.[49]

Some of Franck's observations and ideas deriving from his notion of democracy as a generic "global entitlement" are very relevant to the role of the OAS regarding the promotion and protection of democracy. For example, he suggests that the monitoring of internal elections should be established as a systemwide obligation "owed by each government to its own people and to the other States of the global community."[50] This idea he considers conditional upon the acceptance of a more important obligation, namely, "that all states unambiguously remove the use of unilateral or even regional military force to compel compliance with the democratic entitlement" in the absence of prior authorization by the UN Security Council.

Observation of elections is not new to the OAS. It has observed elections and provided technical assistance in electoral matters since January 1962.[51] However, recent operations have expanded the scope of the OAS in this regard. Since 1989 the OAS has monitored electoral processes in Nicaragua, Haiti, Suriname, Paraguay, El Salvador, and Peru. The creation in 1990 by the OAS General Assembly of the Unit for Democratic Promotion provided the hemisphere with an institutional framework to facilitate technical assistance, exchange of experiences, and election monitoring.

Franck also suggests that a neutral multilateral normative regime be established to authorize and supervise collective action if and when such action is deemed necessary.[52] In the hemisphere, the normative basis for such a regime is provided by the OAS Charter, the TIAR and the Santiago Commitment to Democracy. In the cases of Peru, Guatemala, and Haiti, the OAS debate on the political situation could not be prevented by resorting to the traditionally broad anti-interventionist principle. The disposition to place on the regional agenda "threats to democracy" was proven in Guatemala and Peru. In the former case, the OAS's strong reaction probably rested in a widely shared view that in the political context existing in

Guatemala such a reaction would be successful. In the Peruvian situation, the OAS response reflected the existence of different perceptions as to how to react to the "Fujimorazo." Limited influence more than outright confrontation appears to have been the path followed by the OAS. Fujimori's reaction to the OAS's restrained approach further contributed to the removal of Peru from the hemispheric agenda. Haiti, on the other hand, showed that the OAS could isolate a dictatorship and adopt measures of political and economic coercion. Such measures, as in the case of Haiti, could further justify the resort to armed force under the UN universal umbrella.

The combined impact of OAS legal developments and OAS actions concerning democracy stands in stark contrast to its prior practice, which was dominated by the principle of nonintervention. In the new situation, neither friends nor foes of democracy can ignore the regional dimension. At the same time, OAS member states have yet to develop to the full extent the possibilities of regional action to support democracy. No consensus exists to resort to armed force, even when, as in Haiti, all other measures fail. Currently, any effort to build support in that direction appears premature.[53]

There are, of course, other coercive measures that a regional organization such as the OAS might consider. In fact, as noted earlier, the OAS has amended its charter to authorize the suspension of any member state whose democratically constituted government has been overthrown by force. This political step could perhaps be matched by others, such as suspending bilateral diplomatic relations, freezing state assets, cutting off access to financial institutions, and cutting sea and air links. Selective economic sanctions might take a toll on the illegitimate government, while minimizing the adverse effect on the population.

The Haitian case seems to have translated into practice the powers of the OAS to adopt political and economic means of pressure. Heraldo Muñoz notes that it is necessary, however, to reinforce those means so that they move from authoritative recommendations to watertight, enforceable, economic and political coercion.[54] In addition, while no conditions exist to use armed force, regional peacekeeping operations do not meet the same opposition, since they require agreement by the relevant political actors. As in the case of economic and political measures, peacekeeping by the OAS would require institutional developments still lacking at the regional level.

The cases of Guatemala, Peru, and Haiti also show a need for a strong UN Secretariat, empowered to take political initiatives. While this is, in many cases, a question of political will and leadership, an enhanced political role for the secretary-general also requires personnel and institutions that can provide the technical and operational basis for political action.

However important the adoption of coercive measures, peacekeeping operations, and political crisis management may be for the OAS, and indeed for any multilateral organization, there are other equally important issues at stake in pursuing the democratic goal. The firefighter approach cannot be the only way to fight a fire; promotion and protection of democracy requires, together with sanctions, prevention. A fundamental task for the OAS and its members should be to foster representative democracy, a task that involves encouraging policies that will develop jobs, literacy, health care, and market reform. In short, the need exists to address the underlying causes of social, economic, and political instability. As Larry Diamond points out, "countries that are trying to institutionalize democratic government must receive economic assistance to help them weather painful economic reform and the training and technical support to make democracy function effectively."[55] In this respect, the Unit for Democracy needs to play a more meaningful role. In coordination with OAS political bodies and its human rights regime, the unit could strengthen training and technical assistance. Including nongovernmental organizations in its activities would multiply its impact in building civil societies.

Prevention also includes strengthening the regional institutions and mechanisms that protect and promote human rights. By acting on individual complaints against human rights violators, the Inter-American Commission and its court are useful instruments for international remedial action early on when a government starts to violate human rights norms. At the same time, international adjudication of human rights is a way to improve democracy by enlarging the scope and interpretation of domestic rights, expanding and consolidating democracy. Through its country reports, the Inter-American Commission also plays the useful role of bringing to the attention of governments and the public serious rights violations. Although it is underfunded and understaffed, the Inter-American Commission's system of protection of human rights is key to preventing breakdowns in democracy.

The first responsibility to achieve a democratic society remains mainly a domestic challenge. As in the case of human rights, however, the international community has an important role to play. A wide range of measures are available to the international community, ranging from denial of political legitimacy to various coercive measures, both reactive (punishing those who interrupt democratic processes) and preventive (strengthening democratic rule, expanding and giving content to democracy).

Shared democratic values exist today as never before in the hemisphere, but their development is not lineal, and success cannot be taken for granted. Guatemala, Peru, and Haiti prove the need for international action to protect and promote democracy. They also prove that the role of the OAS has been insufficient. It seems that national democratic elites have not yet fully understood to what extent their future is linked to the protection and promotion of democracy in other countries. As a result, the OAS expresses a vision of national interests that limits it potential. The challenge for the future is to strengthen those shared values, giving shape and content to a hemispheric community organized on the basis of democratic values, along with the institutions and mechanisms needed for its protection and development.

6 Nongovernmental Organizations, Democracy, and Human Rights in Latin America

Kathryn A. Sikkink

Nongovernmental organizations (NGOs) form a crucial link in international and regional efforts to promote democracy and human rights. Although they rarely bring about changes by themselves, in every important case of democratization in Latin America, NGOs have been initiators of concern, providers of information, and lobbyists for change and are a central part of the transnational issue network promoting democracy.[1] These organizations are most effective when they work cooperatively to bring pressure on repressive governments, help raise issues, and pressure other governments, financial institutions, and international organizations to take action. Because NGOs often work behind the scenes and do not always claim credit for their successes, their importance may be overlooked or underestimated.

My discussion here relies on a definition of democracy put forth by Larry Diamond (chap. 3), which includes basic civil and political rights. I evaluate the activities of NGOs in promoting elections, the basic rights of the person, and the civil liberties and political rights that ensure that the formal procedures and opportunities of democracy can be meaningfully and safely exercised by the citizenry.

NGOs and Social Movements

Although human rights NGOs, both individually and collectively, have been discussed in many studies, there is sparse theoretical literature on the role of these organizations as actors in the international system or in Latin American politics.[2] The term NGO (or ONG, in Spanish) appears rarely in discussions of Latin American politics, which tend to theorize about social movements rather than such organizations.[3]

Nongovernmental organizations are distinguished from social movements in being more international and professional. They are more likely to be staffed by paid professionals and to have more international connections, more access to information, a greater ability to process information, and greater access to outside funding.[4] Social movements, on the other hand, tend to rely primarily on voluntary staff and have less organizational infrastructure and fund-raising capacity. Social movements also are characterized by their concern with mobilizing mass activities, whereas most NGOs do not attempt mass mobilization.[5]

The importance of professionalization in human rights NGOs is connected to the central role of information in human rights debates. Because the power of these groups derives from information, they must produce reliable and well-documented facts on human rights violations. To provide high quality, rapid, and reliable information on human rights abuses requires investigative and administrative capabilities beyond the reach of many traditional voluntary social movements. Without some professional staff to keep records, verify complaints, and write up and disseminate information, the basic fact-finding mission of the human rights organization is difficult.

Some human rights organizations combine the qualities of a social movement with that of an NGO. Their identities, political actions, and strategies may fit the image of a social movement, while organizationally they resemble NGOs. Amnesty International is the best example of an organization that maintains a large professional staff, raises and administers significant funds, and follows clear and highly structured decision-making procedures yet whose work is carried out by volunteer groups with some local autonomy to set priorities and organize events. Most human rights organizations, however, fit most clearly into the NGO category.

There is a tension within human rights organizations between strategic and professional demands, such as fund-raising and documentation, and their identity as protest, witness, and oppositional movements. In some countries, this tension is resolved by a division of labor, with some organizations taking on the role of protest and denunciation, others focusing on fact-finding, publishing human rights data, and legal work, while still others specialize in direct assistance to victims and their families. In Argentina, for example, the Mothers of the Plaza de Mayo became most associated with protesting the government's human rights abuses, but outsiders looking for well-documented information on these abuses turned instead to the Permanent Assembly for Human Rights or, later, to the Center for Legal and Social Studies (CELS).[6]

This difference relates to the theoretical debate in the social movement literature between strategy and identity-based politics. The strategies and identities of social movements cannot be easily separated, however, since the strategies of movements "entail an underlying collective identity that the strategies themselves construct."[7] Human rights organizations present a clear case wherein shared methodology and shared strategies have led to a shared collective identity, which may be quite different from the initial identities of these groups. Some groups started to use the language of human rights instrumentally, to confront authoritarian regimes or to gain international support, but then these strategies imposed a certain logic upon the organization, reconstructing their identity as a human rights organization. For example, groups that began by denouncing rights violations of only a certain segment of society, such as members of a particular political party, later began to discuss human rights violations of all individuals. Organizations that initially denounced the human rights violations of only right-wing governments later began to speak out against human rights violations wherever they occurred. Because the essence of the human rights movement is the belief that human rights are universal and pertain to all individuals by virtue of being human, the language of human rights imposes a universalist discipline upon organizations that adopt it.

The Evolution of the International Human Rights Movement

The human rights movement has gone through tremendous changes since the early 1970s in terms of its size, the issues it works on, and the manner in which it works. These changes are the result of the movement's responses to new situations of human rights abuses and to a new international context, its evaluations of the effectiveness of its earlier work, and its responses to public opinion and governments.[8] In addition to these changes, there are also important continuities in both the people who work in the movement and the ideas that motivate their work.

We can distinguish three historical periods in the development of a network of human rights NGOs that work on Latin America. Prior to 1973, although there were important precursors for the human rights movement, no large network of human rights NGOs yet existed. The first, dating roughly from 1973 to 1981, is the period of emergence. Activists set up or expanded many key international and domestic human rights organizations, formed connections among groups, and developed the basic methodology of their work. The second period, dating roughly from 1981 to 1990, was a time of consolidation. Many new groups formed, and existing organizations expanded their funding base and membership and experienced some of their most important successes, as many of the key countries in Latin America that had been the focus of their early efforts made the transition to more democratic governments. The third period, from 1991 to the present, is a time of refocusing and retrenchment, as human rights NGOs struggle to respond, in the changing global context, to new forms of human rights violations in the hemisphere.[9]

Because one of the defining characteristics of human rights NGOs is their concern with strategy and effectiveness, the following discussion emphasizes the changing strategies within the movement. One essential aspect of this strategic behavior is the ability to adjust to changing domestic and international conditions. Each of these stages is examined below, contrasting the nature of the movement, the countries that were the focus of its work, and the evolution of the themes and tactics used. (Table 2 summarizes these periods.)

Precursors

NGOs have been the political entrepreneurs of human rights, initiating action on key human rights issues.[10] In two instances, NGOs brought the issue to public attention and promoted international action before the emergence of human rights as a movement.[11] The Red Cross spearheaded the activities that created the law of human rights in armed conflict, and a group of nongovernmental organizations, the Anti-Slavery League, led the campaign to protect the rights of those held in slavery (and eventually to abolish slavery) and helped persuade states to adopt the 1926 convention outlawing slavery.[12] NGOs also played a pivotal role in including human rights language in the UN Charter: at the San Francisco conference where the charter was drafted, these organizations lobbied in favor of human rights, "which was largely responsible for the human rights provisions of the Charter."[13]

The legal norms in the charter and the American Declaration of Human Rights gave the human rights NGOs of the 1970s a solid legal and institutional basis. Although these norms already existed prior to the 1970s, the term *human rights* was not used frequently by social movements to frame their concerns or demands. Essentially, human rights was "created" in the 1970s as an important and shared issue to express the concerns of groups

Table 2. *The Evolution of the Latin American Human Rights Movement*

Stage	Target	Themes	Tactics
1. Emergence: 1973–81	Military dictatorships	Violation of basic rights of person by governments	Documentation, denunciation, and pressure on governments to cut aid
2. Growth and consolidation: 1982–90	Transitional regimes	Democracy, political rights, justice, and impunity	Legal accountability, election observation, and technical assistance
3. Refocusing and retrenchment: 1990 onward	Democratic and semidemocratic regimes	Human rights in armed conflict, endemic human rights violations, and new groups (women, children, homosexuals, indigenous people)	Education, training, globalized advocacy strategies, and multiple institutional leverage arenas

in countries, in both the South and North, and found an echo in policy circles in the United States and Europe.

The Emergence of the Latin American Human Rights Movement, 1973–1981

Human rights NGOs proliferated and increased in diversity in the 1970s and 1980s.[14] Four key NGOs based in the United States that work on human rights in Latin America—Americas Watch, the International Human Rights Law Group, the Lawyers Committee for Human Rights, and the Washington Office on Latin America—were established during this first stage. Existing NGOs, like Amnesty International, experienced dramatic growth. In Latin America, the Servicio Paz y Justicia (SERPAJ), the Inter-American Institute for Human Rights, and many of the pioneering groups in Argentina and Chile were established during this stage. By the end of the period, all the players and mechanisms were in place for the pressure tactics of the movement to begin to have an effect.

The human rights NGO and social movement landscape looked rather different in Europe than it did in the United States. With the major exception of Amnesty International, which was extremely influential through its International Secretariat in London, as well as Amnesty groups in all the countries of Europe, human rights NGOs were somewhat less important in

Europe than in the United States and Latin America. In Europe, church groups, governmental and semigovernmental institutions, and solidarity groups were more important than standard NGOs. European church organizations, especially the World Council of Churches, based in Switzerland, offered crucial early support for fledgling human rights organizations in Latin America. Governmental and semigovernmental organizations, like German party foundations, Dutch, Swedish, and Danish development agencies, and umbrella church organizations that received the bulk of their funding from the government, also played an important role. Europe was also extremely important to the solidarity groups established by political exiles from Latin America.[15]

The 1973 coup in Chile was a watershed event in the creation of human rights NGOs. Membership in existing human rights organizations grew in response to the Chilean coup, and new organizations were created. The U.S. section of Amnesty International, for example, expanded from three thousand to fifty thousand members between 1974 and 1976.[16] Chilean organizations formed to confront government repression, especially the Vicaria de Solidaridad, became models for human rights groups throughout Latin America and a source of information and inspiration for human rights activists in the United States and Europe.[17] A few human rights groups existed in Latin America before 1973, but they never reached the level of development attained by those established later.[18] The coups in Uruguay in 1973, in Argentina in 1976, and the upsurge of repression in Brazil in the late 1970s gave further immediacy and impetus to the growth of human rights NGOs.

Internationally, the 1970s offered a more conducive atmosphere to the issue of human rights: détente diminished superpower conflict, allowing other foreign policy issues; the human rights covenants came into force, providing additional normative and institutional basis for the consideration of human rights; and the Carter administration gave human rights a higher profile internationally.

The early human rights NGOs responded mainly to massive violations of basic rights by military dictatorships, focusing their efforts on the so-called rights of the person, including freedom from execution, torture, and arbitrary imprisonment. The focus on the rights of the person found sympathy in the liberal ideological tradition of Western countries, where the human rights movement had the bulk of its members. It was also consonant with the human rights problems in the movement's earliest target countries: Chile, Uruguay, Argentina, and Brazil.

During this period, the human rights movement developed its basic strategies and tactics. The great bulk of NGO activity revolved around documentation and denunciation: gathering, publishing, and disseminating information about human rights violations and calling upon governments to criticize and isolate the worst violators. NGOs provided both facts and testimony—direct stories of people whose lives have been affected. Most important, activists interpreted facts and testimony in such a way as to make political action possible. The primary tactic that human rights organizations developed in this period was to provide information to convince more powerful actors like governments, financial institutions, and international organizations to pressure repressive governments. Elsewhere, I refer to this practice as "leveraging."[19]

The Consolidation of the Human Rights Network in Latin America, 1982–1990

The second period is characterized by the continuing expansion of the numbers of human rights organizations, the growth of existing groups, and their evolving targets, themes, and tactics. By the early 1980s, the regional and international context within which human rights NGOs operated had changed. Internationally, the Reagan administration and the Thatcher administration created a political atmosphere much less conducive to the theme of human rights. Most Latin American governments were suffering their worst economic crisis since the Great Depression, and many were undergoing a process of transition from authoritarian to electoral regimes.

In spite of these apparent difficulties, this was a period of growth and consolidation for NGOs that worked on human rights in Latin America. Contrary to the expectation that human rights concerns would disappear when Carter left office, the Reagan administration's indifference to repression in authoritarian regimes actually stimulated human rights NGOs to expand their funds and supporters by consistently opposing human rights abuses throughout the world.[20] From 1980 to 1990, the number of international human rights NGOs doubled.[21] By 1990, more than 200 NGOs based outside the region worked specifically on human rights in Latin America, Central America, and the Caribbean, while 140 international organizations also were identified as being concerned with human rights in Latin America.[22] The combined staffs of the three largest NGOs in the United States doing international human rights work in the 1990s— Amnesty International / USA, the Watch committees, and the Lawyers Committee for Human Rights—grew from approximately 25 in 1981 to more than 200 in 1992, while their combined budgets went from less than $4 million in 1981 to almost $40 million in 1992.[23]

In many Latin American countries, the human rights movement became an important part of the coalition calling for a transition to democracy, and the human rights agenda formed a part of the demands of the political opposition. The number of Latin America human rights organizations expanded dramatically during this period, increasing from 220 in 1981 to 550 in 1990.[24]

Although, previously, NGOs had focused on documenting and denouncing rights abuses by military governments, they now began to address the human rights issues in transitional regimes, increasingly stressing the importance of democracy, political rights, and justice for victims of past human rights abuses. As a result of these changing themes, human rights NGOs also became involved in election and trial observation and monitoring and in calling for legal accountability for perpetrators of human rights violations. Some organizations also began training domestic human rights groups to improve their monitoring of elections and trials.

In this change of themes and tactics, the NGOs were partly following regional political trends and partly responding to a U.S. government initiative. President Reagan's speech to the British Parliament in June 1982 signaled that, instead of simply deserting the theme of human rights, as it had initially attempted to do, the Reagan administration now hoped to refocus the human rights debate more narrowly on elections and democracy.[25] Human rights organizations both resisted this narrowing of the human rights debate and attempted to capitalize on the administration's verbal commitment to support democracy. The groups began to stress the "quality" and "content" of democracy rather than the mere existence of elections; this allowed them to incorporate many of their basic human rights concerns within the debate about democracy.[26] Most of the human rights groups in the region advocated trials for those responsible for repression. When, by the end of the decade, it became clear that legal accountability was extremely difficult to implement in all but exceptional cases, the NGOs began to be concerned with the problems of impunity: the implications of the failure to punish perpetrators of human rights abuses.

This was also the period when the human rights movement gained an important increase in support from public and private foundations. Foundation support was essential to the growth of the human rights movements, because with the exception of Amnesty International, which raises most of its budget from its membership, most human rights NGOs sustain their work on money from private and public foundations. Church-based organizations in Europe and, to a lesser extent, in the United States had provided the earliest financial support for human rights NGOs in Latin America.[27] In this second period, the NGOs began to attract funding from larger and more established foundations in Europe and the United States. The

Ford Foundation was the leader among large U.S. private foundations in initiating an international human rights program. After initiating pilot human rights programs in Chile, Ford decided to make international human rights one of its program priorities in 1978–79.[28] Since that time, Ford has maintained a substantial human rights grants program, funding numerous human rights NGOs in the United States, Latin America, and elsewhere.

Other foundations, as well as government funding agencies in Europe and the United States, also initiated programs funding human rights. By the early 1990s, fifteen to twenty major U.S. private foundations were making regular grants for human rights work, while another twenty foundations gave occasional support for human rights. Another extremely important source of funding for human rights groups in developing countries has been grants from government agencies, such as the international development agencies of Sweden, Canada, and the Netherlands. Both Sweden and Norway now have special agencies designed to fund NGO human rights work.

During this period, NGOs began to work more effectively with regional and international human rights organizations. Individuals with more experience working within the UN system began to offer practical, political, and procedural advice and training to new NGO participants who hoped to participate in the activities of international organizations.[29]

The Refocusing and Retrenchment of the International Human Rights Network in Latin America, 1991 Onward

The present transition of the human rights movement in Latin America is partly the result of its success and partly the result of changing regional and international circumstances. Many of its initial demands have been incorporated into government policy and into the work of international organizations, which now condemn human rights abuses in a manner unimaginable twenty years ago. Their main challenge is how to adjust their definitions and strategies to fit changing global and regional conditions. With the end of the Cold War, governments can no longer use the same geopolitical justifications to excuse their repression or their support for abusive regimes. "Yet, ironically, there was a simplicity to much human rights advocacy in the Cold War era that has also been lost."[30] Superpower competition often made NGO leverage more effective by heightening the salience of the issue, attracting the attention of the international press, and providing the large aid flows to abusive governments that were an obvious target for NGO lobbying efforts.[31] Most human rights violations in the hemisphere are no longer gross violations by military dictatorships but are the more problematic and complex violations under elected regimes. With the exception of a few cases like Haiti and Peru, world attention with human rights has turned to other regions and problems.

Some organizations have responded to the new context by closing their doors. The most symbolic move was the Chilean Catholic church's 1992 decision to close Vicaria de Solidaridad, perhaps the most renowned human rights organization in Latin America. In its place, the church is opening a new office to work on issues of poverty in Chile. Many other human rights organizations are facing difficulties securing adequate funding for their ongoing work on human rights and democracy. Some foundations are shifting resources out of human rights work in Latin America to human rights work in other regions and to other issues, such as environmental issues.[32] The human rights groups in the Southern Cone, for example, experienced a significant decrease in external funding in the late 1980s and early 1990s. Once the process of transition to democracy has been completed, domestic NGOs sometimes lose contact with the international NGOs as the human rights situation in their countries are perceived as less important or less dramatic.[33] New themes that have taken on increased importance are (1) the issue of impunity, (2) rights violations by both governments and insurgents in situations of armed conflict, (3) endemic human rights violations under electoral systems, and (4) rights violations of specially vulnerable groups, including women, children, homosexuals, and indigenous peoples.

The Watch committees led the way in this change by focusing on humanitarian law in their human rights work. Influenced by their work in El Salvador in the 1980s, Americas Watch began in the 1990s to measure combatants' practices against international laws of war. They later applied the lessons learned in El Salvador to their work in other parts of the world.[34] Their decision to monitor the application of the Geneva Convention allows them to investigate the range of human rights abuses that occur in situations of civil war or armed conflict and to report on the human rights practices of guerrilla forces as well as of governments. The members of Amnesty International also recently have approved a change in their mandate that allows them to look at human rights violations caused by both governments and insurgents in the context of armed struggle.

In Latin America, the investigation and denunciation of endemic human rights violations under formally elected governments include Mexico, Brazil, and Colombia.[35] This work is consistent with the concern about not only the formal mechanisms of democracy but also the quality or content of democracy. Such endemic abuses include routine use of torture, violence related to land disputes, violations of freedom of the press, vigilante executions, and poor prison conditions. These issues are often more difficult for the movement to work on, because it is harder to pinpoint responsibility and because they may get less sympathy from domestic groups.

In addition to new themes, the human rights movement is refocusing its work on new groups. During the emergence of the movement, the main concern of the human rights movement was with victims of political repression, often political leaders, students, and union leaders, and likely to be male and middle class. In the current period, the human rights movement is increasingly turning its attention to women, street children, homosexuals, and indigenous people. In the 1991 meeting of its International Council, Amnesty International voted to consider as prisoners of conscience persons imprisoned solely because of their homosexuality.[36] Americas Watch has developed a new program dedicated to the defense of the rights of women. Groups in Argentina and Brazil have turned their attention to the problems of the rights of children and adolescents.

With the end of the Cold War, human rights NGOs have worked to globalize their advocacy by identifying multiple arenas for leverage. In addition to focusing on influencing U.S. government aid flows to repressive governments, they also work to influence debates and policies in Tokyo, the European Union, the World Bank, the Organization of American States, and the many organs of the United Nations.[37] They continue to rely on documentation and denunciation. In the countries where gross violations of the basic rights of the person have continued, such as Peru and Haiti, these tactics are likely to continue to be necessary and effective. In addition, some NGOs are engaging new or enhanced work on human rights education, training and technical assistance,[38] public opinion and the media, the use of new technologies such as fax and computer networks, and treatment and reparation for victims of torture and repression.

The Effectiveness of International Measures

We know very little about the effectiveness of human rights pressures by NGOs because there are few systematic studies of NGO influence. To undertake such an evaluation, the first task is to define what we mean by a successful or effective human rights movement. Human rights work can have a short-term impact, a medium-term impact, and a long-term impact. Because it often takes place behind the scenes, the impact is extremely difficult to document. In the short term, a successful human rights movement is one that has an immediate impact on the victims of human rights violations: it saves life, stops torture, and helps get political prisoners released from prison, limits police abuse, et cetera.

In the medium-term, the movement is effective if it contributes to (1) the strengthening of regional and international human rights organizations, (2) destabilization and delegitimization of authoritarian governments, (3) the redemocratization of the government, and (3) the reinforcement of linkages among human rights groups in Latin America, the political opposition, and policymakers and NGOs elsewhere in the world.[39] Alicia Frohmann (chap. 10) describes this last impact in Chile, where the links forged between human rights NGOs in the United States and members of the domestic political opposition diminished distrust toward the United States and helped Latin American elites gain a more complex view of the decision-making process of the U.S. government.

A potential long-term impact of the human rights movement would be to help transform the cultural and moral context both globally and in countries where violations are occurring. For example, when human rights groups denounce abuses, they may help undermine a culture of impunity that perpetuates rights violations. Many human rights organizations are increasingly focusing on human rights education in the hope of making the long-term impact of deterring human rights abuses in future generations.

Before moving on to a discussion of specific countries and issues, it may help to clarify general points about the possibilities for international influence in favor of human rights and democracy.[40] International pressure does not work directly to change international human rights practices. Rather, it works indirectly by entering into the decision-making calculus of key political actors at crucial points.[41] In her chapter on Mexico, Denise Dresser discusses the importance of "indirect support" for strengthening democratic institutions and practices (chap. 15).

Many theorists of transition to democracy assert that transitions always begin as a direct or indirect result of divisions within the authoritarian regime itself, principally between hard-liners and soft-liners.[42] It is exactly at this point of decision within the authoritarian regime, when civil society is still severely repressed and not yet actively able to mobilize, that international human rights efforts may help shift the calculations of actors internal to the regime, giving weight to arguments that the soft-liners are making in favor of liberalization. For example, international human rights actions appeared to have the most impact in Argentina in the 1978–79 period and in Uruguay during the 1977–80 period, when severe repression constrained domestic political actors. After the plebiscite in Uruguay in 1981 and after the military initiated dialogue with political parties in Argentina in 1979, external pressure became less central than it had been earlier.

Opponents of a human rights policy sometimes argue that strong human rights pressure fortifies hard-liners and undermines soft-liners. But the evidence from Argentina, Uruguay, Guatemala, Chile, and Mexico does not support this argument. All other things being equal, the stronger the international pressure, the more effective it is. The larger the number of actors putting on pressure and the wider the range of policy options employed, the more likely there is to be an impact. In particular, the combination of political and economic pressure is more effective than political pressure alone. Since the soft-liners can use international pressure to fortify their positions vis-à-vis hard-liners, more forceful pressure creates more leverage in internal negotiations.

Examples of Effectiveness

NGOs are rarely effective in and of themselves in improving human rights situations or helping restore democracy. Rather, NGOs play a special role in interacting with other actors. NGOs are very good at introducing themes and countries and at calling the attention of policy makers, publics, and the press to new issues. NGOs are the initiators and political entrepreneurs of the human rights issue. Whereas other actors often wait until sufficient knowledge and pressure have accumulated before taking a position or action, NGOs are a first-warning device: they locate problems and attempt to turn these problems into public issues. In virtually all the key cases of human rights abuses in the region in the last twenty years, early NGO action played a crucial role in bringing the issue to the attention of global and national public opinion. Foreign governments placed pressure on human rights violators only after NGOs had identified, documented, and denounced human rights violations and pressured foreign governments to become involved.

NGOs were influential in Chile because they contributed to a shift in U.S. policy at a time when the United States was the single most important external actor in Chile. Mainly due to the efforts of NGOs, the U.S. Congress began to criticize human rights abuses under the Pinochet dictatorship, as Alicia Frohmann discussed in her chapter on Chile. And NGOs brought human rights abuses in Argentina and Uruguay to the attention of the press and U.S. policy makers in the late 1970s. In the early 1980s, NGOs focused public attention on violations in El Salvador and Guatemala. The international NGO community was one of the key actors in the resolution of the Salvadoran crisis, because, aided by press coverage of the shocking human rights abuses, they made El Salvador a domestic issue in their countries, gaining an unusual amount of political leverage.

Human rights NGOs are more able to heighten the salience of a country or issue and bring it into the policy debate when their information is good, when they engage human interest, and when they connect human rights issues to domestic policy debates. For example, the Argentine government's responsibility for the practice of disappearances was revealed only through intense labor by many NGOs working collectively. Human rights organizations provided the definitive evidence necessary to mount the international human rights campaign against the Argentine military. Without this information, foreign governments would not have been able to bring diplomatic pressure to bear on the Argentine government.

In the case of Mexico, lower level but endemic human rights abuses persisted for decades without any pressure or comments from foreign governments.[43] Before domestic and international NGOs started working on Mexico, there was almost no international awareness of the human rights situation in Mexico. As the chapter by Denise Dresser discusses in great detail, in the late 1980s, and early 1990s, domestic social movements joined with international networks to pressure for political liberalization. Only after NGOs both inside and outside of Mexico began to document human rights abuses and bring them to the attention of the press and policy makers did the Mexican government begin to take measures to improve its human rights practices.[44] To get good information, international NGOs need to have mutually supportive relationships with strong NGOs inside the repressive country. In Mexico, the absence of strong domestic human rights NGOs before the mid-1980s made it difficult to document ongoing abuses in that country.

Strong symbolic action is the main tool used by human rights NGOs to convey the human story and capture imaginations. Domestic human rights groups most effectively carry out symbolic action, which international NGOs can then reflect and project internationally. The Mothers of the Plaza de Mayo, for example, were powerful because they engaged in symbolic action, but the image would have been lost had it not been picked up by the international press and international NGOs. Another effective way that NGOs interact with other actors is through the discovery of policy pressure points. For example, the ability of international and domestic NGOs to bring Mexican human rights abuses to the attention of U.S. and Mexican policy makers and public opinion was enhanced by the opening of negotiations over the North American Free Trade Agreement. The Salinas administration was concerned that Mexico might be subject to heightened scrutiny from the U.S. administration and Congress during trade negotiations and ratification debates.[45]

A similar point of leverage emerged in the case of labor rights in Paraguay. After the coup against Stroessner, Paraguay was lobbying to have certain trading privileges with the United States restored under the general system of preferences (GSP). Human rights NGOs in the United States helped two important Paraguayan labor leaders come to the United States to testify against about ongoing violations of labor rights. Without this work, Paraguay might have had its GSP reinstated immediately. Because of the increased attention, however, the U.S. ambassador to Paraguay criticized the Paraguayan Congress for its slow process in reforming the labor code, which has since occurred.[46]

International NGOs first brought the case of human rights abuses in Guatemala to public attention in the 1970s. Their early work on Guatemala was hampered, however, because of the absence of any domestic human rights organizations in that country and because the military and elites in Guatemala were indifferent to international public opinion and sanctions. It was not until the early 1980s that human rights organizations emerged in Guatemala, and one of their most important efforts of the international NGOs was their promotion and protection of domestic human rights monitors. The combination of international and domestic pressure on Guatemala led to the return to electoral politics in 1985, with the election of Vinicio Cerezo as president.

But Guatemala was still far from being a democracy, lacking the second and third elements of Diamond's definition of democracy: power was not effectively exercised by elected officials, because the military evaded executive control, and continuing human rights abuses made it impossible for citizens to meaningfully and safely exercise the procedures and opportunities of democracy. Nevertheless, electoral politics and a somewhat improved human rights climate allowed a more vibrant political and civil society to grow. Although the civilian presidents didn't control the military, the Congress and the judiciary began to gain some independent life, and NGOs, parties, and grassroots social movements developed throughout the country. When President Serrano carried out a "self-coup" in May 1993 by closing Congress and the judiciary and censoring the press, international pressure combined with the newly emergent political and civil society to force the military to step in and remove Serrano from power.

Many more human rights organizations, both domestic and international, were now working on human rights violations in Guatemala. While in the 1970s, there had been no domestic human rights organizations, in the early 1990s there were at least five, as well as the human rights ombudsman's office established by the government. Internationally, many human rights NGOs were publishing reports on human rights practices in Guatemala in the early 1990s. Immediately after the self-coup, two networks of

European NGOs disseminated information on developments in Guatemala that they received from their counterparts in the country. These networks then coordinated a lobbying effort to pressure their governments and the European Political Cooperation to take a strong position in opposing the Guatemalan coup.[47]

Later, Germany announced it would suspend $78 million of aid to Guatemala, and the Dutch also conditioned their aid on the restoration of parliamentary democracy. The United States immediately suspended all military and police aid and most economic aid to Guatemala and said it would press for sanctions against Guatemala at an emergency meeting of the OAS. One of the most powerful sanctions, however, was the threat by the United States to withdraw Guatemala's trade benefits under the GSP. It was this threat that apparently got business leaders to join other groups in civil society to press for Serrano's removal.[48] Once Serrano was out, politicians, under pressure from organized citizens in the streets, unexpectedly elected Ramiro de Leon Carpio, the former attorney general for human rights, as the new president of Guatemala. To most observers of Latin American politics, this scenario was surprising. For decades, Guatemalan regimes had been the most severe violators of human rights and the most impervious to international human rights pressures. What had changed? Diamond's point that democracy is not a categorical but a continuous variable helps make sense of the Guatemalan situation (chap. 3). The Guatemalan case illustrates some of the ways in which a society can move along the continuum from less democracy to more democracy and the role that international forces play in that process.

The Guatemalan case also shows that internal forces must be the promoters and protectors of democracy but that external groups can offer crucial support and assistance in fostering the growth of political and civil society. The case of Guatemala also suggests that international action must be prompt and forceful and that a combination of economic and political pressure is more effective than political pressure alone.

Perhaps the most significant contribution of the human rights NGOs has been in helping to incorporate human rights as a necessary and permanent part of global discourse and U.S. policy. NGOs not only put human rights on the public agenda, they also helped keep it there.[49] One leader of an important human rights NGO, Michael Posner, said, "we have won a spot at the table. Lip service must be paid to human rights. Even if we don't always prevail, a lot of energy goes into dealing with us. Human rights is often dealt with improperly, but it is always there, it doesn't go away. The government has to come to terms with us."[50]

Another key long-term impact of NGOs is on changing understandings of sovereignty. The doctrine of sovereignty has been discussed in depth elsewhere in this volume (chaps. 1 and 2). Discussions of changes in sovereignty often include only international law and the practices of international organizations and states. Because sovereignty is a set of intersubjective understandings about the legitimate scope of state authority, reinforced by practice, the activities of NGOs also can question the basic premise of state sovereignty: that it is nobody else's business how a state treats its subjects.[51] Every report, conference, or letter of the human rights movement underscores that the basic rights of individuals are not the exclusive domain of the state but are a legitimate concern of the international community. When states respond to NGOs by changing their rhetoric and by changing concrete state policies, it demonstrates shifting state understanding and practices about the scope of state authority.

Examples of Ineffectiveness

Human rights NGOs are less effective in two kinds of cases: (1) where the countries are "too big or too important to be complicated by human rights" (i.e., where the perceived national security interests of the United States or another country are at stake), or (2) where essentially the countries are not important enough, where no constituency exists to press for change.[52]

Most examples of the "too big or important" category come from outside Latin America—China, Saudi Arabia, Pakistan, Israel, Turkey—which may help explain why human rights pressure has been more effective in Latin America than elsewhere in the world. But there are numerous cases in Latin America where perceived U.S. national security concerns have impeded effective human rights actions, in particular in Guatemala and El Salvador. The national interests of other countries also may hamper NGO human rights work. For example, Soviet-Argentine trade led the USSR to frustrate NGO efforts to strengthen UN action on Argentine human rights violations.[53] NGOs have a better track record converting countries in the "not important enough" group into countries where human rights can become a central issue. Two countries once seen as lacking a constituency—Somalia and Haiti—by early 1992 were on the front page of every major newspaper. The human rights community helped provide the information and the testimony to heighten the salience of these countries.

Human rights NGOs are less effective where they confront well-organized and powerful domestic lobbies and most effective where they can ally with such lobbies. NGOs have always been more effective at securing cutoffs in economic and military aid than at embargoes on commercial sales or trade. Foreign aid does not have a strong domestic constituency; to gather the needed majority for military and economic aid cutoffs, human rights advocates often allied with conservative members of Congress who opposed foreign aid in general. But when human rights NGOs lobbied to cut off commercial sales or government credits for domestic sales, they came up against domestic business lobbies and often lost. For example, human rights groups helped secure cutoffs in military and economic aid to Argentina, but when they attempted to block an Export-Import Bank loan to Argentina to help it purchase turbines from the Allis-Chalmers Corporation, business lobbies helped overturn the legislation. Likewise, attempts to block commercial sales of aviation equipment to Latin American military governments have come up against powerful business lobbies. In the case of human rights in Mexico, human rights NGOs allied with the environmental lobby and labor organizations to confront the probusiness lobby.

Unfortunately, there is no direct correlation between the severity of human rights abuses and the degree to which NGOs are effective. International NGOs that initiate concern over human rights practices depend on information from domestic NGOs. Paradoxically, the network may not function well in many countries where it is most needed; domestic NGOs exist only where governments allow them to exist and where people have the time, money, and education to denounce and document human rights abuses. The most repressive governments may simply eliminate those domestic NGOs that are the crucial links for the network to function.

Conclusions

Although many of the conclusions in this study are tentative, it suggests four conditions under which human rights NGOs are most effective: (1) when NGOs have convincing information and are able to mobilize human interest, (2) when target countries have important domestic human rights organizations, (3) when the national security concerns of superpowers and strong counterlobbies are absent; and (4) when possibilities for leverage exist.

The Latin American human rights movement emerged as a response to the gross violations of human rights throughout the hemisphere in the 1970s. Early NGOs, such as Amnesty International, the Vicaria de Solidaridad, and the Madres de la Plaza de Mayo, were inspirations and sources of information, strategies, and tactics for other groups throughout the hemisphere. In this sense, a process of learning took place, with the diffusion of a certain form of human rights organizing. This process was given impetus by the emergence and growth of the human rights movement in the United States and Europe during this period.

With many Latin American countries' transition to formal electoral regimes, the human rights movement has entered a new era. The current phase of refocusing and retrenchment is in part a product of the movement's success and in part a product of the very definitions and strategies that proved instrumental in responding to situations of human rights abuse. As the region moves into a new phase, there is a need for new definitions and new strategies that can respond to the changing international and domestic context. Human rights NGOs served effectively as carriers of human rights ideas, initiators of concern, providers of information, and lobbyists for change. Their influence was important in the early campaigns, the precursors of the current human rights movement. Later human rights NGOs contributed to the implementation and continuity of human rights policy in the United States and Europe. In Latin America, human rights NGOs became part of the coalition pressing for redemocratization, providing the political opposition with legitimacy and a powerful set of symbolic messages. Today, NGOs are taking on a range of new issues, especially the problem of how to enhance the quality and content of democracy under formally elected regimes.

Human rights NGOs are not powerful in any common sense of the word. Their influence is directly the result of the reliability of their information and the resonance of their arguments with the concerns of policy makers. But on the issues of human rights and democracy, small but well-organized human rights NGOs have played an important role. These organizations, however, do not wield influence independently but tend to work through other state and nonstate actors. By providing information to international or regional organizations, or by placing pressure on governmental actors, they are able to play a substantial behind-the-scenes role. Progress in the human rights issue would not have happened without the activities of these organizations, but they are only one link in the chain of international pressure for human rights and democracy.

7 The International Donor Community

Conditioned Aid and the Promotion and Defense of Democracy

Joan M. Nelson and Stephanie J. Eglinton

The present challenge for the international community regarding Latin America is to assist in the consolidation of democratic reforms. In mid-1994, every country except Cuba and Haiti was ruled by a government put in place by reasonably fair elections. Many of these elected governments, however, remain precarious. Established democracies as well as fragile new democracies face serious strains from economic adjustment and, in some cases, from drug cartels and terrorist groups.

Other chapters in this volume examine the roles of the United Nations, the Organization of American States, and nongovernmental organizations in responding to this challenge. This chapter focuses on an instrument rather than an organization: foreign economic assistance and, more specifically, the conditions attached to such aid as an approach to defending and helping to consolidate democracy. Conditionality is a contentious instrument, not least because it is often viewed as an invasion of the recipient nation's sovereignty. Yet in the post-Cold War era the United States and many other aid donors are increasingly inclined to attach conditions to aid to encourage not only economic but also political and social reforms. International development assistance agencies such as the World Bank and the Inter-American Development Bank are much more hesitant to attach conditions to their aid but are being urged by some of their wealthy member nations (especially the United States) and by some nongovernmental organizations to move in this direction. This chapter reviews donors' changing policies and programs, examines the major ways in which conditions can be linked to aid, and briefly surveys the effectiveness of these several approaches.

Democracy and the Development Agenda

The United States has long tried to use economic aid, among other instruments, to promote democracy and human rights protection. But these efforts—for instance, programs to strengthen the judiciary—have usually been fairly minor themes in aid programs directed largely to other goals. The Alliance for Progress of the 1960s was a more ambitious but indirect approach, seeking to promote democracy by encouraging social and economic reforms. During the Cold War, of course, anticommunist objectives often led the United States to use aid to support authoritarian governments. Thus President Clinton's announcement in May 1993 that he would make promotion of democracy and human rights the main elements of his policy toward Latin America marked a significant departure from earlier approaches.

The United States is not alone in this new emphasis on promoting democracy. The wave of political openings throughout Latin America, the remarkable transitions from communism in Eastern Europe, and democratic initiatives in sub-Saharan Africa have generated growing acceptance of competitive democracy and respect for human rights as global norms. The new prevailing assumption is that specific institutional arrangements may vary, but one-party systems and military governments are anachronistic.

At the same time that democracy has become increasingly accepted as a global norm, ideas regarding the relation between democracy and economic development have altered. During the 1970s and 1980s, many believed that democratic governments' capacity for responsible economic management was handicapped by electoral calculations and popular demands for immediate benefits. The example of the East Asian "tigers" (Korea, Taiwan, Singapore, Hong Kong) was used to support the argument that authoritarian regimes were more likely to manage their economies to promote growth. By the 1980s, however, it was increasingly obvious that many authoritarian governments were inefficient and corrupt as well as repressive, while some democracies were able to manage their economies quite well. Analysts comparing economic performance in many countries find no clear evidence of any link between form of government and either long-term growth or short-term ability to carry out stabilization measures.[1]

Moreover, the critique of excessive state economic regulation and the emphasis on free markets and private enterprise emerging during the 1980s bolstered a revised view of democracy as compatible with, indeed conducive to, economic growth: democracy and markets, it was optimistically argued, went hand in hand. Sound macroeconomic management and good basic infrastructure and services (including education and health programs) required honest and competent governments. Good governments, in turn, were promoted by open debate, active media, and democratic competition.

By the early 1990s, these intellectual and ideological trends merged with other strands to produce a greatly broadened concept of development itself. Many now assert that not only economic growth and political freedom but also social equity and environmental protection are inextricably entwined: in the long run, progress on any one of these fronts cannot be sustained without progress on the others. In short, at the same time that democracy is accorded much higher priority by the United States and other wealthy democracies, it is also viewed as part of a broad, integrated concept of sustainable development.[2]

Dissenting views, of course, persist regarding the value of representative democracy, though much less in Latin America than in Africa, the Middle East, and East Asia. With regard to Latin America, the most heated debates concern not the objectives but the means by which outsiders can and should seek to promote democracy. Even among enthusiastic supporters of democracy, there is considerable disagreement on the extent to which external intervention in the affairs of any nation is warranted to accelerate political reforms. Until quite recently—and in the view of many, still today—pressure to promote changes in political institutions and processes was regarded as a clear invasion of the accepted boundaries of national sovereignty. Yet others, even within the poorer nations (particularly political dissidents challenging restrictive governments), favor foreign intervention. They argue that aid has long had the effect (whether or not intended) of supporting incumbents, including dictators. The use of aid to support or press for political reform therefore is not new intervention, they conclude, but intervention directed toward more desirable goals.

Democracy and Aid Agencies

By the early 1990s, reoriented post–Cold War foreign policies and broadened concepts of development led aid agencies to reconsider their policies and approaches for promoting political reforms. The United States and other industrialized democracies announced new measures to more aggressively support global democratic trends. Multilateral donors, especially the World Bank, were also pressed to give higher priority to political reforms, even though their charters prohibit the consideration of non-economic factors. The undersecretary for international affairs of the U.S. Treasury indicated in May 1993 that the United States would urge the multilateral banks to consider democracy and human rights in their aid allocations and loan operations.[3] These pressures prompted controversy within the Executive Board of the World Bank, not only between industrial and developing countries but also among board members representing industrial democracies. (We return later in this chapter to the question of the role of multilateral aid agencies.)

Aid donors use three general approaches to help promote political development: (1) direct support, (2) indirect support, via encouraging economic growth, and (3) pressure to encourage policy reform.

Direct support is not a new approach but has recently received more attention and resources. Through technical assistance and specially designed projects, donors seek to strengthen democratic institutions and processes, such as judiciaries, legislatures, the press, political parties, and electoral systems.

For example, the U.S. Agency for International Development (USAID) made democracy building a principal program focus in its Democracy Initiative of 1990. The initiative distinguishes four main areas of support: strengthening democratic representation, supporting respect for human rights, promoting lawful governance, and encouraging democratic values. USAID also stated its intention to consider the implications for participation and democracy in its full array of aid activities and to take into account progress toward democracy, respect for human rights, and good governance in its allocation of funds to developing countries.[4] Examples of such USAID projects in Latin America include (1) a project in Bolivia to install automated data-processing equipment for voter registries and to train electoral personnel prior to the 1989 elections, (2) a training project to improve the performance and accessibility of Guatemalan judicial services, and (3) a project to broaden participation in and to strengthen democratic labor unions in El Salvador.

Direct support activities compose the bulk of donors' democratization efforts. Most of these are relatively noncontroversial, as long as the activities are clearly nonpartisan. To strengthen political parties and electoral procedures, some governments have created private endowments to channel assistance through NGOs. The National Endowment for Democracy (NED) was established by the U.S. Congress in 1983. The NED is a private organization that receives an annual federal appropriation to provide grants to support democratic institutions, mostly through four core grantees associated with the Democratic and Republican parties, labor unions, and business groups.[5] Similarly, the British Westminster Foundation for Democracy and the Stiftungen of the German political parties channel nongovernmental aid to promote political development.

Indirect support for democracy, through encouraging economic reforms and helping to restart growth, is at least as important as direct support efforts. Assistance cannot by itself produce growth, and growth alone is no guarantee of democracy. But where fragile democracies are tackling difficult economic reforms, adequate economic assistance greatly improves the chances both for growth and for the consolidation of democracy. Especially in poorer countries, support for growth may be particularly important as a complement to donor pressure for sound macroeconomic management and market-friendly economic reforms, because these reforms, while likely to pay off with faster growth eventually, strain democratic institutions in the short run.

Finally, donor governments and agencies can directly pressure governments to make certain policy reforms that would contribute to competitive politics and wider respect for human rights. Linking aid to political reforms—the focus of this chapter—is one such form of pressure. Conditionality is of course highly controversial. The following section examines the instrument of conditionality generally and three specific forms of conditionality used by the international donor community to promote political reforms.

Conditioned Aid

Two main considerations have contributed to recent calls for greater use of aid conditionality to promote democracy. First, the debt crisis and its aftermath triggered a rapid increase during the 1980s of IMF conditionality and World Bank loans based on economic policy reforms. These loans are widely viewed as having powerfully shaped recipients' economic policies. That view is common even among many NGOs and other groups that disagree with the content of the reforms required by the Bank and the Fund. Why not, they began to ask, use the same approach to promote political reforms? Increased conditionality is also encouraged by a second set of factors: constrained aid budgets and aid fatigue in the wealthy democracies, coupled with demands from the public, legislators, and NGOs that aid be targeted to those who use it best and denied to repressive, corrupt, or inefficient governments.

Despite these attractions, the use of aid conditions to promote democracy runs serious risks. First, donors know much less about how to encourage democracy in the unique circumstances of each country than they know about some aspects of economic policy: for instance, how to contain hyperinflation. There is a real danger of insisting on measures that turn out to have unanticipated and adverse side effects.

Second, the technique of conditionality (as separate from the goals it may be used to promote) is usually resented by aid recipients because it is considered an invasion of sovereignty. Conditionality focuses on reforming policies rather than supporting institutions. It presupposes that the donor knows best what is good for the recipient and reflects power inequalities between the donor and recipient. While many governments now agree that blatant human rights abuse is appropriate grounds for international action, most remain highly sensitive about international intervention in their political institutions and procedures.

Third, especially in countries where democratic procedures have been only recently established or reestablished, outsiders' requirements (as distinct from technical assistance, advice, and financial support) regarding delicate and complex political reforms risk destroying the credibility of the democratic process itself. Especially in fragile new democracies, it is imperative that the people of the country feel that they or their government, and not outsiders, are responsible for choices and actions. Strong pressure becomes appropriate only if and when a government itself subverts existing democratic procedures or institutions, as occurred in Peru, Haiti, and Guatemala during 1991 and 1992.

These risks are inherent in conditioned aid. Nevertheless, conditionality can be quite effective in promoting specific reforms or discouraging anti-democratic moves. To better understand both the potential and the limits of conditionality for encouraging democracy, it is useful to distinguish three different forms of conditionality: allocation criteria, sanctions, and conditions attached to specific loans. Bilateral donors have taken the lead in developing criteria that allocate aid according to progress toward political and social, as well as economic goals and in using sanctions to discourage repression. The IMF and the World Bank have much greater experience in using conditions attached to specific loans (called policy-based loans by the World Bank) to influence policies, although thus far they have used this approach almost entirely to promote economic rather than political reforms.

Allocation Criteria

In 1990 and 1991, many bilateral donors, including the United States, announced policies of concentrating their aid on those poorer countries

Beyond Sovereignty

that not only adopt sound economic policies but also are moving toward more democratic politics, more vigorous efforts to help the poor, and better environmental policies. Several smaller donors, including Canada, the Netherlands, and the Nordic countries have long considered recipient countries' performance with respect to human rights and democracy when determining aid allocations. In 1991, Germany announced new criteria for aid that included respect for human rights and participation in the political process. Even Japan, traditionally reluctant to link aid with the policies of recipient governments, issued an Overseas Development Assistance Charter in 1992 that included human rights and progress toward democracy among the principles that would guide the future allocation of its aid.

These policy statements suggest that donors plan to gradually shift the allocation of their concessional aid programs to favor countries making progress on human rights, good governance, and democracy, while providing reduced or no support to countries that do not show progress. The approach is appealing because it is less interventionist than other types of conditionality. In principle, allocation criteria establish a standard that is uniform for all aid recipients. Potential recipients are assessed on policies and performance they have chosen, without direct external influence.

Several donors began to implement this approach in the early 1990s. Within USAID, the bureaus responsible for different geographic regions developed separate complex systems to score recipient performance. US-AID's Bureau for Latin America and the Caribbean allocated part of its budget among countries according to a formula based on recipients's adjustment policies (assigned a weight of 50% in the formula), degree of democratic government (20%), level of its social indicators (20%), and environmental policies (10%). In determining progress toward democracy and human rights, the bureau considered independent human rights reports and Freedom House's indexes of civil and political rights. By 1994, however, this formula had been dropped in favor of a more flexible assessment of each country's own policies and the effectiveness of AID programs in that country.

In practice, the reallocation of concessional aid to favor political reformers and penalize nonreformers was and remains more ad hoc than systematic. Bilateral donors are not likely to pursue performance-based allocation vigorously and consistently for three reasons: the difficulty in developing political indicators, the bureaucratic and legal constraints on aid agencies, and most fundamentally, conflicting foreign policy considerations.

The complexity of political reforms make it difficult to determine the precise criteria to gauge levels and trends of human rights, governance, and democracy. If some aspects of a government's performance improve while others do not, which aspects are most important? Should fixed criteria be used for all recipients, or should trends be considered so that each country is judged against its own record?

Bureaucratic and legal constraints will also hamper major reallocations. As most bilateral donors face shrinking aid budgets, it will be difficult to implement systems of allocation criteria consistently, particularly to reward good behavior. Aid officials often are restricted in how they can allocate funding for developing countries. From the late 1970s, for example, nearly half of U.S. bilateral assistance has been committed to Israel and Egypt alone, and the remainder is constrained by a large number of congressionally legislated earmarks. Despite wide agreement on the need for a basic overhaul of aid legislation, efforts in 1993 and early 1994 to draft a new law proved abortive. In 1995 the continuation of most aspects of U.S. foreign aid is in question.

Finally, attempts to promote political reform through allocation criteria will be impeded if the reallocation of aid conflicts with other diplomatic, commercial, financial, or security interests of the donor. These sometimes competing interests remain important in the post–Cold War era; indeed, some concerns such as trade promotion and fighting drug trafficking, have probably intensified.

Sanctions

When allocation criteria are not implemented systematically, conditionality is likely to take the form of sanctions: punishing a few blatant abusers by withdrawing aid and perhaps rewarding a few excellent performers with increased assistance. Aid sanctions are the most dramatic and publicized form of aid conditionality. Donors are increasingly willing to suspend assistance to governments that violate universal standards of human rights. More recent and more tentative is the international agreement that competitive democracy is an appropriate goal worldwide and, furthermore, is a legitimate issue for external intervention.

Serious violations of human rights or blatant antidemocratic steps—a military coup or an aborted election—are the most appropriate situations for conditionality in the form of aid sanctions. Backsliding is intrinsically a sharper target for pressure, because it is clear what the government has done that now must be undone.

The U.S. experience linking assistance to the human rights records of recipient countries (since the mid-1970s) and the decisions of the international donor community (in the early 1990s) to withdraw aid to Haiti, Peru, and Guatemala in response to antidemocratic events offer some lessons on the limits and potential of sanctions to promote or defend democracy and human rights. The U.S. policy regarding human rights protection and aid is based on legislation stating that no economic or security assistance should be provided to "any country the government of which engages in a consistent pattern of gross violations of internationally recognized human rights."[6] These laws were passed in 1974 and have been implemented inconsistently over the past twenty years, reflecting differing priorities among administrations, conflicts between Congress and the executive, and tensions within government agencies. Most significantly, human rights objectives often have been subordinated to economic, security, and other foreign policy concerns. The United States was more likely to confront a government regarding the treatment of its citizens if the nation was neither an important trading partner nor a strategic player in the Cold War.

Despite its limitations, the U.S. policy of conditioning aid on respect for human rights did contribute over time to a heightened awareness and attention to human rights concerns and much closer monitoring of human rights abuses. Other industrial democracies have increasingly followed the U.S. lead in officially linking aid to human rights.

On several occasions in the early 1990s, the donor community acted in concert to defend participatory democracy, not merely human rights narrowly defined. After military leaders overthrew Haitian President Jean-Bertrand Aristide in September 1991, the United States and other members of the Organization of American States cut aid, imposed a trade embargo, and entered into protracted negotiations to restore the nation's first democratically elected president to power. As discussed in more detail elsewhere in this volume (see chap. 8), three years of such efforts were not sufficient to dislodge the Haitian military and their civilian allies. Only the threat of imminent U.S. military intervention (approved by the United Nations) forced the Haitian military to step down and leave a clear field for Aristide's return.

Intervention in Peru was more promptly effective. In April 1992, President Fujimori of Peru instigated a "self-coup" in which he suspended the constitution and closed the Congress and the courts, claiming that these institutions were hindering his efforts to fight corruption, drug trafficking, and the Shining Path guerrillas. International donors quickly suspended aid; soon afterward, Fujimori agreed to constituent and municipal elections, which were held in October 1993. While Fujimori continued to dominate politics and to manipulate the rules in his favor, fully competitive elections were held in April 1995. When President Serrano of Guatemala attempted his own Fujimori-style coup in May 1993, he set off a rapid chain of events—encouraged by the suspension of international aid—that left both the president and vice president in exile and the former human rights ombudsman in charge of the nation.

In sum, aid sanctions to promote and defend democracy in Latin America have had variable success: in Guatemala they forced a relatively rapid return to competitive electoral politics; in Peru they prevented the consolidation of authoritarian rule and kept the door open to the restoration of democrative government; in Haiti, however, they damaged ordinary Haitians far more than their military oppressors.

Several factors can make the difference between effective and ineffective sanctions. Coordination among donors (discussed more in a later section) can be vital. The point is illustrated by the failure of the hemispherewide trade embargo to persuade Haiti's military leaders to relinquish power. Even within the hemisphere, the embargo was not rigorously enforced, and many European nations did not cooperate. Only after twenty-two months, when the UN Security Council voted to impose a global embargo, threatening the flow of oil from Europe, did Haiti's rulers agree to negotiate. In Peru, Fujimori feared that the negative response of the bilateral donors would jeopardize his efforts to mend relations with the international financial institutions. Guatemalan businessmen advocated a leader who would signal a return to democratic principles after the coordinated donor withdrawal of aid threatened their access to certain trade preferences.

The internal characteristics of the targeted country also influence the effectiveness of conditionality. One consideration is the strength and unity of its democratic forces. External pressure may lead to some political liberalization but will do little to achieve democratization in countries lacking democratic organizations and structures. While Peru and Guatemala have some experience with competitive politics, weak opposition forces and institutions in Haiti contributed to the prolonged political crisis. A second internal factor is the attitude and capabilities of the antidemocratic forces that the international donors hope to influence through conditionality. Because Haiti is so poor, it would seem to be vulnerable to external pressure, but Haiti's coup leaders, interested solely in self-aggrandizement, were quite indifferent to the costs the sanctions inflicted on the nation's poor and for the future development of the nation. However, the UN threat to institute a global freeze of their foreign bank accounts hastened their agreement to negotiate.

The case of Haiti, in particular, poses an interesting further question regarding political conditionality and donor responsibility. Once donors have conditioned aid with respect to democracy, how far are they willing to go in pressing for political liberalization? Promoting durable democracy in Haiti will be an expensive and long-term task. The nation will need to build the institutional framework necessary for a democratic society, including a civilian police force, a professional military, and a reformed civil service and judiciary—long-term tasks requiring not only aid but also sizable and sustained external presence. The limited UN presence that replaced the transitional US force in spring 1995 lacked the capacity to address these challenges effectively. Donors in general have appeared more willing to halt aid to penalize democratic backsliding than to undertake the long-term and costly tasks of building democracy through support for institutional and economic growth.

The bilateral donors have taken the lead in imposing aid sanctions in reaction to human rights violations or antidemocratic steps. Should the international financial institutions—the IMF, the World Bank, and the IADB (or its counterparts in other regions) join bilaterals in suspending loans to clear abusers of recognized norms of behavior?[7] That question is the topic of considerable debate.

The charters of the international financial institutions prohibit political considerations in the allocation of their funds.[8] In other words, neither their staff nor their boards should permit their preferences regarding types of political systems nor their (or their home governments') special ties or hostility to particular governments to influence their judgment on lending or withholding funds or projects. However, they should and do take into consideration political circumstances that affect the probable success of a loan. For instance, the IMF might postpone a stabilization loan because an election is approaching and the current government predictably will fail to curb spending and credit. Or the World Bank might shelve consideration of an irrigation project because endemic rural violence would gravely hamper carrying out the project.

It is not clear how far the international agencies should extend the principle—indeed, the responsibility—to take into account political circumstances that may affect the success of their programs. The multilateral agencies, and particularly the World Bank, have participated in the new thinking we described earlier in this chapter regarding the nature of sustainable development and the links between participation, democracy, and economic development. Indeed, in the late 1980s the World Bank took a leading role in spotlighting the importance of better governance as a requisite for economic growth and poverty reduction.

Concern about governance focuses attention not on individual rights but on the institutions and operations of the government and on the commitment and capacity of countries to govern responsibly and responsively.[9] Good governance, like human rights, can be interpreted narrowly or broadly. The World Bank has defined poor governance fairly narrowly as a lack of transparency, accountability, and predictability in politicians' and bureaucrats' behavior and as the absence of the rule of law. But this definition led inexorably to wider issues. Transparency requires not only open competition for public contracts but adequate information on government projects and programs and, therefore, freedom of the media. Accountability entails not only effective financial accounting and auditing but penalties on corrupt or inept politicians. That in turn implies some form of election and the freedom of association and speech that make such elections meaningful. A predictable rule of law requires an independent and competent judiciary. Thus the notion of improved governance as crucial for economic growth has tended to expand from improved public administration to a series of prescriptions similar to pluralist democracy.[10]

Should World Bank efforts to promote better governance include the use of sanctions? A number of nongovernmental organizations and some of the wealthy democratic member governments of the Bank have urged it to join bilateral donors in suspending or halting aid to governments that seriously violate human rights or that backtrack on progress toward democracy. Responding to the traditional stance that the Bank is barred by its mandate from political considerations, they argue that the Bank should more broadly interpret its Articles of Agreement.[11] Bank staff, particularly the Legal Department, continue to debate where the line should be drawn between permissible and prohibited issues for Bank attention.

In practice, the World Bank has considered sanctions on a case-by-case basis, choosing to get involved in some situations, especially where political circumstances strongly affect the viability of loans. In several recent cases involving African nations, the World Bank has found itself pressured to take an unambiguous stance, because it chairs the donor consultative committees that coordinate aid for the nations. This was particularly clear at the consultative meeting for Kenya in November 1991. In response to the increasing repression and corruption of President Daniel Arap Moi, donors decided to withhold $350 million in assistance to Kenya. Though the World Bank cited the government's economic mismanagement as the basis for its loan suspension, as chairman of the consultative group it conveyed to the Kenyan government the bilateral donors' consensus that aid would not be restored until progress was made toward multiparty democracy and respect for human rights.

Similarly, at the May 1992 consultative group meeting for Malawi, donors froze $74 million in nonhumanitarian assistance. The World Bank press release stated that the donors were seeking "tangible and irreversible evidence" from the Malawian government of "progress in the area of basic freedom and human rights." One month later, however, the World Bank approved a new loan to Malawi.

By the time the revised ideas regarding the links between improved governance, democracy, and development had gathered impetus in the late 1980s, authoritarian regimes had been replaced by elected governments in most of Latin America. Therefore, the IADB has not had to wrestle with interpretations of its mandate as much as has the World Bank. Traditional Latin American sensitivities to external intervention continue to strongly influence the IADB, and it has been reluctant to address issues of democratic governance. However, the IADB did join other donors in suspending lending to Peru after President Fujimori's *autogolpe*.

Conditions Attached to Specific Loans

Aid agencies (bilateral and multilateral) always attach certain requirements to project loans or grants, designed to make sure the funds are used for the designated purpose and are not wasted. Conditionality, however, refers to a different kind of requirement: the government receiving the loan must carry out specified policy reforms before any funds are released or before second or later portions of the funds are released. In contrast to allocation criteria, which are more or less uniform for all potential aid receivers, specific conditionality is tailored to the circumstances of the country and related to the particular goals of the loan.

The IMF has always used this form of conditionality to encourage countries in economic difficulties to adopt stabilization policies. In the 1980s the World Bank used the approach (which it calls policy-based lending) to press its clients to reduce state intervention in the economy and to encourage a more vigorous private sector. These reform conditions were (and are) usually linked, not to project aid, but to fast-disbursing nonproject assistance. Nonproject aid supports the recipient's balance of payments and economy in general, and it is therefore appropriate to link such aid to policy reforms designed to improve the management and performance of the economy as a whole. Moreover, if the borrower fails to follow through on its agreements, the second or third slice of a nonproject loan can be readily delayed. In contrast, delaying or suspending funds on a half-built project is extremely costly.

A few of the larger bilateral donors have also used specific requirements attached to nonproject loans to encourage economic reforms. Most smaller bilateral donors provide all of their assistance in the form of projects and do not engage in policy-based lending.

As concern with governance and commitment to democracy has increased in the past few years, there has been some discussion in both the larger bilateral donors and the World Bank about the possibility of using policy-based loans to promote better governance or progress toward democracy. Most donors have been very cautious about the approach, even though at first glance it seems to offer a means to exert strong pressure to bring about specific high-priority reforms. Specific requirements attached to loans are more intrusive than general criteria guiding aid allocations: when such requirements focus on political rather than technical economic reforms they are particularly likely to prompt strong resentment. The multilateral aid agencies are also restrained by concerns about the boundaries of their mandates, as we noted in discussing aid sanctions.

Moreover, in Latin America in particular, under present conditions policy-based loans may not exert much leverage. Nonproject loans contingent on negotiated policy reforms are attractive to governments that badly need foreign exchange, because the loans help to meet crucial import needs that they cannot cover through commercial trade and financial flows on reasonable terms. During the 1980s, after foreign investment and commercial credit to most of Latin America disappeared in the wake of the debt crisis, many governments faced acute shortages of foreign exchange. More recently, in part as a result of economic policy reforms in many countries and in part because of changing international economic circumstances, private capital has been returning to many Latin American countries. In the mid-1980s, Latin American countries were struggling with massive net negative financial flows.[12] In 1991 and 1992, in contrast, net inflows from the rest of the world to Latin America totaled approximately $80 billion.[13] Some Latin American countries, of course, remain extremely poor and have not shared in this reversal. Nevertheless, many countries (despite the Mexican debacle of early 1995—and its ripple effects) are in much less acute financial difficulties than they were a few years ago, and the leverage of specific or allocational conditionality is correspondingly reduced.

Despite these various constraints, both multilateral donors and some of the major bilateral donors may attempt to promote better governance and strengthened democracy in the next few years by modest use of policy-based loans. To the extent that they experiment with this approach, they can benefit from World Bank and IMF experience with promoting economic reforms by conditioning loans on prespecified measures. Assessments of this experience suggest that policy-based loans are most effective when they are focused on reforms that (1) can be easily monitored, (2) can be enacted by a small number of government officials, (3) can be accomplished in a single step, (4) break bottlenecks and open the way for further reforms, and (5) are based on strong technical consensus. Results are much less good where the required reforms involved complex institutional changes, the cooperation of several or many agencies and people, and many steps or stages. Such reforms are also more difficult to monitor.

The fundamental logic underlying these points applies as much to political as to economic reforms. However, most of these criteria are difficult to meet in the complex process of consolidating democracy. Participation and competitive democracy require not only enabling action by governments but also motivation, organization, and appropriate behavior on the part of much of the society as a whole. How democratic reforms work out in practice will be largely shaped by the nature and degree of the organization of civil society. Representative governments can take a multitude of forms. New democracies can learn a great deal about institutional arrangements and procedures from more established systems, but patterns of participation and political competition appropriate to cultural, social, and political traditions and circumstances must evolve from within.

Nevertheless, conditionality may be appropriate in certain situations, especially related to narrowly defined human rights abuse and specific measures to improve governance. For example, a condition requiring the release of political prisoners can be carried out by a decision of top political leaders. But if human rights are being widely violated by autonomous vigilante groups or undisciplined police or military, central government officials may lack the power to contain them, and conditionality may be futile. Specific regulations that restrict freedom of press or the formation of unions might be appropriate targets for conditionality. Such reforms often can be revised by a few key officials, and it is easy to monitor whether they have been changed. In contrast, conditionality is probably not a useful way to press central government agencies to consult with local citizens' committees on local projects.

Toward International Consensus: Donor Coordination and Multilateral Norm Setting

Conditioned aid, particularly in the form of sanctions, requires coordination among donors. More generally, donors' efforts to support and encourage democratic development will be more effective if different donors complement each others' efforts or, at a minimum, do not work at cross-purposes. Although recipient nations may feel coordination is tantamount to ganging up on them, coordination can help reduce confusion and con-serve resources, including the time and energy of both donor and recipient officials.

Donor Consultative Group meetings, chaired by the World Bank, have emerged as the principal forums for donors to collectively consider and react to specific countries' political performance. We noted earlier how discussions of human rights, democracy, and governance at the Consulta-tive Group meetings for Kenya and Malawi led to the suspension of aid for Kenya by all the major donors and for Malawi by all except the World Bank. Donor groups for many of the poorest countries are chaired by the UN Development Programme and are known as Round Tables. Round Tables may begin to play a role similar to the Consultative Groups in incorporating political issues into their aid discussions and coordinating donor responses to progress in individual countries.

The Development Assistance Committee (DAC) of the Organization for Economic Cooperation and Development (OECD), with a membership of twenty industrialized nations, is the main channel for donor efforts to develop general guidelines (as distinct from decisions about specific coun-tries) regarding democracy and human rights and aid policy. By late 1993, DAC members had endorsed a rather detailed framework of shared princi-ples and areas for action regarding political reforms. The framework clear-ly notes that each country's traditions and circumstances are unique but affirms that good governance, participatory development, human rights, and democratization are interlinked. To encourage these goals, DAC mem-bers stated their intention to rely mainly on "deepened and strengthened policy dialogue" and direct support but noted also that they might cut or suspend aid in response to human rights violations, "brutal reversals from democratization," or in cases where "complete lack of good governance renders efficient and effective aid impossible."[14]

International support and pressure to encourage democracy will be more effective to the degree that not only wealthy but also poorer nations can agree on desirable goals and standards for political evolution. International and regional associations that include representatives of both wealthy and poor nations or of developing nations only are increasingly discussing goals, norms, and standards for improved governance, human rights pro-tection, broadened political participation, and competitive politics. Norm-setting efforts are usually slow and frustrating and often appear more symbolic than practical. Yet over time they can encourage stronger reform efforts in some countries and can also help to guide and legitimize external support and pressure, including conditionality where necessary. When recipients are pressured by their peers instead of or in addition to wealthier nations, they may be more willing to focus on the merits of the norms rather than on the issue of the legitimacy of external pressure.

As Domingo E. Acevedo and Claudio Grossman discuss in more detail in this volume (chap. 5), the OAS has been increasingly active along these lines. It now provides support for election and human rights monitors in Latin America. With the passage of Resolution 1080 in 1991, the OAS created specific guidelines on how to respond to recalcitrant members. In the case of clear threats to human rights or democracy, the General Assembly must call an emergency meeting within ten days and develop a coordinated plan of action. The measures were implemented in the cases of Haiti, Peru, and Guatemala. In addition, a revision of the OAS charter in December 1992 states that any government that comes to power through a coup may have its membership suspended.

Regional efforts at coordination of economic and political reforms in Central America are another example of multilateral approaches to setting targets and monitoring. The San José Accords were initiated in 1984 as a forum for discussion between Central American governments and the European Community and its member governments. Initially focused on security and peacemaking, the annual ministerial-level meetings more recently have emphasized issues of development, regional integration, and democratization. The Central American foreign ministers meet in advance of the annual conference to coordinate their positions. By the late 1980s, their consultation was reinforced by the evolving Esquipulas process, in which the five Central American presidents come together to discuss issues of common concern.

The Larger Challenge for Donors: Growth, Equity, and Democracy

Despite the apparent victory of democracy throughout Latin America, both Latin Americans and the donors who seek to support them face immense problems of completing and consolidating political reforms. The difficulties flow from many sources, but one major set of threats to consolidation of democratic openings and to well-established democracies as well results from the incomplete economic reforms and slow economic and social recovery from the deep depression and disintegration of the 1980s. Paradoxically, while completed reforms (including revived and restructured social services) and economic recovery are crucial to democratic consolidation, democratic pressure may complicate or short-circuit those very reforms. Many of the measures still needed in many countries threaten sizable groups with vested interests in old arrangements. Moreover, there is a growing backlash that blames continued poverty and paralysis on reforms already taken rather than on a failure to follow through with difficult second-phase institutional reforms needed to capitalize on more stable and open economies.

Despite the backlash, several recent elections (including Brazil in November 1994 and Peru and Argentina in April 1995) clearly endorsed continued efforts to contain inflation and reorient economies. But in the medium run, voters will demand more than improved stability. It would be tragic if the hard-learned lessons of the 1970s and 1980s regarding both democratic government and economic management were to dissolve into new cycles of populist expansionism and inflation followed by economic stringency and political repression, similar to the cycles of the 1970s. Latin American governments and external donors together must focus urgently on measures that provide some reassurance to middle and working class voters that the new economic and social policies can offer concrete improvements in their lives. Conditionality may have a modest role in encouraging some of these measures, such as reorienting and upgrading social services. But the needed reforms are complex and multistage; they involve multiple agencies, painful trade-offs, and the cooperation of both private and public agencies and groups. Therefore they demand vision, skilled and committed leadership, and sustained and adequate external support, including aid but also appropriate trade and other economic policies in wealthy nations.[15] Conditionality cannot substitute for nor bring forth these requisites.

Sustaining democracy, in short, is neither a quick nor a cheap endeavor. The role of conditions attached to aid is at most quite modest. However, aid that provides support and is accompanied by information and advice based on relevant expertise and experience can make a contribution, especially in the poorer countries of the hemisphere.

III *Practice and Policy*

National, Transnational, and Foreign Actors

8 Haiti

Sovereign Consent versus State-Centric Sovereignty

Anthony P. Maingot

"Democracy" said the president of Haiti to the United Nations, "has won out for good, the roots are growing stronger and stronger." This was on 25 September 1991. One week later, President Jean-Bertrand Aristide ("Titide," to his followers) was deposed by a coup d'état. The regime of the only internationally monitored freely elected president of Haiti had lasted seven months.[1] The nearly 70 percent of the Haitian electorate who cast their votes for the changes Aristide promised had been robbed of their hopes. So had the other 30 percent, who voted for other candidates. Together they had struggled since at least 1986 to establish the rules of law in Haitian politics, that is, to establish the principle of democratic legitimacy, here called sovereign consent. Haitians have paid a heavy price in blood and standards of living for their efforts.

It is not a trivial matter that this reversal of a process of democratic empowerment of the masses should have come four months after the members of the OAS signed the Santiago Commitment to Democracy and the Renewal of the International System. This declaration was only the latest step in what Fernando Tesón (chap. 2) calls the most exciting development in international law: a redefinition of state sovereignty and new emphasis on human rights and the principles of democracy. While it would be adventurous to argue that there is universal acceptance of this new normative system, there is a growing consensus that the consent of the people, expressed in free and fair elections, is the locus of sovereignty.[2] This we call sovereign consent. And, this warns Tesón, is no passing whim: "The lesson is, perhaps, that the gradual dilution of state sovereignty is not just one more historic phenomenon. . . . It is, rather, a moral imperative."

As uplifting and hope-inspiring as this trend might be, the Haitian case stands as testimony that norms and values do not automatically translate into actions. Despite the fact that, as Tom Farer argues in chapter 1, Haiti is arguably the most telling case of a country which is recognized to need outside assistance, both to reinstate their democratic mandate and then to defend it, there is no consensus on how this should be done. Certainly, as Domingo E. Acevedo and Claudio Grossman note in chapter 5, it is premature to expect the OAS to arrive at any consensus of forceful intervention. Two students of the OAS agree that there will not soon be a consensus for the threat or the use of force as a last resort "in any imaginable case."[3] And this, as Acevedo and Grossman imply, despite the fact that it might well be the only effective alternative to tyranny.

Multinational military action to restore President Aristide was eventually approved by the UN Security Council (see appendix to this chapter); bypassing thereby the collective responsibility of the OAS. Haiti thus exemplifies a more generalized paradoxical situation in Latin America where a functioning regime for the promotion and protection of human rights coexists with major and wide-ranging violations of those rights. David Forsythe notes a fundamental paradox: "Latin America manifests a conflicted political culture. There is an abstract commitment to human rights, including democratic political participation, periodic leadership supportive of these values by small states and the Inter-American Commission on Human Rights, and spasmodic attention to these values by the most powerful hemispheric state—the United States," but without the same underlying political commitment to implement these rights.[4]

It is important for Haiti and for the rest of the Hemisphere to reexamine the issue of how legitimate authority could have been reestablished. What were the chances that the democratic hopes of the Haitian people could have been restored by either internal forces or through international pressures short of the threat and use of force? What exactly did the Haitians, both pro- and anti-Aristide, understand when they heard President Clinton warn that "we will not now or ever support the continuation of an illegal government in Haiti."[5]

None of these questions can be argued without addressing that nation's history. On that score, one has to understand the Haitian version of the three "limiting factors," which Forsythe hypothesizes hinder the fuller implementation of the rhetoric advocating human rights and democracy: (1) Latin Americans' resistance to U.S. leadership, expressed through their emphasis on state-centered sovereignty, (2) the unwillingness of governing elites of states with large underclasses of Indians or blacks to extend the principle of human rights to these masses, and (3) the legacy of the Cold War, when the United States put security and geopolitics above a concern for democracy and human rights.[6]

The need to explore and reflect on the broader implications of these limitations are clear. But there are lessons of Haitian history that have to be addressed in order to understand the failure of third parties, especially the United States and the inter-American system's attempts to force political changes on the island.

This chapter deals with three aspects of Haitian history that should be considered in any review of policy on that country: (1) the contemporary legacy and relevance of how Haitians view the U.S. occupation, which lasted from 1915 to 1934, (2) Haitian economics and demographics, and (3) an assessment of the rise and fall of President Aristide. The basic conclusion is that, given the weight of this history, Haiti could not have achieved a transition, much less the entrenchment of democracy, without active, perhaps even forceful, outside intervention. The basic value judgment is that the limitations set by both hemispheric history and Haitian experience made hemispheric support for such forceful action improbable. Given this reality, we also conclude that until such time as there is a much wider acceptance of the principle of sovereign consent and a willingness to use force if necessary to defend and promote it, the Hemisphere will settle for inconclusive half measures in cases where democratic governance are violated.

The U.S. Occupation: What Kind of Precedent?

In Michel S. Laguerre's monumental *The Complete Haitiana: A Bibliographic Guide* (1982), there are 650 entries under "U.S. Occupation." If it does nothing else, such a bibliographic reference reminds us that Haiti was under U.S. military occupation longer than any other country in the Caribbean. This nineteen-year occupation did little more than leave a bad memory, which all Haitian groups use to their own advantage. It warrants a review with an eye to similarities and differences with the humanitarian intervention initiated in September, 1994.

That the motives which impelled President Wilson to intervene in Haiti—to act as a moral policeman—had little to do with economics is evident. This did not mean, however, that American capital was not interested in profit. Some U.S. investors, according to Ludwell Montague, had an exaggerated notion of Haitian resources.[7] But even Montague agrees that it was fear of a foreign occupation that determined U.S. actions; Germany, whose settlers had the greatest investments in Haiti, was perceived as the greatest geopolitical threat. When the Americans intervened in that island in 1915 they had no major investments there. In fact there were only two significant foreign ownerships of land: an English investment on 10,000 acres and a German one on 7,100. The Americans would acquire these and others, but by 1927 a report of six "disinterested" Americans who opposed the U.S. occupation showed all major agricultural projects losing money. Only banks and utilities were profitable, and these only for a short spell.

Woodrow Wilson acted as the regional policeman in the face of a breakdown of political order in Haiti, and this led to the occupation. Haitian historians do not hesitate to describe the years before the American occupation as bordering on chaos. "Anarchy," says a popular text, "was permanent, generalized, and getting worse every day; the country was on the edge of a precipice."[8] They had four presidents between May 1913 and July 1915. The last of these, Vilbrun Guillaume Sam, had all the political prisoners in the National Penitentiary massacred then sought sanctuary in the French Embassy. An infuriated mob pulled him out of the legation and lynched him. The U.S. Marines landed that same day. Not surprisingly many Haitian intellectuals initially welcomed the Marines.[9] That welcome was soon exhausted as American unilateralism, impatience, and disdain for the Haitians revealed itself.

The dangers of half measures was evident then; it is one of the dangers today. "The result of the arbitrary measures adopted," says Montague, "was a system that had neither the virtues of a treaty regime based on true agreement nor those of a clean-cut military administration . . . but only the bad features of both."[10] With the United States not willing to take on outright "imperial" duties, policy was left to local U.S. commanders, whose character colored that policy. Reports of their arrogance, of their bullying even of the presidents they put in the palace, began to filter out to the American public. Even Republican presidential candidate Warren Harding took up the criticism in the 1920 campaign: "I will not empower an Assistant Secretary of the Navy to draft a constitution for helpless neighbors in the West Indies and jam it down their throats at the point of bayonets borne by United States Marines."[11]

Also catching the attention of American civil rights groups, such as the National Association for the Advancement of Colored People, were the racial attitudes of the occupation forces generally and particularly of one of its main commanders, Colonel Littleton W. T. Waller, who would write insulting notes to the Haitian president. Not surprisingly, historians would later discover just how deep the racial attitudes of men like Waller went. "They are real niggers and no mistake," Waller wrote to a friend, "What the people of Norfolk and Portsmouth would say if they saw me bowing and scraping to these coons, I do not know. All the same I do not wish to be outdone in formal politeness."[12] Haitians, of course, saw through this "politeness" and made the Americans' generalized lack of respect for them individually and collectively the basis of a strong nationalist movement, the Indigenous Movement. This movement became the incubator not just of a protest literature but, indeed, of black nationalists such as François Duvalier, who would tyrannize Haiti from 1957 to 1971.

Those who have studied the occupation from the Haitian perspective agree that racial antagonism was probably the single most important reason why the Americans failed to achieve anything of enduring value despite some significant contributions to improved health, roads, and infrastructure in general.[13] The racism that characterized the occupation administration turned Haitians of all classes and skin color against Americans. As David Nicholls points out, "Paradoxically, the Americans unintentionally succeeded . . . in uniting all Haitians under the name 'black.' "[14]

This is one big difference from the situation today. First, the U.S. civil rights movement has brought about a definite change in U.S. military attitudes, and second, major leaders of the U.S. black community supported strong measures to return Aristide to power. Finally, Aristide himself enjoys the legitimacy and credibility among the masses, which made intervention popular, at least in its initial stage. As reassuring as all this might sound, there are two flies in the ointment.

First, there is nothing in Aristide's past attitudes or in his statements after his overthrow that indicate that he would have ever called openly for a military intervention. Indeed, the recent UN intervention eventually occurred without such a public request. Second, it is well established that initial attitudes toward a popular intervention do not guarantee the same attitudes toward a longer occupation. This is clearly one lesson from the Haitian case. Even the Marine war against the notorious mercenaries from northern Haiti, the *cacos,* turned Haitians against the Americans. These bandits were always available to any member of the Port-au-Prince elite who wished to overthrow an existing government and were a major cause of the political instability that was a factor in the U.S. decision to intervene.

The present-day Ton Ton Macoutes, or *attachés,* come to mind. Certainly Haiti would be much better off without such elements, then and now. The problem is that the war against the *cacos,* especially against Charlemagne Peralte from Hinche in the Artibonite plains of central Haiti, turned into one of those irregular, guerrilla wars invariably accompanied by atrocities. For nineteen years, says Hans Schmidt, the U.S. Marines fought people they defined as "savages" and their tactics "frequently degenerated into torture, systematic destruction of villages, and military tactics tantamount to genocide."[15] In 1919 alone the marines killed 1,861 rebels and had killed 3,250 by the end of five years of occupation. The marines lost 14 men during that period, only one in actual combat.[16]

It comes as no surprise, therefore, that resistance leaders such as Charlemagne Peralte should emerge as heroes to politicians such as Aristide. In his presidential inaugural address, Aristide referred to Peralte three times, once asking rhetorically, "Charlemagne Peralte's young people, do you feel Charlemagne Peralte's blood really flow in your veins?"[17] It is often useless to debate historic figures who strike deep nationalist chords. It could hardly be argued, however, that Peralte was fighting for democracy. He was a regional *caco,* of which there are still many in Haiti. In Haiti, the least of the problems facing any intervention is the military; it is the regional chieftain, the *chef de section,* and his followers in the rural areas that represent the toughest challenge to a restored democracy.

Again, the problem is not purely military. By far the greatest harm done to Haiti's political future was the attempt to modernize the state materially but utilizing—indeed, reinforcing—some of the worst features of the traditional exploitation of the peasantry. This was the case with the 1916 decision to reinstate the *corvée,* a provision of the ancient rural code that forces peasants to contribute a few days a year of free labor to keep the roads open. The Americans decided to build a modern road system with that method even though this meant moving peasants long distances from their homes and food plots. Testimony by a perspicacious U.S. officer indicates the risks involved in the modernization-at-all-costs mentality:

> The results of this exploitation of labor were two: First, it created in the minds of the peasants a dislike for the American occupation and its two instruments—the marines and the gendarmerie—and, second, imbued the native enlisted man with an entirely false conception of his relations with the civil population. As the corvée became more and more unpopular, more and more difficulty caused the gendarme to resort to methods which were often brutal but quite consistent with their training under Haitian officials. I soon realized that one of the great causes of American unpopularity among the Haitians was the corvée.[18]

While the earlier Haitian situation was kept before the eyes of Washington largely through the efforts of the NAACP and especially of its executive secretary, James Weldon Johnson, the United States was also involved in Nicaragua and the Dominican Republic. Even though major segments of both countries harbored a "Yankeephobia," which would come into play

later in the century, the Nicaraguan case is especially relevant. This raises the final point about the U.S. occupation of Haiti: it took place in the context of multiple U.S. interventions. Each intervention fed a generalized hostility and suspicion of U.S. motives. In such a context, the emotional and symbolic overwhelmed whatever good was done at the level of public health, infrastructural development, and demilitarization. This is especially true when, as was the case of Haiti, little was done to restructure the economy in any fundamental way.

Despite Harding's ringing critique of the Wilsonian doctrine of moral policeman of the Caribbean, neither he nor his fellow Republicans who followed him in the White House removed U.S. troops from Haiti. This would not occur until 1934, under pressure from changes in the world order that threatened the United States. The Good Neighbor Policy was launched because the threats mandated the friendship of Latin America. The end of unilateral interventions was one of the conditions for that friendship.

The upshot of all this is that the U.S. occupation of Haiti has to be studied in terms of what should *not* be done by external parties. The task for third parties cannot be redoing Haiti in their own image; it has to be about allowing democracy a chance to work in Haitian terms and for Haitian ends. None of this implies abandoning a universalist definition of what democracy means; it does imply a realistic assessment of what such a democracy can actually accomplish once enthroned. A review of the nature of the Haitian economy tells us why.

The Economy and Demographics

In Haiti, economics has to be discussed along with demographics and ecology. It is not a new issue; it goes back to the nature of the postplantation economy. Since independence, the radically reformed landholding system has been characterized by generalized peasant ownership and subsistence agriculture. This system certainly spared the Haitian peasant the horrors of the typical Latin American *latifundio*. It was, however, harsh on the ecology and not conducive to accumulating surpluses, which could be invested elsewhere. The Haitian economy was characterized by very few pockets of tightly (i.e., family) controlled wealth based in coffee or commerce. Opportunities for employment were largely in government— governments that, crucially, were sustained and financed by squeezing the peasants and the few concentrations of wealth.

The consequences of this economic situation began to be manifested with alarming clarity after World War II. The growth of Port-au-Prince

Table 3. Changes in Rural and Urban Populations, Haiti, 1950–1982

	Population (thousands)			Annual Growth Rates (%)	
	1950	1971	1982	1950–1971	1971–1982
Urban (more than 5,000 population)	255	707	1,042	5.0	3.6
Port-au-Prince	152	507	720	5.9	3.2
Ten towns of more than 10,000 population in 1982	98	180	235	2.9	2.5
Other towns of more than 5,000 population	5	26	97	8.2	12.7
Rural	2,831	3,623	4,011	1.2	0.9
Total	3,097	4,330	5,053	1.6	1.4

Source: World Bank, "Haiti: Policy Proposals for Growth," 26 Apr. 1985, 5.

allowed politicians to use the masses as veritable "steam rollers" (*rouleurs compresseurs*) to intimidate their enemies. This rural-to-urban migration has accelerated (see table 3). By the 1980s, Haiti was dotted with small urban areas, all in direct contact with the all-important capital city, which Haitians call "the Republic of Port-au-Prince."

It is not that the cities have that much to offer in terms of jobs, schooling, health services; rather, there has been an accelerating deterioration of the rural, peasant economy. Haiti's situation is bad by any comparative standards: the annual growth of Haitian agricultural production during the early 1980s was 1.2 percent; for South America it was 3.3 percent; while the total for the Third World was 2.9 percent.[19]

Haiti is quickly shifting from being a rural and agricultural country to a country where the rural sector cannot sustain life, either of the urban population or, indeed, their own. *Minifundio,* or as the French call it, *une paysannerie parcellaire,* describes a situation where 72 percent of landowners possess less than one hectare. The traditional, and usually partly optimistic, studies of the peasantry have been replaced by a pessimistic literature, which engages in debates over the residual value or lack thereof of the "atomization" of the peasantry. Atomization refers to the system of *multiculture,* or mixed cultivation, for family consumption, local needs, and external markets. Paul Moral, for instance, saw this as promoting "disorder"; he called it a system of *grappillage* (*grapiye* in creole), which means literally, "grab wherever you can." One of the experts close to President Aristide, George Anglade, on the other hand, sees Haitians turn-

Table 4. The Deteriorating Haitian Resource Base

Year	Population (thousands)	Arable Land (hectares)	Arable Hectares per Person	Consumption of Fuel Wood (thousand cubic meters)[1]
1938	2,500	540,000	0.216	
1954	3,400	370,000	0.109	8,869
1970	4,300	225,750	0.052	13,125
1980	5,500	225,750	0.041	20,000

Source: Compiled from USAID Library, Port-au-Prince, 1980.

[1]Represents 75% of all wood consumption.

ing necessity (i.e., survival) into a virtue. Whatever the merits of *minifundia* may be, there is one consequence with which no one argues: Haiti imports more and more of its food—importation of foodstuffs increased 300 percent between 1973 and 1980 and continues to grow.[20]

The decline of the Haitian countryside goes beyond food cultivation. The pressure on the land and its wood resources continues its inexorable march toward total ecological disaster (see table 4). This deteriorating resource base is an ongoing structural situation and can be redressed only with a dramatic reduction in population pressure on the land. Migration, mostly to the Dominican Republic, certainly relieves the pressure but cannot be regarded as a structural solution. The "boat people" who tried to reach Florida were numerically a minor part of the flow, although they drew most of the attention; this is a political issue that, whichever way it is decided in the U.S. courts, will have minimal impact on the economic situation.

Structural improvement can come about in only two ways: in the short term, by an urban industrialization program to absorb the "excess" rural workers; in the long term, by a dramatic reduction in the birth rate. Neither appears likely to occur soon, especially not the latter. The trend is clear. The population is growing at an annual rate of 3.1 percent, certainly extraordinary even in Third World terms. There is no evidence, however, that either of the two factors that reduce fertility is operating: natural birth control, resulting from substantial increases in the standard of living, or artificial birth control. Only 7 percent of Haitian women practice artificial birth control. This compares poorly with the 55 percent who do so in neighboring Jamaica.

The known demographic facts are that Haitians will not reach a net reproduction rate of 1 percent until the year 2030, and even after that, actual population size will not become stationary until the year 2145, at which point it will stand at seventeen million. In the West Indies, Arthur

Lewis constructed a model of the urban industrialization needed to absorb the excess labor of the rural areas.[21] However, the dimensions of the problem in the West Indies pales in comparison to the situation facing Haiti. Data in table 4 help explain what a growth of these dimensions implies in the context of a shrinking land base. If Haitian migration agitates the American mind today, with the population standing at an estimated 6.5 million (with an additional one million abroad), what will it be when that population triples and the resources vanish? Change has to occur in Haiti, not Miami or New York. What, then, can one expect from the peasant in terms of action toward social change?

Alain Rocourt speaks for many social scientists when he says that the Haitian democratic process cannot advance without the participation of the peasantry, fully 80 percent of the population. Yet, how to get them involved? It was the city, he says, that brought about the fall of Duvalier. "It was as though the peasantry had not really been concerned, as though it had been on the sidelines of history, solemnly watching the events."[22] There is considerable evidence that, at least in the 1986 overthrow of Jean-Claude Duvalier, the fast-growing medium and small towns played an important role (see table 3).

In the final analysis, however, it is events in Port-au-Prince that determine political outcomes. This is not an exclusively Haitian problem, but it certainly does require an exclusively Haitian solution. There are a number of projects being tried in the rural areas, but they are invariably small-scale, or pilot. One particularly candid student, Marie-Michele Rey, admits that these rural projects are like "a drop of water in the sea."[23]

It is evident, therefore, that the crisis in Haiti's countryside affects the whole country, including urban areas, which have been—and are—the epicenters of Haitian politics. The difference is that virtually all significant political activity used to take place in the one urban area, Port-au-Prince, while now it is taking place in every town of over 10,000 people. Control of Port-au-Prince, however, continues to be the key to power. The reality is that a mobilized Haitian peasantry can vote (and thus is a democratic resource), but they cannot either overthrow dictators or defend democrats. The rise and overthrow of President Aristide attests to that. The implication is that the foreign troops that restored him to power will be the main guarantors of his survival.

The Rise and Fall of President Aristide

Restoring President Aristide to office was the preferred course of action for two fundamental reasons: first, it would reinforce the principle of democratic legitimacy as no other available option could; second, there was no broad political solution possible without it. Without a political solution, there will be no end to social and economic instability and, certainly, little international interest in contributing significantly to the latter. Here is a rare case where the law of necessity works toward a moral end.

As compelling as both these reasons were there was nothing easy about it. The problems began with Aristide himself—his personality, his close allies, and perhaps fundamentally, the nature of the movement that took him to the presidency.

Born in 1954, Aristide was the son of an educated and devoutly Catholic Haitian family. After joining the Salesian teaching order, he did advanced studies in the Dominican Republic, Israel, and Canada. Thoroughly influenced by the more radical wing of the Latin American Theology of Liberation, Aristide was an early member of what came to be known as the Ti L'egliz (Little Church). His antagonism to the established church hierarchy was equaled only by his dislike of both the local bourgeoisie and the United States. To Aristide, the United States was always the "cold country," which he blamed for most of Haiti's ills. Preaching from St. Jean Bosco church in the slum La Saline, Aristide frequently used biblical passages to preach rebellion. On the right of the common people to defend themselves, Aristide would quote from the Gospel of St. Luke (Luke 2:36) "And he that hath no sword, let him sell his garment, and buy one."[24]

Neither Aristide nor his followers seemed to have accumulated any swords. His followers defended him through a willingness to die for him— a human shield appeared to be his only protection. No one can read Amy Wilentz's account of Aristide and not be moved by the apparent total and unconditional devotion of Aristide's followers, even as he seemed to welcome martyrdom.[25]

On 11 September 1988 armed thugs attacked his services at St. Jean Bosco church, killing thirteen people and wounding over seventy. Father Aristide had to be forcibly moved to safety by his parishioners. Whether due to raw courage or some irrational side of his personality, Aristide's many brushes with, and miraculous escapes from, death have become part of his charisma; Msieu Mirak (Mister Miracles), they call him. It would be a true miracle, indeed, if such constant confrontations with brutality and death did not affect his personality. It appears to have done just that. The following account in *Newsday* (the foreign journalist group closest to Aristide) has been corroborated by others. "Nervous by disposition, Aristide suffers from periodic prostrations that leave him virtually out of touch with the world around him. He has on occasion appeared catatonic, almost haunted, as if totally overwhelmed by some frozen image of the most recent blood-letting."[26]

It is important that Aristide never gave the appearance of being one of the conventional seekers of formal political office. In fact, he made a distinct point of dismissing constitutional and party politics as irrelevant. Asked as late as May 1990 whether he had political ambitions, he responded, "I do not suffer from that sickness." And yet he constantly advocated and called for political change. In an interview in Mexico in June 1990, Aristide portrayed the elections, which were only five months away, as an imperialist U.S. scheme, "a farce." The candidates who had decided to run were all "on their knees at the feet of the U.S." General Abraham who promised to respect the results, was "a faithful dog of any imperialism." Citing events in Nicaragua and Mexico, Aristide said that the struggle was an international one to unmask U.S. imperialism.[27]

So sudden and unexpected was Aristide's entry into the 1990 electoral campaign that he was not listed in the 29 May 1990 election handbook prepared by the National Democratic Institute for International Affairs, nor does he appear as a significant candidate in the most used Haitian electoral handbook.[28] Indeed, even the left-of-center Catholic human rights organization, Puebla Institute, thought that the attention Aristide was getting in the foreign press could be explained by the priest's flamboyance. In any case, Puebla thought that it was "far disproportionate to his importance in Haiti."[29]

His was more a messianic movement than a campaign. When the head of the Salesian order attempted to have Aristide sent to the Dominican Republic, the Movement des paysans de Papaye (MPP) sent him a petition on 12 January 1989, bearing 18,552 signatures, which read as follows: "We declare with all our force, with all the force of our faith, that the words of Father Aristide, are the words of the God of Life, of the Prophet Isaiah. They are the words of Jesus Christ, Son of the God of Life."[30]

"You see," Aristide told a veteran Haiti watcher, "I don't have to campaign. It's the people who will do the campaigning." He had, he said, "accepted this rendezvous with history." He was "one with the Haitian spirit." "Titide's not like the others," exclaimed a marketwoman, "he does not have any woman, so he wouldn't be spending the country's money on fancy cars and diamond necklaces. He's pure."[31] Nothing here, therefore, of the traditional Haitian-Caribbean macho man. Not even the red cock they adopted as their symbol could dispel the aura of purity and cleansing the Se Lavalas movement invoked. He won close to 70 percent of the vote, with 85 percent of the registered electorate voting. He swept every section of the island. It was a national victory.

The elections had gone remarkably smoothly. This fact alone, and despite the situation of near anarchy in the society and bankruptcy of the state, gave Aristide several advantages in addition to his massive popular support. To wit: (1) The 7 January 1991 attempted coup by former Duvalierists under Roger Lafontant was squashed by loyalist troops and massive public protests. His most dangerous known enemy now sat in jail, and many others were in flight. (2) The international community responded enthusiastically to his victory. President François Mitterand received him in Paris (the first Haitian president so invited); the United States restored, and doubled, its direct aid to the Haitian government, suspended since the aborted elections of 1987. Carlos Andrés Pérez of Venezuela had received him in Caracas with promises of substantial future assistance. (3) The leading opposition figures, Marc Bazin and Louis Dejoie III, pledged loyal opposition.

Problems, however, became evident from the start. Surrounded by ideologues and idealists, all equally amateurish, Aristide never seemed able to distinguish friend from foe. Worse, he never seemed interested in the profane art of political maneuvering, the only way to increase one's allies and reduce or neutralize one's enemies. "He is not a natural strategist. He is not much of a team player," remarked one who knew him well.[32] In fact, he seemed to exult at turning allies into opponents. Midway through the Aristide administration, a source in the Presidential Palace told the press: "An adversary you can argue with is better than a blundering ally."[33]

His five early acts of commission or omission weakened Aristide's hand in the beginning and raise the question of whether even an Aristide can break the persistence of certain traits of the island's political culture. If he could or would not during his first seven months in power, will he be able to now that he is back in power?

1. *His penchant for raising generalized apprehensions by speaking metaphorically and allegorically.* Consider the following passage in his inaugural address: "One finger does not eat okra, as days go by, donkeys will stop working for horses. . . . If one finger does not eat okra, whether they like it or not, no matter what, stones in water will get to know the pain of stones in the sun."[34]

2. *His failure to speak out forcibly against mob violence by his followers.* The practice of Pere Lebrun (placing a burning tire around an enemy's head) was never sufficiently condemned. Over one hundred perceived Aristide enemies were killed after the failed Lafontant coup d'état; the Papal Nunciature and Haiti's oldest cathedral were burned to the ground; and the papal nuncio and his Zairean deputy were beaten and made to walk nearly naked down the street. Aristide's already strained relations with the church's hierarchy deteriorated dramatically.

3. *His 4 April arrest of former president Pascal Trouillot on vague and*

unsubstantiated conspiracy charges. Fear of arbitrary arrest spread through the already leery opposition ranks.

4. *His sweeping—and by his own admission, unconstitutional—purges of the army top command, including the forced retirement of Brigadier General Hérard Abraham, who had managed the peaceful transfer of power.* During his Inaugural Address, Aristide admitted that Article 264.2 of the 1987 Constitution did not permit the president to make the kind of changes he was asking for; he called on General Abraham to make the changes as a patriotic act. His official biographer explains the event: "The suddenness of the decision was surprising but the moment was well chosen. How could the army react in the face of a man whose popularity was at its zenith and whose international legitimacy was uncontested?"[35] Another case of shifting commitments? Traditional Haitian military apprehensions about civilian intentions intensified.

5. *His sudden and, some say, intemperate and threatening request that the "monied classes" contribute millions of dollars to the state.* He gave them four days to do so. It reminded some of Duvalier's notorious *contributions voluntaires* (voluntary contributions) campaigns.

All of this, however, could have been managed or at least explained away if Aristide had not committed his most costly error: marginalizing, then antagonizing, and eventually attacking, his own political party and its followers within the legislature. It was this behavior that best reveals not only Aristide's modus operandi but indeed how soon and completely he had picked up the very conventional Haitian emphasis on the presidency as the only significant office. In fact, the post-Duvalier Constitution of 1987 had specifically reduced the president's power by providing for a split executive, with a prime minister in charge of day-to-day functions and accountable to Congress. Aristide ignored this, which set Congress against him.

Although holding only 40 of the 110 seats in Congress, Aristide's National Front for Change and Democracy (FNDC) initially controlled the presidency and other significant posts in that legislature. It is with this group that Aristide had his major confrontations, as they attempted to exercise the checks and balances on the executive that is the single most important feature of the 1987 Constitution. Many parties had participated in drawing up that Constitution and took their role in the new politics seriously. They were indignant at not being consulted about appointments and policies and at being left out of even informal consultation.

Not surprisingly, it was Aristide's own FNDC legislators who began calling for the resignation of Aristide's prime minister, René Preval, and it was these legislators who were violently threatened with individual Pere

Lebruns if they proceeded with their plans. Under pressure from the executive, the FNDC lost control over the parliament, control shifting to minor opposition parties. One of these, the minuscule National Patriotic Movement—November 28 (MNP-28), secured the presidency of the Senate; its leader, Dejean Belizaire, soon turned into a formidable opponent of Aristide. Later, Belizaire would emerge as one of the legislative leaders opposing Aristide's return to the presidency.

By early May the complaints about Aristide's style were becoming a chorus. He was, they said, surrounded by incompetent "yes-men" and that he did not "trust people." Others spoke of a "Jekyll and Hyde" personality. Human rights activist, and Aristide supporter, Jean-Claude Bajeux summed up the situation: "Aristide," he lamented, "has established himself as the parish priest of the National Palace."[36]

Be all this as it may, no one was predicting a significant political crisis. Don Bohning in the *Miami Herald* speaks of an army "brought under civilian control," control over the "feared" chiefs of section, and general optimism among business people.[37] Similarly, Howard French of the *New York Times* describes the Haitian success in securing US$442 million from a consortium of lenders led by the World Bank and quotes the U.S. ambassador as saying of Aristide, "He has gotten off to a very credible start. The process is well begun."[38] Even members of the formerly skeptical business community were cheered by what they thought was a new realism in Aristide's actions. In September, Vice President Quayle's wife visited Haiti. It all seemed to corroborate the ratings given Haiti by a major U.S. risk analysis service, Political Risk Services, which in April 1991 ranked Haiti less risky than the Dominican Republic and equal to Jamaica in turmoil risk, financial transfer risk, investment risk, and export risk.[39]

In September, Aristide made a triumphal trip to the United Nations and received the keys to the cities of New York and Miami. On 30 September, the day after his return to Haiti, Aristide was overthrown by what appeared to be a rabble of soldiers and police. The *ti soldats* brutally suppressed public protests, and the president was courageously freed from detention and escorted to the airport by the French and American ambassadors. He had been in the Presidential Palace for seven months.

The elements that the White House, the OAS, and the UN had to work with, thus, were (1) a population deeply suspicious of outsiders, a legacy in no small part of the long U.S. occupation (which had to be overcome with support from Aristide, whose approval of intervention was imperative); (2) an economy that bordered on being a total ecological disaster; (3) a population that wanted democracy—defined more in human rights than in institutional terms—but that had no way of defending it; and (4) a major actor whose charisma was based on attacking the very factors (U.S. intervention, elections, respect for the Constitution of 1987) that he now needed for a restoration. All this led to two fundamental questions. First, could there be a return to constitutional politics without armed external intervention? Second, given the fact of that intervention and restoration of Aristide, could there be a democratic consolidation without the continued presence of that external actor? The answer to the second question will weigh heavily on those who favored the military restoration of Aristide.

Answering these questions requires the building of scenarios, and, in Haiti, the best scenarios are those drawn from an analysis of some of the most enduring and respected views on Haitian political culture.

Can There Be Democracy in Haiti?

Few countries of the Caribbean have been as studied as much as Haiti.[40] Invariably the quest, of Haitians and outsiders alike, has been to explain the island's lack of progress. What is evident from this often excellent literature is that, in the Haitian case, an accurate diagnosis does not guarantee a solution.[41] In his classic treatise *The Haitian People,* James Leyburn expresses a common despair: "How conceivably might this problem be dealt with?" His solution: the "moral imperative" of U.S. and European assistance. To Mats Lundahl (*Peasants and Poverty: A Study of Haiti*) the solution lies in changing the elite's antipeasant bias. He concludes by asking, however, whether that bias would ever change. This tendency to end studies on Haiti with a rhetorical question is evident also in Robert and Nancy Heinl's *Written in Blood*: "Are the Haitian people living endlessly in a perverse continuum, oblivious of their past, doomed always to repeat a history that has been written in blood?" This is also the position of Alain Tournier's *Quand la Nation demande des comptes.*

Is the explanation to Haiti's intractable problems to be found in the island's culture? Accurately or not, that is precisely where many scholars have located the problems. Some, like Aristide, see that culture as a strength. As he told the UN General Assembly on 25 September 1991, the "Ninth Commandment" of democracy in Haiti is fidelity to its culture. "No truly deep change can be accomplished democratically," he said, "without an articulation of the indigenous values that are closely linked with any genuine socio-cultural fabric." Few other observers have been so sanguine about the relationship of Haitian culture to democratic consolidation. According to an early Haitian observer, Emmanuel Edouard, the incessant struggle for the state, the major employer of the urban bourgeoisie, had perverted the political culture. To work for the state was "to be in politics," and that meant to be eternally distrustful, false, and conniving. To steal from state revenues, he maintained, did not engender reprobation but outright envy. A bifurcated moral sense was the result: one reserved for public service, that is, matters of state, the other for private and especially family affairs.[42]

This theme of the dual cultural system became a common one in Haitian studies. One of the earliest of the serious outside scholars to point to cultural imperatives of the Haitian status was anthropologist Melville Herskovits, who took his cue from Haitian J. C. Dorsainvil's comment that Haitians "to an astonishing degree . . . live on their nerves."[43] Herskovits concludes that what is involved is a need to reconcile two cultural traditions that often are in inner conflict: the African and the French. To indicate its structural nature, he calls it "socialized ambivalence": rapid shifts in attitude toward people and situations. The same person will hold in high regard a person, an institution, an experience, or even an object that has personal significance to him and simultaneously manifest great disdain and even hatred for it. "In its broader implications, as a matter of fact, it is entirely possible that this socialized ambivalence underlies much of the political and economic instability of Haiti."[44] It is difficult to ignore Aristide's own duality vis-à-vis a range of things, not the least of which was his "privileged" education, when he was "happy to speak the language of Pascal."[45]

Many others have noticed this tendency to rapid shifts in loyalty. Robert Rotberg's approach is social-psychological, with heavy emphasis on the "paranoic" aspects of Haiti's politics. He attributes the tendency toward sliding commitments to the pervasive rivalries, suspicion, and intrigue that characterize rural and urban Haitians alike.[46] Lawrence Harrison, citing Rémy Bastien, puts the blame squarely on vodun, its promotion of irrationality, listlessness, and inaction. Vodun, say Bastien and Harrison, is the great bulwark of the status quo.[47]

Two problems immediately suggest themselves. First, vodun is a peasant religion, and peasants do not and never have conducted Haitian politics. Second, if vodun favors the status quo, how does one explain Aristide and the Se Lavalas movement for structural change? Indeed, how to explain the truly impressive post-1986 political mobilization of the Haitian countryside, which made the electoral registration, the Constitution of 1987, and the enormous voter turnouts in 1987 and 1990 possible? It is one of the real weaknesses in Aristide's position that he never supported this grassroots mobilization until it became evident that he could lead it. This contributed to its personalization rather than its institutionalization.

It is clearly not the mass of Haitian peasants who brought the great democratic political experiments of post-Duvalierist Haiti to a halt; it was the elites, military and civilian, the 15 percent (all urbanites) who live off the government budgets, and the rapacious *chefs de section*. All were inadvisably threatened at once by Aristide's proposed sweeping reforms. For 200 years the meager yet amazingly munificent cow called the state has nurtured a small elite and a much larger middle sector. The Kingdom of Heaven might well belong to the 85 percent who are Aristide's beloved poor, but the key to the kingdom of this world is held by the 15 percent who use the state to avoid joining the great unwashed. This key eluded Aristide when first in power, even though it appears that, theoretically at least, he understood the structural nature of Haitian politics. Haiti's political situation, he wrote in July 1992, is a product of a long course of traditional politics, which he says created a "political paradigm." "The rules," he explained, "are rigid: The more power an individual or institution amasses from money or weapons, the greater the chances of winning: strength comes from an ability to impose one's will on others."[48]

Again, it is one thing is to understand the world, another to operationalize that understanding. Aristide's followers have neither money nor weapons. Their strengths, despite their numbers, are potential ones and, at least up to now, realizing that potential has depended on the international community's willingness to fund, supervise, and militarily guarantee free elections. Aristide, however, never reconciled himself to this reality, preferring to understand his electoral victory as a fundamental change in the paradigm of Haitian political culture. Before and after his election in 1990, his attitude toward any external involvement was, paradoxically, the key to understanding both his popularity with the masses and his inability to use that external factor pragmatically and instrumentally for the benefit of those very masses. His views on the nature of economic development will illustrate and serve as prelude to the conclusion.

Contrary to all serious studies that see the Haitian peasant as a petty capitalist, Aristide's perception is that they live "in a form of socialism related to their own roots."[49] He recalls his youthful surroundings as "a communitarian existence, a 'socialist' reality on a small scale." This, despite the fact that his mother was one of those informal traders Haitians call a Madam Sara. "She bought and sold," he writes, "moving from one business to another according to the economic conditions . . . [giving their house] the air of a commercial establishment." Next to advice and orders "coming from outside," what he admits to hating most is liberal economics, which he calls "economism." Economic events in Haitian history are interpreted through that lens. He denies, for instance, that the 1987 slaughtering of the entire Haitian porcine population was intended to combat an epidemic of African porcine fever. There was no such emergency; rather, its purpose was "to draw into the cities the abundant and cheap labor force necessary for the assembly plants." At its height, the assembly industry employed some fifty thousand people in a capital city with more than a million and a half inhabitants.

Aristide has repeatedly asserted that in development he would follow the wishes of the peasants themselves, listening to those in touch with "popular consciousness" rather than those who bring foreign models to be executed by foreign specialists. The problem is that without those foreign models and foreign specialists there can be no structural transformation of Haitian politics and, thus, no consolidation of democracy. Such a structural transformation requires a massive foreign economic and technical intervention for the simple reason that in Haiti the problems of political economy and political culture are tightly intertwined.

Conclusion

The legacy of U.S. interventions in the Caribbean now haunt those who would assist Haiti in two ways. First, it crystallized an absolute and categorical principle of sovereignty, which lies not in the people but in the state, no matter who governs or misgoverns that state. The recent changes in perception about human rights and sovereign consent—that "moral imperative" that Fernando Tesón speaks of—have not been enough to overrule this attitude. In fact, the only cases in which such steadfast positions on absolute sovereignty have been ignored is when U.S. vital interests have been perceived to be threatened. The existence of a Cold War climate in the Caribbean made such cases relatively clear-cut for Washington policy makers: the Dominican Republic in 1965, Grenada in 1983, and Panama in 1989 illustrate that reality.

Haiti, however, did not fit the definition of a crisis-level threat to U.S. national security, despite the fears of uncontrolled migration (relatively easily controlled by coastal interdiction) and drug running (was it any worse than what is occurring in many a Caribbean democratic state?). Haiti, from this perspective, was the first major post–Cold War crisis in the Caribbean. As such it reveals a major trend of policy relevance: the international community was much more ready than previously to condemn de facto regimes and call for stringent measures, including embargoes, but not for armed intervention. This was especially the case when the constitutional leader of the country was unwilling to openly call for such an act. Despite

considerable pressure from some political allies who favored such an intervention, Aristide systematically refused for three years, on cultural and
historical grounds, to support that option.

This is one area in which Aristide was consistent, elevating it to something of an operational principle writ large. Before his election, Aristide
told a journalist that the one thing all Haitians agree on, "from Dessalines
to Duvalier," was that there should be no foreign intervention of any sort.[50]
In his autobiography he is equally adamant. "We have not reclaimed our
dignity within Haiti," he writes, "in order to accept any kind of subjuga-
tion that may come from without. . . . We will continue to rely on our own
strengths."

As admirable as such nationalist sentiments are, such broad-gauged
definitions of what "intervention" is fly in the face of Haitian reality. This
reality was brought home to Aristide at a three-day "workshop" between
Aristide and one hundred important and "sympathetic" members of Haiti's
private sector.[51] The atmosphere was good, a result of the 3 July signing of
the Governor's Island Agreement between Aristide and the titular head of
the de facto government, General Raoul Cedras. The prospects of the
lifting of the embargo and of substantial foreign aid flowing in created an
upbeat mood. It was an excellent opportunity to understand what Haitians
themselves, in a rare moment of unity and patriotism, felt was necessary to
move their country toward development and democracy.[52]

The first thing that was evident was the total incapacity of the Haitian
state to perform even the most elementary of state tasks. None of the data
used in discussions came from Haitian sources for the simple reason that
there are no credible statistics produced by the Haitian state. A string of
international agencies, NGOs, and PVOs provided the data inputs. (Haitian elites are now totally familiar with a long list of acronyms identifying
these agencies.) There was a general agreement that any long-term development depended on the mobilization of domestic resources. Such an
eventuality, however, depended on a short- to medium-term program involving massive foreign involvement, for the following reasons: (1) Haiti
did not have the kind of public service—either in personnel or in attitude—
necessary for a serious development initiative. A massive brain drain, over-
staffing by untrained but politically connected people, and the fact that
during much of 1993 and early 1994 salaries in several ministries were up
to six months in arrears all contributed to a total administrative disarray.
(2) There were no local savings and no capacity to encourage such savings
or to collect the necessary revenues. (3) Corruption, already widespread
and endemic, was now the operating system of government. Because the
embargo had greatly stimulated smuggling, which was largely in military

hands, the issue was first a political and only second an economic one. Drug corruption permeated the whole system.[53]

The discussions on the probable privatization of a string of state monopolies (electricity, telecommunications, water, ports, the airport) invariably ended in heated discussions of exactly who controlled these monopolies and how to dislodge them. It was not immediately evident whether there was any national, internal capacity to bring about such political changes. Much of the discussion about reform, therefore, took place under a cloud of political impotence. One example will suffice. The meeting discussed an Emergency Economic Recovery Program (EERP), funded from outside and administered through a central implementation unit (CIU). While the EERP and the CIU would be under the jurisdiction of the constitutional prime minister, its overall administration would be under a variety of international agencies.

One can understand the need for administrative rigor and probity if the Haitian state was ever to emerge from the morass it was in. But listening to the plans for the reorganization and "purification" of the bureaucracy, the extraordinary rules and regulations regarding bidding on jobs, material procurement, tax collections, and performance-based criteria for wage and promotion scales, one wonders just how long the "social pact" between foreigner and the entrenched Haitian elites would last. There are great parallels to the economic-administrative housecleaning that took place in the last decade of the U.S. occupation. In that case, it was carried out under military rule. Needless to say, the three-day meeting in July 1993—presided over, as it was, by Aristide himself—made no mention of force.

In light of the contradictions between total dependence on outsiders to administer services such as public health, education, and agricultural extension services and the intense nationalism among the elites, the question is, How can third parties intervene in such a political system? The answer has to be, forcefully or not at all. No half measures such as embargoes have ever brought about a desired course of events in Haiti. Arguably, the most effective use of force over the longer term would have been a national liberation campaign launched by Aristide himself. This he refused to do.[54] All this leads to two conclusions.

First, it became evident that the incapacity to move the usurpers who overthrew Aristide (see appendix) had eroded the prestige of the inter-American system. That system began to lose credibility after its response to the 1987 crisis, a response very similar to its reaction to the 1991 crisis: statements of regret but reassertions of the principles of state sovereignty as an absolute prohibitor of effective international action.

The OAS's position was encapsulated in the statement by Heraldo Muñoz, Chile's ambassador to the OAS, on forceful intervention. Even a request from President Aristide, wrote Muñoz, though "it might be well founded on moral-political grounds," would be "on shaky juridical terrain given the fact that existing law clearly does not allow the use of force, unilaterally or collectively, on behalf of democracy."[55] Aside from the fact that it would have been insouciant, to say the least, to postulate any "juridical terrain" that contravened "moral-political grounds," there was a purely pragmatic question of adjusting reasonable means to historically avowed ends. The OAS continued to ignore Hobbes's fundamental axiom that covenants without the sword are in vain. *Effective*, in this case, had to be defined in terms of the political culture of Haiti, which, as noted, was not susceptible to half measures, certainly not verbal threats and ineffective embargoes.

Muñoz himself admits that sanctions probably work least well when directed against economies in which subsistence agriculture predominates and that, in the case of Haiti, "they have apparently hurt the average citizen without threatening the putschists' control."[56] Basic empathy, logic, and common sense say that there was little to be gained by continuing to condemn a situation without addressing which specific policies could lead to enduring solutions. The next step would be to analyze the implications—both in law and morality—of those policies over the short, medium, and long terms.

The second conclusion is that, when both international organizations and the legitimate government it was attempting to restore held on to state-centric concepts of sovereignty, there was only a remote chance that the international community would opt for a forceful intervention without extraordinary cajoling from a major power. For three years Haitian elites, including Aristide, held on to an excessively narrow definition of sovereignty, even for a state-centric one. Who holds political office and how it is acquired, defended, or restored—not who feeds, clothes, and heals the children or gets seed to the peasants—is what defines sovereignty in their eyes. Such a definition was certainly a travesty in the case of Haiti, a country where the embargo brutalized the general population even as its futility for policy ends was patently evident.

Those who adhere to a traditional, state-centric concept of sovereignty have to consider how this can coexist with two fundamental Haitian realities. First, for all practical purposes Haiti has already lost sovereign control over critical parts of its economy and society to foreign agencies.[57] The UN Development Program ranks Haiti 137th among the 173 nations of the world in terms of health, education, and purchasing power. More than 450 NGOs perform most of the duties in public health, education, and the daily feeding of nearly one million children. Second, any serious effort to reform that society will undoubtedly involve an even greater and more direct foreign presence and, thus, an even greater retreat from sovereign control, at least for the medium term.

Haiti is not the only case where continued adherence to such a limited state-centric definition of sovereignty will only ensure that further and further inroads into sovereign consent and control will take place. A key question for our age is, What should one call a state where there is a sovereign office but no capacity to perform any of the duties any civilized society requires from that officeholder?

Appendix: Calendar of Haitian Political Instability

1957–71	Rule of François (Papa Doc) Duvalier.
1971	Jean-Claude (Baby Doc) Duvalier inherits rule.
7 Feb. 1986	President Jean-Claude Duvalier overthrown by General Henri Namphy.
29 Nov. 1987	General elections called off after massacre of voters.
17 Jan. 1988	Leslie F. Manigat is "elected" president. General Namphy installs himself as commander of the armed forces and General Regalá as minister of defense. Manigat makes attempts at reducing corruption in military and civil service and attempts to counter moves by General Namphy by siding with Colonel Paul.
19 June 1988	General Namphy overthrows President Manigat, with critical support by General Lhérisson and Colonels Avril, Augustin, and Charles.
17 Sept. 1988	General Namphy is ousted by a coup ostensibly led by noncommissioned officers under Sergeant Joseph Hébreux. General Prosper Avril is declared president.
1 Apr. 1989	Attempt to overthrow Avril fails.
Mar. 1990	General Herard Abraham overthrows the Avril government.
Dec. 1990	Free elections won by Aristide.
30 Sept. 1991	Aristide overthrown. He had governed for seven months.
8 Oct. 1991	Justice Joseph Nerette is sworn in as provisional president by military. OAS imposes full embargo.
24 May 1992	President Bush orders return to Haiti of boat people heading for the United States. President Clinton later continues policy.

25 June 1993	Resolution 841 of UN Security Council imposes worldwide oil and weapons embargo on Haiti because it represents a threat to international peace.
3 July 1993	Governors Island Agreement signed, calling for return of President Aristide by October 30.
25 Aug. 1993	Robert Malval, prominent businessman, wins parliamentary approval to create transitional government.
11 Oct. 1993	U.S. ship *Harlan County*, taking U.S. and Canadian military trainers, as per Governors Island Agreement, leaves Haiti without carrying out mission. Embargo reimposed.
6 Nov. 1993	Senior aid to Prime Minister Malval acknowledges that military control has not been weakened. "This is a strange game. I don't think anybody has a plan. It's like a dogfight. Everybody is fighting against everybody" (*New York Times*, 6 Nov. 1993, 4).
15 Dec. 1993	Robert Malval resigns as prime minister.
6 May 1994	UN Security Council Resolution 917 establishes comprehensive economic sanctions against Haiti, not to be lifted until President Aristide is restored.
31 July 1994	UN Security Council Resolution 940 authorizes a multinational force to use "all necessary means" to restore the president and a stable government.
17 Sept. 1994	President Clinton holds backs invasion of Haiti while former President Jimmy Carter, Senator Sam Nunn, and General Colin Powell negotiate with military junta.
19 Sept. 1994	U.S. troops land peacefully after a general amnesty. They agree to the return of President Aristide.

9 El Salvador

Lessons in Peace Consolidation

Patricia Weiss Fagen

The twelve-year war (1980 to 1992) in El Salvador was a consequence of social inequalities and closed avenues of political participation, reinforced by state terror and repression. The insurgents promised—or threatened, depending on one's perspective—to bring about a vastly changed society at the expense of the privileged elite. What accounts for the length and destructive intensity of the war in El Salvador, however, had less to do with the support or resistance to particular models of change than with the Cold War optic, in which the prospect of social change, even in that small and weak country, could be turned into a global precedent. The war would not end until both domestic forces and international backers agreed that it should. This occurred, and opened the way to a peace accord signed in January 1992 by the government and the Farabundo Martí Liberation Front (FMLN) and blessed by the international community. The challenge of the peace process under way since that time is to prove that it is possible, through political negotiations and reconciliation, to reinforce democratic and participatory structures and spread economic benefits more widely.

The Salvadoran peace process has been a test case for the peacemaking and peace-building capacity of the international community, led by the United Nations. The UN has had a longer and more encouraging experience with the former than with the latter. The tragically frustrated attempts to end ongoing conflicts in Bosnia and Somalia aside, international efforts through the UN have been relatively effective where a genuine commitment exists to resolve armed conflict. Peace, albeit sometimes fragile or only relative, has also been restored with international assistance in Cambodia, Eritrea-Ethiopia, Mozambique, Namibia, Nicaragua, the Occupied Territories, parts of Somalia, and for the second time, Angola. Although conflicts persist, there are serious negotiations toward peace in process in Liberia, Georgia, Guatemala, and Sri Lanka as well. As of mid-1994, the UN Secretariat was overseeing eighteen missions engaged in peacekeeping activities, and its field presence had tripled since 1988.[1]

Once peace treaties have been signed, successful transitions from war to peace must be achieved in war-torn countries like El Salvador, not only for the well-being of their long-suffering populations but for the sake of general international stability. Therefore, the effectiveness of international interventions to this end is a matter of concern and attention for the United Nations, governments, and a wide spectrum of other agencies. The role in the Salvadoran peace process demonstrates rising expectations and the demands on the international system and the extent to which the nature of peacekeeping has changed. Once understood to require limited observation and treaty verification, establishing peace now entails active participation and programmatic responsibilities that extend well into the post-conflict period. That the UN would have been so prominently involved in bringing about a peace settlement in a Central American civil conflict and, subsequently, to have established its presence to ensure compliance with a series of domestic agreements would have been unimaginable before the end of the Cold War.

While the major powers are far from having surrendered their basic decision-making powers to the UN, the latter has become a leading force worldwide in the diplomatic and operational pursuit of peace. Regrettably, UN member states have mandated peacekeeping operations for which they have not assured adequate resources or political support.[2] A basic hypothesis of this evaluation is that peace agreements are more than likely to "unravel" unless respected "third parties" are on the scene to mediate, apply pressure, and press for actions neither side wishes to take.[3] A related assumption is that, to reinforce the political will of authorities to sustain necessarily painful political and social transformations, economic resources must be sufficient and, to some degree, conditioned on progress in peace-related areas.

El Salvador as a Test Case

El Salvador is one of the poorest countries in the Western Hemisphere, with a long history of social injustice and violence. The conflict, as is common in civil strife, ended without clear victory. The warring parties may have decided against achieving goals by military means, but their mutual hostility did not diminish. Most of the issues that led to the war remained to be resolved when the peace was signed, and the compromises would not be forthcoming easily.

The successful conclusion of armed conflict in El Salvador contrasts sharply with the experience of neighboring Nicaragua, where sporadic conflicts persisted and peace arrangements failed to take hold. Nicaragua and El Salvador emerged from war to face the same dire situations: over a decade of strife had created economic ruin, affecting both productivity and infrastructure, and the task of rebuilding fell to widely distrusted governments and a much weakened civil society. Hundreds of thousands of people were uprooted and resettled in areas far from their places of origin.

Why has El Salvador been the more successful of the two neighbors in holding fast to peace and moving toward reconciliation? There are, of course, historic, political, and economic factors that distinguish the two cases. Nevertheless, the major advantages of the Salvadoran peace process were, first, a comprehensive peace treaty, second, the international peace presence, and third, the broader international support for projects directly benefiting the war-affected population.

Compare the peace arrangements in Nicaragua in early 1990 with those of El Salvador in 1991–92. In Nicaragua the positive achievements of an internationally monitored cease-fire and demobilization were diminished by the absence of a comprehensive peace accord. The United States, far and away the major donor, initially lent support intended to favor only its former ideological allies, thereby distorting rehabilitation and impeding reconciliation at the outset. In El Salvador—whose conflict was no less profoundly affected by the Cold War—both internal and external actors eventually pushed for a UN-mediated peace, which established mechanisms for dealing with a wide range of divisive issues. Potential donors, then, could direct their assistance in line with what had been agreed, while urging both sides to accept the necessary compromises. The structure of the UN mission in El Salvador, never contemplated for Nicaragua and unprecedented at the time, is seen now as a model for other situations, most immediately Haiti and Guatemala.

While El Salvador may be seen as a test case of what can and cannot be achieved through international interventions, it has been a difficult laboratory of operations. It is difficult to judge the peace process in terms of success or failure. Changes have taken place in El Salvador that were unthinkable even at the end of the conflict but that were nevertheless short of the ambitious objectives proclaimed in the peace accords. These accords went well beyond simply establishing conditions for ending the war. They included measures to open the political process, to redefine the purposes and functions of national security organizations, and to create a framework for addressing basic economic and social needs of the poorest sectors. They propose to create and strengthen democratic institutions that will respond to the needs of the poor and promote human rights in a country where such institutions have been weak and in a context of postconflict polarization and distrust. The UN was involved in every aspect of the process.

The experience illustrates the fundamental importance of coordinating efforts among international actors, not only the secretary-general's Observer Mission in El Salvador (ONUSAL) but the full UN system, donors, regional entities, and nongovernmental organizations. Very soon after the signing of the accords, it became clear that, in addition to the political and diplomatic skills of the peacekeepers, the technical and operational capabilities of other entities would also be essential to funding and implementing agreed-upon projects. As will be shown, because coordination was not built into the accords, mechanisms of cooperation had to be worked out spontaneously as needs arose.

The Background to Peace

The peace accords signed by the government of El Salvador and the FMLN were successfully negotiated over a period of more than two years, between 1990 and 1992, after twelve years of civil war, possibly seventy-five thousand dead, about a fifth of the population of approximately five million people living outside of the country as refugees or exiles, and hundreds of thousands more displaced from their homes. The physical destruction of infrastructure and productive capacity was close to $1.5 billion.[4]

A combination of regional and international pressures, domestic events, and geopolitical changes brought the parties to the peace table. Beginning in 1983 the Contadora process, propelled by Mexico, Venezuela, Colombia, and Panama and later reinforced by Argentina, Brazil, Peru, and Uruguay sought grounds for ending the then regionwide conflict.[5] A more influential agreement was the Procedures for the Establishment of a Firm and Lasting Peace in Central America, known as Esquipulas II, which was signed on 7 August 1987 by the five Central American presidents, who agreed to end aggression and military support to insurgents and called for regional cooperation in verifying peace and overall democratization. Esquipulas II asked for UN and OAS participation and for the UN to support a regionwide effort on behalf of uprooted populations. This resulted in an innovative regional initiative called CIREFCA, combining reconciliation and dialogue with international assistance to refugees, repatriates and displaced persons.[6] Another initiative, signed during the same month, was the Arias peace plan, a framework for peace in El Salvador and Nicaragua, proposed by President Oscar Arias of Costa Rica and formally approved by the Central American presidents.

While these regional efforts seemed promising, their success was undermined by political opposition and by escalated U.S. military assistance to the Salvadoran government and the Nicaraguan contras, along with the continuing ability of the left in both countries to obtain arms and support from the Soviet bloc. Periodic discussions between the government and the FMLN brought no significant results. In November 1989, as El Salvador entered its second decade of civil conflict between the government and the armed guerrilla forces of the FMLN, the latter launched a powerful offensive and, for weeks, held the capital city, San Salvador, which had been calm for years. The military attacked the neighborhoods where the FMLN was entrenched, with a high civilian cost; they were unable to protect either citizens or property. In the midst of the offensive, military operatives assassinated six highly respected Jesuit priests and two women.

The national and international repercussions of these incidents, combined with an awareness of the likely impact of profound changes occurring in other parts of the world, propelled the pursuit of peace. The murder of the Jesuits was greeted with horror everywhere and embarrassed the U.S. government, which had boasted of the increasing "professionalism" of the Salvadoran military. It strengthened the case for the opposition to U.S. military assistance to El Salvador. Then, with the end of the Cold War, U.S. politics turned inward and there was less enthusiasm for pursuing rightist victories in Central America. On the left, the collapse of the Soviet Union, the 1990 Sandinista electoral loss, and the progressive weakening of the Cuban economy affected resource flows to the FMLN, which, although very well stocked with arms and ammunition, nonetheless stood to lose important allies. When consulted by the secretary-general, both Soviet and Cuban governments expressed approval of the proposed negotiations.[7]

Soon after the 1989 FMLN offensive, first the FMLN and then President Alfredo Cristiani approached the United Nations, recalling UN support for the Esquipulas agreement, and asking the secretary-general to help achieve a peace agreement.[8] The secretary-general accepted and initiated a prolonged and complex series of negotiations between the government and the FMLN. From the first it was understood that the United Nations not only would lend its auspices to the negotiation process but would also verify compliance with the agreements reached. This was subsequently made explicit in the language of the accords. Although conservatives considered the Organization of American States politically more reliable, the government, the FMLN, and the United States by this time favored the UN because of its peacekeeping experience, operational capacity, and diplomatic leverage and the fact that it was acceptable to both parties.[9] That the UN had established a positive presence in the region through the ongoing projects of CIREFCA and other economic initiatives was helpful.

The Peace Accords

Many analysts have reviewed the stages of the Salvadoran peace negotiations.[10] The long period during which the secretary-general's representative, Alvaro de Soto, skillfully guided discussions and the two sides presented proposals regarding issues in contention helped to build confidence and mutual respect and to accustom both the government and the FMLN to solving disagreements through compromise. Key agreements reached in the staged negotiations that took place between April 1990 and December 1991 were aimed primarily at the reincorporation of the FMLN into national life and the transformation of the security forces. However, as noted above, the accords were broad in scope, including calls for social justice as well as for political and judicial reforms. The major accords included the following:

1. At the time of the initial meetings between the government and the FMLN in Geneva, and with their agreement, the secretary-general designated four Friends of the Secretary General: Mexico, Spain, Colombia, and Venezuela, who would serve as advisers during the negotiations and as mediators thereafter. All four had established relations with both sides in the conflict and had permanent missions in the country.

2. On 26 July 1990, the government and the FMLN, meeting in Costa Rica, signed the San José Agreement on Human Rights. Agreeing to a range of measures for the protection of human rights, the parties also provided for the establishment of a UN observer mission to monitor compliance in these human rights areas. Following the completion of the peace accords, that mission would expand its mandate to oversee overall compliance with the full range of agreements. The UN Observer Mission in El Salvador, ONUSAL, opened its doors a year later, on 26 July 1991, with Iqbal Riza as chief of mission.[11]

3. In talks in Mexico that ended in April 1991 the negotiating parties agreed (1) to establish a Commission on the Truth to investigate past major human rights violations and to make recommendations, (2) to create a new Supreme Electoral Tribunal and implement general electoral reforms so that

the voting process would be broader and more legitimate than had previously been the case, (3) to produce a national reconstruction plan with the participation of both the government and the FMLN for the areas damaged by war, and (4) to restore public administration that had been replaced in the course of the conflict. As these and other agreements required constitutional reforms, the parties also agreed to a formula by which the postelection National Assembly would ratify amendments made by the existing Assembly.

4. By far the most thorny questions concerned how the FMLN was to be integrated into national security structures and what would happen to the Salvadoran armed forces: reduction in numbers? modification of the officer corps? a change in its mandate? The military and the government steadfastly refused to agree to the FMLN insistence on power sharing and direct participation in the military. A compromise was reached, linking the question of the armed forces to the creation of a new National Civilian Police force accompanied by a police training academy (the National Academy for Public Security), in which the FMLN would participate.[12] The government agreed to reduce the armed forces in size, to abolish the security police and intelligence structures, and to disband the rapid deployment infantry battalions. It would accept the conclusions of an ad hoc commission of civilians created to identify those individuals the military should remove on human rights grounds. The FMLN agreed to dismantle its military structure entirely, in order to integrate itself as a legal political entity. In the interim, the FMLN would be represented in a provisional political decision-making mechanism, COPAZ (see below). Once its demobilization and disarmament were verified, it could function as a regular political party. The demobilized FMLN combatants were to be reintegrated into the economic and social fabric through favorable land transfers and other reintegration programs.

5. The complex and historically divisive land questions were discussed during the final negotiating sessions in New York, which produced a rather hastily contrived framework for effecting land transfers to the FMLN and its supporters. This framework legitimized FMLN occupancy in the conflictive zones under its control but also recognized the legality of titles held by existing owners, from whom the land would have to be purchased.

6. The parties agreed to establish a National Commission for the Consolidation of Peace, COPAZ, with participation from government, political parties, and the FMLN, and with the presence of observers from the archbishop and ONUSAL. COPAZ was intended to be the major forum for verifying compliance and resolving diverging views regarding time frames and interpretations and was charged with drafting whatever legislation was needed for the accords. Ultimately, it was able to fill its role only in part.

At midnight on 31 December 1991, the Salvadoran government and FMLN representatives signed a preliminary peace treaty. The formal peace agreement was signed ceremoniously in Mexico City on 16 January 1992. The cease-fire went into effect on 1 February.

Following through with the Agreements

El Salvador entered the first phase of peace consolidation with what appeared to be many advantages.

—*A comprehensive agreement.* The signed peace agreement was unusually thorough, both in touching upon and providing frameworks for resolution of major points of contention, establishing the time frames in which both sides were to fulfill their obligations, and providing for national institutions with mandates for democracy and social justice.

—*The political will to negotiate and compromise.* Both parties had sought a political solution to their conflict, and the process itself had promoted and rewarded negotiation and compromise between them.

—*An adequate UN peacekeeping presence.* ONUSAL was adequately funded and staffed in three (later four) divisions, whose activities were coordinated by the special representative named by the secretary-general. All staff were Spanish speaking. While its size and visibility was at times used by its enemies to whip up nationalist sentiment, the ONUSAL staff could be present throughout the country, which (another advantage) was small and, for the most part, lacking in major logistical barriers.

—*A relatively strong UN mandate to ensure compliance with the agreements.* Although accorded the status of observers, ONUSAL could and did take an active role in investigating problems, seeking solutions to disagreements, and engaging the relevant parties in dialogue toward solutions. Following demobilization the military sector was reduced, and as elections approached a new electoral unit arrived. The departure date of ONUSAL was tied to the completion of the accords. Salvadorans on both sides respected the secretary-general, who took direct responsibility for resolving particularly difficult problems.

—*International support for peace, expressed both politically and financially.* During the war, the international community was divided on the question of El Salvador, with major U.S. support going to the government and the military and far smaller quantities of European support made available to the left. When the peace accords were signed, however, all donors weighed in heavily with both sides to encourage compliance.[13] The Four Friends who had assisted the negotiation process continued to play an effective mediating role with both sides and helped to mobilize financial resources. The United States subsequently joined the group of Friends; its influence was particularly important for maintaining the momentum of compliance by the Salvadoran government and for countering the pressures of the far right, which still opposed the agreements. On the economic side, donor participation in El Salvador has been strong, taking into account the competing demands of other world crises and the general economic downturns in Europe and North America.

—*The commitment of other UN agencies and nongovernmental organizations to the peace process.* While peace negotiations were still in process, the secretary-general asked the UNDP to mobilize funds and deal with the technical aspects of the agreements. The UNDP and other UN specialized agencies in El Salvador redirected their programs to undertake projects related to the peace process. NGOs implemented or participated in the implementation of the majority of the projects that grew directly out of the accords or as a result of the process.

The process was rocky from the outset. Although each side was committed to comply with specific agreements, in practice the agreements proved mutually dependent. Fulfillment of one was linked to compliance with another. Time frames for fulfilling obligations were tight, and there were no contingency plans to deal with the consequences of nonaction or delayed response. Both the government and the FMLN at one time or another flagrantly ignored their commitments, and sources of pressure had to be found to persuade them to reverse course.

The linkage problem was exacerbated by the disparity between both sides' commitments. The government was responsible for taking measures in response to nearly all the agreements: the new police, the recommendations of the Truth Commission, the land that was to be made available to the FMLN and its civilian followers, and so on. Government representatives repeatedly blamed their multiple responsibilities and funding shortfalls for the slow pace of compliance. The FMLN had the opposite problem. Its main responsibilities were to disarm and demobilize. Not to do either of these was to undermine the whole process. Once the FMLN had complied with both, however, it would lose its major source of pressure on its political adversary, the government.

The majority of agreements suffered delays in implementation, sometimes willful, sometimes unavoidable. Each side expressed serious dissatisfaction about the quality of compliance by the other. The FMLN continually accused the government of noncompliance with its many obligations. In addition to the complaints of the FMLN, the government faced, on the one hand, pressure from the political right of its party to concede as little as possible and, on the other, warnings from donors that continued funding required more decisive action.

The negotiated end of the war brought no change in basic government economic policies. The military budget was still high. As it had before and during the war, the government sought to enhance investor confidence by adhering to the structural adjustment policies advocated by the international financial institutions (World Bank, International Monetary Fund, large private banks). Despite the call for social spending specified in the accords, the government adopted conservative economic policies aimed at reducing public sector expenditures and holding down wages. Foreign donors, with minimum government participation, contributed financial support to the peace process. Funding shortfalls crippled or delayed activities essential to major peace-related projects.

Overseeing the peace process proved to be akin to moving across a new terrain without a proper map. To be sure, there was the "map" of the accords, but that document marked only the major arteries. It did not include the streets that connected one artery to the other, and along the way, many bridges had to be built. To build those bridges required collaboration and coordination among national and international entities well beyond the government and FMLN negotiators and ONUSAL.

The UN Response to the Peace Initiatives

The peace negotiations were debated and signed by President Cristiani and other representatives of the Salvadoran government, by the FMLN leadership, and by Alvaro de Soto, the special representative of the UN secretary-general. The international organizations that would implement the eventual agreements had followed the negotiations only indirectly and could make no more than general preparations to respond. Thus, strategies of implementation necessarily awaited the presentation of the final accords. In later reflections, officials of ONUSAL and the UNDP, as well as some economic assistance officials from donor countries, have expressed regret at having been unable to provide, at an earlier stage, more in the way of technical advice, particularly on those issues with developmental implications.

The UN Observer Mission in El Salvador

The Accords gave ONUSAL a central role in observing, following, promoting, and verifying all agreements.[14] It first established its presence through a forty-member human rights mission headed by French jurist Philippe Texier, working in regional offices throughout the country, prior to the signing of the peace agreement.[15] The human rights division gave Salvadorans a first sense of UN monitoring and accompaniment, which undoubtedly facilitated their acceptance of the full mission and its larger mandate.

Besides investigating cases brought to its attention and promoting human rights generally, the ONUSAL regional staff was called on to mediate disputes and resolve potential local flare-ups. A 380-person military unit arrived after the accords went into effect to oversee the cease-fire, ensuring the reduction of government armed forces and the concentration and gradual demobilization of the FMLN and the destruction of its arms. The police unit, which has averaged 300 persons, closely followed the activities of El Salvador's National Police, which was to be replaced by the National Civilian Police (PNC), as established in the peace accords. The National Police was fully disbanded only in 1995, and by that time the ten-thousand-officer target had already proved too small. Except for a brief period in late 1993 to early 1994 (see below), the ONUSAL police unit directly assisted the PNC by sharing resources and advice. In an environment of high crime and insecurity, the ONUSAL police took on much of the responsibility for providing police protection.[16] An Electoral Division was added to ONUSAL from May 1993 to April 1994, to work with national institutions toward establishing a new voter registry and mechanisms for fair and broadly based elections.

A difficulty within the ONUSAL structure, which is common to nearly all such missions, was the overlapping responsibilities of the different sectors. The ONUSAL police and the human rights divisions, for example, frequently addressed the same cases and typically advocated different approaches for handling them.[17] When asked about the impact of ONUSAL in El Salvador's peace process, Salvadorans of many political persuasions and ONUSAL staff tend to agree that its role as mediator was fundamental. Of course, the successful monitoring of the terms of the cease-fire was a sine qua non for everything else that followed, but ONUSAL was able, in addition, to strengthen civil society and overall reconciliation because of its ability to convene the two sides for dialogue. ONUSAL mediation produced solutions, or frameworks for solutions, in disputes between the government and the FMLN, labor and management, landowners and landholders, municipal officials and community residents, and so forth, disputes that ONUSAL leadership believed were related in some way to the peace process.

ONUSAL's mandate differed from that of other recent peacekeeping missions (e.g., Cambodia, Mozambique), whose presence is tied to demobilization and the restoration of order and civilian rule through elections. ONUSAL would remain as long as needed to promote and verify the completion of all the specific agreements by the opposing sides. This somewhat open-ended presence had salutary effects in making it clear that the UN intended to see the process through. Postelection reforms in the judicial and electoral systems and changes in the police leadership certainly owed much to continued UN pressure.

The UN Development Program

In the chapter on national reconstruction in the peace accords, the two parties requested that the UNDP work with the government toward developing an appropriate plan to attend to reconstruction needs in the conflict zones and to mobilize international resources.[18] Generally, the UNDP was charged with overseeing the technical aspects of the peace accords, that is, to prepare the projects and programs mandated by and appropriate to the peace agreements and to mobilize external funding for them. This arrangement meant, first, that the UNDP and ONUSAL would have to work together, second, that the UNDP would become a major channel for international funding for the peace process, and third, that the UNDP would design and carry out projects in coordination with the government, the FMLN, and other agencies of the UN system as well as with nongovernment organizations, where appropriate.[19]

Relations between ONUSAL and the UNDP initially suffered from mutual misunderstandings. Both the peacemakers and ONUSAL underestimated the complexity and technical difficulties of implementing the agreed-upon projects they turned over to the UNDP. The UNDP, on its side, at first inadequately understood the integral relationship between political and technical issues. For example, when putting together a commission to design the National Academy for Public Security (to train the new National Civilian Police), the UNDP assembled the two major donors, Spain and the United States, with the Salvadoran government. Immediately, the FMLN—the other party to the peace agreement that had brought about the academy—expressed its strong displeasure.[20] UNDP took the appropriate corrective measures.

Gradually at first, and then more decisively, the agency revised its previous operating assumptions. None of the parties, including the UNDP itself, had taken sufficiently into account the extent to which bringing it into the process would require a departure from its traditional role as adviser to the government on national development. As essentially technical and economic advisers to government institutions, the UNDP had lacked experience working with implementing partners outside of the government. To assist the peace process, however, meant ensuring FMLN participation in projects and working with an array of national NGOs as well as with the government. As the UNDP tried to adapt, the FMLN and its supporters complained that it was still too tied to the government, and the FMLN indicated substantial displeasure with aspects of UNDP's new role and its relationships with the government's adversaries. At times, the regional UNDP office also felt insufficiently backed by headquarters; UNDP representatives in New York who had followed the peace agreements wanted the UNDP to play a positive role, but top leadership frequently questioned the need for actions that took the UNDP beyond its traditional activities. Ultimately, the UNDP did broaden its relationships and managed to cement diverse working relations with government, a wide range of NGOs, and donors. However, the office remained short of staff and was overextended regionally.

UNDP officials in El Salvador further complained that ONUSAL was turning over to them the management and funding of complex, politically charged, projects without sufficient follow up by ONUSAL. Moreover, when ONUSAL staff failed to require full compliance with the agreed-upon terms (e.g., with regard to reintegration programs for the demobilized FMLN), the UNDP would be criticized for poor performance or poor use of funds.

International donors have channeled much of their assistance through the UNDP to such key democratic institutions and programs as the Academy of National Security, the Supreme Electoral Tribunal, the Human Rights Ombudsman, and a number of programs connected with the reinsertion and training for former combatants and with general national reconstruction. Such activities were altogether new for the UNDP and, by its own account, tested its capacity for flexible response.[21] The training and agricultural programs, moreover, were rendered less effective by the lack of complementary actions that would tie training to the acquisition of land or employment. Former combatants could rarely pay the interest rates on credits or loans, which the government set at nearly full market rates. As shown in the following pages, delays in compliance or partisan political factors complicated virtually every program.

Other UN Agencies

Meanwhile, the other UN agencies with offices in El Salvador (the UN High Commissioner for Refugees, or UNHCR; the UN Children's Fund, or UNICEF; the World Food Program, or WFP; the Food and Agriculture Organization, or FAO; the World Health Organization/Pan American Health Organization, or WHO/PAHO; and the UN Population Fund, or UNPFA) pushed for greater interagency cooperation and broader participation in ongoing UNDP projects. All the agencies, to their credit, redirected programs toward reinforcing the objectives of peace. They did so through separate mechanisms and donor networks, while working closely with both government and ONUSAL. In general, they filled important gaps in government services for war-affected populations.

Working with the government and a range of NGOs and community groups, the UNHCR supervised a nationwide project for restoring civil registries and providing primary documentation, as stipulated in the San José Human Rights Accords—a prerequisite to the exercise of citizen rights, including the vote. As the only UN agency (prior to ONUSAL) permitted to work in the conflict zone during the war, the UNHCR had established good relations with the population there and provided a bridge for other agencies to begin operations in these areas.

PRODERE (Program for the Development of Refugees, Displaced Persons, and Repatriates) focused on regional development and consensus-building projects for returnees and displaced populations with local authorities. The project offered the combined services of the UNDP, the WHO/PAHO, the UNHCR, and the International Labor Organization (ILO) to local initiatives in three regions. UNICEF established water and sanitation projects in the former conflict zones and brought government and private support for educational and health efforts. WHO/PAHO developed working relations with several health-related NGOs to support programs in areas that the government covered inadequately or not at all, while encouraging expanded government health services in the former conflict zones. The WFP provided food for a variety of projects implemented by international agencies, NGOs, and the government (e.g., for former combatants' training programs). It provided emergency food stocks for repatriates and food for work, benefiting displaced persons communities; it also worked with communities in land rehabilitation. The FAO gave technical advice on the land transfer program, which helped produce a revised agreement, and was involved in the training of former combatants.[22]

With the partial exception of the UNHCR, all the UN agencies had to obtain approval from the respective government ministries with which they were associated for the peace-related operations they wished to undertake. Depending on the ministry, the obstacles could be substantial.

With regard to donors, the U.S. government reversed previous policies and threw its substantial weight in support of the peace process. U.S. embassy officials began to build bridges for the first time with the full range of UN agencies, NGOs of the left, and not least, the FMLN.[23] The U.S. Agency for International Development (AID) has been by far the largest contributor to governmental programs in support of the peace effort, followed by the European Community, Japan, Germany, and Canada. The Inter-American Development Bank has supported an important Social Investment Fund (FIS). Funds from European donors, particularly the Nordic countries and the Netherlands, have mainly gone through UN agencies or directly to NGOs. The European Community has implemented its own programs but also funds NGO projects. The Italian government has been the major donor to PRODERE.

Working Together

The UN is an institution with several related parts, but outsiders frequently underestimate the institutional barriers and rivalries that mitigate against closer collaboration. Compared to other major peacekeeping efforts, the relationships among UN organizations in El Salvador on the whole were comparatively positive.[24] However, at the outset of the peace process, there were two quite separate systems: ONUSAL and its components, and the regular UN agencies that had been there before and would remain after the peace mission departed. The peace process in El Salvador benefited from the fact that these two systems—and the donors—shared similar assumptions and managed to work cooperatively. Nevertheless, much of what was accomplished was unplanned and came about thanks mainly to good will, flexibility on the ground, and the willingness of donors to back peace initiatives.

The need to pull together and innovate became obvious at the very beginning of the peace process in order to rescue the demoblization program. The story illustrates both the resourcefulness and inexperience of the international actors: astonishingly, no provisions had been made for food, housing, health care, or training in the fifteen assembly points where the FMLN concentrated its soldiers after the signing of the peace agreements. At the request of the Salvadoran government and the FMLN, ONUSAL and the UNDP quickly assembled an emergency committee, chaired by the latter, that met forty-nine times and cobbled together a plan of action.[25]

For food, the WFP obtained permission from the government to "loan" stocks already in the country to the cantonment centers until the European Community could finance food purchases, which an NGO (CARITAS) distributed. The WHO/PAHO designed health care services for former combatants needing specialized attention, like dentistry, eye care, complicated surgery. These health projects were largely carried out by the medical faculty of the University of El Salvador, a team of NGOs working with the F-16, and the FMLN medical structure. The UNDP mobilized some $3.1

million from fifteen countries.[26] With these funds and its own resources, the international NGO Doctors without Borders installed tents, infrastructure, and sanitation. UNESCO, with the F-16 and the Salvadoran National University, designed a project that brought basic education to the otherwise inactive and bored former combatants. The USAID donated basic-needs packages and construction materials to the demobilizing soldiers. Since none of the plans had taken into account the fact that many of the combatants had families, UNICEF quickly elaborated a project to provide water, sanitation, and some care for the family settlements that grew up alongside the assembly points. The relevant government ministries—Planning, National Reconstruction, Health and Education—backed and complemented the UN-NGO activities.

By all accounts, this interagency emergency project was an operational success. Unfortunately, the agencies did not go on to establish regular mechanisms for coordination. Each entity returned to its separate programs and projects, meeting periodically to discuss issues of common concern.

Another example of successful coordination spearheaded by the UN, but including governmental and nongovernmental entities from left to right, was the combined documentation and electoral registration campaign. One of the most important objectives of the peace process was to ensure full, free, and fair elections in March 1994, which would elect mayors and congressional representatives as well as a new president and vice president. These elections would establish the FMLN as a political force instead of a guerrilla opposition. Success depended on creating a vastly enlarged and more reliable voter registry and the depoliticization of the electoral procedures.[27]

Apart from political will, the two major obstacles to enlarging the voter registries were, first, that hundreds of thousands of Salvadorans lacked basic documentation (birth certificates, identity cards) and hence could not apply for voting cards; and second, that there was an absence of strategies to mobilize potential voters, long disenchanted with rigged elections or still fearful of expressing themselves. Large amounts of assistance from the United States and other donors were devoted to the latter effort, most directed at the Supreme Electoral Tribunal (TSE), a new entity established through the peace process.

A combined campaign of documentation and electoral registration brought together in common action the TSE (supported by the United States and a number of donors and the UNDP), the governmental Salvadoran Institute for Municipal Development (ISDEM) (supported by the

USAID and the UNHCR), the mayors from all municipalities, the regional offices of ONUSAL and its human rights and electoral divisions, and a broad array of NGOs.[28] The success of the documentation-registration campaign was due to the participation of all relevant Salvadoran actors of the political left and right in every municipality of the country.[29] In this first electoral phase, some 80 percent of estimated potential voters applied for voting cards, mostly during high-visibility, documentation-registration days, which lasted until the end of November 1993.

These two examples of ad hoc coordination are not intended as an endorsement of unplanned programs. Rather, they point to the need for UN agency leadership to permit flexibility for their staff on the ground and for donors to build their capacities to respond quickly to unplanned contingencies.

Flawed Institutions and Political Will

UN, donors, and NGOs were often disappointed with the direction of the peace process in El Salvador. The causes combined inefficiencies, competing political priorities, intentional obstruction of certain activities, and last but certainly not least, inadequate resources. Critics argue both about the balance of these factors and the extent to which international pressures might have produced different results.

Demobilization

The first task was to bring about the demobilization of the opposing sides: following the concentration of troops, the FMLN did not meet the agreed-upon schedule for demobilization, which was to occur in five stages between 1 May and 31 October 1992.[30] Each of the first three demobilizations was delayed two months on grounds that the government had not taken the necessary steps to establish the training academy for the National Civilian Police (PNC) and was not effecting land transfers.[31] The delays were not simply politically motivated retaliation on the part of the FMLN. The issues of demobilization and government compliance were in fact linked. Twenty percent of the entrants into the National Academy for Public Security (subsequently the PNC) were expected to be drawn from the demobilized FMLN. The fact that the government delayed for three months in identifying an appropriate venue for the academy meant that there was no training academy to receive them. Likewise, so very few land

transfers had been prepared at the time the first groups were due to demobilize that many would be left with no means of achieving economic self-
sufficiency. This indeed occurred.

Predictably, the Salvadoran armed forces also delayed its reduction of
forces and the dissolution of its special battalions. The demobilization of
the FMLN and the reduction of the armed forces were completed two
months behind schedule, on 15 December. Neither side complied fully
with its promised disarmament. The armed forces failed to retrieve most of
the military weapons known to be in private possession; the FMLN, indicating a persisting lack of confidence that peace would endure, hid substantial quantities of its armament.[32]

The Peace Institutions

The institutions and reforms created through the peace process (the Human Rights Ombudsman, the Supreme Electoral Tribunal, the National
Academy for Public Security, and the National Civilian Police) were innovative and responsive on paper. Together, they constituted mechanisms for
enabling the political participation of long marginalized sectors of Salvadoran society, restructuring organizations that previously had spawned
corruption and arbitrary use of power, and promoting human rights in a
society long characterized by repression. However, in practice, at least at
the outset, these institutions lacked the strength and organizational capacity to fulfill their mandates. Within these institutions, and more clearly
within the governmental entities separate from the accords but essential to
the fulfillment of the peace process (the Secretariat of National Reconstruction, the land bank, the various ministries), were individuals who did not
fully share the goals of the accords and who worked for partisan or personal objectives.

The establishment and deployment of the PNC, a key institution among
those created by the peace process, occurred more slowly than anticipated
due to the delays establishing the training academy. When finally deployed,
the recruits were made to live in substandard conditions, with low salaries
and inadequate equipment and vehicles. Both the government and international funders remained reluctant to pay for these needs.[33] Indeed, in
September 1993 the government-appointed leadership of the PNC told
ONUSAL to suspend its technical assistance to the PNC.[34] Meanwhile,
although contrary to the peace accords, candidates from the abolished
security forces and groups from the government's Antinarcotics Unit were
inducted into the PNC, the latter without passing through the training
academy as required.[35] Only following the 1994 elections was the PNC

leadership changed and its practices modified. By 1995, living conditions had improved somewhat, and the government was partially funding the PNC through its own budget.

Major human rights violations have sharply declined, but the recommendations of the Truth Commission, made public in March 1993, were very slow to be implemented. Eventually, individuals named in the report were dismissed, but actions on recommendations (subsequently reiterated by ONUSAL) regarding changes in the judiciary structure were not presented to the legislature until April 1994, and in a weakened form (the draft laws refer to procedures used in criminal cases, reforms in the penitentiary code, and constitutional reforms relating to the administration of justice). The progress of judicial reforms following the March 1994 elections began positively, with the election of new judges for the Supreme Court and the purging of a number of judges known to be corrupt or inept. Progress then slowed to a virtual halt.

A spate of politically motivated murders prior to the elections, apparently with "death squad" sponsorship, abated thereafter, but as of this writing are unsolved. In December 1993, the government and ONUSAL agreed to the creation of a Joint Group for the Investigation of Illegal Armed Groups with Political Motivation in El Salvador. The Joint Group report, issued in July 1994, confirmed that illegal armed structures still operated clandestinely and were connected to the state security apparatus and that, while the while national leaders wanted an end to death squad type actions, the measures they had thus far taken were insufficient.[36]

The Human Rights Ombudsman, an important accomplishment of the peace agreement, slowly gained space and acceptance. However, while affiliated with the government, the latter provided little financial or other support; groups on the left still question its efficacy.[37] With new leadership in place in 1995, the ombudsman's office promises to become more dynamic.

The Supreme Electoral Tribunal (TSE) replaced an electoral body know for corruption and political bias. The new structure, however, maintained many of the old inefficiencies and some of the politicization as well. Even insignificant decisions had to be agreed to by the magistrates representing its four parties, and it was often virtually immobilized. Moreover, TSE personnel were overwhelmingly political appointees of, and beholden to, these same political parties (two on the right, one on the left, one centrist). The TSE seemed to be working cooperatively with international electoral experts during the registration campaign.[38] But, when it came time to actually provide electoral cards for those who registered, there were strong indications of political bias.[39] The voting itself on 20 March was a logistical nightmare, as the TSE had taken little of the expert advice offered and had barely trained election officials, much less voters. Some of the electoral reforms advocated by ONUSAL were put in place after the elections, including new procedures for appointing TSE members.

The Land Transfer Program

Land transfers were so slowly implemented that the FMLN postponed demobilization three times. Additional delay was caused by the failure of the FMLN to produce an acceptable inventory of land and potential beneficiaries.[40] The process of establishing titles and allocating land was and remains extremely complicated, and funding for the key institution, especially the land bank, is still below estimated needs.

As of the end of 1993, only 8 percent of the land to be transferred was in the hands of the potential beneficiaries. The program accelerated for a time in 1994, largely due to international pressure, but was stalemated again by midyear. By early 1995, some 46 percent of the land had been transferred.[41] The UN regularly criticized government inaction on the land question; in its August 1994 report, it criticized the FMLN, as well, for continuing to relocate or add people to the plots of land in question and for often failing to present documentation needed for transfers.[42] In addition to the complicated mechanisms for titling and approving sales, land transfers have been slowed by the tendency of sellers to insist on far higher prices than those established by the government.

As long as land transfers are bureaucratically and financially mired, potentially productive land cannot be planted, and farmers who lack legal titles receive no credit. Neither landowners nor landholders are able to plan for the future. To date, the majority of communities of repatriates, displaced persons, and former combatants who settled on abandoned land in the conflict zones during the 1980s and early 1990s are still in doubt as to how or whether they will obtain legal title to the places where they have constructed homes and projects. Unfortunately a workable solution to El Salvador's land problems lies beyond compliance with the framework established in the peace accords, but providing land for former combatants and resolving the legal status of present landholders is fundamental for lasting security.[43]

National Reconstruction

The goal of reconstruction is to turn a country divided and at war into a single productive nation at peace. For most of the population affected by the conflict, the transition to peace was or was not on track depending on the changes they saw in their lives when the fighting ceased.[44] The manner in which national reconstruction would proceed would effectively define or redefine relations of power and the exercise of participatory democracy.

The priorities for national reconstruction were established, as stipulated in the peace agreement, in consultation between government and the FMLN. They were (1) integrated development in the former conflict zones, (2) attention to the basic needs of the population most affected by the war and of the former combatants of both sides, and (3) the restoration of infrastructure. The peace accords designated as the target population of the National Reconstruction Plan (NRP) the 35,362 Salvadorans—the demobilized, repatriates, displaced persons, and the poor—living in 115 municipalities affected by the war. These areas had been without government services during the years of conflict, and the population survived largely thanks to private international donors. The peace plan mandated special programs aimed at the reintegration of the FMLN, including scholarships, training, housing, and small enterprises.

A struggle inevitably emerged over the planning process: how funds would be channeled and how projects would be selected and executed. The largest component of the National Reconstruction Plan was executed by the National Reconstruction Secretariat, which received most of its funding from the USAID. In addition to the projects for reintegrating former combatants, as noted above, the secretariat approved funds for municipal improvements and productive projects. With elections looming in 1994, two years after the peace accords, the director of the National Reconstruction Secretariat was unfriendly to measures that might strengthen the voting appeal of local groups on the left; she wanted beneficiaries to depend on and be grateful to the government. For their part, the FMLN and its allies in many communities refused the programs offered by government ministries unless the latter would relinquish full control to entities chosen by the communities, which rarely occurred.

The left wished to retain the structures of grassroots representation it had established during the conflict. Nongovernmental organizations working in zones under FMLN control had gained direct access to modest funds, largely from European donors who supported their efforts during the war years. The NGOs and churches had used the donor funding for small projects in target communities inhabited mostly by persons sympathetic to the FMLN. These projects were consolidated in the framework of CIREFCA after 1989. CIREFCA, jointly sponsored by the UNHCR and the UNDP, was the preferred vehicle of the left for receiving development assistance because of its emphasis on the participation of NGOs and its insistence on dialogue between government, NGOs, and the UN.

CIREFCA, now considered a model for early reintegration and

community-level development in war-torn societies, was an important vehicle of reconciliation between former adversaries. The first formal negotiations between the civilian left and the government over developmental priorities and approaches took place in the context of CIREFCA, as the two sides negotiated a joint document to present to the donors at the Second International CIREFCA Meeting held in San Salvador in April 1992. The negotiations took place because the UNHCR-UNDP officials involved and the donors made it clear that, if the Salvadoran government wished CIREFCA funding, it would have to present its projects to donors in a consolidated NGO-government document.

Once CIREFCA had opened the dialogue between the government and the NGOs, the two sides discussed approaches to the government's National Reconstruction Plan. Locally—encouraged by ONUSAL, UNDP/PRODERE, and other agencies—the former local adversaries came together in reconstruction committees composed of the municipal authorities favored by the government as well as the civilian left leadership. Together, they formulated project requests to the secretariat. This hopeful alliance was not welcomed by the National Reconstruction Secretariat. One after another, the broad-based committees failed because the secretariat ignored virtually all the community projects they presented to it for funding. Secretariat funds were made available mainly to municipal officials loyal to the government, who did not join alliances with the left.[45]

What accounts for these institutional shortcomings and the limited effectiveness of international pressures to keep the two parties in positive movement? Certainly, such problems are rooted in generations of institutional inefficiency and embedded forms of corruption and are not amenable to correction in the very short term. Under the best of circumstances, it will take many years and another generation of political leadership to develop responsive civil institutions and a more mature political culture.

Doubtless, the scarcity of funding for a number of peace institutions has limited their ability to follow through with projected activities. As of May 1994, the UN secretary-general complained of a shortfall of $476 million to cover needs arising from the peace accords for the period from 1993–96.[46] As noted, outside donors, rather than the government, funded these accords. The World Bank consistently voiced support for the peace process but did not encourage the government to materially support its institutions or social projects. To do so, it maintained, would undermine ongoing conservative economic policies. Therefore, bank officials urged, instead, greater donor generosity.[47] Critics argue that this arrangement mitigated against the government's commitments both to peace institutions and to reversing the social conditions that gave rise to the conflict.[48]

Faced with frequently disappointing results from government performance, donors nonetheless acted with restraint in exerting pressure directly on national institutions. The European donors largely avoided confronting this issue by channeling funding through UN agencies and NGOs. The US, as the major bilateral donor, complained and cajoled Salvadoran leadership, but did not reduce support when aid recipients acted contrary to stated U.S. policy.

Evaluation and Lessons Learned

As of this writing in early 1995, the Salvadoran peace process is very much on track. No armed confrontations have taken place since the peace agreement formally went into effect in February 1992. The military has carried out large-scale demobilization and has accepted a far more limited role in governance and, in 1995, even a cut in its budget.[49] The government has retired the major human rights offenders from its ranks. The five factions of the FMLF turned in their weapons and transformed themselves into a political entity that effectively competed for public office. The new police force, drawn from the opposing sides and from the general population, has been established and deployed. Some thirty thousand repatriates and tens of thousands of internally displaced persons have repopulated the former conflict zones. Both national and local actors, from the left and the right, are involved in defining the directions of economic development through their respective organizations, and many are in direct contact with donor agencies. Judicial reform that will improve the treatment of people accused and arrested have been initiated, and the Legislative Assembly plays a larger role in major appointments. The presidential, congressional, and mayoral elections scheduled for March, though flawed, provide a basis for legitimate government and for the political participation of the full spectrum of Salvadoran politics.

Yet, in the aftermath of the long-awaited elections, and in the last months of ONUSAL's presence in the country, achievements are still fragile, and many Salvadorans lack confidence in the democratic and civil institutions created as a result of the peace agreements. Neither the former combatants of the FMLN nor those of the armed forces as yet have benefited from adequate reintegration programs. Indeed, the most visible threats to peace in 1994 and 1995 have been the violent demonstrations by the police and the demobilized members of the armed forces, demanding more money. The vast majority of Salvadorans are extremely poor and have received little from the ongoing national reconstruction effort, which was supposed to undergird the political achievements of peace. Finally, with other worldwide emergencies absorbing millions of dollars of humanitarian aid, international support has dwindled and will continue to do so despite the tasks remaining.

As ONUSAL departs, it will be extremely important to work out smooth transitions with the national and international organizations that will remain. The UNDP, which is already understaffed, will have to play an even more central role vis-à-vis the democratic institutions and the reconciliation process. Reconstruction projects must now be absorbed into national development plans. Peace consolidation in El Salvador is a long-term process.

The problems of interagency coordination, the difficulties in negotiating and implementing coherent projects for which international funds are successfully mobilized, the challenges of transitions—from verifying a cease-fire to overseeing reintegration and reconstruction and eventually development—are common to the effective consolidation of peace efforts everywhere. The preparations for peace in Guatemala, under way at this writing, reflect the fact that the international agencies have learned some lessons from their experiences in El Salvador. They have begun with interagency collaboration and an emphasis on broad-based planning. The various agencies of the UN system working in Guatemala are striving to pull together earlier, in consultation with regional and other concerned governments and the various sectors of Guatemalan society, to devise a workable plan of action to implement an eventual peace agenda. As the United Nations replaces the United States in Haiti, its officials look to past experiences, including that of El Salvador, for lessons in how to maintain the momentum of positive change. Obviously, these learned lessons will be effective only if the national actors are prepared to make the necessary changes.

El Salvador sheds light on opportunities as well as the limits for consolidating peace and rebuilding in a postwar context. The peace came about because the parties to the conflict had the political will to establish it, but it may well have unraveled at several points had there not been ample outside support and pressure to move it forward. Peace missions and international assistance to peace processes are fundamental to consolidating peace and rebuilding. The international presence can lay the groundwork that promotes reconciliation, participation, and sustainable development. No peace mission can fundamentally change economic, social, and political structures or make government accountable to its citizens. The "imperfect" institutions described in this Salvadoran case will be improved only by Salvadorans, if at all. But thanks to the process described here, the changes can be effected in a context of peace.

The United Nations will remain at the center of peace consolidation efforts, and its effectiveness will depend in large measure on international consensus and support. That support is needed for the peace processes under way in many countries—the list of nations is already dauntingly long and, one hopes, will soon be longer as present wars are brought to a close. Support is also desperately needed in the United Nations itself, to improve its ability to create, staff, and provide technical and political support for the large numbers of missions under its jurisdiction. This is not the place to enter into a discussion of inefficiencies and organizational reforms, however necessary they may be. It is important that member nations should not themselves be the cause of inadequate UN responses because they have held back essential resources. Rather, national leaders, international UN officials, regional organizations, financial institutions, and nongovernmental organizations should analyze the challenges and needs of peace consolidation and the rebuilding of societies torn by war and should prepare their agencies, together and separately, to change in whatever ways are necessary to meet those needs.

10 Chile

External Actors and the Transition to Democracy

Alicia Frohmann

Chile has traditionally been a country very open to ideas and influence from abroad. This was true at the time before and during the democratic breakdown, in the sixties and early seventies, and also after the mid-eighties, when the return to democratic government began to loom in the distant future.

External actors played an accessory, even crucial, role both at the time of the breakdown of democracy and during the "democratic moment"— when Pinochet lost the 1988 plebiscite and democratic presidential and legislative elections were held in 1989. The inauguration of President Aylwin in 1990 brought to an end seventeen years of military government and international isolation, and Eduardo Frei Ruiz-Tagle's inauguration in 1994 marked the consolidation of democratization.

The degree of international political isolation the Pinochet dictatorship endured was really quite exceptional, even though the economic model implemented by the military regime was strongly influenced by the "Chicago boys" who maintained close links with neoliberal ideologues abroad. However, this connection did not suffice to legitimate the authoritarian government, and Chile became a showcase for economic reform and liberalization elsewhere in Latin America only after the transition to democracy was achieved.

Influence from abroad seldom took the form of direct political or economic pressure, except during the Unidad Popular years when the Nixon administration and U.S. business interests resorted to all kinds of overt and covert actions to bring about the speedy demise of the Allende government.

Before that, the Johnson administration had poured considerable amounts of foreign aid into making the Christian Democratic government a showcase for democracy and socioeconomic reform.

However, historically the Chilean political system was strongly influenced by external political models and many international trends (modernization and dependency theory, Marxism, the Cuban revolution, and later on, Reaganomics, Eurocommunism, and the failure of the Eastern European socialist models) strongly influenced the intellectual and political debate in Chile during the last decades.[1]

The Breakdown and Resurgence of the Democratic Process

The case of Chile is usually presented as exemplary regarding the early development in the nineteenth century of democratic institutions, such as elected presidents and congresses, political parties, and the competition and rotation of state power.[2] Within this perspective, the history of the development of democracy in Chile seems to have followed an "optimum sequence," which began with the emergence of a national identity relatively early after independence; later in the nineteenth century, authoritative and legitimate state structures were established; well into the twentieth century a "crisis" of participation crystallized, which led to the expansion of citizenship rights to non-elite elements.[3]

According to this interpretation, the early development of democracy in Chile was exceptional by Latin American standards and quite comparable to Western European levels during the late nineteenth and early twentieth centuries. Apparently, Chilean political development would also fit into a more general framework where the "incorporation of non-elite social groups was gradual and regulated by the elite and mass political participation—signaling the transition to a fuller democracy—would be accommodated, as socioeconomic pressures for it crystallized, without elites fearing mortal damage to their interests. Thus, wider democratic competition, when it came, was more subdued and less polarized than it would otherwise have been."[4]

This chapter argues that the politics of negotiation and compromise of the pre-1960s period were possible largely because of the very traditional nature of Chilean society, in which most of the political elites, whatever their ideology or party affiliation, were strongly linked by a combination of family, educational, professional, or business bonds. Most Chileans did not belong to this tightly knit network, and political competition and compromise were, to a notable extent, an *acuerdo de caballeros* (gentlemen's agreement), which only marginally considered other social sectors. The leadership of the parties of the left and, later on, the Christian Democrats were mostly excluded from these social and political networks, which handled most of Chile's affairs.

This apparently harmonious process did not extend into the period of higher levels of democratization of the political system in the 1960s.[5] It was not able to endure the increases of voter registration and participation or the drastic reduction of electoral fraud resulting from the 1958 and 1962 electoral reforms. Voter registration rose from 20.5 percent of the total population in the presidential election of 1957 to 34.8 percent in 1964, and 36.2 percent in 1970; voter participation increased from 16.9 percent in 1958, to 29 percent in 1964, and 30 percent in 1970.[6] Electoral fraud, a long-standing practice in rural areas, was made very difficult by the introduction in 1958 of the *cédula única* (single ballot) issued by the state, which replaced ballots issued by political parties. In 1962, voter registration was made obligatory and permanent.

These changes shifted the relative power of the various political sectors, modifying the margin for negotiation and compromise, breaking the conservative stronghold in the countryside, and allowing for the electoral victory of the Christian Democratic presidential candidate in 1964 and of the Socialist candidate of Unidad Popular in 1970. The changes in the electoral system brought forward political forces that effectively challenged the power base of the hegemonic elites, pushing for reforms that would establish a more egalitarian economic and social system. All this happened within a national and international context with strong tendencies toward ideological polarization and pressures for radical reform.

The commitment of the hegemonic elites to the democratic system did not survive the challenge to their economic and social power base. The challenges to the ruling elites that had occurred earlier in Chilean history (the rise of the middle class, the Frente Popular government) had not threatened their power base so seriously and had been successfully accommodated by the political system. However, after the mid-1960s, the clash between the elites' interests and the reforms advocated by the political sectors that benefited from the increased democratization of the political system was crucial in eroding their commitment to democratic institutions. This is the context in which the violent confrontations of the early 1970s and the military coup of September 1973 took place.

External actors certainly contributed to the erosion of democratic institutions during the Unidad Popular government.[7] For the United States and the Soviet Union, Chile became just another scenario in the East-West confrontation, one more chapter of the Cold War. However, Moscow clearly respected the fact that Chile was within the U.S. sphere of influence and never gave the Allende regime any significant support. The link between the Unidad Popular government and Cuba was much closer and was viewed with great distrust by the Chilean right and by Washington. It was, however, the U.S. government and American corporations that, through numerous overt and covert actions, definitely contributed to destabilize Chilean democracy. They were most active in isolating Chile within the international banking community, financing both violent and nonviolent opposition groups, and actively supporting the Chilean procoup military forces. Although the role of these foreign actors was only accessory, their intervention helped decide a crucial moment in Chilean history.

Even if the composition of the hegemonic power groups changed somewhat during the seventeen years of military rule, these maintained their deep distrust of democracy and its consequences. The Constitution of 1980, sanctioned in a dubious plebiscite, and the political legislation enacted by the military junta are good examples of this distrust. When it became clear that the dictatorship would sooner or later need an institutional framework to replace military rule, the authoritarian regime created institutional mechanisms to bring about the transition to a "protected"— in fact, restricted—democracy. These restrictions were designed to avoid the clashes between the social and economic interests of the elites and those of the political sectors empowered by a participatory and representative democratic system.

How Democratic Is the Present Chilean Regime?

The process of transition to democracy has not yet been completed in Chile, even though there is a democratic government, an open party system, and fair elections. The institutional mechanisms and rules set by the former authoritarian regime strongly restrict the scope of power of the democratic government; and the electoral system does not ensure adequate representation and encourages legislative stalemate and political blackmail by minority political sectors. The transition to democracy has not been completed yet, and thus there is still a considerable margin of action for external actors trying to encourage a strong and working democratic system in Chile.

The various stages of the transition to democracy show precisely the extent and limitations of this process.

The Plebiscite

During the evening of 5 October 1988, when the results of the plebiscite began to be read by the opposition radio networks, and later that night, when the triumph of the no vote was recognized first by television broadcasters and, shortly afterward, by one of the members of the military junta, it dawned on the Chilean people and on the many observers and analysts who were following the event worldwide that the democratic moment had finally arrived for Chile.

The events that led to that crucial day had been carefully programmed by the military regime, in order to legitimize and perpetuate Pinochet's rule until 1997. The Constitution of 1980 provided a legal base for continuation of the authoritarian regime: it provided that the military junta would select a candidate who would be presented in 1988, and the Chilean people would be able to vote either yes (accepting the candidate chosen by the military) or no (rejecting that candidate). If this candidate were rejected, free and competitive elections would be held a year later, and a "protected" democratic system would be established.

Even though public opinion polls prior to the plebiscite had been indicating the possibility of a triumph of the no vote, the final result—with 55 percent rejecting the chosen candidate (the general himself) and 43 percent in favor—took most people by surprise.[8] Certainly, the result was very different from what Pinochet had expected, and this led to some initial uncertainty about whether the plebiscite results would be respected by the authorities.

However, tampering with the election outcome was difficult and risky, given both the national and the international context within which the plebiscite had taken place. The business community and the right-wing parties—both staunch supporters of the military regime—felt that Pinochet had had his chance and had lost; even the military argued "that the result was a personal defeat for Pinochet, but not for the political and economic system that they had created."[9] The events of the following years would more than prove the accuracy of this argument.

There was considerable involvement by international actors in order to ensure a fair election, and during those first days of October 1988 events in Chile—one of the last countries in Latin America under military dictatorship—were being followed closely by public attention worldwide. Thus, at a moment when the political and economic system created by the military needed both internal and external legitimation to deepen the globalization of the Chilean economy, the cost of tampering with the election results would have been very high.

The Constitutional Reforms

During the fourteen months between the plebiscite and the December 1989 presidential and legislative elections, the rhythm of Chilean politics accelerated considerably. The opposition parties transformed the Concertación por el NO into an equivalent coalition, the Concertación de Partidos por la Democracia, a group of seventeen center-left parties, the cornerstone of which was the historic alliance between the Christian Democrats and the Socialists. This alliance would present a viable government alternative in the 1989 elections, with a presidential candidate, Christian Democrat Patricio Aylwin, and a list of parliamentary candidates. The right joined in another coalition, Democracia y Progreso, and with the blessing of General Pinochet himself, chose as its candidate the successful former minister of finance, Hernán Büchi.

Before the election, during the first half of 1989, the government and the opposition negotiated a series of reforms to the Constitution of 1980. Pinochet had sworn never to reform the Constitution, and he yielded on only a few points, which, even if the Constitution remained too undemocratic for the opposition, would make democratic government for the center-left coalition somewhat less difficult than originally planned by the ideologues of the authoritarian regime.

As a result of the reforms, the National Security Council would now be balanced equally between civilians and the military and would lose its virtual veto power over controversial legislation, keeping only an advisory role. The unpopular Article 8, which outlawed "subversive" points of view, was eliminated. Constitutional reform became marginally easier, and the president lost his power to dissolve the lower house. The negotiators were unable to reach an agreement to abolish the institution of the nine senators nominated directly by different institutions of the military regime, making it impossible for the Concertación legislators to win a vote in the Senate without compromise. However, the total number of senators was increased from twenty-six to thirty-eight, thus reducing the eventual influence of the nine. The Ley Orgánica de las Fuerzas Armadas (issued in early 1990, after the election of Aylwin but without taking into account what the military had negotiated with the future authorities) would make civilian control over the military very difficult, and the president continued to lack the power to remove the commanders in chief. Some reforms were approved to increase control by the executive over the designation, promotion, and retirement of military and police officers.

The constitutional reforms were approved by a large margin in another plebiscite in mid-1989, and even if some of the reforms were a comedown for the Pinochet government, this new plebiscite definitely consecrated the acceptance and legitimation of the Constitution of 1980 by the majority of political forces. Thus, both the regime and the opposition gained by the acceptance of the reforms in a fair election.

The parties of the Concertación knew that many aspects of the Constitution and of the Electoral Law were undemocratic and would make both government and constitutional reform very difficult. However, at that point, it seemed difficult to advance in any kind of transition to democracy other than that programmed by Pinochet. The acceptance of the "Constitution and the military-imposed election and political party laws [were] a tactical price for a peaceful transition."[10] The dictates of pragmatism and realpolitik recommended acceptance of the existing rules in the short term and a strong drive to make changes once the general was out of government, even if he would continue to be commander in chief of the army.

The authoritarian regime would not yield regarding the restrictions (*leyes de amarre*) on the institutional mechanisms, which were aimed at ensuring the continuation of the political and economic system they had created. A restricted ("protected") democracy was supposed to have a balancing and stabilizing effect on the political system and would thus avoid possible clashes between the hegemonic power groups and the economic and social interests of the majority, such as those that had occurred in the late sixties and early seventies.

The Electoral System

In the case of the presidency, the electoral system is quite straightforward, and there is a runoff ballot only if no candidate obtains more than 50 percent of the vote. In the December 1989 elections, the candidate of the Concertación, Aylwin, received 55.18 percent of the valid votes; Büchi, the candidate of the right and Pinochet's apparent dauphin, obtained 29.39 percent; and Francisco Javier Errázuriz, a rightist populist businessman, received 15.43 percent. Aylwin was inaugurated in March 1990 for a four-year term. In December 1993, the candidate of the Concertación, Eduardo Frei Ruiz-Tagle, won by a similar margin, underscoring the fact that the electoral system tends to freeze the relative position of the various political forces and to perpetuate the status quo.

The presidency, as such, was strengthened by the Constitution of 1980, whose creators had taken for granted the continuation of Pinochet or some other natural successor to the authoritarian regime. However, given the particular conditions of the Chilean transition—the stalemate in Congress regarding the passage of bills presented by the executive, and the continua-

Beyond Sovereignty

tion of Pinochet as commander in chief of the Army until 1997—the Constitution of 1980 has in fact limited Presidents Aylwin's and Frei's real scope of power.

The peculiar binomial electoral system devised by the authoritarian regime was aimed at securing congressional representation of the right—a numerical minority—well beyond its share of the ballot. Even though the Concertación has consistently won a majority of the seats in both houses, the overrepresentation of the right and the presence until 1997 of the nine senators still designated by Pinochet led to many legislative stalemates during the transition years and to a situation where no laws can be passed without the support of at least part of the right. In this context, it has been almost impossible to enact the constitutional and legislative reforms the Concertación has advocated, which require in some cases a two-thirds congressional majority, for some reforms three-fifths, and for changes in the *leyes orgánicas,* four-sevenths.

Thus, given the present political coalitions and the relative electoral strength of the various parties, the electoral system has worked just as its creators in the military regime had intended, giving minority political sectors the chance to have a disproportionate influence on the political system. It seems likely that, in the medium term, this electoral system might have a destabilizing effect on the democratic process: some political sectors lack representation (the left), while others are overrepresented (the right); political frustration grows because of continuous legislative stalemates and the impossibility of achieving reform; and this eventually leads to the discredit and delegitimation of democratic institutions because of their relative impotence.

The direct election of municipal and regional governments was not contemplated in the electoral system created by Pinochet. Thus local government, which had become a centerpiece of the political system created by the authoritarian regime—administering the schools and health, housing, and poverty programs and thus controlling local political patronage—was supposed to remain an administrative entity, "uncontaminated" by party politics. The authoritarian regime thereby hoped to perpetuate, at the local level, a political power base that seemed difficult to achieve through the party system.

Institutional Reform under Aylwin and Frei

The reform of the Constitution and of those laws that allow only for a restricted democratic system has been a priority for the Concertación from the very beginning. The initial government program of the Concertación actually included the proposed constitutional and legislative changes on page 1:[11]

—Election of both houses by popular vote through a system based on multimember districts and a corrected proportional representation. No more designated senators and an increase of the total number of senators and representatives.

—A guarantee of political pluralism and the punishment of undemocratic behavior.

—Changes in both the composition and the functions of the National Security Council, including the president of the Chamber of Deputies and acting in only an advisory role to the president.

—Presidential power to remove the commanders in chief of the armed forces.

—Direct democratic elections of local government (mayors and municipal councils).

—Increased attributions for Congress, in order to ensure an adequate balance between the executive and the legislative powers.

—Respect for human rights as a constitutional guarantee.

—Reform of both the Constitutional Court and the Electoral Court in order to secure their autonomy and independence.

—Reform of the judiciary.

A measure of the difficulty of bringing about these reforms, which are all relevant to a complete transition to democracy, is the fact that of the above list only direct democratic elections of local government were achieved. The other reforms are still pending. In 1992, the executive presented to Congress a package of constitutional reforms (including many of the above list but, also, a few others, such as equal rights for women and men), but their passage was blocked by rightist opposition.[12] In 1994, the Frei administration again presented a package of six constitutional reforms, which were again blocked. Presenting this package of reforms to Congress has almost become a political ritual for the parties of the Concertación. However, most politicians seem to have accommodated to the present rules, and no serious attempts to mobilize public opinion, in order to achieve constitutional reform, have taken place.

The judiciary and especially the Supreme Court (almost all members are still Pinochet appointees) are a serious impediment to investigations regarding human rights abuses. Many magistrates have maintained strong links with the armed forces and are only too willing to pass on most human rights cases, which usually involve the participation of military personnel, to the military courts, where they are almost immediately dismissed. Magistrates who have tried to investigate cases dealing with *desaparecidos* ("the disappeared"), torture, or summary executions have been suspended or dismissed from judicial service.

However, reform of the judiciary has not been achieved under the Aylwin and Frei administrations. It has also been impossible to work around the 1978 law by which the military regime granted amnesty to all perpetrators or abettors of "political crimes" (i.e., human rights violations) prior to that year. Very little has happened on the judicial level in response to the 2,279 deaths and disappearances reported in 1991 by the Truth and Reconciliation Commission designated by President Aylwin. The idea that justice will be done "within the limits of what is possible" became a leitmotif of the human rights policy of the Aylwin administration. Under Frei, human rights issues have had a very low profile, and the executive has not been able to get the resignation of the chief of the police force after a magistrate accused him of obstructing a court investigation of three political homicides committed in 1985.

Civil-military relations have been strained throughout the process of transition to democracy mainly because of tensions with the army, which still remains under the command of General Pinochet (he was designated by Allende in 1973 and will probably remain until 1997). The extension of civilian control over the armed forces has not really taken place, and the armed forces continues as a state within the state: a budget over which the executive and Congress have practically no control, military courts, and almost complete impunity for human rights abuses.

Every few months Pinochet stages some kind of confrontation with the government, to show that he still holds considerable power. The most serious of these public demonstrations of defiance to civilian authority occurred in May 1993. The main issue was once again the treatment of human rights violations committed under the dictatorship. In response to pressure from the military for a rapid resolution of the issue, Aylwin submitted a bill to Congress, proposing to appoint special magistrates (*ministros en visita*) to deal with these cases and employing confidential proceedings to elicit greater cooperation from implicated military personnel. This was criticized both by the military and human rights advocates, and the bill was finally withdrawn. The crisis of 1994, when Frei was unable to impose early retirement on the chief of the police force, reinforced the perception that a definitive solution to these problems seems unlikely.

The personal popularity of Pinochet has eroded, and even though he is already looked upon as one of the important statesmen of Chilean history, he is viewed by public opinion predominantly as a divisive figure of the past. However, most of the proposed constitutional and legislative changes are perceived by the general as outright treason to the military regime, and this has discouraged some politicians and legislators of the moderate right, who might otherwise consider supporting some of the reforms.

Thus, in spite of the general discourse about political consensus and national reconciliation, it has been impossible during the first years of the transition to bring about constitutional reform or to untie the laws restricting democratic government (*leyes de amarre*). The list of necessary political reforms contained in the 1993 program of the Concertación were thus very similar to that of 1989 and will probably continue the same well into the nineties.[13]

Chile is still a deeply divided country at the political level, and the hegemonic power groups with strong links to the right and the armed forces, although they represent the interests of a minority, continue to exercise a veto power over the political system. Interestingly, ideological differences have diminished considerably, and there is significant consensus on the economic level due to growth and economic stability. Thus, today the political reforms would be unlikely to threaten the economic system, which the right (but also other political sectors) cherishes so much.

Foreign Actors and the Transition to Democracy

Foreign actors may affect the development of internal political and economic conditions either by specific actions or by omission. Sometimes local perceptions as to what the reaction of an external actor might be can have an even stronger impact than a specific action, per se. Thus, the symbolic aspects of the language and practices of international politics become especially important.

The impact of foreign actors on domestic affairs gradually has become an accepted fact in the eyes of many political actors, and only in extreme cases is it denounced as outright interventionism.[14] This is the case especially with issues such as the promotion of democracy and human rights and the protection of the environment, which are increasingly considered by many state and nongovernmental actors as issues of supranational concern, where the concept of the sovereignty of nations is applicable only in relative terms.[15] In Latin America nationalist sentiment has always been strong because of the long interventionist record of the United States and, earlier on, because of European powers. However, a result of changing international power relations and the strong links developed by Latin American opposition groups with nongovernmental actors in the United

States and Europe during the years of military dictatorship, the traditional distrust vis-à-vis these countries has decreased.

Today, Latin American intellectual and political elites, especially those at the center-left of the political spectrum, have a much more complex view regarding the political system and decision-making process in the United States. They know that within this system they can find both adversaries and sympathetic allies and that, when differences arise, lobbying and tactical alliances might be much more fruitful than open confrontation.

External actors definitely have had a role in the process of transition to democracy in Chile. In some cases, such as international support before and during the 1988 plebiscite, this role was specifically defined and clearly recognizable. However, there was also another kind of participation in this process, which occurred over a more protracted period of time and which made an equal or even more important contribution to setting the parameters of the Chilean transition: (1) the international involvement in human rights abuses, (2) external funding of local NGOs, social movements, and political parties, which pushed the process of democratization and prepared for a postauthoritarian government, and (3) a wide range of ideas—from Reaganomics, neoliberalism, Eurocommunism, to the dramatic revision of socialism and neostructuralism—that have strongly influenced local intellectual and policy debates.

Although it was not made explicit, external considerations were also important to the technocratic and business elites who supported the authoritarian regime in deciding on some kind of transition to democracy. The military government had been quite skillful in handling international political isolation and the international pressure regarding human rights and the return to democracy. However, given that the abuses of the Pinochet dictatorship had been publicized worldwide, it was becoming obvious by the mid-1980s that, if the "besieged fortress" mentality continued to predominate and there was no regime change, it would be difficult for Chile to advance further in the internationalization of its economy. Structural adjustment, stabilization, the liberalization of trade and investment, and payment of the foreign debt were looked upon with benevolence and interest by Western governments and the international business community. However, a return to democratic institutions was a necessary complement to a market-oriented economy, especially if Chile wanted to become an attractive location for foreign investors and significantly increase its exports to markets abroad. The international legitimation of the increasingly successful economic model was possible only when the return to democracy had begun.

These considerations were in themselves a result of the global drive for democracy during the second half of the eighties. Conditions were rapidly changing in the Soviet Union and Eastern Europe; in the Western Hemisphere, serious efforts were being made to reach a negotiated settlement and advance toward democracy in Central America; and democratic institutions were once again in place in most countries of South America. The end of the Cold War was being sought by the second Reagan administration with a political discourse focused on democracy. Military dictatorship, even if ushered in with the blessing of the U.S. government, had become a liability for a country striving for development based on the internationalization of its economy. At least in the Western Hemisphere, economic performance had to be buttressed by political legitimation for a county to qualify as an attractive business partner. This is the international context within which the transition to democracy began in Chile.

U.S. Involvement in Chile

The U.S. government was undoubtedly the single foreign actor with the most influence over the beginning, the course, and the end of the Pinochet dictatorship. After the 1973 coup, the Nixon and Ford administrations, urged mainly by national security concerns, played a crucial role in consolidating the military regime.[16]

During the midseventies, as a result of the efforts of nongovernmental organizations (principally churches and human rights groups) and some legislators, the U.S. Congress, in an attempt to restrain internal repression in Chile, began to develop an active critical stance vis-à-vis the Pinochet dictatorship and sought to include human rights issues in U.S. foreign policy. In 1976, Congress suspended military sales to Chile and limited economic assistance until the Chilean government made substantial progress on human rights issues.

The Carter administration made a dramatic shift in U.S. policy toward Chile, not only condemning human rights violations but also voting against virtually all loans to Chile in the international financial institutions. Toward the end of his administration Carter imposed diplomatic, economic, and military sanctions on the Pinochet regime for failing to investigate seriously the murders of Orlando Letelier and Ronni Moffit. This case has continued to haunt U.S.-Chile relations because significant progress has been very difficult to achieve.

It was during the second part of the Carter administration that Pinochet decided to hold his first two plebiscites: the first one, in 1978, to attempt to legitimize the human rights practices of his government, and the second one, in 1980, to ratify the constitution. The military government perceived it was under siege from abroad and reached for both domestic and international legitimation. Although the results of both plebiscites were favorable to the military regime (amid serious allegations of fraud), the impact of the Carter administration's policies on Pinochet's efforts to legitimize his regime should not be underestimated. The effects of Carter's human rights policies are difficult to quantify, but they definitely helped save lives and accelerated the liberation of political prisoners. They also helped to consolidate the international political isolation of the Pinochet regime.

The first Reagan administration's policy of "silent diplomacy" blurred the former assertiveness of U.S. human rights policies, and democratic and humanitarian values became once again subordinate to national security concerns and anticommunism.[17] In Santiago, "silent diplomacy was perceived as a green light for repression" and cordial relations were once again established between both governments.[18]

This honeymoon in U.S.-Chile relations did not last very long. Once the mass social protests began in 1983, as a result of the economic crisis that followed the failure of the monetarist model, the U.S. State Department became increasingly concerned about political radicalization and polarization and urged Pinochet "to continue the political dialogue and to respect human rights."[19] In fact, during the second Reagan administration, the emphasis shifted considerably from silent diplomacy to the active promotion of democracy. The replacement of James Theberge by Harry Barnes as U.S. ambassador to Chile in 1985 signaled a definite change of policy vis-à-vis the Pinochet government. Considerable political and economic pressure began to be applied in order to encourage Pinochet to follow the transition schedule contemplated in the Constitution of 1980. Simultaneously, the opposition forces were approached and also encouraged to accept the terms of Pinochet's constitution. Some specific minor economic punitive measures were applied, such as excluding Chilean goods from the generalized system of preferences, (GSP), ending OPIC insurance for foreign investment in Chile, and abstaining on some international loans for Chile.

Although there was no real consensus in Washington over Chile policy (the hard-liners, led by Jesse Helms, were very favorable to the Chilean military), U.S. involvement in Chile increased as the 1988 plebiscite drew near. The U.S. Agency for International Development and the National Endowment for Democracy gave financial support to various civic groups in Chile who were working to guarantee a fair plebiscite.[20] The National Democratic Institute for International Affairs supported the Concertación por el NO during the campaign. A couple of days before the plebiscite, U.S. Deputy Secretary of State John Whitehead summoned the Chilean ambassador and emphasized the "U.S. government's strong desire to see the plebiscite held as scheduled."[21]

Thus, the record of U.S. involvement in Chile during the dictatorship is very mixed. Generally, at the executive level (with the exception of the Carter years), what prevailed were national security concerns and a Cold War logic that perceived military rule in Chile as the only way to deter the advance of communism. The shift during the second Reagan administration can be explained in various ways. On the one hand, the Cold War was coming to an end, and the administration wished to show that its policy of promotion of democracy was applicable to Chile as well as to Nicaragua and the countries of Eastern Europe. On the other hand, Chile remained one of the last countries in Latin America under military rule, and a stagnation in the process of democratization could easily lead to increased polarization and political violence.

The Conditions of the 1988 Plebiscite

While the United States shifted from support of Pinochet to efforts to bring about his exit, most European countries—with the exception perhaps of Great Britain under Thatcher—actively supported the democratic opposition and offered a haven to many Chilean exiles. In fact, the support of the European socialists, social-democrats, and Christian-democrats, as well as that of the party internationals allowed for the survival as well as the ideological renewal of Chilean political parties. If it had not been for this support, the reconstruction of the political party system after the mid-eighties would have been much more difficult, and it would have been unlikely that Pinochet would have encountered such a formidable opposition coalition in 1988.

In mid-1988, political activity was still very limited, and arrest without warrant and arbitrary censorship were possible because of the continuing impositions of a "state of exception." Political conditions seemed adverse for the opposition, and many analysts believed that electoral fraud was likely. However, a favorable international context helped to liberalize the authoritarian system sufficiently to allow the opposition to campaign successfully for the no vote and to set up a parallel computer system to count votes and scrutinize the official results.[22]

It has rightly been argued that "policies of promotion of democracy by diverse external actors, defined as policies of influence and not of destabilization, may contribute to widen the margin for action of both the liberalizing forces within the regime and the moderate opposition, leaving a space for the formation of a minimum consensus to reestablish a democratic

Beyond Sovereignty

system."[23] Not only did pressure by foreign actors contribute to improving the overall conditions for political activity, but also support and funding for the campaign and the parallel computer network definitely increased the chances for the defeat of Pinochet at the polls. During the plebiscite itself, a host of international observers from the National Democratic Institute for International Affairs and elsewhere worked hard to ensure that the election rules and results would be respected. Over a thousand foreign journalists gathered in Santiago and rapidly transmitted what was going on in Chile to the living rooms of millions of people all over the globe.

Although Pinochet remained in La Moneda for seventeen more months (time that he used to make future democratic government difficult), the 1988 plebiscite signaled the democratic moment for Chile as well as the highest point of overt external influence over the process of democratization. The nature and "quality" of this influence from abroad was special: it worked to ensure that all political actors would be allowed a fair chance, and most of the external actors involved stepped aside once their participation was over. The retribution that was expected was the future integration of a democratic Chile into an international system where democracy and respect for human rights were basic qualifications.

Foreign Actors and the Aylwin Government

The presence of numerous heads of state and delegations from many different countries at the inauguration of President Aylwin in March 1990 symbolized the global sympathy and support for the return to democracy in Chile. After seventeen years of isolation, Chile resumed its traditionally close ties with its Latin American democratic neighbors and with many Western and Eastern European countries that had severed their links with Chile during the dictatorship.

The normalization of bilateral relations with the United States began shortly afterward: by the time of President Bush's official visit to Chile in December 1990, Chilean goods were once again included in the GSP, and OPIC insurance for U.S. investment in Chile had been restored. The Letelier case lingered as a reminder of past problems, but the U.S. administration seemed to be understanding of the difficulties the Aylwin government had in achieving substantial progress in this area.

The U.S. government has made considerable efforts in order to aid the reprofessionalization (i.e., exclusive dedication to specifically military affairs) of the Chilean armed forces and strengthen their commitment to the democratic process. Military exchanges, training programs, joint operations, and some arms sales have helped to thaw U.S. relations with the

Chilean navy and air force. However, the army—which remains Pinochet's stronghold—is still very distrustful and often echoes right-wing nationalist sentiment against the United States.

The enthusiastic response of Chilean authorities to President Bush's Enterprise for the Americas Initiative (EAI), and the fact that the U.S. administration singled out Chile as the first likely candidate from South America to join NAFTA, brought the two nations closer than they had ever been in the past.

Progress toward NAFTA was slow during the Bush administration and the early Clinton years but began to accelerate after the Hemispheric Summit of December 1994. However, these developments helped to buttress the democratic government's image of legitimacy, stability, and economic growth. The efforts of the Aylwin administration to show that democracy can be even better for business than authoritarian regimes definitely was helped by Washington's interest in pointing to Chile as a showcase for economic reform, stability, and growth.

It is difficult to speculate how the Chilean economy would have fared had the dictatorship continued, but it is certainly true that it has prospered since the return to democracy. Transnational actors have played a significant role in leading the economic boom of the post-Pinochet era. The fundamental aspects of the present economic model were clearly established during the latter years of military rule, yet the internationalization of the Chilean economy has made big strides in the wake of the return to a democratic regime. It was only after 1990 that foreign investment (and not just foreign debt conversion) began to escalate. Chile became the first country in Latin America to receive a triple-B investment grade rating from Standard and Poor's, and foreign investment rose 22 percent to US$1.38 billion in 1992, while the GNP grew 10.4 percent. Chilean exports boomed to almost US$10 billion in 1992, and Chilean goods have become attractive because of their high quality.

The international economic legitimacy and success of the democratic government has had both economic and political impacts within Chile itself. It has helped to develop a more positive attitude toward democratic government within the local business community and it has also stimulated local investors to increase their own investments in Chile. International human rights groups, which were so active during the years of military rule, have been very discreet since the beginning of the Aylwin government. They have not participated actively in the efforts to sanction the human rights abuses reported by the Truth and Reconciliation Commission, possibly because of lack of encouragement by their Chilean counterparts.

Another external/internal actor, the Catholic church, had a strong impact on political developments during the dictatorship. At a time of great political and ideological polarization, the church took up the defense of human rights and also engaged in efforts to get political adversaries together at the negotiating table. Since the return to constitutional government, however, the church has been engaging more and more in purely religious matters, and episcopal appointments by the Vatican have become increasingly conservative.

Foreign influence on the intellectual and political debate has been very strong. Members of the Chilean intellectual and political elites are extremely receptive to ideological trends from abroad and participate in many international conferences and seminars, in spite of the country's geographical remoteness and insularity. During the years of military dictatorship, foreign funding was crucial to the survival of intellectual activity and to the development of critical perspectives in the newly created think tanks; these funding agencies were a significant channel for ideas about the nature of democracy, civil society, market forces, and the role of the state.[24] Important issues that must be included in an agenda for development and modernization, such as women's rights, the environment, and consumer issues, were also introduced through these channels. The discussion of topics especially relevant to the transition process—democratic governance, regime reform, and parliamentarism—also received considerable input and stimulus from abroad.

These channels were also instrumental in the renewal of the political thinking of the Chilean left. In this case, however, direct contact with the European socialist parties and the personal experience in exile of many political leaders were also very important in bringing about deideologization and change, which still continue. Without this political renewal, the present stability of the political regime—based on the historic alliance between Christian Democrats and Socialists—would have been very difficult.

After the return to democratic government, the think tanks provided many of the economists, sociologists, and political scientists who joined the administration and became policy makers. Thus, the investment in intellectual activity during the years of military rule did in fact have a long-term impact on Chilean society. Today, the think tanks and the generation and exchange of critical thinking has been weakened, due in part to the exodus of intellectuals to the government ranks and also because of the rather excessive emphasis on consensus building.[25] Growing restrictions on international funding are also having a serious negative impact on these institutions. Nevertheless, whatever the fate of these institutions, intellectual influence from abroad is likely to remain strong in Chile.

Lessons from the Chilean Experience

That the Chilean transition to democracy has taken place over a protracted period, and that a variety of external actors were involved in this transition, make it possible to extract a number of plausible lessons from the Chilean experience:

1. The most important external factor in a democratic transition is an international context that requires competitive, representative, and participatory democracy as the basis for the country's participation in the international system. International organizations and nongovernmental actors have an especially important role in setting the parameters of an international system in which democracy and human rights are issues of supranational concern.

2. The strong interest of most developing countries in achieving a successful internationalization of their economy is an important incentive for democratic legitimation. External actors should keep this fact in mind.

3. At a turning point in the process of democratization (such as the 1988 plebiscite in Chile), the influence of, and even direct pressure from, external actors acquire special importance and visibility. This pressure will contribute to the desired effect, however, only if it is truly exceptional and not just part of a continuous practice. Even if only accessory and complementary to the role of internal actors, foreign and transnational actors may play a crucial role when events are decided by marginal differences. The line between influence and intervention should be drawn very carefully; otherwise, the legitimacy of democratic internal forces is easily jeopardized.

4. The long-term involvement of external actors with internal actors (supporting self-confidence building and intellectual contributions to the creation of viable political alternatives) may often be more fruitful than dramatic gestures or strong direct pressure.

5. Once the initial enthusiasm of the democratic moment is over, external actors should not only emphasize the progress in the process of democratization but also keep in mind the deficiencies that remain. Democratization is an incomplete and ongoing process in most countries making the transition from authoritarian rule. External actors can continue to contribute to this process. Special attention should be paid to difficulties in civil-military relations, which can effectively block the course of a transition process. Internal democratic actors should be aided in "winning" over the armed forces for the cause of democracy.

11 Peru

Collectively Defending Democracy in the Western Hemisphere

David Scott Palmer

Peru has achieved unenviable eminence as the Latin American country in which most economic, social, and political indicators show substantial deterioration since the restitution of democracy in 1980. Why did two successive presidents in the 1980s, both with comfortable majorities in Congress, fail to deal effectively with the challenges of building reasonably responsive central government? What explains the third elected president's surprise 1992 suspension of the constitution and subsequent democratic restoration under new rules? What should be the role of the international community in helping make democracy work in Peru?

The Peruvian case highlights the complexities of getting Latin American democracies established. Clearly, the effective exercise of democracy involves much more than elections alone. However, the attainment of a political process in which open elections are regularly held and the results respected is a central and absolutely essential component. Getting to this point has remained elusive for much of the world, including Latin America.

The Latin American Context

The larger regional redemocratization context of which Peru has been a part is truly remarkable. Between 1978 and 1991 every Latin American country except Cuba either retained or returned to electoral democracy.[1] Mexico, Costa Rica, Colombia, and Venezuela were the only countries that had democratic forms before 1978 and that kept them.[2] Panama is the only case of democracy instituted after U.S. military intervention (on the basis of the May 1989 election exit poll preferences!).[3] Put another way, beginning in 1978 with the Dominican Republic and continuing through Haiti in 1991, no fewer than fifteen of Latin America's twenty countries returned to or established elected civilian government after experiencing one form or another of authoritarian rule.

The decade of the 1980s, as a result, witnessed fewer *golpes de estado* in fewer countries than during any previous decade since independence.[4] There were only seven, in just four countries: in Bolivia in 1980; in Guatemala in 1982 and 1984; in Haiti in 1986, 1987, and 1988; and in Paraguay in 1989. Furthermore, of these seven true *golpes* (the case of Panama is a murky one throughout), four were carried out by militaries to open up the political process to democratic elections and only two were mounted to thwart them. Prior to the 1980s, the decade of fewest nonconstitutional government changes was 1900–1909, when there were eight successful *golpes* in six countries.[5] Put another way, between the 1930s and the 1970s, 104 of the 277 changes in chief executives (38%) occurred through *golpes de estado*,[6] whereas for the 1980s it was about half that level (7 of 37, or 19%).

From 1978 through 1992, there were thirty-three national presidential elections in these fifteen Latin American countries, including second elections in eleven countries and third or fourth elections in five of them. Some four-fifths of these second, third, and fourth national presidential votes were won by opposition parties and candidates. Such victories indicate the challenges of governing during a difficult period as well as an emerging willingness by elites to accept opposition rule. Since the 1976 *golpe* in Argentina terminated a brief and tumultuous period of civilian rule, the Haitian military takeover from President Jean-Bertrand Aristide in September 1991 and Peru with its *autogolpe* (self-staged coup) in April 1992 are the only examples over a seventeen-year period of forced political interruptions in Latin American after open elections were held and civilian governments installed. Clearly, the routinization of electoral procedures has become the mechanism of choice for access to political power in the region.

Although several other countries in Latin America have experienced serious political problems, through 1994 at least all had worked them through short of a total collapse of democratic forms. The Brazilian Congress initiated impeachment procedures against President Fernando Collor de Mello to force his resignation. Venezuela experienced two failed military coup attempts in 1992 and then pursued constitutional impeachment proceedings to bring about the resignation of President Carlos Andrés

Pérez in June 1993. In Guatemala, President Jorge Serrano attempted a Peruvian style *autogolpe* in May 1993, which failed to gather domestic support. He was forced to resign as a result and was replaced after intensive intra-elite consultation and international pressure by a respected human rights advocate, Ramiro de León Carpio.

In spite of such difficulties, however, Latin American countries have made significant advances through procedural stages of democracy since the 1970s. The first stage is to hold open elections and accept the results, the second is to hold subsequent open elections at regular intervals with outcomes considered legitimate, the third stage is reached when an opposition party wins subsequent election and takes office, and the fourth stage occurs when the original party or some other party succeeds via the electoral route. Such a pattern suggests important advances in political development, defined as "the routinization of political procedures and practices."[7]

This political routinization is even more impressive because it has occurred during a period both of great economic difficulty for the region and of lowered barriers to voting, such as literacy and age requirements. Economists consider the 1980s as "the lost decade" for Latin America, with negative net economic growth for the region as a whole each year from 1982 through 1992. At the same time, however, the electorate was expanding, in some cases more than doubling. By the end of the 1980s all citizens eighteen years of age and over, literate or not, could vote in every Latin American country for the first time. Effective response to rapid growth in political participation is difficult when economic resources available to government are declining,[8] which was the case in most Latin American countries in the 1980s. Even so, democratic processes held on almost everywhere. Their routinization served, furthermore, to enhance and legitimate an emerging regional consensus (articulated in the OAS Santiago Commitment of 1991) to apply outside pressure on countries that tried to overturn democracies, such as Haiti (1991), Peru (1992), and Guatemala (1993).

Explanations for Democratization

A number of factors, international, regional, and internal, contributed to and helped reinforce democratization in Latin America. They include the following in rough chronological order.

1. The struggle in the United States between the legislative and executive branches in the 1970s, which gave rise to multiple restrictions on executive branch conduct of foreign policy, including foreign military and economic

assistance conditioned to human rights observance and human rights reporting.[9]

2. The Helsinki Accords of 1975, defining human rights in individual, political, and economic terms, agreed to by both East and West, which substantially raised human rights issues consciousness levels worldwide.[10]

3. The Carter administration (1977–81) decision to put pressure on Latin American military governments to respect their citizens' rights.[11]

4. The establishment in the 1970s of such nongovernmental human rights organizations as the Washington Office on Latin America, the Council on Hemispheric Affairs, and Americas Watch; and their significant impact, along with Amnesty International, on legislation and policy during this period.[12]

5. The growing influence and impact of the Inter-American Commission on Human Rights and the UN Commission on Human Rights.[13]

6. European political foundations' (e.g., Konrad Adenauer, Frederich Ebert) support for Latin American political parties, civilian political leaders, and democratic institution building, as well as increased concern of the Socialist International in promoting civilian governments in the region.[14]

7. The failure of most Latin American military governments—these were long-term regimes (rather than short term or personalistic) and directed by the hierarchy of the military—to accomplish their goals while they were in power.[15]

8. *Desgaste militar;* that is, the wearing down of the military, both individually and institutionally, from trying to be politicians and officers simultaneously over an extended period.[16]

9. Economic problems, even crises, in most of Latin America in the 1980s, resulting from heavy foreign debt burdens, world recession, low commodity prices, and high interest rates.[17]

10. Domestic popular opposition, more and more organized over time, even outraged, which reduced the viability of several military regimes.[18]

11. Internal military divisions over policy, which put additional pressure on that leadership to return to civilian rule.[19]

12. U.S. policy changes in the mid-1980s, which increased support for democracy. (New ambassadors to Chile and Paraguay had instructions to expand ties with civilian oppositions; officials made strenuous behind-the-scenes diplomatic efforts to remove dictators in Haiti, which were successful, and in Panama, which were not.)[20]

13. Military negotiations with civilians over the terms of return to democracy, which enabled officers to retain some influence and to be protected from accountability for abuses committed while in office.[21]

14. In Central America, a combination of developments—elected governments in all five countries after 1985, the failure of the Contadora and Contadora support groups, and U.S. policy paralysis after Iran-Contra—

which gave leaders the space to work issues out among themselves and sign the peace accords.[22]

Looking Back

Theorizing on Latin American Democracy

Studies of Latin American politics tend to concentrate on the difficulties the republics have had in establishing stable and democratic political systems.[23] Nevertheless, the early republics' constitutions set out the principles of democratic rule. Furthermore, between the 1870s and 1920s and from the mid-1940s to the early 1960s, increasing political stability occurred based on democratic norms.[24]

The recent rapid shift in the region to electoral democracy soon led several leading analysts to lay out the most relevant elements to explain these changes and their possibilities for success. One systematic, historical, and case-study-based approach includes ten key components for democracy in Latin America. It concludes, somewhat unexpectedly, that external forces have not been determinate in establishing or sustaining democracy but, rather, serve to enhance democratic procedures and practices where they already exist.[25]

1. The early development of a "partial, elite democracy," in which "political competition precedes the expansion of participation" (8,9).

2. Political elites making room gradually for "autonomous institutional expression of new popular interests" (9).

3. The choice of democracy by political elites preceding the presence of a democratic political culture ("the presence of democratic values among the general public or other elites") (10).

4. Popular commitment to democracy being reinforced by successful performance of democratic systems (11).

5. Strong, democratic leadership at such key junctures as founding, responding to new groups' participation demands, economic crises, and national disasters, thereby enhancing and consolidating democratic forms and values (14–19).

6. The presence of "at least one and eventually two or more parties," which "become institutionalized but not polarized" (21–23).[26]

7. The presence of an authoritative, effective, state operating in a rule of law and with an effective judiciary (26–27).[27]

8. The "early development of a pluralistic, less unequal, autonomously organized civil society to check the power of the state and to give expression democratically to popular interest" (35).[28]

9. Steady, broadly distributed, economic growth (43).[29]

10. The progressive incorporation of new social elements into the national system through urbanization, literacy, and education, without strong opposition by political elites (43).[30]

In practice, however, for all but a few Latin American countries, history has not been democracy's ally.[31] Most gained their independence between 1810 and 1840 but did not quickly establish democratic governance. Authoritarianism or political instability predominated. The political routinization under limited liberal democratic auspices, which took place in the late nineteenth and early twentieth centuries, was swept away with the world economic collapse of the 1930s. Economic growth from the early 1940s to the early 1980s certainly contributed to the relegitimation of democratic modalities after the World War II period but was insufficient to sustain it. New authoritarian regimes emerged in the 1960s, dominated the 1970s, and gradually gave way to democracy in the 1980s.

Peru's political history parallels these regional patterns in a number of ways and indicates that many of the essential components for establishing and maintaining democracy have not been present there.

Peru's Authoritarian Political History

What is now Peru was at the center of both the Inca Empire for some 300 years before 1532 and the Spanish Empire in South America for some 300 years from the 1530s until the 1820s. Both were autocratic, authoritarian, and hierarchical in their political, social, and economic orders. This is the distal historic context from which Peruvian politics evolved after independence.[32]

Independence from Spain was earned in the battlefield, culminating in Ayacucho in December 1824, later than for most Latin American countries. Independence was largely fostered by outside forces and by leaders from other parts of the Spanish or former Spanish Empire.[33] The Peruvians were generally reluctant to separate from Spain; those who were not were mostly of the Creole elite. So independence did not represent for Peru a truly definitive or revolutionary break with its past.[34] While this was the case to a greater or lesser degree for all of Spanish and Portuguese America at the time of separation from colonial rule, the carryover to independence of the authoritarian institutions of successive empires was much greater in what became Peru than in any other former New World colony except Mexico.[35]

This carryover was in large measure because these portions of Spain's empire in America (the center) had been more closely controlled, with attendant larger bureaucracies and administrative prestige and the management of greater resources. The presence of substantial amounts of precious metals and large clusters of indigenous populations ensured such interest by the colonizers. This contrasted with other areas (the periphery), including regions we now know as Argentina, Uruguay, Chile, and Costa Rica, where such resources were virtually absent or evanescent. Therefore, the establishment of limited liberal democratic governments based on the international ideological currents of the period was by and large much harder to effect in the new independent countries of the former Spanish colonial center than in those of the periphery. It is not mere accident, then, that the four Latin American countries where democracy developed in the nineteenth century were Chile, Argentina, Uruguay, and Costa Rica.[36]

Other factors—the local leadership, the geography, British trade and investment, foreign wars, and natural disasters—also affected the degree to which democratic organization and institutional practices evolved in the nineteenth century. However, the patterns of the countries at the former core of the Spanish Empire (Brazil, under Portuguese rule, was a different case entirely) were either authoritarianism (caudillo rule, principally) or instability, where no group proved able to build a consensus for governance based on elite rotation. Mexico, the most unstable of the nineteenth century countries (until the 1870s), was one extreme example. Peru, with no elected civilian government until some fifty years after independence and no routinized electoral succession until the turn of the twentieth century, illustrates a military-dominated mode of governance.[37]

No civilian head of state governed Peru for more than a few months before 1872.[38] The total number of years of elected government rule in Peru from independence through 1993 is about sixty-three, or just 37 percent (compared from 77 percent for Chile). More revealing is the presence since independence of only two periods of elected civilian rule with more than two successive elections for head of state: the five presidents during a nineteen-year period at the turn of the century (1895–1914) and the three presidents over almost twelve years ending with the 1992 *auto-golpe*. Of all the countries of Latin America, only Haiti (with thirty-one), Bolivia (with twenty nine), and the Dominican Republic (with twenty-eight) have had more *golpes de estado* than Peru (26).[39] Instability and authoritarianism have gone hand in hand in Peru since independence.

The country's political record clearly suggests that no routinization of civilian institutions under democratic governance has ever taken place. This, in turn, has inhibited the creation of a democratic political culture, even though the organizations usually associated with democracy— parties, unions, interest groups, and media—have pursued their activities extensively over the years.[40] The lingering tentativeness of Peruvian politics has given rise to alternative formulations to permit effective responses to the dilemmas and challenges of governance. These include personalistic dictatorships, such as Augusto Leguía (1919–30) and Manuel Odría (1948–56), military guardianship (1933–39) or long-term rule (1968–80), and independent civilian "antipolitics" (1992 to the present).[41]

The nineteenth century is also important for Peru in setting the political dynamics of the twentieth. When civilian presidents finally did come to power in the 1870s, they did not acquit themselves well. They were considered partly responsible for the War of the Pacific (1879–83) and its disastrous outcome, by reducing military expenditures, maladroitly handling the emerging crisis with Chile, and abdicating authority (and absconding with funds) as war broke out.[42] The war itself was a political, social, and economic catastrophe for Peru. It impoverished the elites.[43] It impoverished the state as well; in 1870, Peru's national government revenues per capita was the largest in Latin America, and as of 1890 only Bolivia and the Dominican Republic were smaller.[44] Furthermore, the war's aftermath ushered in a period of high dependency on foreign creditors and foreign investors, as the government turned over many of the country's assets to Great Britain to cover its debts.[45]

After a turbulent hiatus, it also ushered in the Aristocratic Republic, which lasted from 1895 to 1919 (interrupted only by one brief coup, in 1914). With regular elections, a limited franchise, and controlled participation, Peru's experience at this juncture paralleled that of Chile in the 1840s and 1850s. Unlike Chile, however, Peru failed to consolidate democratic governance at this time, in large measure because of the unwillingness of elected civilian president Augusto Leguía to play by the rules. He usurped power within a year of assuming office in a 1919 *autogolpe* and ruled for eleven years through three manipulated elections.[46]

Such exercise of political leadership was to be repeated periodically thereafter. In the 1930s and 1940s, long-term Alianza Popular Revolucionaria Americana (APRA) party leader Víctor Raúl Haya de la Torre pursued his quest for political power through elections where possible but also through organized violence and coup plotting with sympathetic military supporters. As a result, the dominant cleavage in Peruvian politics through the 1960s was between APRA and the military. This continuing tension severely retarded the development of democratic politics, that is, a polity progressively more representative and popularly based.[47]

Over Peru's political history the military played a dominant role, except for a brief period during the Aristocratic Republic. During the twentieth century, however, the military shifted from being "the watchdog of the oligarchy" to become a reformist institution.[48] During its twelve years of military rule, 1968–80, the officer corps believed it could modernize the country through substantive change without recourse to parties and politics. It failed. In the officers' efforts to use the government to build new structures of participation and reform, they ran up against resource limitations and popular unwillingness to be manipulated.[49] Economic problems, many of the military's own making, largely undid the reforms.[50] Its most enduring accomplishment, the rapid expansion and legitimation of a dynamic Marxist left party and union organizations, was undone by the left's own internal bickering in the course of the 1980s.[51]

Peru's Most Recent Experience with Democracy

While the country's military governments of General Juan Velasco Alvarado (1968–75) and General Francisco Morales Bermúdez (1975–80) faltered in their reforms, to their credit they opted for an orderly transfer of power back to civilian rule (through national elections for a constitutional convention in 1978 and through the Constitution of 1979). Successive presidential and congressional elections in 1980, 1985, and 1990 brought forth clear winners from three different political parties: Fernando Belaúnde Terry of Acción Popular (AP), then Alan García of APRA, followed by Alberto Fujimori of Cambio 90. The elections were generally perceived to be open, honest, and available for the first time to all adult (eighteen years and over) Peruvians. Between thirteen and seventeen parties and groupings also gained access to Congress through these elections, including substantial representation in 1980 and 1985 by a largely Marxist coalition, Izquierda Unida (IU). Municipal elections nationwide were also reinstituted in November 1980 after a fourteen-year hiatus, with pluralities in 1980 for AP, in 1983 and 1986 for IU, and in 1989 for a conservative coalition, Frente Democrático (FREDEMO). The 1990 electoral process even witnessed for the first time voting for regional legislatures. At one level, then, formal or procedural democracy advanced even as the economy deteriorated and political violence became more widespread.[52]

Peru's outpouring of enthusiasm for civilian democracy in the 1980s can be understood in large measure by the failure of long-term institutionalized military rule. When Belaúnde and his AP majority faltered during their 1980–85 mandate, the electorate turned to the best organized and most unified opposition, APRA and García. Then García and the APRA majority's even more dramatic failure turned much of the population against politics as usual, away from traditional parties and leaders. Fujimori and his belatedly mustered Cambio 90 grouping gained the presidency and about a quarter of congressional seats largely on the basis of their appeal as nonpoliticians. They were perceived as concerned citizens coming to rescue the country from the disasters of politics as usual ("a Peruvian like you," was how candidate Fujimori billed himself). Judgments by his countrymen on his performance, therefore, were based primarily on how well he dealt with the country's massive problems: hyperinflation, economic decline, a growing guerrilla threat, a corroding state, and a total cutoff of credit from abroad. They were not determined by how well he played the political game.[53]

Why did Belaúnde and García fail? Belaúnde's difficulties stemmed from several factors.

1. An insistence on restoring the status quo ante, that is, Peru as it was when he was first president (1963–68) before being ousted by the military. Thus he concentrated on restoring elite privileges and dismantling the military reforms of the 1970s and on regaining access to substantial foreign loans even as economic circumstances deteriorated sharply.

2. Failure to act soon enough to stem the rise of the Shining Path when it was still small, weak, and concentrated in a few highland provinces. This failure was because he feared, quite incorrectly, that the military might use the vehicle of counterinsurgency to take political power once again. Many believe this was the case during Belaúnde's first term, when a successful military campaign in 1965 against a Castro-style guerrilla campaign bolstered that institution's capacity and confidence.

3. The pent-up demand by Peruvians for participation and effective government. Any elected government would have had problems meeting these demands, but Belaúnde exacerbated the challenge by being more responsive to elites than to the masses.

4. The severe world recession of the early 1980s, which depressed prices for Peruvian exports, including oil, at just the time that large foreign debt refinancing bills were coming due.

5. The emphasis by the military on repression of the mostly Indian peasantry in dealing with the Shining Path rather than on intelligence gathering and military protection with economic assistance.

6. Disturbances caused by the warm El Niño current off the Peruvian coast between 1982 and 1984, which temporarily changed the country's normal weather patterns by creating flooding in the north and drought in the southern highlands, thus substantially reducing agricultural production.[54]

García's failures were in many ways more consequential than Belaúnde's because of the enormously high expectations that accompanied his election. He epitomized the young, dynamic, can-do, new political leader of the emerging Latin American democracies. He brought with him a recently reunified reform party of long standing in Peru, known for its strong organization. It seemed a perfect match to help get the country moving again, but by the end of his term he had failed miserably on almost every count, for several reasons:

1. Heavy government patronage for the party faithful who had been waiting in the wings for up to sixty years (some 400,000 jobs in all).

2. Loss of the business community's confidence following a disastrous bank nationalization in 1987 after careful cultivation of business in 1985 and 1986.

3. The prison massacre of 279 Shining Path guerrillas in June 1986 authorized by García and then disavowed as excesses by the police and the military.

4. The suspension of all foreign debt repayments, beginning in early 1988, including obligations to governments, the World Bank, the International Monetary Fund, and the Inter-American Development Bank. By the end of his term the country was almost totally bereft of access to international credit.

5. A dramatic economic collapse during the last half of his term, in which inflation reached four-digit figures for the first time in Peru's history and gross national product declined by over 20 percent.[55]

García's failures reinforced those of Belaúnde to set the stage for the electoral triumph of the political independent Fujimori as well as for his suspension of democracy. On 5 April 1992, President Fujimori announced the "temporary" dissolution of Congress, the Justice Ministry, and the General Accounting Office and assumed emergency powers. At the time, this *autogolpe* made little sense.[56] The economy was starting to turn around. International banks and foreign governments were poised to provide substantial assistance, and some funds already had begun to flow. The opposition-controlled Congress and the president had their disagreements, but still they worked tolerably well together. The Shining Path guerrillas posed a significant challenge, but democracy seemed the best bulwark against their advance. Even though there was generalized disgust for a judicial system unable to perform its mission, many specialists believed it could be remedied short of abandoning the democratic process.

Predictably, most of the world reacted in horror and prepared for the worst—repressive dictatorship and increased chances for a Shining Path victory. In Peru, however, Fujimori's favorable rating in weekly opinion polls skyrocketed. Even so, he was able to turn his *autogolpe* to advantage in a substantive way only after the capture of the head of Shining Path on 12

September 1992. Although the arrest had much more to do with careful police intelligence work than with the suspension of democracy, in its aftermath the decrees upping jail penalties and providing speedy trials for terrorism, now by military courts, could be more easily justified. More than any other event, the capture served to legitimate Fujimori's suspension of democracy. It also served to give Peru's president and his beleaguered government desperately needed political space to bring the country back from the brink of disaster.

Police and military followed up Guzmán's capture with hundreds of additional arrests and rapid trials; hundreds more turned themselves in under a new "lenient treatment" law. Most were from Peru's other guerrilla organization, the Tupac Amanu Revolutionary Movement (MRTA). At last, in this long-festering struggle, accounting for some 30,000 deaths and disappearances and some $24 billion in direct and indirect property damage from 1980 through 1992, the government appeared to be gaining the upper hand. President Fujimori was the clear beneficiary.[57]

National and municipal elections also served to strengthen his position, largely because he organized them to encourage new political groups to register and to keep established parties off balance. The November national-al vote—for eighty Constituent Assembly delegates to reform the 1979 Constitution and then to serve as a congress for the balance of Fujimori's five-year term (until 28 July 1995)—delivered to the president a legislative majority for the first time.[58]

The January 1993 municipal elections represented successes of a different sort. The Shining Path's efforts to disrupt them, a key objective in the guerrillas' long-term take-over strategy, were far less effective than they had been in 1989.[59] The established political parties lost out as well. After most chose not to register for the November vote, they decided to participate in the January elections, fully expecting to gain a new launching pad for success in 1995. However, they fared poorly. Residents of most major towns and cities voted for independent candidates instead.[60]

By means of these votes, President Fujimori succeeded in outmaneuvering the politicians and their parties while simultaneously meeting the OAS demand for timely free and fair elections to restore democracy to Peru. Along the way he also succeeded in forcing into exile his predecessor, Alan García, whose political rejuvenation in early 1992 may have been the proximate cause of Fujimori's 5 April *autogolpe*.

At root, Fujimori's political success is based on his ability to tap into a reservoir of popular discontent over the failure of two successive elected governments. Parties over the course of the decade were not able or willing to meet the needs of their constituents. However, the Shining Path was too extreme for all but a few. Voter turnout rates in successive elections demonstrate the declining relevance of formal democracy in large swaths of Peru's hinterlands for the poorer, more Indian, segments of the population. These same areas also tend to be those most affected by the Shining Path, MRTA, or government military-police repression.[61]

At the same time, political parties did not serve effectively as transmission conduits for popular concerns, and electoral strength did not translate into meaningful government response. Belaúnde's party alliance equated popular support with a mandate to turn back the clock on reforms rather than to make them more responsive to popular needs. García and APRA mistakenly believed that their electoral mandate legitimated implementation of the historic party platform, colossal political patronage, and nationalistic bombast. The vote for Fujimori thus represented popular rejection of the party system and politicians. His support actually increased when his government's initiatives, like the economic shock program, began to produce results, even though they caused even greater hardship for many.[62]

Nevertheless, the Fujimori government was not very successful in responding effectively to citizen needs through 1993. Spending per capita for such social services as education, social security, health, and housing actually declined during the first two and one-half years of his administration.[63] Peru's acute financial crisis was part of the explanation, as was the Fujimori government's lack of administrative expertise. President Fujimori's personalized approach to governing was also an important factor.[64] The office of the president assumed a particularly significant role with this approach but was too small to be able to deal effectively with the enormous challenges it had to face.

With the decline of effective parties on the input side of government and of an effective bureaucracy on the output side, much of Peru's population was forced to find its own solutions to its problems. They turned to local self-help organizations, neighborhood soup kitchens, and nongovernmental entities to give and receive assistance.[65] The result was the emergence of an "informal polity," based on these expanding networks of social organizations at the local level and their leaders.[66] The dynamic was analogous to the informal economy that developed in the 1970s and 1980s to respond to people's needs as Peru's formal economy became less and less able to do so.[67] It is too early to tell if this informalization of politics can be constructively channeled from the grass roots to Peru's political center. If it could, the result might represent a genuine solution to the perennial Latin American problem of political structures in the center, which are endemically unresponsive to the majority of citizens in the periphery.

A less charitable interpretation, however, emphasizes the personalization and deinstitutionalization of the democratic process. The manipulated "normalization" after the *autogolpe,* including national and municipal elections, a new constitution, and a national referendum, represents in this view thinly disguised attempts by Fujimori to legitimate the informalization of politics in order to perpetuate his "antipolitical" mandate. While the result could be technically successful in the short term in meeting some of the population's basic needs, it would remain inherently unstable due to a lack of institutionalization.

The Role of International Actors

Given the particulars of the Peruvian case in the larger context of Latin American political history and democratization, what contribution can international actors make toward democracy's collective defense there? Several sensitive issues are involved. One is a definition of democracy itself: Whose should be used? A second is the principle of nonintervention as a fundamental and historic tenet of Latin American countries' foreign policies. A third is the distinction between collective intervention in response to threats to the peace, breaches of peace, or acts of aggression, on the one hand, and such intervention in response to internal breakdown or a domestically generated threat to democracy, on the other. The former is much easier to justify under international law than the latter.[68]

A fourth sensitive area concerns sovereign and legal international acts and initiatives of governments, which come to have very negative, if usually unintended, consequences for those same states' own democratic governance. Peru's recent experience is relevant and includes massive foreign exchange expenditures for military equipment and the contracting of excessive foreign debt. Does responsibility for extricating such states from their self-induced predicaments rest exclusively with the states' leaders and domestic organizations and institutions? Or should the international community or some entities of that community take major initiatives to deal with such situations?[69]

A fifth area includes cases in which a nongovernmental actor works diligently to undermine fledgling democracies by adducing a higher revolutionary cause. Peru's Shining Path is an example. The resulting dynamic of violent initiatives of the nongovernmental actor creates a cycle of destructive cumulative causation, including inappropriate and repressive initiatives by the democratic government's own agents of authoritative force— the police and armed forces. The violent dynamic also reveals hitherto

Beyond Sovereignty

unobserved institutional weaknesses of the democracy, such as inappropriately trained forces of order or a weak judicial and penal system.[70]

Continuing violent actions by the nongovernmental actor create, over time, a self-fulfilling prophesy: a nominally democratic government that is more and more repressive and less able or willing to follow due process and its own laws. The government's legitimate right to protect itself and its citizens from violent attack is progressively delegitimated by its own actions. In the process, the ideological correctness of the undemocratic actor's violent actions is enhanced and its own legitimacy progressively established. How can the international community contribute to the reversal of this destructive cycle of cumulative causation? Is it sufficient or appropriate to emphasize sanctions against the government, however reasonable the argument that governments need to be held to a higher standard of accountability for violations of their own laws and procedures than nongovernmental actors? What initiatives can be appropriately brought to bear against a nongovernmental actor historically unwilling to respond to external diplomatic pressures?[71]

The role of foreign actors has been quite significant in Peru. However, the record indicates that the effect on democratic procedures and practices has rarely, if ever, been determinate. In fact, Peru's longest period of democratic government, the so-called Aristocratic Republic of 1895–1919, emerged after, not before, the calamitous War of the Pacific. This war included temporary foreign occupation by the victorious Chilean forces, in 1881–83, as well as substantial resource transfers to Great Britain to cover war loans (including the railroads, a large jungle tract, and guano production). The republic's temporary consolidation coincided with economic liberalization and rapid increases in foreign investment.[72] These liberal economic policies continued long after the democratic government's termination in Leguía's 1919 *autogolpe*.[73]

So Peru's one earlier extended period of democratic rule had its roots in hardship and adversity. While reinforced by expanding economic activity based largely on foreign private economic actors, democratic government's demise in 1919 neither resulted from nor occasioned economic collapse. The end of the Aristocratic Republic, like its beginning, stemmed fundamentally from internal rather than external factors. Foreign investors and foreign trade helped stimulate economic growth, jobs, and expanding government resources, except for the 1929–33 period.[74] However, they did not provide a context for democratization in Peru from the 1930s through the 1960s, primarily due to the deep domestic political cleavage between the military (allied with the elites through the 1950s) and APRA.

The strong opposition of the U.S. government during the Kennedy ad-

ministration to the Peruvian military's July 1962 *golpe* (following an inde-
cisive national election) quite probably shortened the junta's rule to just
one year and contributed to the satisfactory conclusion of the 1963 democratic elections with the Belaúnde presidency. However, equally strong U.S.
official support of an American private company's efforts to negotiate a
favorable settlement with the Peruvian government (over nationalization of
Standard Oil's International Petroleum Company subsidiary), including
economic and military assistance cutoffs during peak years of the Alliance
for Progress, certainly contributed to the erosion of democracy and the
military *golpe* of 1968.[75]

While various other, largely domestic, factors were at work as well at
this time,[76] U.S. government pressure helped provoke the military institution's nationalistic response ending the traditional liberal economic
growth model, which Peru had pursued since the late 1880s. However, the
new nationalism soon proved insufficient to generate poles in spite of
nationalizations, reforms, and rapid public sector expansion. U.S. government opposition throughout was important, if not decisive. The failure of
the military's original goal of domestic private and public investment to
finance reforms through improved distribution of economic growth led it
by the early 1970s to turn to newly available outside resources. As a result,
Peru's total foreign indebtedness increased from about $800 million at the
time of the 1968 military takeover to almost $8 billion twelve years later.[77]

The eventual result was exactly the outcome the Peru military had
sought to avoid: a new dynamic of external dependency, which put in
jeopardy both the enlarged state and its reforms. The democracy restored
in 1980 inherited the burden and could not extricate itself. Belaúnde em-
braced refinancing and new loans but got caught in the world economic
downturn of the early 1980s. García adopted a strategy of limiting debt
servicing to a small percentage of export revenues but stopped payments
altogether in 1988, with devastating consequences. Peru's total external
debt exceeded $22 billion by 1990. Fujimori, out of sheer necessity, pur-
sued an international policy of economic reinsertion and a domestic policy
of shock and liberalization. While inflation was brought under control, the
consequence was further reduction of government resources for the rapidly
growing number of needy Peruvians.

In sum, Peru remained trapped in the foreign loan box fully fifteen years
after the first debt crisis outbreak in 1977–78. Both international financial
institutions and foreign governments showed considerable willingness to
help Peru's beleaguered democracy by putting together a substantial refinancing package of some $2 billion and government assistance in excess of
$1 billion. However, when Fujimori suspended democracy in April 1992,

the international community responded almost immediately by postponing implementation of their agreements. One casualty was Peru's incipient economic recovery, now set back by almost two years. Another was the precarious welfare of several million poor Peruvians. The evidence strongly suggests that these setbacks could have been avoided had the country's elected president chosen to maintain democratic governance, however imperfect.

As in the case of Haiti a few months earlier, the international community concurred for the most part in the need to take substantial measures to force Peru back into a democratic mode (see Chapters 5 and 8 in this volume). However, in substantial respects the Peruvian case differs from that of Haiti. Most significantly, the perpetrator of democracy's suspension was the elected civilian president. Of equal importance, the *autogolpe* was in large measure a response to democracy's failures and not to the failure to give democracy a chance. These included virtual economic collapse, substantial reduction in government capacity and bureaucratic paralysis, judicial immobilism, and expanding guerrilla activity. There were also growing human rights abuses as the conflict spread, even though between two-thirds and four-fifths were committed by the insurgents. What was remarkable in Peru was that governments had been able to continue democratic forms for as long as they did and that the suspension of these forms, when it came, was not more convulsive.

Given these circumstances, it is not surprising that the international community's response was mixed. On the one hand, the U.S. government took a strong and decisive stance. This was at least in part because various executive branch agencies as well as the Congress had paid a remarkable amount of attention to Peru's travails under democracy for a country that at no point represented a primary U.S. policy concern.[78] Many officials felt betrayed, perhaps none more so than Assistant Secretary for Inter-American Affairs Bernard Aronson, who was in Lima for meetings, including one scheduled with President Fujimori, at the very time of the *autogolpe*. The United States immediately suspended economic and military assistance, recently approved by Congress after long and difficult negotiations, although humanitarian aid and most of the antidrug program were continued. The U.S. government also used its considerable weight both in the international finance community and in the Peru Support Group (a dozen countries) to suspend some $2 billion in bridge loans, a $420-million new Inter-American Development Bank loan, and several hundred million dollars in the Support Group assistance package. Of the major participants, only Japan chose not to follow the U.S. lead.

On the other hand, the role of the OAS was more modest. The Santiago

Commitment of 1991 stipulated an emergency session of OAS foreign ministers to discuss the threat to democracy in Peru and to decide what measures to take. The resolution of this session lamented the suspension of democracy, urged its expeditious reinstatement, and authorized the sending of an OAS mission to Peru. But it imposed no sanctions nor a specific timetable. In part, this was because Peru's *autogolpe* occurred after the precedent-setting Haitian coup, the first in which the Santiago Commitment provisions were invoked. In spite of intense OAS involvement in Haiti, it had not succeeded in restoring democracy. Furthermore, Peru's interruption was less dramatic and less violent and did not involve a military takeover or the removal of an elected head of state.

Another moderating consideration was the diplomatic skill and experience of the Peruvian OAS ambassador, Luis Marchand, President Fujimori's first foreign minister and a former ambassador both to the United States and to Chile. In addition, Peru's president placated the OAS almost immediately by recognizing its authority, agreeing to respect its deliberations, and appearing before its May 1992 Bahamas meeting of foreign ministers to submit a detailed plan for the restoration of democracy "within a year."

In essence, the OAS accepted the official Peruvian position that the measures suspending democracy reflected the special circumstances then present in the country and that they were temporary. In fact, however, government resources for the poor declined, and government human rights violations increased sharply after 5 April. In addition, President Fujimori overtly manipulated the rules of democratic restoration to ensure an outcome favorable to him. Even so, national elections for a constitutional convention congress were held in November 1992, followed by municipal elections in January 1993. Observer missions under OAS auspices certified the national election's validity, thereby getting President Fujimori, for all intents and purposes, off the OAS hook.[79]

Human rights organizations were not comfortable with OAS certification on procedural rather than substantive grounds. The Washington Office on Latin America, Americas Watch, and Amnesty International emphasized, instead, continuing high levels of disappearances and other human rights violations through 1992. They were also concerned with military impunity and with the absence of due process due to post-*autogolpe* decree laws establishing rapid trials for accused guerrillas in military courts—with hooded magistrates, life sentences, and limited grounds for appeal. While they noted Shining Path abuses, their main focus was on government human rights violations. They relied on Peru's independent Human Rights Coordinator office (Coordinadora de Derechos Humanos) for documentation on abuses; their support helped preserve the Coordinadora's integrity and ability to continue to function.[80]

Although these human rights organizations consistently opposed U.S. military assistance to Peru, they had been unsuccessful in preventing the U.S. Congress from approving some $24 million in such aid in September 1991. This was ostensibly part of the Andean Initiative drug war campaign, but it was justified primarily on grounds of protecting democracy from subversion financed by drug trafficking. Fujimori's *autogolpe* abruptly ended such justification, and military assistance was suspended forthwith by the U.S. government. Voluble opposition by the leading human rights organizations, the capture of Guzmán and key lieutenants, and the election of President Clinton combined to make quite unlikely any renewal of U.S. military assistance in the near future. In fact, the new U.S. administration moved quickly to assert its concerns regarding human rights violations in Peru by working to delay the normalization of Peru's economic relations with the international financial community and to continue suspension of bilateral nonhumanitarian economic aid.

This combination of human rights organization lobbying and U.S. government initiatives may very well have contributed to the sharp reduction in Peruvian government abuses in 1993 and to the Fujimori regime's growing willingness to investigate past violations by its military and police forces. It also illustrates the U.S.-based human rights organizations' view that they can be most effective by making relevant U.S. government agencies and Congress aware of their concerns, which are then reflected in U.S. policy.[81]

While democratic electoral procedures have been reestablished in Peru and the Shining Path's capacity to disrupt the country seems to be waning, external agencies, including the Inter-American Commission on Human Rights, continue to be concerned about the restrictions on due process imposed by judicial reorganization and about the changed procedures for the prosecution of guerrillas after the *autogolpe*.[82] Yet Peru insists that its situation, with a radical guerrilla group threatening to destroy the country and a judiciary incapable of effective response, required extraordinary measures. Swift justice, Peruvian authorities argue, even if sometimes arbitrary and conducted under a military aegis, has lanced the terrorist boil and restored some semblance of security to the country. Extraordinary times require extraordinary measures, they argue. Yet it is also the case that outside governments and organizations have played a key role in keeping political and legal processes in Peru from being even more arbitrary.[83]

As of late 1993, Peru seemed well on its way to both political and economic normalization. The capacity of the international community to influence Peru's prompt restoration of democratic forms was considerable. However, it was less successful in restoring the democratic status quo ante. In large measure this was because President Fujimori's *autogolpe* had substantial popular support.[84] Most Peruvians blamed the democratic process itself and its elected leaders for putting their country into the parlous state they believed Fujimori was trying to overcome. In short, the Peruvian case makes clear the limits of international sanction for violations of democratic procedures and practices when those violations have high levels of public approval and when democracy itself is seen as part of the problem.

For the United States, Peru presents a complex set of back-burner foreign policy issues which defy quick or easy resolution; specific U.S. foreign policy objectives involving democracy, human rights, guerrillas, drug trafficking, economic liberalization, and immigration intertwine here. Over the past several years, American policy makers have spent an inordinate amount of time worrying the Peru bone without a lot of visible success. So the temptation may be great for the United States to write Peru off with such moral justifications as Peru's continuing human rights abuses or a shift in the U.S. "drug war" priorities.

That would be a bad mistake. More lives will be saved and more people's precarious situations improved if the United States moves to normalize relations. Concretely, this means a leadership role in restoring hundreds of millions of dollars of aid through the Peru Support Group and in encouraging the international financial institutions to complete, posthaste, the long-awaited $2 to $3 billion international economic reinsertion process. Peru must have both to regain real economic growth.

In turn, economic growth will reinforce efforts now under way within Peru to promote economic liberalism, strengthen government welfare services, reduce drug trafficking, eliminate the guerrilla threat, and increase the population's access to politics. Such normalization would also give the United States greater leverage on both the human rights and drug trafficking issues. In short, nuanced pragmatism rather than strident moralism makes the most sense in U.S. dealings with Peru.

12   *International Support for Democratization*

A Map and Some Policy Guidelines
Derived from the Four Case Studies

Anita Isaacs

The topic of international support for democratization has attracted the considerable attention of both scholars and policy makers in recent years. While scholarly efforts to unravel the dynamics of democratic transition have been motivated by the search for a paradigm to explain the democratic tide that has surged of late, policy makers have been driven by the need to formulate new responses to a rapidly changing international environment.

The rich detail and analysis contained in the case studies presented in this section do much to advance our thinking on both these fronts. The analysis of the successes and failures of democratization in Haiti, El Salvador, Chile, and Peru enable the reader to construct a map, locating the diverse actors involved and tracking the varied external influences. After studying this map, the reader is also in a position to suggest guidelines designed to help steer members of the international community engaged in democratization efforts along a policy path. While not the most obvious, direct, or easiest of routes, the one offered may well be most likely to lead eventually to the preferred destination.

Mapping the Terrain

The Players

It is widely accepted that the contribution of external actors to democratization has been relatively minor. To the extent that the international community has made a difference, it has done so at the margins, encouraging and nurturing a domestically rooted process of regime change.

Certainly, the case studies presented here confirm the secondary importance of external actors to the twin processes of democratic transition and consolidation. As each case suggests, the assistance of external players has seemed most significant when it has come in response to a domestically inspired effort at political transformation. Thus, as Alicia Frohmann notes in her review of the Chilean experience, the contribution of external actors to the process of transition was most apparent through the assistance they provided during the 1988 plebiscite. The technical assistance offered, as well as the presence of international observers during the plebiscite, served to guarantee a free and fair vote and results that were respected. The Chilean electorate voted no in October 1988; the international community was able to help ensure that the Chilean popular will was respected. Similarly, as Patricia Fagan notes in her analysis of El Salvador, the international peace process was pursued in response to domestic requests for assistance. Indeed, it was only when internal and external actors agreed on the need for mediation that genuine progress could be made in translating weariness with war into support for peace and, ideally, also for democracy.

By contrast, the examples of Haiti and Peru reveal how difficult it is for the international community to encourage democratization in countries where the democratic commitment of popular or powerful sectors of the population is less than wholehearted. As noted by Anthony Maingot, elite intransigence, coupled with the powerlessness of the Haitian peasantry, stymied sustained international effort to negotiate the restoration to power of the first democratically elected president in Haitian history, Jean-Bertrand Aristide. It was only at the very last minute, when faced with the reality that force would indeed be used, that the Carter mission succeeded in persuading the Haitian military leadership to step down. In the Peruvian case, extremely high levels of domestic popular support both for the "Fujicoup" and for the Fujimori government's counterinsurgency effort enabled Fujimori to pay lip service to international calls for a prompt restoration of democracy while, in actual fact, gaining international acceptance for his self-styled and gradual process of return to representative democracy. Fujimori, moreover, achieved the outcome he desired: his election (in April 1995) to another term as president.

But the case studies offer the reader much more than a simple confirmation of the secondary influence of international democratization efforts; they also highlight the diverse character of the many international participants in that process. Not surprisingly perhaps, the U.S. government has been a key political actor. Although its contribution to democratic break-

Beyond Sovereignty

down in Chile and to the deterrence of democracy in Central America are most notable, U.S. government support for democratization, during the Carter interlude and from the mid-1980s onward, did play a part in facilitating democratic transitions. Yet the U.S. government has not been the sole government actor. As Fagen points out in her study of El Salvador, Latin American governments, through their involvement in the Contadora and Esquipulas initiatives (which were opposed by the United States), established the basis for a negotiated political settlement to the Central American crises. On one occasion—to wit, the UN-brokered peace in El Salvador—those efforts have produced dramatic results and lessons, which are likely to be applied to current UN efforts in Guatemala and Haiti. In the case of Peru and Haiti, however, for reasons that reveal both the historic weakness of the OAS and its membership's reluctance to abandon stato-centric views of sovereignty, the OAS response was insufficiently categorical to secure either the restoration of Aristide or the relinquishing of dictatorial powers by Fujimori. In a different vein, Palmer notes Japan's reluctance to sanction publicly the Fujimori government in the wake of the *autogolpe,* as evidenced by its refusal to heed U.S. pressures to suspend economic aid.

Intergovernmental actors have also been actively involved in democratization efforts. To be sure, the United States has shown a recent willingness to work through the offices of multilateral institutions in an attempt to promote democratization, even in this hemisphere. On one occasion, to wit the UN-brokered peace effort in El Salvador, those efforts have produced dramatic results. In the cases of Peru, however, for reasons that reveal both the historic weakness of the OAS as well as its membership's reluctance to abandon stato-centric views of sovereignty, the OAS response was insufficiently categorical to secure the relinquishing of dictatorial powers by Fujimori.

NGOs have also worked diligently to encourage democratization. Private independent foundations, as well as publicly funded institutions (such as the National Endowment for Democracy and European party foundations), have sought to assist democratic transitions. They have been joined in that endeavor by private voluntary organizations, whose efforts have been more focused at the grassroots level. And, as hinted at in several of the case studies, the international financial and business communities have a critical role to play, not least in the contribution they might make to the ongoing process of democratic consolidation.

Finally, as Frohmann remarks in observations about Chile—observations that might hold as true for El Salvador during the 1980s or for Peru today—the exile community is another international participant in the process of democratization. The exile experience, as well as the bridge that this community provides between the international and domestic political realms, enable the political leadership in exile to nurture democratic transition in unique ways.

The Instruments

The mention of actors immediately raises the question of the instruments that are either available to or employed by each of these players in their efforts to encourage democratization. The diversity of instruments is at least as striking as that of the actors themselves, ranging from those designed to have a punitive effect on democracy's usurpers to those intended to reinforce democracy and reward would-be democratizers.

At the punitive extreme lies intervention. Several of the essays in this volume begin to craft a persuasive argument for the use of force in defense of a redefined, less statocentric, notion of sovereignty. Yet the case studies are equally convincing in underscoring the difficulty in mobilizing support for intervention. As the Haitian experience reveals, the inability to clearly define U.S. interests provoked opposition among members of Congress and the U.S. public, which persisted even after the mission was under way. Moreover, the lukewarm regional reaction to the U.S. intervention in Haiti reminds us how fiercely resistant Latin Americans remain to U.S. military involvement in the hemisphere, no matter how well intentioned. Punitive measures are thus better reduced to diplomatic pressure and to the enactment of sanctions. The latter ranges from the suspension of military and economic assistance, as seen most recently in the case of Peru, to the imposition of an embargo, as witnessed in the Haitian case.

At the other end of the spectrum, the instruments available to reinforce and reward democratization are more varied and imaginative, a reflection in large measure of the diverse international players. As Frohmann notes, for instance, the political exile community assists democratization through the transmission of ideas. The political learning acquired by Chilean exiles exposed to European social democracy was thus critical for the renovation of the Chilean political left, facilitating accommodation among that country's political parties and culminating in the successful NO campaign.

The particular contribution of NGOs and voluntary organizations, explored by Kathryn Sikkink elsewhere in this volume, has also been observed by the authors of these case studies. As Palmer notes, international human rights organizations played a critical role in focusing international attention on the crises in Latin America and in making these crises a domestic policy concern. The larger foundations, public and private, European and U.S.-based, were also important international players. For the most part, these institutions have worked at the elite political level, supporting research on democratic construction and reconstruction, supporting the dialogue among long-standing political adversaries, or providing technical assistance to political parties and to those responsible for the electoral process. Voluntary organizations have played as central a role; by helping to mobilize and organize marginal sectors of society, they helped nurture a growing civil society, which is vital for the sustenance of democracy. Moreover, as noted in the Peruvian case, these new communal organizations tended to compensate for the weakness of formal political institutions by providing alternative vehicles for articulating local interests.

The tasks of easing stabilization and stimulating economic recovery require an active and concerted effort on the part of a set of international actors, including foreign governments, international financial institutions, and foreign investors. The challenges are substantial. Fragile democratic regimes must struggle initially to ensure that the burdens of austerity are not so unevenly spread or hard felt as to diminish popular support for democratic governance. They subsequently face the uphill battle of spurring renewed economic growth, a prerequisite for establishing effective leadership credentials. To meet these challenges successfully, however, they must count both on foreign investment and on significant economic and technical assistance, which governmental and intergovernmental actors are best placed to provide.

The Timing

The question of timing is also raised by these four case studies. Its answer is an imprecise one. The moment when external actors can aspire to contribute to democratization appears to be a prolonged, almost continuous one. It begins as soon as (if not sooner than) a democratic regime has been overthrown, and it continues well beyond the "magic moment" associated either with transition elections or with the transfer of power, as the international community may be called upon to assist fragile elected regimes undertake the subsequent, difficult process of democratic consolidation. At every stage along the way, different external actors play different parts, entering and exiting the stage as their roles assume varying degrees of visibility and importance.

Thus, by way of illustration, the work of the international human rights community in documenting the violations that tend to follow the imposition of a dictatorship can be critical in focusing immediate international attention on abuses and in mobilizing an international response. Those pressures can also help guarantee the physical survival of leading democratic opposition figures, who are likely to become central players in an eventual transition. Along similar lines, throughout the period of dictatorial rule, NGO and voluntary organizations are engaged in efforts to enable a dialogue to take place on achieving a transition to democracy and establishing a viable democratic regime. They also strive to empower new political actors to participate in that dialogue and in the eventual transition and consolidation process. The willingness of foreign governments, acting both bilaterally and multilaterally, to send signals of disapproval to the authoritarian leadership, whether through diplomatic channels or through the skillful imposition of sanctions, can help deter an authoritarian takeover or persuade authoritarian rulers to carry through with a transition. Timely responses by external actors (governmental, multilateral, nongovernmental) to democratic requests for assistance, whether with electioneering in Chile or internally brokered mediation in El Salvador, can also support the transition in its most critical moments. And sustained international private and public assistance in the aftermath of the transition can make a considerable difference in enabling the long-term survival of democratically elected regimes.

Some Policy Guidelines

In highlighting the diverse external actors, the varied democracy-promotion instruments employed, and the real and possible impacts that these actors and instruments have on democratization, the analysis presented in these cases studies, and more generally in this volume, breaks new ground. Upon reflection, moreover, it seems to me that one can draw more general conclusions, offered here in the form of a travel advisory, to guide the actions of those members of the international community able and willing to assist in the democratization effort.

    1. *Let Latin Americans be the guides.* Each of these essays is explicit in accenting the indigenous roots of democracy. By emphasizing the extent to which external actors have made a difference and the limits of their effectiveness, these studies support the notion that democracy cannot be imposed. It is only when domestic conditions are ripe that external assistance yields results. Along similar lines, several of the essays also caution the international community against working from a clearly defined notion of democracy; external actors must bear in mind that history and traditions, as well as the current challenges that each of these countries faces, will influence the specific shape that democratic governance assumes.

2. *Accept that there is not a single path.* Related to the above point, these cases underscore the difficulty of constructing a regional, let alone a global, democracy-promotion policy. The radical differences that emerge from a reading of the recent history of the four Latin American countries explored here make it patently clear that international efforts to support democracy must be tailored to meet the specific needs of each country. Thus, in many respects the needs of Chile, for instance, with its long history of reasonably democratic political party politics, will differ from those of Haiti and El Salvador, which have little prior experience with representative democratic practices. By the same token, the internally mediated peacemaking effort that was required in El Salvador will not, in all likelihood, enable a return to democracy in Peru.

3. *Detours are to be expected.* Democratization is a long-term gradual process. In many instances it requires the abandonment of authoritarian traditions and practices and widespread popular adherence to new, more representative ones. This takes considerable time and effort and is marked by gradual conquests by the civilian leadership and, also, by occasional setbacks. If international actors are truly to contribute to the process, their commitment and assistance must be both sustained and sensitive to the challenges and obstacles.

4. *Resist the temptation to take a seemingly more direct route.* The U.S. government should avoid recourse to intervention as a means of promoting democracy. The domestic opposition that intervention is likely to generate in the United States will only be matched by that which it would trigger among Latin American nations, who over the years have experienced too many ill-fated and ill-intentioned U.S. interventionist adventures. It is not, however, only because of the opposition and bad feeling that intervention would inspire all around, that the U.S. government should refrain from calling for intervention, even as a measure of last resort. It is also because such a course of action would not achieve the desired democratization effect. Precisely because democracy cannot be imposed (as the Haitian case is likely to confirm), intervention will not lead to the establishment of a viable democratic regime.

5. *Travel with your colleagues.* International actors are gradually beginning to search for ways of nurturing democracy collaboratively. Since the early 1970s, NGOs and voluntary organizations have been actively involved in efforts to strengthen democratic opposition to dictatorships on the continent. Unfortunately, for much of this same period U.S. government interests and policy worked to sustain authoritarian rule, thereby limiting the effectiveness of those efforts. Similarly, in a world that was still viewed through a Cold War lens, foreign government and multilateral involvement in the Western Hemisphere continued to be strongly resisted by the United States. The current foreign policy disarray notwithstanding, the end of the Cold War, the advent of the Clinton administration, and the financial constraints

faced by the United States could usher in a promising new era in international relations in the hemisphere, one in which external actors and Latin American governments cease to be viewed by the U.S. government as potential adversaries but rather as partners.

6. *Pack and carry your own bags.* While the potential for collaborative efforts is promising and more likely to enhance the prospects for democracy than the adversarial alternative, external actors are most effective if they play to their own audiences. Each should emphasize its own area of expertise and be given the freedom by others to maneuver within that sphere. Thus, for instance, the U.S. government and its agencies should focus on strengthening bilateral relations with democratically elected governments and on using diplomatic channels to send clear and unambiguous signals about the consequences (short of intervention) that would ensue should the leadership decide to stray from the democratizing path. NGOs and voluntary organizations, meanwhile, should maintain their efforts to strengthen civil society and to encourage critical thinking and dialogue within the nongovernmental sphere and between those outside and inside government. While there certainly continues to be a need to broaden political participation and to criticize government policy openly, that task is best left to NGOs, which have a long history of involvement, strong ties to the local communities, and thus considerable legitimacy. In addition, the experiences of El Salvador, Haiti, and Peru, which tell us much about the history of the OAS and U.S.–Latin American relations, may yield insights into ways in which democracy may be strengthened in the hemisphere, with the OAS serving as a reasonably effective instrument in pursuit of such a goal.

7. *Respond to Latin American calls for assistance along the way.* The policies pursued by external actors should reflect the fact that democracy is not acquired overnight but is a long, complicated and inherently fragile process. This reality underscores the need to be sensitive to the particular challenges that each individual country faces and to tailor international efforts accordingly. But it also highlights the importance of not neglecting Latin America once the transition process is deemed complete. Thus, efforts must be made to ensure the viability of representative political institutions, whether political parties or the judicial system; to encourage the subordination of the military to civilian authority; and to assist the processes of economic stabilization, recovery, and growth. The task is indeed Herculean, and much of it is necessarily a local effort. Nevertheless, a case of international players working in concert and dividing responsibilities among themselves can certainly contribute. For example, through the assistance that they provide to their local counterparts, international NGOs and PVOs can continue to stimulate policy relevant debate and discussion in each of these areas. Foreign governments, either working in tandem with—or under the auspices of—UN agencies, can offer technical assistance to those Latin

American governments seeking, for instance, to reform their judiciary or to empower civilians to manage defense policy. Foreign public and private investment can provide an essential stimulus for renewed economic growth, thereby assisting a civilian political leadership challenged to demonstrate its effectiveness.

A Concluding Remark

As this analysis suggests, the road to stable democracy in Latin America is a long, circuitous one, fraught with obstacles, and with no guarantee of safe arrival. If the challenges that this poses for the civilian leadership on the continent are enormous, the consequences for the international community are also significant. A concerted, responsive, sustained, and sensitive effort to nurture fragile democratic regimes is necessary—a collaborative effort, in which local actors must take the lead but in which the entire cast of external actors may be called upon to play secondary roles. The tools are many, including various forms of assistance, advice and pressure.

Nevertheless—and whatever the outcome in Haiti—the interventionist tool need not be used, not even in response to a redefined notion of sovereignty. Instead, the challenge for Latin Americans and their international partners lies in patiently nurturing the process of democratic transition and consolidation, tackling obstacles as they arise, and building gradually, through sustained political, economic, and social reform, a popular commitment to representative democracy. Once this is achieved, one may well find that, rather than being at odds with each other, state and popular notions of sovereignty eventually intersect.

13 External Pressures and Domestic Constraints

The Lessons of the Four Case Studies

Karen L. Remmer

The case studies presented in this volume highlight the ways in which domestic conditions facilitated or limited international efforts to promote and defend political democracy in Latin America during the late 1980s and early 1990s. The external political environment was relatively constant across the four cases, but the efficacy of outside pressures ranged from the limited (Peru), through the secondary or complementary (Chile), to the critical (El Salvador and Haiti).

To explain these outcomes, each of the case studies emphasizes particular features of national political life. Inter alia, the successes and failures of external pressures are explained in terms of political culture, elite interests and values, strategic leadership choices, presidential personality and popularity, civil-military relations, coordinating efforts among international actors, the administrative capacities of the state apparatus, political violence and repression, the perceived costs and benefits of nondemocratic alternatives, national security threats, the strength of civil society, the orientation of the church, particular alignments of political forces, economic conditions, climatic changes, and demographic pressures.

The sheer number of explanatory factors introduced in the four studies offers a useful caution against simplistic theories of democracy. Likewise, it is helpful to be reminded of the variability of the democratic experience. Quite apart from the broad range of socioeconomic conditions associated with political democracy, formal institutional arrangements, party structures, systems of interest group intermediation, social bases of regime support, and many other important features of democratic political life differ significantly from country to country. Such variations not only shape the impact of democratic rule upon local populations but also condition the capacity of international actors to defend competitive political institutions.

The difficulty is that case studies establish a fragile basis for developing useful policy guidelines, much less theoretical generalizations about the conditions under which collective action is likely to succeed at promoting and protecting democracy. Precisely because they underline the complex and combinative nature of political life, studies of macropolitical outcomes in individual countries at particular points in time privilege the unique and contingent over the general and structural, inhibit the integration of data from regional and international levels of analysis, and constrain opportunities for developing propositions that transcend specific national experiences.

The entire body of literature on democratization in post-1979 Latin America evidences these limitations. Conceived largely within a case study format, research has yielded long lists of potentially relevant variables but few testable theoretical generalizations or predictions about the emergence or sustainability of political democracy. Studies of Ecuador variously attribute the transition from military to civilian rule of the late 1970s to the opposition of the business community, policy divisions within the military, and the disruption of petroleum income. To explain the breakdown of military rule in Argentina, analysts emphasize the importance of economic failure, military defeat in the Falklands/Malvinas conflict, military factionalism, and the loss of regime legitimacy. Peruvianists cite still other factors, including rising civilian unrest, economic policy failure, military disunity, the pressures of the Carter administration, declining state autonomy, and General Velasco Alvarado's poor health. And so on. The nearly simultaneous breakdown of authoritarianism across Latin America thus ends up being portrayed as the result of multiple distinct and unrelated processes of interaction between particular actors and shifting political conjunctures. The resulting array of complex and often contradictory interpretations of individual transitions establishes no basis for understanding why the political face of the entire region was transformed between 1979 and 1989.

To explain the common process of democratization, it is obviously necessary to place individual national experiences within a broader comparative context. The importance of specific events, leadership decisions, or particular configurations of social forces or institutions cannot be assessed on the basis of research that ignores general patterns of similarity and difference or that analyzes individual countries in total isolation from one another. Likewise, to draw lessons about the conditions under which various forms of collective action are likely to promote and sustain democracy, the recent experiences of countries such as Chile, El Salvador, Haiti, and Peru need to be nested within a broader analytical framework that addresses key questions about variation through time and across cases.

From a historical perspective, what stands out about the contemporary situation is less the conditioning impact of domestic forces than the extraordinary capacity of outside actors to shift the political momentum in the direction of democratic options and to maintain that momentum through time in the face of apparently insuperable obstacles and repeated setbacks. A decade ago, who could have predicted that a nation such as Haiti, so completely lacking in democratic political experience, so incredibly impoverished and underdeveloped, and so otherwise deficient in the traditional list of democratic prerequisites, would even experience a reasonably open and competitive presidential election, much less that the winner would be permitted to assume office? Until very recently, El Salvador would also have garnered a high ranking on any list of least likely democracies, further emphasizing the importance of international involvement. After more than a decade of socioeconomic disintegration, Peru might not be far behind.

Although the case is not discussed in this volume, note should also be made of Guatemala, where international pressures recently registered an important victory over long-standing national traditions of authoritarianism and abuses of human rights. During the 1980s a leading specialist on Guatemalan politics predicted: "There is no possibility of a centrist solution . . . the only two realistic alternatives are a continuation of the reactionary class dictatorship or a takeover by the forces of the guerrillas and their sympathizers."[1] That democratic institutions of any kind have emerged in such a country speaks to the importance of analyzing how regional and international changes have interacted with local forces to reverse the preexisting political dynamic.

In short, it is comparatively easy to identify domestic factors that limit or constrain the development of political democracy in countries such as El Salvador, Haiti, Peru, and Guatemala. Accounting for recent democratic advances without reference to the international context, on the other hand, is highly problematic. This theoretical asymmetry runs through all of the country studies presented in this volume, including the chapter on Chile, which emphasizes the restrictions that the institutional mechanisms and rules of the Pinochet regime imposed on political democracy. Hence, while the case studies place considerable emphasis upon domestic factors, collectively they underline the importance of understanding how and why changes in the regional and international context have worked in favor of representative government. In attempting to understand this trend as well as its varying impact on important countries, it should be emphasized that the key theoretical issue is not the relative importance of domestic as opposed to international variables but, rather, varying patterns of interaction across time and space.

Three major sets of changes may be briefly identified to account for the increased effectiveness of external pressures on behalf of political democracy: the transformation of the global economy, the related breakdown of the Soviet Union, and the expansion of political links between Latin America and the rest of the world. On the economic side, shifts in international financial markets dating back to the oil shocks of the 1970s exacerbated the fragility of authoritarian regimes across the region and paved the way for the restoration of democratic governance. The timing and pace of this process varied considerably across the region, depending upon economic structure and the institutional and social bases of authoritarian rule; nevertheless, by 1990 authoritarian rule had disappeared from most of the region, creating a new and widely shared interest in the defense of democracy. Democratization thus established new bases for collective political action, which in turn reinforced the momentum of the democratization process.[2]

Along with the emerging regional political consensus, changes in the global economy created new opportunities and instruments for the promotion of democratic goals. The economic crisis of the 1980s generated strong pressures for economic reform, enhanced the role of official international lending institutions, and reduced the parameters of economic choice. In the process new linkages were created among Latin American economies, establishing new foundations for political cooperation; commercial and financial ties between Latin America and the rest of the world assumed new importance; external actors obtained new levers, notably conditional lending, for influencing political outcomes within the region; and domestic financial and business elites, who have posed the most serious threat to representative government in the past, gained assurances that their interests could be protected under democratic rule.

The breakdown of the Soviet Union and the related transformation of the international political system reinforced these developments by undercutting extremist forces at both ends of the political spectrum, thus fostering political moderation and consensus and facilitating the construction of broad political coalitions around democratic institutions. Of particular importance was the decline in the perception of national security threats. The end of the Cold War limited the incentives and justifications for the overthrow of democracy, removed a major source of policy ambivalence and inconsistency on the part of the United States, and helped shift the balance of power in the region away from the military.

The broadening of political linkages between Latin America and the OECD nations and the expanding networks between NGOs, political parties, and trade unions strengthened prodemocratic values and actors and helped to coordinate internal and international activities on behalf of political democracy. As Kathryn Sikkink documents in her chapter on NGOs in this volume, the international human rights movement played an important role in this process.

The net impact of these changes was that (1) the interest in the promotion of democracy became more widely shared across the region than at any time since the onset of the Cold War, (2) the instruments of collective action available to the international community became more powerful, and (3) the interaction between prodemocratic domestic and international actors became more pronounced. These changes in international interests, instruments, and interactions account not only for the unprecedented breadth, depth, and durability of the democratization process in the region as a whole but also for variations in the impact of international pressure across individual countries.

International involvement has proved most effective in Latin America when the collective interest in the promotion of democracy has not run up against competing policy goals, when the instruments of coordinated economic pressure have posed the most serious threat to the local business community, and when the interactions between local and international prodemocratic forces have most effectively blurred the lines conventionally separating domestic and international politics, thereby establishing the basis for the emergence of a common set of political strategies and tactics. These conditions were met most fully in Chile, where the perpetuation of the Pinochet dictatorship came to be seen by the United States as a threat rather than a guarantor of political stability, where the process of economic reform had created a business community strongly oriented toward the expansion of international trade and investment, and where the democratic opposition, the Catholic church, the U.S. government, the National Endowment for Democracy, European political parties, and many other prodemocratic forces converged around an electoral strategy designed to terminate authoritarian rule.

At the other extreme is Peru, where the rise of a serious guerrilla challenge undercut the shared interest in the protection of democracy by raising questions of regional security and stability. The economic strategy pursued by Peru up through the end of the 1980s was also diametrically the opposite of Chile's, creating a business community that was more tenuously linked to the international system and thus far more threatened by the Sendero Luminoso than by the prospect of diminished access to external markets. The dependence of the Peruvian economy upon continued international aid and lending was critical, but its effectiveness was limited by the ambivalence and confusion generated by Fujimori's immediate response to international political pressures, the orthodoxy of his economic program, and the severity of the internal security challenge. Also important was the relative paucity of linkages between Peruvian political actors and the international community and the related inability of prodemocratic actors to agree upon a common formula for confronting the *autogolpe*.

The contrasts between El Salvador and Haiti may be similarly explained. The failure of international pressures to effect the restoration of President Aristide without resorting to military action reflected the thin and fragile nature of the linkages between Haiti and the rest of the world community, the limited capacity of conventional instruments of trade and financial pressure to alter the preferences of an inward-oriented and rent-seeking economic elite, and the ambivalent orientation of U.S. policy makers. Deep-seated pessimism about the capacity of Haiti to maintain electoral democracy, doubts about the leadership capacities of President Aristide, pressures from U.S. business interests operating in the assembly sector in Haiti, and fears about immigrant pressures combined to produce a cautious and equivocating policy stance. As documented so effectively in the chapter by Patricia Weiss Fagen, high levels of external involvement meant that the boundaries between international and domestic politics were far more attenuated in Salvador, the leverage of external actors far stronger, and the pressures of the United States more consistently in tune with the strategies of other prodemocratic forces.

By placing the cases of relative success and failure in a comparative framework, it thus becomes apparent that the differential impact of international pressure is not merely a function of the relative favorability or unfavorability of the domestic terrain; what counts is the pattern of interaction between domestic and international forces or, to put it more broadly, the way in which a nation is situated within the international community. The point is not that domestic factors are irrelevant or even secondary but, rather, that their importance is conditioned by the regional and international context in which they operate.

Although more consistent with traditional theoretical frameworks, nation-centric explanations are less helpful for understanding the patterns of similarity and difference that emerge from the case studies. For example, with the transition to competitive rule secure in Chile, the country's relatively high literacy, its prolonged constitutional tradition, and its strong political parties might all be cited to account for political democratization. But those same factors did not prevent the emergence and consolidation of the Pinochet dictatorship, nor did they allow Chile to make an early, easy, or full transition back to democratic rule. The Chilean transition of 1989 was among the last in the region. As emphasized by Alicia Frohmann, that transition also left many authoritarian bulwarks untouched, including General Pinochet, who remained in charge of the Chilean army.

Prospects for the collective defense of democracy in the Western Hemisphere thus need to be assessed within regional and international rather than a strictly national framework of political action. The relative efficacy of external involvement depends upon the consistency with which the shared regional interest in democracy is pursued, the levers of influence available to the international community, and the density of organizational networks linking domestic and international actors. On all three counts, the capacity of external actors to promote political democracy in the hemisphere has increased, creating a new basis for optimism about the sustainability of democratic institutions.

Optimism about the future of electoral democracy in the Western Hemisphere, however, must be tempered by realism. Competitive electoral processes may not only coexist with, but also help to legitimate, severe social inequalities, gross administrative corruption, and misguided policies. The spread of democratic institutions is not a panacea for poverty, social injustice, political violence, or anything else. Nor can it be assumed that we have arrived at the "end of history," in which old tensions between capitalism and democracy have been permanently superseded: even though the recent triumph of neoliberal economic paradigms makes it seem that capitalism and democracy are mutually buttressing, conflicts over state and market roles continue to threaten political democracy. To cite but a few illustrations, international drug markets have created powerful economic actors that defy state control and thereby prejudice human rights, civilian control of the military, and other central elements of democratic governance across the entire Andean region. In countries such as Venezuela, state actors have led the resistance to market-oriented reforms, jeopardizing the stability of democratic institutions in the process. Also illustrative of the destabilizing tensions between state and market roles are the actions of the world banking community, which has sanctioned elected governments pursuing policies considered prejudicial to international capitalism.

Finally, the collective defense of democracy and human rights collides not merely with traditional notions of sovereignty but with the rising claims of subnational and supranational ethnic, fundamentalist, and nationalist movements. As an increasingly important source of political conflict, such movements pose major challenges to multilateral efforts designed to promote three central and mutually reinforcing sets of political outcomes: demilitarization, democratization, and the peaceful settlement of disputes.

IV Two Impending Challenges

14 Cuba in the International Community in the 1990s

Sovereignty, Human Rights, and Democracy

Jorge I. Domínguez

After governing Cuba for over a third of a century, President Fidel Castro, in the early 1990s, had only one remaining achievement: the construction of Cuba's sovereignty. His claim to have held the nation's flag aloft in dignity and defiance against all odds remains at the core of his political appeal and strength. It is the instrument through which he hopes to rally Cubans to support his government at its hour of greatest peril.

Lost in the debris after the collapse of the Soviet Union are other claims to lasting significance that Castro might have made as recently as the mid-1980s. Cuban economists have calculated that the nation's global social product—the widest measure of Cuban economic performance—fell somewhat during the second half of the 1980s and then, catastrophically, in the early 1990s; in particular, Julio Carranza estimates that Cuba's global social product in real terms fell 3.6 percent in 1990, 24 percent in 1991, and about 15 percent in 1992.[1] As a result of such economic decline, the Cuban government's crown jewels—its performance in health and education—were tarnished beyond recognition. Textbooks and medicine became scarce; in 1993, a severe health epidemic that affects the eyes and limbs broke out. The nation's life has been grinding to a halt, awaiting a miracle.

In the early 1990s, however, the construction of Cuba's sovereignty remained an accomplishment of special significance to adults between roughly the ages of forty and seventy. Some of them had participated in acts of resistance against Fulgencio Batista's government in the 1950s; many more had participated directly in the tasks that defined the revolutionary government in the early 1960s. They rallied to defend the government against the Bay of Pigs invasion in 1961; they hunkered down in the trenches to defend Cuba against a U.S. invasion in October 1962. The younger among them tasted the thrill of military victory in the successful war in Angola in 1975–76 and in Ethiopia in 1977–78. Together with Fidel, they built the revolution, they defeated the United States, and they projected Cuba's power well beyond the oceans surrounding Cuba.

imp of sovereignty

For these men and women who built the revolution, sovereignty is not just an abstract concept. It defines as well who they have become as human beings. Especially in the early 1960s, the massive upheaval that this authentic social revolution brought to the country reshaped their lives. Cubans met in classrooms and in clinics, in the cane fields and in militia training camps, in rallies and in endless meetings. They argued, they worked, they volunteered, to accomplish the impossible. Though an ill-organized and inefficient government often wasted the fruits of such extraordinary dedication, Cubans met each other in depth and understanding and, in so doing, created a national sovereignty that provided intense meaning to their lives.

Reason 4 little opp.

For many Cubans, long unhappy with Fidel Castro's policies and with his government's performance, loyalty to the Revolution—necessarily capitalized to express this thought—and to Cuba itself has held them back from actively joining an opposition that, in the early 1990s, was still portrayed by Castro's government as being the agent of the United States.[2] To oppose Fidel meant to oppose national sovereignty, which is the revolution's central legacy; to oppose national sovereignty was to deny the very meaning of their lives. No wonder Castro's new slogan for the 1990s was: "We must save the homeland, we must save the Revolution, we must save socialism." Far better than anyone, he understood the power of the word *homeland* to save the revolution and socialism.

The meanings of sovereignty in the world today can be understood along a spectrum, at one end of which it is associated with production and at the other with consumption. In the European Union, for example, sovereignty is much closer to the production end of this spectrum. Countries invest their sovereignty to gain other ends: peace between France and Germany; fiscal and monetary discipline in Italy; democratization in Spain, Portugal, and Greece; peaceful communal coexistence in Belgium; and economic growth everywhere. The sovereignty of the member countries of the European Union is deliberately penetrable everywhere; its main use is its surrender for the sake of greater gains.

In Cuba, sovereignty is a consumption item. Certainly for Cuba's leaders and for many of their supporters, there is no greater goal. It is unthinkable to surrender it consciously. The enjoyment of sovereignty is an end in itself. To think about Cuba's future, its further democratization, and its relation to the international community, it is essential to recall the continuing importance of sovereignty and its meaning as an organizing concept for Cuba's recent political and social history.

In this chapter, I consider, first, some pertinent norms established in Cuba's constitutions to show that Cuba is normatively committed to active engagement with the international community in the assertion of its sovereign rights. Just as Cuba asserts its right to participate in the world, its own constitution commits it to listen when the international community speaks. Then, I examine the recent practice of international institutions and conferences to show that the United Nations especially, and the Latin American governments more gingerly, have also asserted their right to address both domestic circumstances in Cuba and U.S. policy toward Cuba; Cuba's actions suggest at least partial acceptance of such international jurisdiction. Finally, I turn to the future, considering crises already under way in Cuba or that may quite plausibly occur, turning then to the steps that the international community might take to foster a peaceful transition toward pluralist democracy.

Norms in the Constitution: Internationalism and Nationalism

One result of the collapse of the communist world and the transformation of Cuba's international environment was the revision of Cuba's constitution. From 1959 to 1976, Cuba was governed by a makeshift Fundamental Law, based in part on the 1940 Constitution but mostly on ad hoc amendments issued over the years. A new constitution was approved by national plebiscite in 1976, and a major revision was approved by the National Assembly in 1992.

The normative changes between the 1976 and 1992 documents shed light on official Cuba's self-portrait. In general, the 1992 Constitution eliminates nearly all references to international communism. It purges the text of many social class references and replaces or modifies them with national symbols. It shifts from an emphasis on armed international conflict toward the peaceful resolution of disputes and economic and political cooperation while explicitly acknowledging the pertinence to Cuba of the UN Charter. And it seeks especially to identify Cuba with Latin America.

In the Preamble to the 1976 Constitution, Cubans were guided by the "victorious doctrine of Marxism-Leninism." In the Preamble to the 1992

Constitution, they are guided by "the corpus of José Martí's ideas and by the political and social ideas of Marx, Engels and Lenin." In the 1976 Constitution, Cubans acknowledged "the fraternal friendship, the assistance and the cooperation of the Soviet Union and other socialist countries." This reference is absent from the 1992 Constitution, understandably so, given that the Soviet Union and most socialist countries no longer existed. Gone as well from Article 12 is the reference to basing Cuba's relations with the remaining communist countries on "socialist internationalism." The 1992 Constitution, in short, recognizes the passing of the era when communist countries played a significant role in the world.

Perhaps more noteworthy are the normative shifts between the texts that emphasize nationalism at the expense of socialism in a domestic context. In 1976, Article 1 defined the Republic of Cuba as a "socialist state of workers and peasants." In 1992, Article 1 substitutes the word "trabajadores" (people who work) for "obreros" (workers, a narrower social class meaning). To make sure that the point is clear, the new Article 1 adds words borrowed from Cuba's national hero, José Martí, to explain that this state is "organized with all and for the good of all." In 1976, Article 5 described the Communist Party as the "organized Marxist-Leninist vanguard of the working class." In 1992, the same article describes the party as "heir to Martí as well as Marxist-Leninist" and, in that context, is "the organized vanguard of the Cuban nation." The 1992 Constitution, therefore, appeals to the nation as a whole far more than its predecessor did.

Despite the marked shift toward nationalism from the 1976 to the 1992 text, the 1992 Constitution retains a significant commitment to internationalism that is unusual for constitutions in the world today. And yet, this residual internationalism has a somewhat different tone and character from the one evident in the 1976 text. In both texts, Article 12 describes this internationalism.

In 1976, Article 12 opened with a reference to Cuba's "solidarity in combat," a reference to its own international troop deployments. That phrase is gone from the 1992 text. The first operative paragraph in 1976 was equally militant in its condemnation of imperialism. In 1992, the paragraph remains but has been dropped to fourth place. The first operative paragraph in 1992 is an expanded version of the old fourth paragraph, proclaiming Cuba's vocation for peace among all states, big and small, based on respect for sovereignty, independence, and self-determination.

The decline in the constitution's martial emphasis is evident even in the clause that condemns aggressive war (the eighth clause in 1992, third in 1976). In 1976, the text affirmed the legitimacy of "wars" of national liberation; in 1992, "wars" has been replaced by "struggles." In 1976, the text affirmed that Cuba had the internationalist duty to "assist" the victims

Beyond Sovereignty

of aggression; in 1992, the text affirms only that Cuba has the duty to express its "solidarity."

The second operative paragraph in 1992 (fifth in 1976) has also been greatly expanded. It describes the "principles on which Cuba bases its international relations" and now includes previously absent references to "international cooperation . . . the peaceful resolution of disputes based on equality and respect." More important, the paragraph indicates that Cuba's international relations are also based on "the other principles proclaimed in the Charter of the United Nations and other international treaties to which Cuba is a party." There was no reference to the U.N. Charter in the 1976 Constitution.

The third operative paragraph in 1992 (eighth in 1976) is a much changed discussion of Cuba's wish to become better integrated with Latin American countries. In 1976, such integration was conditioned upon Latin America having been freed from "external domination and internal oppression," while its objective was the "common struggle against colonialism, neocolonialism and imperialism." All the words in quotations are absent from the 1992 text. Instead, the 1992 text focuses on a "common identity" as a basis for "economic and political integration to achieve a genuine independence." This thought appears also in the Preamble of the 1992 text, which retains the words "the fraternal friendship, the assistance and the cooperation" (applied in 1976 to the communist countries) but applies them for the first time to the peoples of the world "especially those from Latin America and the Caribbean."

In sum, the Constitutions of 1976 and 1992 call attention to Cuba's evolving understanding of its role in the world. Cuba affirms its national sovereignty more than its Marxism-Leninism and the inclusiveness of nationality more than the militancy of class politics. Cuba remains committed to an active international role, but in the 1990s the role is more oriented toward Latin America than toward the nearly defunct communist world. Cuba seeks more peaceful engagement and economic cooperation than participation in war. Cuba explicitly accepts the pertinence of the UN Charter for its own Constitution.[3] Cuba's 1992 Constitution commits its government and people not only to participate in the world community but also to listen to its counsel and its norms.

Norms in the Constitution: Democracy and Human Rights

Cuba's Constitutions of 1976 and 1992 have a fairly extensive bill of rights, duties, and fundamental guarantees. Symbolically, the first rights listed are economic and social rights. There is a fairly detailed discussion of the right to work, to vacations, to social security and other forms of public assistance, to occupational health and safety, to health, education, and sports. In the second segment of this constitutional chapter are found political rights. These articles are conditioned in one or two ways. Within some articles (for example, Article 53 of the 1992 Constitution, on freedom of expression), the political right is conditioned to serve "the ends of socialist society." More generally, Article 5 asserts the supremacy of the Communist party and Article 62 of the 1992 Constitution asserts that "none of the liberties" can be exercised "against the existence and goals of the socialist state, nor against the Cuban people's decision to construct socialism and communism."

Cuba's constitutional formulations in its bill of rights call attention to three important conceptual distinctions in the official understanding of democracy in Cuba. Moreover, this official understanding has substantial (though difficult to measure) support in the population.

1. Democracy in official Cuba is majoritarian, not liberal. Cuban leaders claim that their political system is democratic because it expresses the will of the majority. Participation is significant to this understanding of democracy, but the notions of opposition or contestation have little meaning. It is possible for the majority to exercise its "dictatorship" over the minority in order to achieve majoritarian ends and, in so doing, for the political system, in this view, to remain democratic. This understanding of democracy led Plato to fear the rule of the mob and led Rousseau to seek to understand and defend the "general will" as the organizing concept for politics. In practice in the twentieth century, a purely majoritarian and illiberal understanding of democracy has turned out to be a sham.[4]

2. The understanding of democracy in Cuba tends to be consequentialist, not anticipatory. That is, democracy is to be measured by its results in advancing majoritarian goals, not in the rules that may be set up in advance. A consequentialist understanding of democracy focuses on substantive outcomes with regard to ownership, distribution, welfare, and similar concepts. A political system deserves to be called democratic only if it ensures these consequences. In contrast, an anticipatory view of democracy, as Przeworski's formulation notes with blunt clarity, institutionalizes uncertainty. Democracy is to be understood as a "contingent institutional compromise" in which "no one's interest can be guaranteed." It is the rules set in advance, not the consequences of government action, that mark a political system as democratic.[5] This anticipatory view of democracy prevails in Western Europe, North America and has at last considerable support in Latin America, where there is nonetheless also strong support for a consequentialist understanding of democracy.

Beyond Sovereignty

3. A third feature of the official understanding of democracy in Cuba, but one that has especially widespread support in the population, is that decisions ought to be made by consensus rather than by rules of procedure that could create minorities and oppositions. The effect of this emphasis on consensus is the need to call meetings frequently and to have them last long. In contrast, in other countries votes tend to settle decisions, and there is much greater toleration of the existence of oppositions.[6]

In the early 1990s, these understandings of democracy remained important and had begun to turn against the government. The consequences of government policies arguably no longer benefited most Cubans in the midst of rapid economic decline. The views of the majority of Cubans, as always, were difficult to determine but the evidence available called attention to considerable dissatisfaction.

A poll conducted in 1990 on behalf of Cuba's Communist Party found, for example, that only 20 percent of Cubans thought that the food supply was good and only 10 percent thought that public transportation was good (these answers were given before the end of Soviet support for Cuba's economy).[7] No doubt the level of criticism may have been understated by such a poll, but even so, criticism had already become substantial and open, and it no doubt only heightened as the economy fell in the early 1990s.

The reliance on consensus as the means to reach agreement had eroded less, however. Even among human rights and opposition activists, the search for consensus was especially important. Human rights and opposition groups often preferred to fragment, creating smaller new groups within which consensus could be achieved, than to expand the boundaries of tolerable views within existing groups.

International Institutions and Cuba's International Environment

In the early 1990s, a continuing feature of Cuba's international environment remained the decades-old U.S. trade embargo and associated policies that have sought Cuba's international isolation.[8] The enactment of the so-called Cuban Democracy Act in the fall of 1992 sought, among other steps, to tighten the U.S. embargo on Cuba by imposing sanctions against U.S. firms whose subsidiaries located in third countries traded with Cuba.[9] The effect of these U.S. policies on Cuba was compounded by the termination of assistance from the communist countries.

For the first time since U.S. economic policies to punish Cuba were adopted in 1960, in the fall of 1992 the UN General Assembly called upon the U.S. government to end its embargo on Cuba. Cuba introduced the resolution and actively sought its approval. In a clever maneuver, the Cuban delegation revised its own draft to omit any specific reference to the United States. Nonetheless, the resolution that the General Assembly approved mentioned "having learned of the recent promulgation of measures . . . aimed at strengthening and extending the economic, commercial, and financial embargo against Cuba"; the only such instance was the enactment of the U.S. Cuban Democracy Act. The General Assembly's resolution then "urges States which have such laws or measures to take necessary steps to repeal or invalidate them as soon as possible."[10] In November 1992, the resolution carried by fifty-nine ayes, three nays (the United States, Israel, and Romania), and seventy-one abstentions. In the fall of 1993, a similar resolution carried eighty-eight to four (the United States, Israel, Paraguay, and Albania), with fifty-seven abstentions (many Caribbean countries shifted from "abstain" to "yes").

In July 1993, the third Iberoamerican Summit of heads of government (including all the Spanish-American countries, Brazil, Portugal, and Spain) met in Bahia, Brazil. In this case, the resolution aimed at the lifting of the U.S. trade embargo on Cuba mentioned neither the United States nor Cuba, though it was plain what the unanimous heads of government meant. As in the case of the vote in the General Assembly, Cuba actively sought the approval of this measure.

Not all recent actions by international institutions or conferences have been equally welcomed by Cuba's government. In 1988, the UN Human Rights Commission sent a special delegation to Cuba to look into human rights conditions. The Cuban government cooperated with this delegation. Subsequently, however, the Cuban government refused to accept other delegations. In 1991, the Human Rights Commission appointed a special representative and, in 1992, a special rapporteur. The special rapporteur found ample evidence of substantial human rights violations in Cuba, whereupon the General Assembly adopted a resolution expressing profound regrets about "the numerous uncontested reports of violations of basic human rights and fundamental freedoms" described by the special rapporteur.

The resolution also called upon Cuba "to cease the persecution and punishment of citizens for reasons related to freedom of expression and peaceful association; to permit legalization of independent groups; to respect guarantees of due process; to permit access to the prisons by national independent groups and international humanitarian agencies; to review sentences for crimes of a political nature; and to cease retaliatory measures

Beyond Sovereignty

towards those seeking permission to leave the country."[11] The General Assembly approved its resolution on the condition of human rights in Cuba on 2 December, that is, eight days after it had approved its resolution concerning the U.S. trade embargo on Cuba. (In the fall of 1993, the General Assembly reaffirmed this resolution.)

These actions were, of course, not contradictory, in particular because the special rapporteur on his own had called attention to the U.S. trade embargo as an obstacle to political opening in Cuba:

> While not overlooking the urgent need for specific measures [for the Cuban government to take], as proposed above, the Special Rapporteur nevertheless wishes to point out that any analysis concerning the situation and implementation of human rights in Cuba must, as a point of departure, accept the fact that the government is, and has for a long time been, surrounded by an international climate extremely hostile to many of its policies and, in some cases, even to its very existence. . . . A policy vis-à-vis Cuba based on economic sanctions and other measures designed to isolate the island constitute, in the opinion of the Special Rapporteur, at the present stage, the surest way of prolonging an untenable internal situation, as the only remedy that would be left for not capitulating to external pressure would be to continue desperate efforts to stay anchored in the past. International sanctions, especially if accompanied by conditions implying the adoption of specific measures, be they political or economic, are totally counterproductive if it is the international community's intention to improve the human rights situation and, at the same time, to create conditions for a peaceful and gradual transition towards a genuinely pluralist and civil society.[12]

In short, the United Nations had evolved a complex but consistent position with regard to Cuba and to Cuba's relations with the world. In the first instance, the United Nations asserted its jurisdiction to comment on both U.S. policy toward Cuba and the Cuban government's treatment of human rights within its borders. The General Assembly called upon the United States to lift its economic sanctions on Cuba and upon Cuba to stop violations of human rights and to observe the principles of the UN Charter on such matters as freedom of expression and freedom of association (a charter that Cuba's government had voluntarily, in 1992, inserted in the country's own constitution). The U.N. special rapporteur linked these two aspects explicitly in his own report, all the while insisting on the proper respect for Cuba's sovereignty.

UN involvement in Cuba is likely to continue. Its Human Rights Commission will retain its concern for conditions in Cuba. The General Assembly resolution on the trade embargo "requests the Secretary-General to prepare a report on the implementation of this resolution and to submit it for consideration by the General Assembly at its forty-eighth session." The various dimensions of the Cuban question will remain on the U.N. agenda, therefore.

The United Nations has jurisdiction with regard to human rights but not with regard to the shape of domestic political systems as a whole. The Organization of American States, on the other hand, enshrines in its own charter its commitment to democracy. In the early 1990s, the OAS took additional steps—especially its 1991 Santiago Commitment (Resolution 1080)—to activate its support of democracy (as detailed in other chapters in this book). The Guadalajara Declaration signed by the heads of government at the first Iberoamerican summit (held in Guadalajara, Mexico, in July 1991) also affirmed their commitment to democracy and human rights. None of these statements mentioned Cuba specifically; however, Cuba joined in the issuance of the Guadalajara Declaration.

On 23 October 1991, the presidents of Colombia, Mexico, and Venezuela—known as the Group of Three—met in Cozumel, Mexico, and invited President Castro to join them. Castro gave a detailed account of Cuba's international and domestic policies. On that basis, the Group of Three welcomed the Cuban government's decision to invite investment from Latin American countries and decided to "encourage" the "reforms aimed at broadening political participation" that Castro had outlined. In turn, the Group of Three pledged to work for "the prompt and full reintegration of Cuba into the Latin American family." They "offered to mediate between the government of Cuba and the countries [otherwise unnamed] with which Cuba might have differences" to settle their disputes.[13]

At one level, the Group of Three merely endorsed Castro's proposals for domestic and foreign policy initiatives. More subtly, the very nature of the meeting could be interpreted to mean that Castro accepted the Group of Three's right to comment on Cuba's domestic affairs and was prepared to accept voluntarily an obligation, however limited, to report on Cuba's domestic conditions to the three presidents.

In short, the institutions of the inter-American system, and Latin American international practices, are in principle now more capable of shaping the domestic political circumstances of countries in the region. While Latin American governments have not expressed themselves collectively as pointedly as the United Nations has with regard to human rights conditions in Cuba, they have the potential for doing so and, in particular, enjoy a special receptivity within Cuba. President Castro has had no other meeting similar

Beyond Sovereignty

to the one with the Group of Three at Cozumel. The Cuban government's evolving self-understanding, as we have seen, seeks to emphasize its Latin American identity and, therefore, seems more willing to respond to and listen to the concerns of Latin American leaders who treat Cuba with appropriate international respect.

Possible Imminent Crises for Cuba

In the spring of 1993, Cuba faced a medical emergency. A poorly understood disease severely affected the eyes (leaving some blind) and limbs. Inappropriate nutrition seemed related to the incidence of the disease; at issue was not hunger (some well-fed high officials were afflicted as well) but a vitamin B-complex deficiency. The international community responded with shipments of medicines and vitamins; many health personnel from the World Health Organization, the Pan American Health Organization, the U.S. National Institutes of Health, and private entities contributed their time, effort, and resources to combat this disease. The response of the international community, therefore, spanned a range that included international organizations, the United States and many other governments, and private individuals.

This is not likely to be Cuba's only humanitarian emergency. For years there have been incidents of ordinary people seeking to leave Cuba without the exit permit that the Cuban government has required. Beginning in mid-1993, Cuban border guards fired to maim Cubans who attempted to seize vessels unlawfully to take them to U.S. shores. Some Cubans were killed. In some cases (the best documented occurred in Cojímar, near the city of Havana), local citizens rioted to protest the border guard shootings. The largest riot occurred in Havana in 1994; it was followed by Cuba's suspension of the exit permit requirement and the migration of more than thirty thousand people by boat and rafts to the United States. (U.S. officials took them to the Guantanamo Naval Base.) In September 1994, Cuba and the United States agreed on measures to prevent such migrations, including Cuba's reimposition of the exit permit requirement. As Cuba's conditions continue to worsen, violence may become more frequent.[14]

In the history of U.S.-Cuban relations, there have been three major massive illegal migrations, one through Camarioca harbor in 1965, the more dramatic one through Mariel harbor in 1980, and one in the summer of 1994. In the first two cases, the Cuban government opened a Cuban port to free emigration and invited Cuban-Americans to pick up their relatives.

Even if there is no repetition of such incidents, the prospects for violence and drownings in the Straits of Florida are likely to remain high, drawing the concern of the international community generally and of the United States in particular.[15]

Speculatively, other crises may lie just over the horizon. The final collapse of East Germany's regime was closely associated with massive and uncontrolled emigration and with instances of border guard shootings of East German citizens attempting to cross to West Germany. Although the Cuban government has repeatedly handled emigration crises quite effectively, given the changed world and changed domestic circumstances a Cuban emigration crisis could escalate out of control and be followed by massive violence from state security forces and rioting citizens.

Might there also be a military coup in Cuba's future? The Cuban armed forces have been extraordinarily loyal to President Castro and to his brother, Armed Forces Minister Raúl Castro. They have led the armed forces to repeated military victories on African battlefields, and they have honored and rewarded officers and soldiers who have served the nation and its government bravely and effectively. Moreover, the armed forces in communist countries proved remarkably loyal to civilian authority even during times of regime change. In the communist countries of Europe, only in Romania did a military coup bring about regime change, and only in the Soviet Union was a military coup attempted to prevent the democratic transition. Everywhere else, the armed forces did not overthrow the communist parties, and then they obeyed the new civilian authorities.

Nonetheless, as Cuban officers witness the collapse of the nation's economy and the loss of decades of effort to construct a better future for all, some might choose to take up arms against the Castro brothers, holding them responsible for the lack of sufficient change under these quite different circumstances. Continuing with this line of speculation, the Castro brothers and the forces that would still remain loyal to them are likely to resist. In the context of the mid-1990s, the forces loyal to the government are likely to remain sufficiently powerful; they are also likely to prevail.

Would the international community, the U.S. government, and Cuban-Americans in southern Florida stand idly by if violence on such a scale breaks out in Cuba? What would happen if neither side within Cuba is strong enough to bring the struggle to a quick conclusion and a protracted civil war takes hold in Cuba? Suppose some Cuban-Americans decide to participate on the anti-Castro side; suppose the Cuban navy or border guards shoot and kill such U.S. citizens in the Straits of Florida. What would be the response of the U.S. government?

Beyond Sovereignty

The McKinley Option

On 11 April 1898, U.S. President William McKinley explained the grounds on which he justified a U.S. military intervention in Cuba, as follows:

> First. In the cause of humanity and to put an end to the barbarities, bloodshed, starvation, and horrible miseries now existing there, and which the parties to the conflict are either unable or unwilling to stop or mitigate. It is no answer to say this is all in another country . . . and is therefore none of our business. It is specially our duty, for it is right at our door. . . .
>
> Fourth, and which is of the utmost importance. The present condition of affairs in Cuba is a constant menace to our peace and entails upon this Government an enormous expense. With such a conflict waged for years in an island so near us . . . [and given] the expeditions of filibustering that we are powerless to prevent altogether, and the irritating questions and entanglements thus arising—all these and others that I need not mention, with the resulting strained relations, are a constant menace to our peace and compel us to keep on a semi war footing with a nation with which we are at peace.[16]

There were many other reasons, of course, for the U.S. declaration of war in 1898, but the ones cited above bear an eerie resemblance to a future Cuba may be about to enter. McKinley's first reason was the need for humanitarian intervention; McKinley's fourth reason was the entanglement of the United States in a prolonged Cuban civil war, through, among other ways, the uncontrollable "filibustering" expeditions that some Cuban-Americans might mount.

In the 1990s as in the 1890s, the pressures on the United States to intervene militarily and unilaterally in a country "right at our door" may be irresistible. The principal alternatives to the McKinley option are (1) to let a Cuban civil war run its course and to accept its outcome, and (2) to organize a collective international response through existing international institutions, principally the United Nations and the Organization of American States.

The task of military intervention in Cuba under the auspices of an international organization remains daunting, however. Even if the country is divided and engaged in civil war, the side loyal to the government is likely to retain impressive firepower as well as considerable loyalty. Only the United States has the military capacity to ensure the success of such an international project, and even the United States would need to commit very substantial forces to achieve the collectively defined objectives.

Fostering Peaceful Democratization in Cuba

No one could possibly wish for outcomes such as those described in the previous section. For Cuba, the United States, Latin America, and the rest of the international community, the task must be to foster a peaceful transition toward pluralist democracy in Cuba and avoid the circumstances that might lead to the McKinley option or even to its collective security alternative.

There is a start, already. The actions of the UN General Assembly with regard to human rights in Cuba and U.S. policy toward Cuba set an appropriate framework for related international and domestic changes. The U.S. government ought to heed the General Assembly's call in order to facilitate the prospects for openings in Cuba, and the Cuban government should act to open up its politics consistent with the General Assembly's recommendations.

The Group of Three have a new window of opportunity. By a coincidence of the electoral calendar, Colombia, Mexico, and Venezuela held presidential elections between December 1993 and August 1994. In all three countries, new presidents have been installed in office who are fresh and capable of following up on the initiatives launched at Cozumel in 1991. Consistent with the Cozumel Declaration and with the subsequent U.N. General Assembly and Iberoamerican Summit statements, the Group of Three ought to press for a change in U.S. policy toward Cuba and for political openings within Cuba. In each case, they ought to engage the presidents of Cuba and the United States, dealing with each with the respect to be accorded to a head of a sovereign state.

A change in U.S. policy toward Cuba is almost certainly required before substantial, peaceful democratization is likely to gather strength in Cuba. Only if the United States sheds the image of the enemy will it be possible for those Cubans who seek to democratize their nation's politics to shed the image that they are agents of the enemy. The unfreezing of U.S. policy toward Cuba is likely to foster the unfreezing of Cuban domestic politics. Opposition becomes possible only when there is no risk that one's children will consider it treason.

President Castro has already made concessions which he once would not have dreamed possible. A socialist regime founded in 1960 on the expropriation of foreign property had in the 1990s shifted to search eagerly for, and to welcome, foreign direct investment. A revolutionary regime born in defiance of the United States turned in 1993 to legalize the holding and use of the U.S. dollar for many routine economic transactions in Cuba. In short, Castro has demonstrated that he can change course when he has no alternative. No one has to assume that Castro would want to make changes, nor need one assume his benign interest in such matters; in the early 1990s, Cuba's conditions were such that Castro has had to make decisions against his own publicly admitted preferences. It is likely that he will have to make more such decisions and that he will make them more readily if there are inducements.

To induce Castro to make changes in the structures of the political regime will require, however, a careful attention to respect his personal dignity and Cuba's sovereignty. Conditioning U.S. policy changes on Cuba's domestic policy changes is a good recipe for failure. Cuban politics ought to change consistent with the preferences of Cubans themselves and with the goals and practices set forth in Cuba's own 1992 Constitution (which require mainly, though not exclusively, the deletion of Articles 5 and 62). Cuban leaders ought to be informed, however, that the opening up of domestic politics will be associated with generous changes in U.S. policy and with equally forthcoming international assistance.

Other Practical Steps

The U.S. government can take a variety of modest unilateral steps that will serve its own interests and foster Cuba's peaceful democratization. First, the U.S. government should stop assisting the Cuban government's censorship of information and ideas to the Cuban people. The Clinton administration did take a first step in this direction; in late 1994, the U.S. government authorized normal telephone communications on a commercial basis. The U.S. government ought also to sign a civil aviation agreement with Cuba to authorize scheduled airline flights, which would also carry mail directly between the two countries. The U.S. government should establish academic, cultural, and artistic exchanges similar to those that long existed between the United States and the communist countries and that helped train many who would become the agents of political and economic transition in their home countries. The U.S. government ought to permit the opening of U.S. and Cuban news bureaus in Washington and Havana. The U.S. government ought to authorize the export to Cuba of facsimile machines and equipment to permit the flow of electronic mail.

Second, the U.S. government ought to convey clearly to the Cuban people that they need not fear military aggression from the United States. President George Bush made the first key unilateral statement to such effect on 20 May 1991; up until then, U.S. pledges against a military invasion of Cuba had occurred only in the reciprocal context of U.S.-Soviet understandings heir to the 1962 missile crisis. In May 1993, Secretary of State Warren Christopher issued a similar statement.[17] Such intentions need to be conveyed credibly and palpably through confidence-building measures. The Clinton administration has begun to adopt such measures.[18] In the spring of 1993, for the first time ever, a U.S. officer at the Guantanamo Naval Base, under orders from the base commander, communicated to his Cuban counterpart an aspect of forthcoming U.S. military exercises at the base. The specific aspect of the exercises that was revealed to the Cuban side in advance had been, in fact, a routine procedure that Cuban forces had observed U.S. forces perform in earlier maneuvers. Thus the political intent of this prior notice was plain.

A related confidence-building measure was evident in the spring 1993 discussions between the coast guards of both countries, the first comprehensive discussions held since the late 1970s. Given that a possible U.S.-Cuban military accident is most likely to begin by involving the coast guards, such sustained professional communication is especially important. Also in the spring of 1993, the two governments held discussions over migration to expedite and facilitate the implementation and existing agreements and, therefore, to make drownings and violence less likely. Meetings about migration became routine in late 1994 and 1995.

The international community can play an important role in strengthening such confidence-building measures. With the consent of the U.S. and Cuban governments, UN or OAS military and civilian observers could be present at all U.S. military maneuvers in Guantanamo or near Cuba; better still would be the inclusion of Cuban military observers. Looking further into the future, these international institutions could eventually play a constructive role in the eventual return to Cuba of the Guantanamo base area.

Third, the U.S. government should continue to permit humanitarian donations to Cuba (begun late in 1992) and should also authorize licensed, limited sales of food and medicine to Cuba to prevent a worse humanitarian crisis. The United States should support the continued engagement of international organizations in maintaining and improving the level of health and nutrition of the Cuban people. These actions respond to universal human values and would also communicate to Cubans that the United States does not wish disease or starvation upon them.

Fourth, the U.S. government should also engage the Cuban government in practical discussions, such as how to address their shared interests as neighbors in reducing the pollution of the waters in the Straits of Florida, improving early warning systems about Caribbean hurricanes, protecting migratory species, and deterring drug trafficking through or around Cuban air space and waters. Most of these issues can be addressed in the wider context of the Caribbean and Gulf of Mexico region and within the framework of international conventions. This wider multilateral focus could facilitate the evolution of eventual U.S.-Cuban bilateral agreements. Beyond the intrinsic merit of such agreements, they would further convey to the Cuban people that the United States has no hostile intent toward them.

Latin American governments can take steps, also. They should sponsor Cuba's entry into the International Monetary Fund and the World Bank provided Cuba meets all the normal conditions for entry; on that basis, the United States should support Cuba's application. Though the current Cuban government would gain some financial resources, it could do so only if it were to adopt the kinds of economic policies that would in themselves represent spectacular economic and political changes in Cuba.

Latin American governments should continue to include Cuba within the Latin American caucus in the United Nations and its family of specialized agencies. The OAS should invite the Cuban government to become a permanent observer of its meetings. Especially after the adoption of the Santiago Commitment in 1991, however, the OAS has been evolving into an institution that includes only substantially democratic regimes; Cuba's political regime remains quite distant from the operating standard for current OAS members. Therefore, Cuba should be invited to rejoin the OAS as a full member only after it implements further democratizing steps. Then, but only then, should Cuba also be invited to join the Inter-American Development Bank. This was the practice of the European Community in its relations with Spain, Portugal, and Greece; only after the installation of pluralist democracy were these three countries admitted to the community.

The OAS can volunteer specific assistance to Cuba in the planning, organization, and monitoring of local and national elections. Cuba's February 1993 elections set one important precedent: the Cuban government invited the international press to be present on election day. The OAS should ask the Cuban government to modify that invitation to permit the OAS to become involved in Cuba's next elections along the lines of OAS involvement in other countries. The fact of OAS involvement must be well disseminated so that ordinary Cubans would know. In time for the next elections, Cuba's electoral law ought to be changed to permit the full exercise of the freedom of association that is unambiguously guaranteed by Article 54 of Cuba's 1992 Constitution; this should permit the organization of opposition parties and their freedom to campaign to propagate their views.

These and similar steps that the international community can take emphasize peaceful intent and democratic objectives. Individually and collectively, these steps provide inducements for economic and political openings in Cuba that respect the nation's sovereignty and that seek to permit its people to exercise their democratic self-determination. None of the steps proposed in this section is coercive.

Conclusions

The workbook for civic education for the fourth grade in Cuba's primary schools includes a variety of activities. In one, children are asked to rearrange the words that appear scrambled on the page. The correct answer (translated into English) says: "We support the peoples that *luchan* for their liberation." The Spanish word *Luchan* can be translated as *struggle,* which need not include violence; but in this case, the workbook communicates the unmistakable hint that *luchan* be translated as *engage in combat,* because each of the words is emblazoned on the side of an army tank.[19]

Since Cuba's first civil war in 1868, Cubans have sung a national anthem that ends with the words: "to die for the homeland means to live." There have been variations in the intensity of patriotic feelings, but its strength today should not be underestimated. Many Cubans, young and old, believe that the nation's sovereignty is worth defending, by armed force if necessary.

One long-standing target of such nationalism has been the United States. Fidel Castro's clearest comment on this point was made before the Second Congress of the Cuban Communist Party in December 1980. Across the centuries, he said, "the United States has been the sworn enemy of our nation. . . . Imperialism has never stopped attacking our Cuban national spirit, putting it to the test."[20] He did not say the U.S. government, or the president, or the CIA, nor did he limit the comment to his own government, the communist regime, or the revolution that he led. His point was broader, deeper, and hence more resonant.

For the international community and for the United States, the worst outcome with regard to Cuba is the McKinley option, which entails death, destruction, and indefinite turmoil. The common task, therefore, is to avoid another president of the United States feeling compelled to say, as McKinley did in 1898 in asking the U.S. Congress for a declaration of war: "I have exhausted every effort to relieve the intolerable condition of affairs which is at our doors." Nor should anyone look upon a collective military intervention in Cuba under the auspices of an international organization as a desirable alternative, though it would clearly be preferable to unilateral U.S. intervention.

The central task for the international community is to support the conditions for peaceful change in Cuba and, simultaneously, to act to foster such a change. The United Nations, the Organization of American States, the Iberoamerican Summit, and the Group of Three, among others, have begun to take such steps. This chapter suggests some additional steps that should be taken and some reasons why Cuba may choose to respond constructively to such initiatives.

In asserting its sovereignty, Cuba also asserts its internationalism even in the formal text of its constitution. The 1992 Constitution accepts the applicability of the Charter of the United Nations and, in general, is markedly less bellicose than its 1976 predecessor. The Cuban Constitution's bill of rights section is adequate in many ways as a step toward democratization, once Articles 5 and 62 are deleted and related changes are made.

Cuba's own constitutional norms and the recent actions of its government and its president commit it to listen and to respond to the properly articulated concerns of the international community, especially of Latin American countries that respect Cuba's sovereignty. Cuban actions at the United Nations, the Iberoamerican Summit, and the Cozumel meeting of presidents signal a readiness to engage international institutions and certain Latin American presidents in helping to chart Cuba's future. These changes in the 1990s in Cuba's norms and in the actions of its government, and the new interest in Cuban affairs evident in international institutions and conferences, suggest the possibility of important changes in Cuba and in its place in the international community. The time has come to advance the speed of change.

Cuba's fourth grade civics workbook also asks children to rearrange other words that appear scrambled on the page. These say that "Cuba belongs to the socialist community."[21] They now know that this is no longer the case. Cuba's leaders know it as well. Cuba is poised for change because its world has changed.

The international community ought to foster additional changes that would in time make Cuba more democratic and that would avert the dangers of violence and war in or around Cuba. The time has come to think of Cuba not as an isolated pariah but as a sovereign nation in the international community. As such, Cuba deserves respect, and for this among other reasons, the U.S. government should change its policies toward Cuba. For its part, the Cuban government ought to comply with the UN General Assembly directive to Cuba to respect human rights, and Cuba should advance toward further democratization to comply with the norms that have come to prevail throughout much of Latin America.

15 Treading Lightly and without a Stick

International Actors and the Promotion of Democracy in Mexico

Denise Dresser

Among Mexico's great historical mysteries is the seduction that the country's politics has exercised over foreigners during turbulent times. Ambrose Bierce went to war with Villa; John Reed chronicled the upheavals of insurgent Mexico; Malcolm Lowry dragged his contemplative stupor through the canteens and jails of Oaxaca in search of a cause; and students of the Mexican Revolution owe a debt of gratitude to Tannenbaum's perceptive pen.[1] Few of these men went to Mexico with a detached, clinical attitude. Instead of treating Mexico as a museum piece, they viewed it as a country that could and should be changed.

After more than sixty years of detached neglect, external actors are resurrecting the hopes and aspirations that inspired those who crossed the border to participate in, write about, or contribute to a democratic crusade. In the 1990s, transnational networks of nongovernmental organizations are making a variety of contributions to social and political change in Mexico. The Mexican state is being transformed from above and below by domestic and external forces attempting to dislodge Mexican complacency with one-party rule. The Mexican state may control territory, force, and resources, but it can no longer monopolize legitimacy. Mexican social movements have formed international alliances with NGOs, international organizations, foreign reference publics, international media, and other groups concerned about Mexico's political future. Pressure from above and from below has led to a broad array of institutional changes and has thus fueled greater political liberalization.

More often than not, Mexico is overlooked when the international promotion of democracy comes to the fore. Since the revolution, the international system was accustomed to dealing with a Mexico that could be neglected.[2] Foreign governments and multilateral organizations were used to interacting with a politically and economically predictable country, where the myth of revolutionary legitimacy was strong and pressures for political opening were weak. Enjoying steady economic progress and governance by the cohesive and durable Institutional Revolutionary Party (PRI), with its remarkable capacity for coopting dissidents and managing domestic conflicts, Mexico was generally perceived as one of the few bastions of stability in Latin America.

Mexican exceptionalism and predictability came to an abrupt halt in the decade of the 1980s. In response to an unprecedented crisis, Mexico underwent a multidimensional change that remade the country's political economy. Economic liberalization forged ahead at a rapid pace, leaving behind vintage sociocultural conventions and economic institutions. The Salinas term clearly marked a watershed in Mexican history, as state elites self-consciously strove for the country's inclusion in the First World via the North American Free Trade Agreement.

Despite the government's attempts to preempt political change, disaffected social movements began to push for greater opening, transparency, and accountability in the exercise of public power, culminating in the Chiapas upheaval of 1994. The unprecedented burst of guerrilla activity, followed by the assassination of the ruling party's candidate in March of the same year, raise questions about Mexico's protracted democratic transition and fueled the enactment of significant electoral reforms. The reforms led to the cleanest presidential elections the country had experienced since the creation of the PRI in 1929.

The timing of the Chiapas revolt, its impact on international awareness, and the relatively clean elections suggest that integration into the world economy has become a catalyst for democracy in Mexico. As globalization proceeds apace, Mexico is increasingly exposed to the influence of an embryonic "transnational civil society."[3] Each successive wave of democratization across the world has contributed to the emergence of formal nongovernmental organizations and informal networks devoted to the promotion of human rights, the protection of minorities, the monitoring of elections, the provision of economic advice, and the promotion of governmental accountability.[4] Mexico now hosts a democracy network: an extraordinary variety of international election observers, professional associations, foundations, religious and social movements, and NGOs working together to promote democracy in Mexico.

This chapter explores the role that external actors play in amplifying the impact of domestic movements for political change in Mexico. The main argument is that the impetus for democracy has not emanated solely from the state, civil society, or international influences. The relation between civil society and the Mexican state has been mediated by the international system; change has come about due to pressure from above and from below.[5] In the area of human rights and political rights, domestic social movements have joined forces with international networks of organizations to press for greater political opening. The success of the Mexican democracy network resides in its capacity to work outside of official government-to-government channels and promote democratization in an indirect fashion.[6]

The Mexican case illustrates how understandings of sovereignty are being redefined across the globe and the role that transnational actors play in this development.[7] The activities of the prodemocracy network have led to a slow, important, and permanent redefinition of Mexican sovereignty. As Kathryn Sikkink argues, "if sovereignty is a shared set of understandings and expectations about the authority of the state and is reinforced by practices, then a change in sovereignty will come about by transforming understandings and practices."[8] In Mexico, the democracy network has helped develop new understandings about citizenship, political participation, and government accountability. These new understandings, in turn, have spurred new political practices that have undermined authoritarian rule.

Mexico's Splendid Isolation from International Scrutiny

Until the 1980s, Mexico's interactions with the international system were guided by the principle of revolutionary nationalism, defined by four broad series of attitudes and postulates: (1) a mistrust of the superpowers (particularly the United States), accompanied by xenophobia and anti-imperialism, (2) state ownership of land and natural resources, control of petroleum, and legal limitations on foreign investment, (3) a strong interventionist and protectionist state, and (4) a premium on Mexican identity as an inexhaustible source of political energy.[9] For half a century Mexico opposed intervention in the internal affairs of other countries, even when this stance forced it into uncomfortable confrontations with the United States. Mexico displayed firm support for the principle of self-determination and cultivated its image as a progressive international force. As a result, Mexico's authoritarian regime was able to consolidate and evolve in a climate undisturbed by international concern.

The widespread lack of attention devoted to Mexico's political development also reflected U.S. policy. Since Mexico's revolutionary upheaval in 1910, the promotion of stability became the central objective of U.S. policy toward its southern neighbor.[10] The persistence of a strong central government in Mexico was acceptable to the U.S. government because strong authorities were perceived as necessary to ensure the prosperity of American interests. The persistence of a benignly authoritarian political system based on a one-party monopoly caused little dismay. Concern for democracy invariably took second place to political stability and the promotion of a stable investment climate.

When after more than forty years of systematic growth, the Mexican economic model floundered, Mexico's splendid isolation came to an end. Faced with the country's worst crisis since the Great Depression, and no longer able to rely on foreign loans or oil revenues to cover the import bill, the Mexican government had little choice but to embark on a new development strategy.[11] Since state-guided import-substituting industrialization was no longer deemed capable of serving as the engine of growth, the government placed its hopes in the market and in Mexico's ability to compete in the international arena. Thus, Mexico undertook a sophisticated diplomatic strategy that subtly linked macroeconomic stabilization with debt renegotiation and free trade.[12]

During the 1980s economic recovery became the focal point of government strategy, leading to the economization of foreign policy, particularly regarding the United States.[13] Mexican leaders attempted to harness interdependence between Mexico and the United States and to hasten convergence between the two countries. Mexico's state elite gambled that greater integration with the United States would increase perceptions of a permanent shift in Mexico toward more open, liberal economic policies and that the end result would be a large inflow of new capital and the return of capital that fled the country during the "lost decade." Because capital was a major constraining factor on Mexican economic growth, the added inflow would accelerate growth and thus improve living standards. By appealing to the United States via a free trade agreement, government leaders hoped to consolidate Mexico's great leap forward. By tying the Mexican economy to the international arena, the Salinas administration, in power from 1988 to 1994, hoped to ensure that its economic and political vision would survive the pendular policy shifts of future *sexenios*.

Free trade negotiations also had a political dimension closely related to the course of events in Mexico. Mexico's political elite hoped that free trade would institutionalize the political predominance of an emerging center-right coalition in the Mexican polity. The political equilibrium (favorable to the PRI) and the economic equilibrium (favorable to the private sector) that state managers established under Salinas were perceived as fragile and jeopardized by economic setbacks and the regrouping of fragmented opposition forces. In the perspective of modernizing state elites, a dynamic market economy operating in conjunction with the United States would help undermine support for the left and strengthen pro-Salinas forces. Economic growth became Mexico's containment policy: the success of the country's economic reforms would enhance the PRI's position and steal away banners from the opposition.

Keeping one eye on the Soviet Union, president Salinas deliberately delayed the process of political reform, avowedly in order to safeguard the institutionalization of his economic policies.[14] In the Salinas perspective, economic reform would eventually lead Mexico to become more democratic.[15] Inspired by this line of reasoning, Mexico's leaders instituted Mexico's economic reform in a context of tightly controlled political liberalization.[16] It is undeniable that the political system underwent a process of evolution and reform during the Salinas term. Elections became more competitive, electoral reforms were negotiated, the ranks of the opposition swelled, and the National Action Party (PAN) earned three state governorships. However, throughout the *sexenio* power was concentrated in the presidency; the PRI continued to dominate elections through clientelism, fraud, and intimidation; the state still imposed limits and restrictions on the opposition; and at the end of his term president Salinas handpicked his successor. Government critics, especially on the left, suffered frequent harassment and abuse of human rights, and the system displayed low official tolerance for dissent, from whatever source.[17]

The Salinas strategy of economic reform first, political reform second, was strongly supported by what Mexican analyst Lorenzo Meyer calls "the American factor." Both the Bush and Clinton administrations met Salinas's overtures in search of support for greater economic integration and Mexico's economic model with enthusiasm.[18] The U.S. government hoped that market-oriented reforms would open opportunities to American exports and investment, reactivate the economy thus curbing Mexican migration, and expand U.S. influence in Mexico. The United States was also anxious to invest in the success of Mexico's economic reform program in order to ensure the political stability of its southern neighbor. From the perspective of the U.S. government, the Salinas administration's promotion of economic reforms and a modern diplomatic stance was a timely development. The political salience gained by the left-leaning Party of the Democratic Revolution (PRD) in the 1980s had raised concerns about Mexico's political and social stability. Therefore U.S. officials lent support to Salinas's management of the economy and tended to ignore persistent electoral fraud and human rights abuses.[19]

The extensive rapprochement that followed the change in administrations in each country—the arrival of presidents Bush and Salinas—marked a pivotal change in U.S.-Mexican relations. Beginning with the renegotiation of Mexico's debt in 1989–90, followed by the Brady Plan for debt reduction and finally by the NAFTA initiative, the Bush administration made a broad effort to support the Salinas government. The cordial climate in U.S.-Mexico relations that prevailed throughout the Bush term managed to subsist even when conflicts arose over drug trafficking. It appeared that the two presidents had tacitly agreed to place difficult issues on the back burner and not allow them to sully what Salinas proclaimed as a "new era of friendship between Mexico and the United States."[20]

Mexico, in the context of the free trade rapprochement, began to follow a generally accommodating foreign policy vis-à-vis the United States. Mexico decreased its activism in Central America, softened its criticism of the U.S. invasion of Panama, provided increased oil exports, abstained in a UN vote on human rights in Cuba, accepted Chinese immigrants headed for the United States, and sacrificed a seat on the UN Security Council.[21] Mexico's new foreign policy sought, in the words of Salinas's foreign minister, Fernando Solana, to "understand and accept the growing globalization of the planet [and to] choose a strategy accordingly."[22] A central component of the country's economic diplomacy was the avoidance of diplomatic conflicts with the United States that could jeopardize the free trade negotiations.

Newly elected president Bill Clinton waged an all-out battle in 1993 to assure the passage of NAFTA in Congress. Throughout the NAFTA debate, Clinton adopted the Salinas stance on Mexican democracy, considering it an inevitable by-product of free trade. A democratic opening would ineluctably follow economic development in Mexico via NAFTA. During his debate with Ross Perot, Vice President Gore recognized that Mexico was not yet a "full democracy" but that, through the leverage provided by free trade, the United States could encourage Mexico down the right path. According to U.S. officials, by choosing integration with the United States, Mexico had the vision and the courage to follow the American path, becoming a partner of the land of Jefferson and democracy.

Mexico under Attack, at Home and Abroad

Mexico's aggressive undertaking of economic diplomacy toward the United States contributed to mitigate U.S. concern about the country's authoritarian regime. But in the United Nations, the Organization of American States, and other forums, the Mexican government was forced to exercise defensive diplomacy whenever the issue of democracy arose. In the face of mounting international criticism, Mexican officials resorted, with increasingly less success, to the principles of nonintervention and the defense of national sovereignty. Despite the Mexican government's defensive maneuvers, Mexico's political system began to encounter unprecedented critical scrutiny from abroad.

Minister of Foreign Affairs Fernando Solana outlined clearly the Salinas administration's policy on the international aspects of Mexican democracy when he denounced "the pretensions of ideological hegemony" in the world, which sought to make universal "democracy for export, in which commercial manipulation becomes a substitute for the autonomous political will of the voters." Throughout his tenure, Solana declared that the problems of democracy would have to be resolved by Mexicans "and not by specialized observers from Atlanta or Milwaukee who tell us how to do things." Foreigners will not be allowed "to teach us [Mexicans] what democracy is."[23] President Salinas himself spelled out the government's position in several State of the Union addresses, including the September 1993 message to the nation, in which he declared: "Our democracy is sovereign. One does not imitate nor subordinate oneself to foreign criteria. Discussion of our democracy knows no bounds and has only one decisive judge: the Mexican people."[24]

In 1990, Mexico's lack of democracy was called into question for the first time at a regional forum by Guillermo Endara, president of Panama, who launched a direct diatribe at Mexican electoral practices. Well-known Latin American writer Mario Vargas Llosa contributed to swelling criticism of Mexico's lack of democracy when he coined the definition "perfect dictatorship" during a series of televised roundtables in 1990.[25] Also in 1990, the Inter-American Commission on Human Rights issued its first critical report of Mexico in response to a complaint filed by the PAN. The commission expressed concern over the violation of civil rights as a result of irregularities in the Durango and Chihuahua state elections held in 1985 and 1986. In response, the Mexican government argued that any determination to offer an opinion on electoral matters "would . . . violate the principle of non-intervention."[26] The commission answered by asserting that electoral matters—given that political rights formed part of the Convention of the Rights of Man—did fall within its domain and that, therefore, the Mexican position was unfounded.

Throughout the Salinas term, Mexico's idiosyncratic concepts of sovereignty led it to serious differences with governments across the hemisphere.

The suspension of Panama from the Group of Eight in 1988 because the "enforcement of democratic institutions" had been compromised was strongly opposed by Mexico. Mexican diplomats rejected any military action by the OAS to reestablish democracy in Haiti after the 1991 coup that deposed President Jean-Bertrand Aristide, despite the fact that Mexico condemned the coup. Inside the Group of Three, Mexico tried to distance itself from Venezuela's open calls for the establishment of the "universal concept of democracy in Cuba."[27] When the OAS voted in December 1992 for the automatic suspension of members who overturn democratic rule, Mexico cast the sole dissenting vote.

During the Salinas period, Mexican leaders instituted a fundamental conceptual change in the way they viewed the world. Sovereignty was redefined as economic strength and international competitiveness. However, as Mexico's defensive attitude regarding the external promotion of democracy underscored, the rethinking of sovereignty did not extend to domestic politics. The Mexican government was willing to open the country's economy to Latin American capital but, at the same time, was reluctant to submit its political system to Latin American scrutiny.[28] Mexico offered leadership in the region in return for muted criticism regarding its political system. Official Mexican policy recognized an interdependent world of free trade agreements and unrestricted foreign investment but, simultaneously, resorted to nationalism and sovereignty to defend a suspect political system.

In 1994, a peasant uprising in the southern state of Chiapas called into question the main tenets of the government's "modernizing authoritarian" strategy.[29] On New Year's Day, approximately fifteen hundred armed and uniformed men flooded into San Cristóbal de las Casas, Ocosingo, and several other small towns in the state. Headed by a mysterious, hooded leader named Subcommander Marcos, the rebels declared war on Salinas, voiced their opposition to NAFTA, and vowed to seize control of the government. After five days of sporadic combat, leading to more than one hundred deaths, the Mexican army resorted to targeted air strikes. After violence extended to Mexico City and other areas of the country, Salinas opted for a bargaining stance that led to containment of the conflict.

The revolt was the product of long-standing grievances, which exploded into violence because they lacked democratic channels for expression.[30] In response to mounting peasant discontent, federal and state authorities had done little but increase public spending and provide social compensation for political problems.[31] Chiapas revealed the weaknesses of an economic modernization strategy that attempted to buy social peace at the expense of democratization. Ultimately, the lack of institutionalized mechanisms for generating consensus for economic reform in Mexico rendered the "Salinastroika without PRIsnost" formula untenable.

Mexico's time-honed stability was further jeopardized by the assassination of the ruling party's presidential candidate, Luis Donaldo Colosio, in March 1994, which propelled the country into a period of unprecedented uncertainty. The PRI appeared unstable, economic dislocations loomed, and the government's credibility was weakened by public perceptions of PRI involvement in Colosio's death. The ruling party faced numerous problems: a stagnant economy, a hastily chosen replacement candidate, a discredited president, increased drug trafficking and public insecurity, and a disaffected and suspicious citizenry.

As a result of these challenges, the Mexican government's defensive position in relation to the international system changed dramatically during Salinas's last year in office. Domestic political turbulence ignited by Chiapas and the Colosio assassination convinced state elites that a relatively clean, competitive, and peaceful presidential election was the only way to ensure the consolidation of the country's neoliberal reform. The key challenge for the Salinas technobureacuratic team became how to imbue a PRI victory with domestic and international credibility. Whereas in the past international scrutiny of Mexico's elections had been strongly rejected, during the last six months of 1994, international supervision of the August 1994 election was actively pursued.

Mexico's position regarding the role of international actors also shifted as a result of external pressures, principally from the United States. After the Chiapas uprising and the Colosio assassination, the Clinton administration began to assume a more proactive stance regarding the promotion of Mexican democracy. This change in U.S. policy from detached neglect to growing concern was fueled by NAFTA. During the free trade debate in 1993, the Clinton administration had used a large amount of political capital to promote the virtues of integration with Mexico and had linked free trade to democratic opening south of the border. The Clinton team had also talked about "enlarging" the global community of market-oriented democracies, and Mexico could not be an exception. In the past, the costs of overlooking Mexico's authoritarian regime were almost insignificant, but North American integration heightened those costs. From the perspective of the U.S. government, Mexico was no longer an exotic anomaly but part of the North American community. Events such as the rebellion in Chiapas called into question the political system of a free trade partner, and thus forced the United States to respond.

The Mexican government's about-face regarding the role of international actors was also fueled by pressures from domestic organizations. In the wake of the Chiapas rebellion, human rights and democracy activists successfully drew international attention to the flaws in Mexico's political system. As the international system became more aware of human rights violations and electoral irregularities in Mexico, international organizations demanded an explanation. Confronted with mounting criticism, the Mexican government attempted to justify its actions. This led to a constant process of "exposing violations, demanding explanations, and providing justifications," which in turn changed government practices.[32] By pressuring the Mexican government, the domestic and international NGO alliance altered the country's political system and redefined age-old notions of Mexican sovereignty.

The Mexican "Democracy Network"

In recent years, the issue of democracy in Mexico has become part of an incipient, yet growing, international issued network.[33] The late 1980s and early 1990s have witnessed the emergence of a transnational social movement bound together primarily by shared principled ideas and beliefs about what is right and what is wrong about the Mexican political system.[34] The Mexican democracy network includes domestic and international electoral observer organizations, international NGOs, private foundations, groups of scholars, international secretariats of political parties, and some sectors of the national and international media.

Mexican prodemocracy social movements are key parts of this nascent network. Prodemocracy groups in Mexico have achieved their impact through the use of information and the promotion of citizen participation to change government institutions. At the heart of their crusade is the desire to change public perceptions and behavior at home and abroad. They provide information and direct international attention to specific local situations (such as Chiapas) and add a human dimension to the abstract concept of democracy. Increasingly, they find counterpart organizations across the border with which they communicate and collaborate.[35] This unprecedented transnationalization of civil society is important because it may be setting the foundations for political evolution in Mexico.[36]

Initially, human rights advocacy was the centerpiece of Mexican and international NGO activity. The international human rights network had developed by the mid-1970s, but the more blatant violations in Central America and the Southern Cone were the main focus of its concern. Mexico did not elicit attention, given the presence of a civilian elected government, the use of sophisticated Mexican diplomacy that kept international organizations at bay, and the government's avowedly progressive position on international human rights. With the fall of the military dictatorships and the emergence of democratic rule in the 1980s, however, human rights violations decreased in many countries that the network had targeted in the past.[37] Attention then veered to the less visible cases of human rights violations, such as Mexico's.

Among the key events that fueled the emergence of the human rights network was the founding, in 1984, of the Mexican Academy for Human Rights to focus on the problems of Central American refugees in Mexico. Over time, the academy began to develop a domestic agenda, which currently spans human rights and political rights. The 1985 earthquake was another critical juncture that gave impetus to Mexican NGOs and their allies in human rights organizations. Alliances between groups in civil society and international NGOs eroded traditional perceptions in Mexico that politics had to be channeled through the PRI and also led the NGO sector to incorporate governmental accountability into its demands.[38]

Since 1988 human rights and prodemocracy NGOs in Mexico have flourished largely as a result of changes in Mexico's political economy, including economic liberalization and increasingly contested elections. According to Sergio Aguayo, head of the Mexican Human Rights Academy, the country's integration with the United States opened "windows of vulnerability," which the NGO sector has attempted to exploit. During the Salinas term, sovereignty was redefined not only by the Mexican government but also by forces in civil society. NGOs perceived that economic integration would force Mexico to accept the rules of the international game and to rethink its politics, its human rights practices, and its sovereignty accordingly.[39]

In the aftermath of the turbulent 1988 election, the international human rights network began to devote even more energy and attention to Mexico. In collaboration with recently formed domestic human rights groups, foreign NGOs such as Amnesty International and Americas Watch placed the issue of human rights abuses in Mexico at the top of their international agenda. Persistent human rights abuses and the prospect of a free trade agreement made human rights a more salient issue both in Mexico and abroad. In 1990, Americas Watch released a seminal report documenting human rights violations, and shortly thereafter the U.S. Congress held its first hearings on the human rights situation in Mexico.[40]

Beginning in 1991, many Mexican human rights NGOs began to redirect their focus to the electoral arena. The fraudulent midterm elections, particularly in the states of San Luis Potosí and Guanajuato, were a turning point for civic organization in favor of democracy. Civic groups such as the Movement for Democratic Change (Movimiento para el Cambio Democrático), and the Association of Citizens United for Democracy (Asociación de Ciudadanos Unidos Para la Democracia) carried out independent electoral observations and produced critical reports on the process that stressed the PRI's fraudulent practices in the states.[41] They also undertook electoral observations in twelve other states and attempted to disseminate the right to free and fair elections as a basic human right.

Citizen mobilization in the context of the midterm elections led to a growing convergence between human rights organizations and pro-democracy groups. Leaders of human rights organizations began to view political rights as human rights and, thus, subject to international promotion and protection. Human rights advocates broadened the range of their concerns to the controversial arena of Mexican electoral practices and began to judge Mexican elections according to international standards of transparency and credibility. Democracy thus became a nonsovereign issue, that is, not restricted to the exclusive domain of the Mexican government.

The independent Mexican Commission for the Promotion and Protection of Human Rights illustrates the phenomenon of growing political awareness among human rights organizations. Funded partly by the National Endowment for Democracy, the commission currently handles over 500 cases and considers itself an alternative source of information to the government-sponsored human rights organization. Since its founding, the commission has established close ties to social movements, the PRD, and international organizations such as Americas Watch and Minnesota Human Rights Advocates. It distributes its reports among these organizations and participates in international briefing sessions. The commission's president, MariClaire Acosta, has testified in the U.S. Congress regarding human rights in Mexico. By drawing domestic and international attention to the abuses committed by the Mexican federal police, the commission has contributed to a government crackdown on abusive police officers.

The commission also belongs to a Mexican network of thirty-six human rights organizations known as the National Network of Civic Organizations, "All the Rights for Everyone" (Red Nacional de Organizaciones Civiles, "Todos los Derechos Para Todos"). Its members seek to protect dissidents, reveal patterns of repression, and build domestic institutions to safeguard human rights. The ultimate goal of these organizations is to "generate accountability." Therefore, according to Acosta, the human rights agenda is also a political agenda: "The focus on human rights has raised public consciousness. It has led to emergent citizens' movements across Mexico and has also offered the Mexican population a form of citizen resistance to the government."[42]

Network members believe that individuals can bring about political change by documenting electoral irregularities and violations of political and human rights. Activists such as Sergio Aguayo, José Agustin Ortiz Pinchetti, MariClaire Acosta, Julio Faesler, and Adolfo Aguilar Zínser have interpreted events and rendered testimony in a fashion that has enabled them to have an impact on the country's political debate. Their moral commitment, powerful testimony, and appeals to democratic principles have captured the imagination and harnessed the energy of significant sectors of the Mexican population.[43]

The Mexican democracy network has strengthened the concept of citizenship and citizen participation in politics.[44] Traditionally, political activities in Mexico had been monopolized by political parties and the government. NGOs, however, have promoted citizen participation in electoral observation exercises and postelectoral marches against the government, with successful results. New organizations devoted exclusively to the promotion of democracy, including the Council for Democracy and Women Fighting for Democracy, have gained strength and visibility: 138 of these organizations, representing twenty states, banded together to create the Convergence of Civic Organizations for Democracy (Convergencia de Organizaciones Civiles por la Democracia).

In March 1993, several members of the Federal District Assembly, academics, and opposition party leaders organized a plebiscite to consult public opinion about the possibility of an elected government in the city. The organizers invited 300 prominent citizens to form a Support Council for the Citizen Plebiscite. The plebiscite was conceived as a citizens' effort to pressure the government into incorporating the results of the referendum as part of the agenda for political reform. Approximately 320,000 people went to the 2,400 *casillas* (polling booths) in schools, churches, and shopping centers. Opposition parties subsequently used the plebiscite's results to pressure the government into devising a new system of governance for the city. The plebiscite set another precedent for citizen participation that successfully redefined the boundaries of the politically possible.

The Mexican prodemocracy movement has developed a two-pronged tactical approach that combines political theater in Mexico with lobbying in the United States and collaboration with international organizations.[45] To generate domestic and international awareness, the network engages in symbolic forms of public protest and electoral vigilance, including the organization of so-called parallel elections in the United States and prodemocracy marches in Mexico City. The network's strategy is to direct domestic and international attention to antidemocratic practices, with the hope that greater vigilance and protest will force the Mexican government to promote substantive change. As a democracy activist explained: "International interest regarding democracy in Mexico will only continue if the costs of supporting an antidemocratic government in power begin to grow. We can raise those costs."[46]

Citizen mobilization in the early 1990s set the stage for widespread independent electoral observation during the 1994 presidential race. As Sergio Aguayo, cofounder of the Civic Alliance, explained: "From 1991 to 1994 we observed 15 state and local elections, organized five quick counts and, in March of 1993, the first-ever 'Citizens' plebiscite' in Mexico City. Around that time we decided that we should organize a national coalition to observe the electoral process of 1994."[47] Months before the election, citizen groups undertook critical studies of structural conditions that continued to preclude electoral fairness, including biased media coverage, vote buying, and coercion. On 21 August, over twenty thousand Mexicans participated as election observers from diverse organizations, including Civic Alliance/Observation '94. The Civic Alliance coordinated the activities of three hundred NGOs and civic groups, placed observers at polls throughout the country, conducted quick counts of the results, and produced a postelectoral report that highlighted the persistence of electoral irregularities, particularly in the Mexican countryside.[48]

The Mexican democracy network involves three publics: "participants, powerholders and bystanders."[49] Traditionally weak groups have been able to influence government policies by using public protest to attract the attention of "reference groups," that is, international organizations and activists, who in turn, have pressured Mexican leaders. Transnational alliances between Mexican democracy activists and their counterparts abroad, including human rights monitors, lawyers, representatives of religious communities, and international electoral observers, are contributing to expand the frontiers of political change by magnifying domestic demands for democracy beyond Mexico's borders. Transnational linkage has also strengthened the domestic clout of Mexican opposition organizations by connecting them to the political influence of their foreign allies.[50]

For example, in 1992 the Mexican Human Rights Academy invited a group of observers from the Carter Center to observe, in a nonofficial capacity, the elections in the state of Michoacán. The Carter Center produced a report on the activities carried out by domestic observers. Subsequently, the Carter Center released a document entitled "Electoral Reform in Mexico," based on the findings of a delegation visit in 1993. The widely disseminated report concluded that, while positive, the electoral reforms undertaken during that year fell short of establishing a foundation that would "give all parties and all the people of Mexico confidence that a genuinely free and fair election would occur in 1994."[51] The Carter Center's report gave international resonance to many of the complaints voiced by opposition parties and NGOs in Mexico and contributed to a subsequent reversal of the Mexican government's opposition to international observers.[52]

Domestic organizations such as the Civic Alliance have been able to expand their influence and visibility through collaboration with the National Endowment for Democracy (NED). Leaving behind its traditionally meager involvement in Mexican politics, since 1992 the NED has funneled grants to several civic groups that participate in opposition politics.[53] The Mexican grantees are known among democracy activists for their support for electoral democracy and their promotion of citizen participation.[54] The grants have supported training sessions for election monitors, quick counts during local elections, publications, conferences, and some infrastructure development.[55] NED support also helped the Civic Alliance to disseminate its views in Washington policy-making circles, and strengthen its credibility as a nonpartisan organization during the 1994 presidential election.

Members of the Convergencia Democrática and the Washington Office on Latin America have also developed a series of joint activities. The Washington Office on Latin America and the Mexican Academy for Human Rights collaborated in a joint report on the 1994 Mexican presidential election, calling their effort "one symbol of the growing desire of civil society in Mexico and the United States to promote more democratic and humane societies."[56] The Convergencia also sponsored three trinational meetings in Washington and the establishment of a task force on Mexican democracy as part of the activities of the Latin American Studies Association. The purpose of these activities has been to define a shared political agenda for Mexico and to expand the definition of democracy in Mexico beyond a narrow focus on elections.

These transboundary alliances in favor of democracy underscore that the Mexican government can no longer monopolize the pace, timing, and implementation of measures to promote democracy in Mexico. Domestic and international actors have propelled Mexico into an era of reconceptualized sovereignty, in which the Mexican state has begun reluctantly to accept that the violation of human rights and political rights can no longer be considered an exclusively domestic problem.

The democracy network is gradually strengthening domestic NGOs, altering political discourse, creating a more auspicious environment for political reform, and educating foreign publics about Mexico's political situation. External and internal actors are mounting a legitimacy challenge to the Mexican state; a legitimacy challenge is the ability of social movements to weaken the state's power by eroding its mandate in the eyes of its domestic and international allies.[57] By delegitimizing the Mexican state at home and abroad, domestic and international forces are gradually fueling the Mexican transition.

The Mexican government's response to the international spotlight has ranged from public relations campaigns and defensive nationalist posturing to specific policy innovation. Government officials have tried to deny the legitimacy of international concern over human rights and democracy, to discredit opposition activists by suggesting that they are engaging in anti-Mexico campaigns, and to mobilize nationalist public opinion against avowed interference in internal affairs. When that piecemeal strategy has failed to placate international criticisms, the government has tried to defuse international and domestic opposition by collaborating with some segments of the democracy network while, simultaneously, proceeding with business as usual. The third tactic has entailed making concrete improvements in the electoral laws in response to international and domestic pressures.[58]

Throughout his term, president Salinas exhibited great sensitivity to the country's external image and to the deleterious effects of international complaints regarding problems with human rights and democracy. To a large extent, the Mexican government's creation of the National Commission on Human Rights in June 1990 was a direct response to pressures from the democracy network. The Salinas administration was worried that Mexico might be subjected to intense criticism from the U.S. Congress in the midst of the free trade debate. The National Commission was installed to lessen international scrutiny in the wake of reports released earlier that year by the OAS and Amnesty International, detailing persistent human rights abuses.

As part of a sophisticated international public relations campaign, Salinas often resorted to preemptive actions to generate approval for his administration's policies toward human rights and political reform. Creating the National Commission on Human Rights served to preempt the issue by making it appear that the Mexican government had its human rights problem under control.[59] Since the formation of the commission, the government has taken several concrete steps to improve human rights practices. The Salinas administration, in the absence of international pressures, would have been unlikely to make these changes of its own accord.[60]

The Mexican government's sensitivity to international criticism has heightened the importance of a critical, and yet oftentimes inadvertent, member of the democracy network: the press, both international and in the United States. In the aftermath of the Nicaraguan elections, which were closely watched by international observers, the U.S. press began to make recommendations for supervised Mexican elections in view of the proposed free trade region. Partly as a result of irregularities in the mid-November elections in Mexico state, an important segment of the foreign press began to intensify its criticism of the Mexican political process. For the first time since the 1988 election, some of the criticism was directed toward Salinas personally. This marked a significant contrast to the generally supportive attitude of the foreign press during the first two years of his tenure, when reporters tended to make negative judgments of the PRI, on the one hand, and positive evaluations of Salinas, on the other.

The U.S. press may have influenced the outcome of the 1991 midterm elections, including the downfall of two turbulently elected governors, through influential editorials that called into question President Salinas's commitment to political liberalization.[61] As the *New York Times* bureau chief in Mexico explained: "Objectively there was not enough strength in the opposition in San Luis Potosí and Guanajuato to force the PRI to give in. The new element was the concern over the foreign press. The government got rid of Aguirre the day the *Wall Street Journal* editorial came out, but before that they called several foreign correspondents to brief them on what was about to happen. The event seemed more directed to the foreign audience than the local one."[62]

Given that Mexican politics can no longer escape the unforgiving spotlight of the international media, international exposure is contributing to political change. As a renowned political analyst remarked, "If the Mexican press writes something critical about Mexico it has an even greater impact when it is reproduced in the United States. U.S. coverage magnifies the impact of domestic criticism and forces the Mexican government to retrace its steps."[63] For example, in February 1993 select guests at a dinner hosted by prominent financier Antonio Ortiz Mena were asked by President Salinas to contribute an average of $25 million to the PRI's 1994 presidential campaign. When local furor over the "millionaire's banquet" was reported in the *Wall Street Journal* and on the front page of the *New York Times,* one week after a Mexican business daily broke the story, the

Beyond Sovereignty

PRI reversed course and announced self-imposed limits on individual campaign contributions.

The same boomerang effect occurred in 1993 after prominent political columnist and radio host Miguel Angel Granados Chapa was fired for interviewing opposition candidate Cuauhtémoc Cárdenas on his show. The event caused a stir in Mexico, but not until it was covered by the U.S. press did the Mexican government remove the public official who had pressured the radio station into removing Granados Chapa. Thus, growing exposure to the media may be forcing the Mexican government into a modicum of accountability. As a Mexican political columnist argued: "The foreign press has played a crucial role as a representative and a creator of international public opinion. Public opinion in Mexico is irrelevant to the Mexican government. The government has transferred its political nerve center to the United States, because it is so dependent on foreign investment. As a result, public opinion in the United States matters to the government when in Mexico it doesn't."[64]

Ten years ago, most Mexican newspapers would not have printed politically controversial stories for fear of government retaliation, and most U.S. papers would have ignored them. During the last several yeas, they have made headlines on both sides of the border. By revealing flaws in the Mexican political process, the foreign press is contributing to create a pro-democracy environment in the United States and beyond.

The Mexican government is aware of the democratizing power of the international press and has attempted to harness it through sophisticated cooptation strategies. Foreign reporters in Mexico marvel at their extraordinary access to high-level government officials, and president Salinas himself gave interviews to foreign journalists approximately once every week and a half (a privilege rarely granted to the Mexican press). Salinas even chose to announce major policy innovations, such as allowing external revision of Mexico's voters' registration list, to the foreign press with the hope that, by granting journalists privileged access to information, they would adopt a progovernment stance.[65] However, despite the government's courtship, since the presidential *destape* (the hand-picked selection of the president's successor) in November 1993, foreign correspondents began to file increasingly critical stories, focusing on the lack of political change in Mexico.

In the case of the Chiapas rebellion, press and media coverage of the Mexican military's bombardment of the Chiapas hillside spurred international concern and led to an influx of human rights organizations from abroad. CNN dissemination of events in Chiapas undoubtedly raised the costs of the government's initial military response. Scenes of government repression in Chiapas captured international attention and underscored the potential power of the electronic media to curb human rights violations and to fuel political change. Media coverage generated a tide of international criticism and brought the traditionally secondary issue of Mexican democracy to the fore.[66] Events in Chiapas revealed that the Mexican government was no longer capable of monopolizing information or of keeping international and domestic actors from covering the conflict. In addition to the foreign press, Mexican and international NGOs sent their representatives to the state, where they cooperated to release periodic communiqués on the evolution of the crisis.[67]

The Zapatista National Liberation Army (Ejército Zapatista de Liberación Nacional, or EZLN) demonstrated a sophisticated awareness of the role and power of the international press and other transnational actors. The guerrillas chose to rebel on 1 January, the first day of NAFTA's enactment, when international attention would be focused on Mexico. By voicing their opposition to the agreement, the Zapatistas added a transborder dimension to the rebellion. Throughout their crusade, EZLN leaders made deliberate efforts to court the domestic and international press. Guerrilla commanders sent journalists glossy pamphlets describing their demands, organized press conferences, and faxed wrenching statements from Subcommander Marcos describing the roots of the revolt. Their communiqués requested media assistance to alert the world about the "genocide" taking place in Chiapas. The EZLN also called upon the citizens and government of the United States to undertake "solidarity actions" and to suspend all military and economic aid to the Mexican government.[68]

Mexico's integration into the North American region rendered the Mexican government accountable to constituencies beyond its borders and raised the political costs of repression. The Mexican government ultimately opted for a political solution in Chiapas, due to a combination of internal and external forces and because violence was spreading beyond the state. In response to mounting domestic and international pressure, Salinas removed Interior Minister Patrocinio González Garrido, known for his hard-line stance, and replaced him with Jorge Carpizo, an internationally respected lawyer and human rights advocate. Salinas also named the former mayor of Mexico City, and short-lived foreign affairs minister, Manuel Camacho, as commissioner for peace and reconciliation in Chiapas. In addition, Salinas sent a National Commission on Human Rights team to investigate human rights abuses, declared a unilateral cease-fire, and offered amnesty to the rebels. The dual message was that the government would attempt to solve the Chiapas crisis in a negotiated fashion and that Carpizo had been designated to ensure the impartiality of the 1994 presidential election.

By forcing the government to allow truly competitive elections, Chiapas opened a window of opportunity for domestic and foreign actors in favor of democracy. The revolt led to the signing of an unprecedented preelectoral Pact for Peace, Democracy, and Justice among political parties, including the traditionally reticent leftist Party of the Democratic Revolution (PRD). The accord, subsequently voted into law, called for "legal and credible" elections during the August 1994 presidential race and established measures designed to create a level playing field among parties, including limits on campaign spending, scrutiny of party financing and expenditures, equal access to the media, and the creation of an "army of electoral observers." The Colosio assassination provided further impetus for political reform by pushing all political parties to the realization that a clean and peaceful presidential election was necessary to ensure political stability.

U.S. policy toward Mexico also contributed in an indirect fashion to political evolution by pressuring the Mexican government into sponsoring clean elections. Through its public statements, private diplomacy, and financial support for election-related activities, "the Clinton administration went farther than any of its predecessors in devising and articulating a policy designed ostensibly to support Mexican democratization."[69] U.S. contributions to democratic change in Mexico were targeted mainly on electoral observation, via the National Endowment for Democracy, the National Democratic Institute, and the International Republican Institute. These organizations channeled funds to Mexican election observers, provided technical assistance to the Federal Electoral Institute, and assembled a high-profile delegation of foreign visitors.[70]

Pressures from above (by the U.S. government and international electoral observation groups) and from below (by domestic observer organizations) forced the Mexican government into accepting the presence of international "visitors" during the August presidential election.[71] In the past the Mexican government had viewed domestic observers as a nuisance and international observers as an unacceptable infringement on Mexican sovereignty, but the need to provide credibility to a predictable PRI victory led to unprecedented concessions.

In May 1994 the Mexican government invited a technical team from the United Nations to train and coordinate the activities of local observers. Although the late invitation precluded the possibility of a UN-sponsored national observation of the kind conducted in South Africa, UN staff provided funding and technical training to national observers and issued an evaluation of the Mexican electoral system. UN assistance to domestic observation efforts raised the political salience and credibility of organizations such as the Civic Alliance and contributed to mitigate government accusations of partisanship against domestic observer groups.

It was in the area of scrutiny, accountability, and vigilance that international actors, particularly international visitors, played a significant role during the election. International visitors helped to reduce the PRI's capacity to commit fraud, limited the partiality of the Federal Electoral Institute, and ensured greater transparency in the electoral process. The combined presence of international and domestic observers may have also minimized campaign violence and encouraged voter participation. Thus, international observation served to legitimize a PRI victory when such a victory would have not been credible otherwise.

The 1994 presidential election marked a significant step in Mexico's unfinished transition to a more competitive, democratic system of governance. However, even though the centrality of elections was widely recognized, one of the major parties, the PRD, did not accept the results, and several groups (including the Zapatista rebels) continued to disqualify the rule of law and to reject established institutions and political organizations. Although the elections were generally perceived as clean and free, the structural inequalities of the political system, such as the lack of a level playing field among parties, prevail. The main challenge for international and domestic actors will be to maintain the momentum for political reform and to ensure democratic consolidation.

Prescriptions for Treading Lightly and without a Stick

Pressures from a burgeoning democracy network have contributed to modifying understandings about how the Mexican government should use its authority over its citizens and to changing specific political practices. International actors and forces are an integral part of this network, whose power and influence continue to evolve. External pressure has proven to be most effective when it intersects with domestic actors pushing for political change. Therefore, indirect support to strengthen democratic institutions and practices may be the most positive form of external assistance in aiding democratic consolidation in Mexico.

Indirect support cannot be expected to foster democratic rule directly, but in tandem with domestic actors, it can strengthen civil society, encourage pluralism, and inform the decisions of pro-democracy elites.[72] What follows are suggestions that would enable foreign assistance to "fit" with Mexico's specific circumstances. In Mexico, forces operating against democracy are identifiable and strong, while forces in favor of democracy are relatively less organized and diffuse. External support can help strengthen prodemocracy actors and, thus, enable greater political opening.

As Sikkink argues, the countries most susceptible to network pressures are those that aspire to form part of the community of nations as a normative community.[73] Mexico's modernizing technobureaucrats are greatly concerned with the international image of Mexico and the damage done to that image by widespread reports of human rights violations and democratic failings. International members of the democracy network could take advantage of such technobureaucratic sensitivity to multilateral condemnation, underscoring that international criticism can affect a country's power, prestige, and commercial interests. Heightened international disapproval of Mexico's political vagaries could alter the balance of power within the Mexican elite and enhance the power of that faction in favor of broader political opening. International pressure spearheaded by the press, by international human rights advocates, and by multilateral organizations could be used as leverage against the Mexican government.

Given that the position of numerous international actors regarding the promotion of democracy in Mexico hinges on U.S. policy, that policy may have to be clarified. The Clinton administration's hands-off approach toward the 1994 presidential elections was frequently contradicted by the administration's clear endorsement of the Mexican government. Throughout the presidential campaign, U.S. officials constantly praised the Mexican government for its efforts to institute electoral reform and all but predicted that the election would be the cleanest in Mexican history. U.S. officials studiously avoided making any public statements on the flaws of the electoral system, creating the impression that electoral fairness had been achieved—thus undermining many of the opposition's valid concerns about the lack of a level playing field among parties.

Indirect assistance to the electoral process occurred at the margins of official U.S. policy and did not lay the foundations for a clear stance in the future.[74] The depth of Washington's commitment to democratic consolidation in Mexico (beyond relatively clean elections) remains unclear. The U.S. government has not yet articulated a strategy for assisting Mexico to strengthen its democratic institutions, nor has it decided how much it wants a fully democratic Mexico or how much it is prepared to invest in that outcome.

U.S. policy can contribute to Mexico's political evolution by nurturing independent organizations and institutions and by emphasizing the protection of human rights. The U.S. government has already taken innovative steps in that direction by instituting a new assistant secretary of state for global affairs and a new assistant secretary of defense for democracy and peacekeeping. The task of enhancing democratic rule south of the border, however, will require every instrument available, including a cadre of sympathetic diplomats. In Chile, an important ingredient for the country's transition to democracy was U.S. Ambassador Harry Barnes, who skillfully used U.S. policies to support a democratic transition. Much could be accomplished in Mexico if the U.S. ambassador became a strong supporter of political rights and independent prodemocracy organizations.

The United States can also contribute to political evolution in Mexico by expanding and redefining the role of the National Endowment for Democracy. The endowment's focus has been on poll watching and quick counts, obviously important tasks in Mexico, where fraudulent elections are the norm. But the effectiveness of these activities is limited due to the size of the country and because so much of the fraud and distortion of the political process takes place well before the election. If the problems that preclude a level playing field among parties remain unaddressed, quick counts and election observers risk "validating election results in cases where the voting itself was relatively free of overt fraud, even though the combined irregularities over time might add to an unfair election climate."[75]

In tandem with U.S. policy, domestic and international NGOs may be the best vehicle for reform by promoting public awareness, pressuring the government, and raising the calculus of Mexico's leaders.[76] Mexican NGOs have fueled international concern for democracy in Mexico by providing documentation and reports to international and regional organizations. The prodemocracy movement in Mexico will have a maximum impact if it is backed by a network of sympathetic international actors.

In the case of human rights, it was only after the NGOs inside and outside of Mexico began to document human rights abuses and bring them to the attention of the press and policymakers, and only within the context of the free trade negotiations, that the Mexican government made concrete changes to improve its human rights situation. Challenges from above and below have thus had a clear impact in Mexico. External support could enable internal prodemocracy groups to develop similar strategies to garner international attention. Because the power of NGOs derives from information, they must produce reliable and well-documented testimony on electoral irregularities and the broader violation of political rights. External funding and training would assist these prodemocracy groups in the task of gathering, systematizing, and disseminating politically relevant information.

Another way of strengthening Mexico's domestic NGOs and the democracy network as a whole would be the presence of Mexican democracy activists in Washington, D.C. In the human rights arena, NGOs have exerted influence on U.S. human rights policy by providing information to the U.S. Congress and by lobbying its members. Prodemocracy NGOs could develop a similar strategy and begin to link Mexican activists to U.S. policymakers and journalists. Groups linked to the democracy network could serve as sources of information for U.S. policymakers other than Mexican public officials. Mexican NGOs could also counteract inertial tendencies in the U.S. government's policy toward Mexico by creating an institution (a "democracy NGO central") in Washington for information gathering and lobbying.[77]

Transnational NGOs can play a critical role in connecting Mexican democracy movements to an emerging "democracy regime." The Mexican prodemocracy movement, for example, might benefit from closer ties with transnational NGOs such as the Washington Office on Latin America, Amnesty International, and the Human Rights Watch. International NGOs could sponsor meetings with their Mexican counterparts to discuss strengthening democracy in Mexico through more effective electoral vigilance. International meetings and conferences could strengthen the transnational democracy network, facilitating linkages and serving as a focal point for NGO organizing and information sharing. International conferences could be used to train domestic electoral observers and elaborate what the head of the Human Rights Academy calls a "Manual and Code of Conduct for International Electoral Observers in Mexico."

Foreign donors such as the Ford Foundation, the Inter-American Foundation, and the MacArthur Foundation also have a significant role to play in Mexico's transition. They could contribute funds for public opinion studies, civic education campaigns, independent research centers, and programs to bring opposition leaders together to discuss policy options. Such meetings might enhance the ability of political actors to work together and lay the psychological bases for relations of sociability among political opponents. External funding might also help the opposition develop modern campaign techniques, particularly the use of polls and focus groups.[78] Donors could also promote independent scholarship on electoral systems and laws and on how to decentralize government and combat corruption.

To raise the profile and salience of the need for political change in Mexico, measures could be taken by members of the democracy network to strengthen the independent press and media. International organizations could provide scholarships and training for Mexican journalists abroad. International donors and NGOs could also reinvigorate programs to monitor, enhance, and defend freedom of the press and to assist and train journalists, editors, and newscasters. By strengthening independent coverage and analysis, international actors could contribute to the development of a more democratic political culture in Mexico.[79]

Finally, organizations such as the OAS have an indirect role to play in the promotion of Mexican democracy. The existing human rights regime has laid the groundwork for applying multilateral pressure to Mexico. Although the general effectiveness of Latin American regional organizations is uncertain, their activities may have the cumulative effect of stigmatizing Mexico as a pariah state where democracy and human rights and corruption are concerned. Diplomatic pressure from regional organizations might dislodge the Mexican government's traditional opposition to full-fledged international observers.

Diplomats from regional organizations might be able to reach private understandings, in which democratizing measures are not publicly linked to external actors and the Mexican government does not seem to be caving in to international pressure. The OAS can volunteer specific assistance in the monitoring of electoral processes. By involving the OAS, the democracy network would thus interpose a regional organization that is legitimate in the eyes of the Mexican government and public. Many Mexican NGOs consider the OAS and the United Nations indispensable allies, whose role and credibility need to be strengthened in order to pressure the Mexican government.

Thus, external support could significantly contribute to Mexico's transition to democracy in ways that are diverse, complex, and not always obvious. Certainly, the decisive actors in Mexico's transition process will be internal rather than external, and the internal evolution of the Mexican situation will determine the timing and pace of greater political opening. But external actors can amplify domestic demands, strengthen domestic organizations, and create a favorable international climate for democratic consolidation. By not intervening directly, international forces can make positive and worthwhile contributions to democratic governance in Mexico.

The Mexican case underscores the importance of transnational linkages in influencing political change. The impact of such NGOs as the United Nations, Americas Watch, Amnesty International, the international media, and transnational NGOs has been unmistakable. The combined activities of organizations devoted to the promotion of human rights and democratization has led to the gradual emergence of a transnational democracy network pushing for greater political change.

Mexico's integration with the world has entailed not only the movement of goods and capital but also the flow of communication, people, and ideas, a flow that is affecting the nature and dynamics of the Mexican political system. International networks, civic associations, and overlapping local, regional, and global organizations have become part of the Mexican political process. Globalization is altering the Mexican government's constituencies, the meaning of accountability, the form and scope of political participation, and the meaning of the country's sovereignty.[80]

International attention has undoubtedly helped raise the costs of conducting fraudulent elections in Mexico, but ensuring the fairness of the electoral process is only one among many necessary steps to consolidate democratic governance. The persistence of clientelism, corruption, biased media coverage, presidentialism, and an unfair playing field among political parties suggests that Mexican democratization still has a long way to go. However, the intersection of domestic and international attention has proved to be a catalyst for reform. Grassroots pressure combined with international criticism has forced the political system to move in a democratizing direction and will continue to do so in the future. The task for international actors and their Mexican allies who advocate democratic rule is to ensure that the ballot box becomes an enduring and effective fulcrum for change.

Notes

Chapter 1   *Collectively Defending Democracy*
in the Western Hemisphere

1. See, for example, the various authors in David Collier, ed., *The New Authoritarianism in Latin America* (Princeton: Princeton Univ. Press, 1979). The term seems to have originated with Guillermo O'Donnell; see his *Modernization and Bureaucratic Authoritarianism: Studies in South American Politics,* No. 9, Politics of Modernization Series (Berkeley: Institute of International Studies, University of California, 1973).

2. In the course of my two terms as a member of the Inter-American Commission on Human Rights (1976–83), during which the commission investigated the general (and generally miserable) condition of human rights in virtually every country with an authoritarian government, I frequently encountered the mind-set I have described. On the rise and fall of various economic models in the modern history of Latin America, see John Sheahan, *Patterns of Development in Latin America* (Princeton: Princeton Univ. Press, 1987).

3. See, for example, O'Donnell, *Modernization and Bureaucratic Authoritarianism.*

4. Larry Diamond, Juan J. Linz, and Seymour Martin Lipset, eds., *Democracy in Developing Countries: Latin America* (Boulder: Lynne Rienner, 1989), xvii.

5. However, in her comment on the case studies, Karen Remmer does make a persuasive case for the proposition that the external environment is the decisive variable for explaining the broad renewal and resilience of democracy in the 1980s. See chap. 13, this volume.

6. *Restatement (Third) of Foreign Relations Law of the United States,* sec. 201 (1986).

7. See Richard B. Lillich, ed., *International Law of State Responsibility for Injuries to Aliens* (Charlottesville: Univ. Press of Virginia, 1983).

8. See Ian Brownlie, *International Law and the Use of Force by States* (Oxford: Clarendon, 1963), 3–18.

9. At Nuremberg, Professor Jahrreiss for the defense argued that "every state is sole judge of whether in a given case it is waging a war of self-defense." International Military Tribunal, *Trial of the Major War Criminals before the International Military Tribunal, Nuremberg, 14 Nov. 1945–1 Oct. 1946* (Nuremberg: International Military Tribunal, 1947–49), 17:469. When the defense alleged specifically that the invasion of Norway was an act of self-defense, the tribunal treated this as raising a question of fact and concluded that the criterion of immediate necessity was not satisfied. Lawrence D. Egbert, "International Military (Nuremberg), Judgement and Sentences," *American Journal of International Law* 41 (1947):

206. Still the single best study of the place of self-defense in the discourse of international law during the nineteenth and the first half of the twentieth centuries is Derek Bowett, *Self Defence in International Law* (Manchester: Manchester Univ. Press, 1958).

10. William Edward Hall, *A Treatise on International Law* (Oxford: Clarendon, 1917), 302–3 (implicitly).

11. See Thomas M. Franck, "The Emerging Right to Democratic Governance," *American Journal of International Law* 86 (1992): 49–52.

12. Randall L. Schweller, "Domestic Structure and Preventive War: Are Democracies More Pacific?" *World Politics* (1992): 253–69; Steve Chan, "Mirror, Mirror on the Wall . . . Are the Freer Countries More Pacific?" *Journal of Conflict Resolution* 28 (1984): 617–48. Compare Karl Deutsch et al., *Political Community and the North Atlantic Area* (Princeton: Princeton Univ. Press, 1957). For the original argument, see Immanuel Kant, *Perceptual Peace,* trans. Ted Humphrey, rev. ed. (Indianapolis: Hackett, 1983), 107–39. But see Christopher Layne, "Kant or Cant: The Myth of the Democratic Peace," and David Spiro, "The Insignificance of the Liberal Peace," both in *International Security* (1994): 5–49, 50–86, respectively.

13. John C. G. Rohl, *Germany without Bismarck: The Crisis of Government in the Second Reich, 1890–1900* (Berkeley: Univ. of California Press, 1967).

14. See John J. Mearsheimer, "Back to the Future: Instability in Europe after the Cold War," *International Security* 15 (1990): 5–56.

15. See Gregor Athalwin Zierman, *Education for Death: The Making of the Nazi* (London: Oxford Univ. Press, 1941); Werner Richter, *Re-Educating Germany,* trans. Paul Lehman (Chicago: Univ. of Chicago Press, 1945); Erika Mann, *School for Barbarians* (New York: Modern Age Books, 1938).

16. See, for example, Jessica Tuchman Mathews, "Redefining Security," *Foreign Affairs* (1989): 162.

17. See, for example, James Malloy, ed., *Authoritarianism and Corporation in Latin America* (Pittsburgh: Univ. of Pittsburgh Press, 1977).

18. See Tom J. Farer, *The Grand Strategy of the United States in Latin America* (New Brunswick: Transaction, 1988), 23–31.

19. Stephen Schlesinger and Stephen Kinzer, *Bitter Fruit: The Untold Story of the Coup in Guatemala* (New York: Doubleday, 1982); Piero Gleijeses, *Shattered Hope: The Guatemalan Revolution and the United States, 1944–54* (Princeton: Princeton Univ. Press, 1991).

20. Robert D. Crassweller, *Trujillo: The Life and Times of a Caribbean Dictator* (New York: Macmillan, 1966); Arturo Espaillat, *Trujillo: The Last Caesar* (Chicago: Henry Regnery, 1963), 7.

21. See Franck, "Democratic Governance," 63. See also Farer, *Grand Strategy,* 79–85, 112–22.

22. See OAS, *The Inter-American Commission, 1972–1982* (Washington, D.C.: OAS, 1984), 333–35.

23. This was, for instance, a main theme of the Argentine military leaders I interviewed during the 1979 "observation in loco" conducted by the Inter-American Commission on Human Rights, of which I was then a member.

24. Robert A. Pastor, *Condemned to Repetition: The United States and Nicaragua* (Princeton: Princeton Univ. Press, 1987).

25. For a nuanced and detailed account, see ibid.

26. See UN GAOR, 42d Sess., Agenda Item 34, UN Doc A/42/521S/19085 (1987), reprinted in "Costa Rica–El Salvador–Guatemala–Honduras–Nicaragua: Agreement on Procedure for Establishing a Firm and Lasting Peace in Central America," *ILM* 26 (1987): 1166–74 (Esquipulas II, signed by five Central American presidents).

27. See "Carter to Monitor Elections Next February in Nicaragua," *New York Times,* 9 Aug. 1989; Franck, "Democratic Governance," 71–72.

28. Tim Golden, "UN Report Urges Sweeping Changes in Salvador Army," *New York Times,* 16 Mar. 1993. For a discussion on the Salvadoran peace accords, see George Vickers, Jack Spence, et al., *Endgame: A Progress Report on Implementation of the Salvadoran Peace Accords* (Cambridge, Mass.: Hemisphere Initiatives, 1992).

29. See, generally, Indar J. Rikhye and Kjell Skjelsbaek, eds., *The United Nations and Peacekeeping* (New York: St. Martin's, 1991).

30. OEA, "The Serious Crisis in Panama in Its International Context," Ser F/II.21, Doc 8, Rev 2; Ser F/II.21, Doc 45 (1989).

31. R. W. Apple Jr., "Bush's Trip on Panama," *New York Times,* 11 May 1989.

32. OAS, "Serious Events in the Republic of Panama," CP/Res 534, 800/89 (1989). On 22 Dec., the resolution was passed twenty to one, with five abstentions.

33. OAS, "Resolution on Representative Democracy," AG/Res, 1080, XXI-0/91 (4 June 1991).

34. See Howard W. French, "Sixteen Haitians Slain in Week of Strife," *New York Times,* 28 May 1992; Stephen Kinzer, "Two Chilean Exiles Go Home to a Rousing Welcome," *New York Times,* 6 Sep. 1983.

35. SC Res 841 (16 June 1993), Res 861 (27 Aug. 1993), and Res 917 (6 May 1994).

36. Howard W. French, "US, Its Blockade of Haiti Failing, Studies Other Means to End Crisis," *New York Times,* 29 Jan. 1992.

37. Hall, *A Treatise on International Law,* 301.

38. Ibid., 302–3.

39. See Rikhye and Skjelsbaek, *United Nations and Peacekeeping.*

40. See Abraham F. Lowenthal, *The Dominican Intervention* (Cambridge: Harvard Univ. Press, 1972); Piero Gleijeses, *The Dominican Crisis: The 1965 Constitutionalist Revolt and American Intervention,* trans. Lawrence Lipson (Baltimore: Johns Hopkins Univ. Press, 1978), 260–63.

41. Peter Hakim, "Saving Haiti from Itself," *Washington Post,* 31 May 1992. See also "The Caribbean: Bad to Worse," *Time,* 10 Feb. 1992, 32.

42. See Kenneth Freed, "In Sanction's Wake," *Los Angeles Times,* 20 Dec. 1993.

43. Linda Robinson, "Tough Guys Don't Blink," *U.S. News & World Report,* 16 May 1994, 36.

44. Nathaniel C. Nash, "Peru Chief Orders New Mass Arrests," *New York Times,* 8 Apr. 1992.

45. OEA, "Support for the Restoration of Democracy in Peru," Ser F/V.2, Mre/Res 1/92 (13 Apr. 1992).

46. Nash, "Peru Chief Orders New Mass Arrests." See also "Peru's Leader Bars Appeals by Ousted Judicial Officials," *New York Times,* 29 Apr. 1992.

47. Nathaniel C. Nash, "Peru's Leader Facing a Test in Vote Today," *New York Times,* 22 Nov. 1992.

48. OEA, "Restoration of Democracy in Peru," Ser F.V.2, Mre/Res 3/92, Corr 1 (14 Dec. 1992).

49. See, for instance, Kenneth Anderson, *Maximizing Deniability: The Justice System and Human Rights in Guatemala* (Washington, D.C.: International Human Rights Law Group, 1989); Human Rights Watch, *Civil Patrols in Guatemala* (New York: HRW, 1986); Lawyers Committee for Human Rights, "Judge Yolanda Perez Ruiz," Lawyer-to-Lawyer Network, New York, 1994.

50. See Ibrahim Shihata, *The World Bank in a Changing World* (Dordrecht: Martinus-Nijhoff, 1991), 53–93.

51. One can still detect a residue of it in the Bush administration's tepid response to the overthrow of President Aristide (a leftist populist calling for radical change) and to the continuing drumbeat of hostility to Aristide one can detect around some of the edges of official Washington.

Chapter 2   *Changing Perceptions of Domestic Jurisdiction and Intervention*

1. UN Charter, Art. 2(7).

2. The traditional Cold War view of nonintervention is reflected in, among other sources, the "Declaration of Principles of International Law Concerning Friendly Relations and Cooperation among States in Accordance with the Charter of the United Nations," GA Res/2625 XXV, UN GAOR/Supp 28, 1970, UN Doc A/8028: 121.

3. See Fernando R. Tesón, *Humanitarian Intervention: An Inquiry into Law and Morality* (Dobbs Ferry, N.Y.: Transnational Publishers, 1988), 205–14. For a classic overview of the principle of nonintervention, see Anna Van Wynen Thomas and Aaron Joshua Thomas, *Nonintervention: The Law and Its Import in the Americas* (Dallas: Southern Methodist Univ. Press, 1956). See also Tom Farer, "The Regulation of Foreign Intervention in Civil Armed Conflict," *RCADI* 142 (1974): 291; the essays collected in Hedley Bull, ed., *Intervention in World Politics* (Oxford: Clarendon, 1984); and those in Nigel Rodley, ed., *To Loose the Bands of Wickedness: International Intervention in Defence of Human Rights* (London: Brassey's, 1992).

4. L[assa] Oppenheim, *International Law: A Treatise* (London: Longmans, 1955); see also C. Arellano García, *Derecho Internacional Público* (1983), 465–66.

5. International Court of Justice, "Case of Military and Paramilitary Activities in and against Nicaragua (Nicaragua vs. the United States)," Merits, Judgment of 27 June 1986, *ICJ Reports* 14 (1986): 107–8 (hereafter *Nicaragua Case*).

6. I discuss these elements of intervention at some length in Tesón, *Humanitarian Intervention,* chap. 10.

7. Hersch Lauterpacht, *International Law and Human Rights* (London: Stevens, 1950): 166–73; see also Djura Nincic, *The Problem of Sovereignty in the Charter and in the Practice of the United Nations* (The Hague: Martinus-Nijhoff, 1977), 161–70; and D. R. Gilmour, "The Meaning of 'intervene' within Article

2(7) of the United Nations Charter—An Historical Perspective," *International and Comparative Law Quarterly* 16 (1967): 330–51.

8. "Exclusive" jurisdiction may or may not be "domestic" jurisdiction, although, technically, those areas where the state is legally free may not concern domestic matters. For example, choices regarding foreign policy are not domestic but they may be legally discretionary and, thus, within the exclusive jurisdiction of the state. Thus, for example, Res 2625 (see note 2, above) prohibits intervention in the *internal* or *external* affairs of other states. Although the issue is a general one of the permissible limits of state influence, technically only intervention in internal affairs gives rise to issues of *domestic* jurisdiction.

9. If the aggrieved state responds instead by invading the wrongdoer (as opposed to merely retaliating) this will of course be a violation of the principle of nonintervention as well.

10. Most of the scholars in the pre-UN era favored this view. See, e.g., Theodore Woolsey, *International Law*, 4th ed. (New York: Scribner's, 1874), 50; Paul Fauchille, *Traité de droit international public* (Paris: Rousseau, 1922), 396–97.

11. Thus, for example, a commentator opines that it "has always been considered that the constitutional, political, and social organization of a state is essentially a matter coming under the latter's sovereignty, i.e., within its domestic jurisdiction." Nincic, *Problem of Sovereignty*, 186. The essentialist view is supported by the wording of Art. 2(7) of the UN Charter. For the difference between the UN Charter and Art. 15(8) of the League of Nations Covenant, see the excellent discussion in Hans Kelsen, *Principles of International Law* (New York: Rinehart, 1952), 196–98. Because, unlike the covenant, Art. 2(7) makes no reference to a UN organ with powers to decide jurisdictional matters, some early commentators read Art. 2(7) as leaving that decision to the state concerned. See, e.g., Kelsen, *Principles of International Law*. As it turned out, UN practice has not followed this interpretation. See Rosalyn Higgins, *The Development of International Law through the Political Organs of the United Nations* (London: Oxford Univ. Press, 1963), 65–67; see also *International Court of Justice Report, 1950*, Art. 2(7), no bar to rendering advisory opinion.

12. The classic citation for this proposition is the dictum by the Permanent Court of International Justice in the Nationality Decrees Case: "The question whether a certain matter is or is not solely within the jurisdiction of a state is an essentially relative question; it depends upon the development of international relations." *Permanent Court of International Justice Report, 1923* (Series B), 23.

13. The International Court of Justice seems to have adopted an intermediate position. For the court, there is a presumption that a matter traditionally described as a matter of domestic policy falls within the exclusive domestic jurisdiction of the state; see *Nicaragua Case*, 131. This approach is quite close to the essentialist view of domestic jurisdiction. That presumption, however, can be rebutted by a showing that the state has bound itself internationally (through custom or treaty) with respect to such issue; see *Nicaragua Case*, 131. This view is a concession to the legalist position. Thus the court held that whether or not the government is freely elected is a matter presumptively falling within the domestic jurisdiction of the state; but there is no principled obstacle to a state committing itself to holding free elections. Ibid. I criticize the court's view in Fernando R. Tesón, "Le Peuple, C'est

Moi: The World Court and Human Rights," *American Journal of International Law* 81 (1987): 173–83. See the discussion below.

14. The essentialist view of domestic jurisdiction is thus a version of anti-cosmopolitan nationalism, and it will stand or fall with it. If, for example, one believes that state sovereignty is not autonomous or original but rather derivative from more basic moral principles such as individual dignity and human rights, then the essentialist view of domestic jurisdiction in this all-or-nothing form is harder to defend. I defend a derivative concept of sovereignty in Fernando R. Tesón, *The Philosophy of International Law* (Boulder: Westview, forthcoming). If one has a derivative definition of state sovereignty, one can make distinctions regarding state sovereignty and the conditions under which it has normative weight against foreign intervention. These distinctions will be based, perhaps, on different degrees of domestic legitimacy.

15. Some writers clearly saw this weakness of the legalist position. It is not enough to say that domestic jurisdiction ends where international jurisdiction starts; nor is it possible to say that UN organs may decide the issue on a case-by-case basis. A policy or principle is needed to decide in individual cases whether or not a matter is within the domestic jurisdiction of states. Rosalyn Higgins, in her seminal discussion of domestic jurisdiction of more than thirty years ago, proposed the policy that "states must be made responsible when their actions cause substantial international effects." Higgins, *Development of International Law,* 62.

16. See, e.g., ibid.; Felix Ermarcora, "Human Rights and Domestic Jurisdiction," *RCADI* 124 (1968): 371, 436. The most famous case is that of South Africa, which—contrary to widespread opinion that the basis for the exercise of UN powers was the "international effects" test—is and was a human rights case. Maintaining and enforcing a system of apartheid is not a valid domestic jurisdiction choice for a state, regardless of whether it is deemed to produce international effects.

17. The UN General Assembly routinely adopts resolutions concerning human rights; among the recent ones are: A/Res/46/242 (Bosnia); A/Res/46/133 (El Salvador); A/Res/46/134 (Iraq); A/Res/46/132 (Myanmar/Burma); and A/Res/46/136 (occupied territories).

18. See, generally, Burns Weston, "Human Rights," in *Human Rights in the World Community,* ed. Burns Weston and Richard Pierre Claude, 2d ed. (Philadelphia: Univ. of Pennsylvania Press, 1992), 14.

19. This was the virtually unanimous view before 1948. See Gregory H. Fox, "The Right to Political Participation in International Law," *Yale Journal of International Law* 17 (1992): 539, 549–69.

20. The classical view is summarized in American Law Institute, *Restatement of Foreign Relations,* 3d ed., 201(d).

21. See Preamble to the UN Charter.

22. See "International Covenant on Civil and Political Rights," Art. 25, UN TS 171, 179; "American Convention on Human Rights," Art. 23, 36 OAS TS 1, OAE/Ser L/V/II.23, Doc 21, Rev 6, both in *ILM* 9 (1970): 673, 682, respectively; Protocol 1 to the *European Convention for the Protection of Human Rights and Fundamental Freedoms,* 213 UN TS 262, 264; and Art. 13, "African Charter on Human and Peoples' Rights," both in *ILM* 9 (1981): 58, 61, respectively.

23. I summarize here the argument I made in Tesón, "The Kantian Theory of

International Law," *Columbia Law Review* 92 (1992): 53, 74–81. The argument relies on the seminal research by Michael Doyle, "Kant, Liberal Legacies, and Foreign Affairs," *Philosophy and Public Affairs* 12 (1983): 205, 213, 323.

24. See, e.g, the *Declaration on Principles of International Law,* note 2, "Every State has an inalienable right to choose its political . . . system."

25. Fox, "Right to Political Participation." See also Thomas M. Franck, "The Emerging Right to Democratic Governance," *American Journal of International Law* 86 (1992): 46. It is important to emphasize, however, that the International Court of Justice's rejection of the principle of democratic rule in the Nicaragua Case was mistaken in 1986 for the Americas and is bad general international law in 1994. See Tesón, "Le Peuple, C'est Moi."

26. I do not pass judgment here on the *unilateral* enforcement of democracy (the cases of Grenada and Panama are possible examples). See, generally, Tesón, *Humanitarian Intervention.* But those precedents, especially when added to the Haitian case, at the very least reinforce the proposition that democratic rule is no longer part of the domestic jurisdiction of states.

27. For those who argue against humanitarian intervention, see ibid., 128 n5; for those who argue for humanitarian intervention, see ibid., 129 n7. Space prevents me from discussing separately the legitimacy of collective hard intervention. The conclusion in this section, however, applies, a fortiori, to measures adopted by the Security Council under Art. 41 (measures not involving the use of force.)

28. See ibid. Also see Louis Henkin, *Right v. Might: International Law and the Use of Force,* 2d ed. (New York: Council on Foreign Relations Press, 1991), 37, 41–44; Lori F. Damrosch, "Commentary on Collective Military Intervention to Enforce Human Rights," in *Law and Force in the New International Order,* ed. Lori R. Damrosch and David Scheffler (Boulder: Westview, 1991), 215, 217–21.

29. See, e.g., Thomas Oppermann, "Intervention," in *Encyclopedia of Public International Law,* ed. Rudolf Bernhardt, 3d ed., vol. 3 (Amsterdam, N.Y.: North Holland, 1987), 233, 235: "The raison d'etre of the nonintervention rule is the protection of the sovereignty of the State."

30. An example of this position is Tom J. Farer, "Human Rights in Law's Empire: The Jurisprudence War," *American Journal of International Law* 85 (1991): 117–27. (While sympathetic to intervention in cases of brutal repression, the UN Charter does not authorize unilateral humanitarian intervention).

31. See Tesón, *Humanitarian Intervention,* chap. 8.

32. See, e.g., Vladimir Kartashkin, "Human Rights and Humanitarian Intervention," in Damrosch and Scheffler, *Law and Force,* 202, 208; Jost Delbruck, "A Fresh Look at Humanitarian Intervention under the Authority of the United Nations," *International Law Journal* 67 (1992): 887. While reluctantly believing that unilateral humanitarian intervention is banned by the UN Charter, Tom Farer has a more sympathetic view of collective humanitarian intervention. See, in addition to Farer, "Human Rights in Law's Empire," Tom J. Farer, "An Inquiry into the Legitimacy of Humanitarian Intervention," in Damrosch and Scheffler, *Law and Force,* 185, 191, 198–99.

33. See, e.g., Barry M. Benjamin, "Unilateral Humanitarian Intervention: Legalizing the Use of Force to Prevent Human Rights Atrocities," *Fordham International Law Journal* 16 (1992–93): 120–58. An inherent problem with unilateral intervention is that it may be done for self-interest or political gain—although this

may be more closely monitored by modern technology; Nancy D. Arnison, "International Law and Non-Intervention: When Do Humanitarian Concerns Supersede Sovereignty?" *Fletcher Forum for World Affairs* 17 (1993): 199, 201. Collective humanitarian intervention is preferable to unilateral action, although collective action also may suffer from the potential for abuse and mixed motives.

34. See, e.g., Peter Malanczuk, *Humanitarian Intervention and the Legitimacy of the Use of Force* (Amsterdam: Het Spinhuis, 1993), 26. The decision of what constitutes a "threat to peace" is a political one, subject to Security Council discretion.

35. See, e.g., Theodore Meron, "Commentary on Humanitarian Intervention," in Damrosch and Scheffler, *Law and Force*. In the same volume, Lori Damrosch finds the arguments for collective humanitarian intervention stronger than those for unilateral action, but she is still is not free from doubt. See Damrosch, "Commentary on Collective Military Intervention," 219.

36. This was the position taken by Libya in the Lockerbie case. See *International Court of Justice Report, 1992*: 114, 126; reprinted in *ILM* 31 (1992): 665, 671.

37. This was the case of Haiti before Res 940, in which the Security Council imposed economic sanctions under Art. 41. The Haiti case is fully discussed below.

38. For a general discussion of the legitimacy of Security Council decisions (mostly from a procedural standpoint), see David D. Caron, "The Legitimacy of the Collective Authority of the Security Council," *American Journal of International Law* 87 (1993): 552–88.

39. The discussion that follows is taken from the seminal work by Ronald Dworkin, *Taking Rights Seriously* (Cambridge: Harvard Univ. Press, 1978), 31–39.

40. Compare the Lockerbie case, *International Court of Justice Report, 1992*: 126–27, which rules only that Security Council decisions prevail over contrary treaty obligations by virtue of Art. 103 of the UN Charter, thus not excluding the possibility that the Security Council may act ultra vires.

41. See, e.g., Judy A. Gallant, "Humanitarian Intervention and Security Council Resolution 688: A Reappraisal in Light of a Changing World Order," *American University Journal of International Law and Politics* 7 (1992): 881–920.

42. See Malanczuk, *Humanitarian Intervention and the Legitimacy of the Use of Force*, 25.

43. I argue that the text of the UN Charter is inconclusive on this issue. For a more thorough discussion of this point, see Tesón, *Humanitarian Intervention*, chap. 7.

44. UN Charter, Preamble.

45. A well-known example is, of course, the voting practice in the Security Council.

46. See, among others, Damrosch, "Commentary on Collective Military Intervention," 218.

47. See, e.g., Nigel Rodley, "Collective Intervention to Protect Human Rights and Civilian Populations: The Legal Framework," in Rodley, *To Loose the Bands of Wickedness*, 14, 28, 40. Although the winds of change may be blowing in the direction of collective humanitarian intervention, the threat to international peace will probably be required.

48. See Tesón, *Humanitarian Intervention*, pt. 1.

49. See, e.g., Rep. Lee Hamilton, "When It's Our Duty to Intervene," *Washing-*

ton Post, 9 Aug. 1992; "multilateral consideration would guard against aggression, prevent hasty or capricious intervention, and enhance the effectiveness of subsequent action."

50. For a discussion with abundant documentation of the first stages of the UN action against Iraq, see J. Norton Moore, *Crisis in the Gulf: Enforcing the Rule of Law* (New York: Oceana, 1992), 3–281.

51. See Kevin McKiernan, "Kurdistan's Season of Hope," *Los Angeles Times Magazine,* 23 Aug. 1992, 28; Jonathan C. Randal, "Against All Odds: Resistance to Saddam," *Washington Post,* 7 Apr. 1991. In addition, confiscated Iraqi materials have provided comprehensive documentation of massive human rights violations. See Amy Kaslow, "Documents Give Evidence of Atrocities against Iraqi Kurds," *Christian Science Monitor,* 10 June 1992, 1; and Jeanne Kirkpatrick, "It Is Appropriate to Speak of Genocide," *Washington Post,* 2 Mar. 1992. See also UN Doc S/Res/688 (5 Apr. 1991); Gallant, "Humanitarian Intervention," 57; David J. Scheffer, "Toward a Modern Doctrine of Humanitarian Intervention," *University of Toledo Law Review* 23 (1992): 253–93; and Rodley, "Collective Intervention," 28–34.

52. UN Doc S/Res/688 (5 Apr. 1991), 68.

53. See, e.g., Malanczuk, *Humanitarian Intervention and the Legitimacy of the Use of Force,* 18.

54. David Scheffer, "Toward a Modern Doctrine of Humanitarian Intervention," *University of Toledo Law Review,* 23 (1992): 258.

55. See, e.g., Mary Ellen O'Connell, "Commentary on International Law: Continuing Limits on U.N. Intervention in Civil War," *Indiana Law Journal* 67 (1992): 903, 907–8, which argues that Res 688, together with Res 678, gave coalition members the authority to use "all necessary means" to secure peace in the area that included the Kurdish region.

56. For a list of Iraq's multiple violations of international law, see Moore, *Crisis in the Gulf,* 66.

57. For the Security Council action that led to Res 794, see Scheffer, "Toward a Modern Doctrine," 66.

58. See Don Oberdorfer, "The Path to Intervention," *Washington Post,* 6 Dec. 1992, A1, A35. The brief account that follows is borrowed from Jeffrey Clark, "Debacle in Somalia," *Foreign Affairs* (America and the World, 1992/93), 109.

59. UN SC Res 794, UN Doc S/Res/794, Preamble.

60. For a recent description of the distinction, see Boutros Boutros-Ghali, "Empowering the United Nations," *Foreign Affairs* (1992): 89.

61. UN SC Res 794, para. 10. For the language that follows, see para. 7 and the Preamble.

62. See O'Connell, "Commentary on International Law," 908.

63. See generally, Richard Lillich, *International Human Rights: Cases and Materials,* 2d ed. (Boston: Little, Brown, 1991), 767–83.

64. UN S/Res/794, Preamble.

65. Ibid. The same language was used by the Security Council in its recent imposition of nonforcible sanctions against Haiti.

66. OAS Ser G/CP/Res 489, Doc 720 (1987).

67. A/Res/46/7, 2.

68. S/Res/841 (1993). This resolution expressly relies on the previous OAS and UN General Assembly resolutions.

69. See also the reimposition of sanctions by the U.S. government, Bureau of

National Affairs, *International Trade Reporter* 10 (1992): 1756 (available on LEXIS); and S/Res/841 (16 June 1993).

70. See S/Res/940 (1994), para. 4.

71. See "2,000 U.S. Troops Land without Opposition and Take over Haiti's Ports and Airfields," *New York Times,* 20 Sept. 1994.

72. See, e.g., S/Res/841, Preamble.

73. See Tesón, *Humanitarian Intervention,* chap. 6.

74. The complete text of the address is reprinted in *Washington Post,* 16 Sept. 1994. I quote from there.

75. People who talk about the national interest tend to have, in my view, a noticeably narrow definition of what national interest should be, and typically is, in a democracy. Why would citizens of a democracy define national interest as only strategic, economic, or political advantages over other nations? It seems to me that, typically, a democratic government also advances the national interest if it is responsive to the moral indignation that citizens feel when confronted with serious violations of human rights outside the state's borders.

76. For a thorough discussion of intervention by consent, see David Wippman, "Treaty-Based Intervention: Who Can Say No?" *University of Chicago Law Review* (forthcoming).

77. See Elaine Sciolino, "On the Brink of War: A Tense Battle of Wills" *New York Times,* 20 Sept. 1994.

78. See Vienna Convention on the Law of Treaties, Art. 52.

79. See UN Charter, Art. 2(4)

80. See, generally, Judith Gail Gardam, "Proportionality and Force in International Law," *American Journal of International Law* 87 (1993): 391–413.

81. For an account of the changes of opinion by Aristide, see Deborah Zabarenko, "Aristide Thanks U.S., Gets Assurances on Haiti," *BC Cycle,* Sept. 1994 (available on LEXIS).

82. See Thomas M. Franck, "Legitimacy in the International System," *American Journal of International Law* 82 (1988): 705, 706.

83. See Michael Walzer, "The Moral Standing of States: A Reply to Four Critics," in *International Ethics,* ed. Charles Beitz et al. (Princeton: Princeton Univ. Press, 1985), 217. Walzer's principle is "always act so as to recognize and uphold communal integrity." Michael Walzer, "The Rights of Political Communities," in Beitz et al., *International Ethics,* 165, 181.

84. See Tesón, *Humanitarian Intervention,* chaps. 3 and 4.

85. Another important UN precedent is the case of Rwanda. On 22 June 1994, the Security Council adopted Res 929 authorizing member states to establish a temporary multinational operation of a "strictly humanitarian" character. In furtherance of this resolution, France occupied Rwanda and attempted, with varying degrees of success, to put an end to the horrendous situation in that country. See "Equatorial Guinea and Congo Support French Intervention," *BBC Monitoring Service—Africa,* 25 June 1994 (available on LEXIS).

Chapter 3   *Democracy in Latin America*

I would like to thank David Collier, Michael Coppedge, Thomas Carothers, Barbara Geddes, Jonathan Hartlyn, Kevin Middlebrook, Philippe Schmitter, and

Michael Shifter for the enormously helpful critical comments and suggestions they gave me on a draft of this chapter. Needless to say, they bear no responsibility for the logical and empirical flaws that may remain.

1. Abraham Lowenthal, "Latin America: Ready for Partnership?" *Foreign Affairs* 72 (1992–93): 75.

2. Address to the nation on Haiti, 15 Sept. 1994, *New York Times,* 17 Sept. 1994.

3. Heraldo Muñoz, "The OAS and Democratic Governance," *Journal of Democracy* 4 (1993): 29–38.

4. On the mounting problems of electoral integrity in the Dominican Republic, see Jonathan Hartlyn, "Explaining Crisis-Ridden Elections in a Fragile Democracy: Presidentialism and Electoral Oversight in the Dominican Republic, 1978–1994"; and on electoral fraud in Peru under Fujimori, see Cynthia McClintock, "Classifying the Regime Types of El Salvador and Peru in the 1980s and 1990s," both papers prepared for the 1994 Annual Meeting of the American Political Science Association, New York, 1–4 Sept.

5. Human Rights Watch, *World Report, 1993* (New York: HRW, 1992), 127; Human Rights Watch, *World Report, 1994* (New York: HRW, 1993), 115.

6. Philippe C. Schmitter, "Interest Systems and the Consolidation of Democracy," in *Reexamining Democracy: Essays in Honor of Seymour Martin Lipset,* ed. Gary Marks and Larry Diamond (Newbury Park, Calif.: Sage, 1992), 158.

7. Samuel P. Huntington, *Political Order in Changing Societies* (New Haven: Yale Univ. Press, 1968).

8. I am grateful to David Collier for calling my attention to this essential insight.

9. By "disloyal," Linz means behavior that questions the legitimacy of—or challenges the rules or existence of—a democratic regime. Juan J. Linz, *The Breakdown of Democratic Regimes: Crisis, Breakdown, and Reequilibration* (Baltimore: Johns Hopkins Univ. Press, 1978), 17–32.

10. Larry Diamond, Juan J. Linz, and Seymour Martin Lipset, eds., *Democracy in Developing Countries: Latin America* (Boulder: Lynne Rienner, 1988, 1989), xvi. This definition draws heavily on, and is essentially equivalent to, Robert A. Dahl's concept of polyarchy. See his *Polyarchy: Participation, and Opposition* (New Haven: Yale Univ. Press, 1971).

11. Philippe C. Schmitter and Terry Lynn Karl, "What Democracy Is . . . and Is Not," *Journal of Democracy* 2 (1991): 75–88.

12. Joseph E. Ryan, "The Comparative Survey of Freedom, 1993–94: Survey Methodology," in Freedom House, *Freedom in the World, 1993–1994* (New York: Freedom House, 1994).

13. Each country was assigned 0 to 4 points for each of the nine items on the political rights checklist and for each of the thirteen items on the civil liberties checklist (ibid., 674–75.) One confusing feature is that the raw point scores vary directly with freedom, whereas the two summary measures vary inversely. A more serious problem is that the 0-to-4 point scheme represents a change in the methodology of the survey (which assigned 0 to 2 points per question in the previous four years). The survey notes a few changes in country freedom scores from year to year that have resulted from these modest changes in methodology.

Some critics may worry about more subtle changes in the method, which may now apply stricter standards of evaluation at the "freer" end of the scale for each measure. To the extent that this is true, it is possible that some of the deterioration in regime scores may be an artifact of the change in methodology. This concern is sensible but is, I believe, allayed by the survey's acknowledgement of changes in scores that result explicitly from changes in its methodology and by the accumulation of qualitative evidence and evaluations that reinforce the depiction of an overall trend toward deterioration in democratic performance in a number of countries.

14. Freedom House rates a country as free if its combined score on civil liberties and political rights is 5 or lower; as partly free if its combined score is between 6 and 11; and as not free if its combined score is between 11 to 14. For countries with combined scores of 11, the raw point scores distinguish between partly free and not free. The full classification scheme is 60–88 points for a ranking of free; 30–59 points for partly free; and 0–29 points for not free (ibid., 675). A striking but little noticed observation in the 1993–94 survey is that, even as the number of free states declined in 1993 from 75 to 72, "the number of democracies continued to grow, increasing from 99 at the end of 1992 to 108 as 1993 drew to a close" (ibid., 5). This judgment can only be based on extremely superficial criteria for democracy, which trivialize the concept and confuse both scholarly and policy considerations.

15. Diamond, Linz, and Lipset, *Democracy in Developing Countries*, xvii.

16. Dahl, *Polyarchy,* table A-3.

17. For a more comprehensive checklist of empirical questions, see Freedom House, *Freedom in the World, 1993–1994,* 672–73.

18. Samuel P. Huntington, *The Third Wave: Democratization in the Late Twentieth Century* (Norman: Univ. of Oklahoma Press, 1991).

19. Guillermo O'Donnell, "Delegative Democracy," *Journal of Democracy* 5 (1994): 55–69. See also his earlier and more extended version, "Delegative Democracy?" Working Paper 173, Kellogg Institute, Notre Dame University, Mar. 1992.

20. See Lowenthal, "Latin America: Ready for Partnership?" 83; and Francisco C. Weffort, " 'New Democracies': Which Democracies?" Woodrow Wilson Center for International Scholars, Washington, D.C., Jan. 1992, 41.

21. O'Donnell, "Delegative Democracy," 62; see also Weffort, " 'New Democracies,' " 39–40.

22. Weffort, " 'New Democracies,' " 40.

23. O'Donnell, "Delegative Democracy," 61–62.

24. Larry Diamond, "The Globalization of Democracy," in *Global Transformation and the Third World,* ed. Robert Slater, Barry Schutz, and Steven Dorr (Boulder: Lynne Rienner, 1993); and in *Freedom Review* 26 (1995): 5.

25. Inter-American Dialogue, *Convergence and Community: The Americas in 1993* (Washington, D.C.: IAD, 1992), 23.

26. Karen L. Remmer, "Democratization in Latin America," in Slater et al., *Global Transformation and the Third World,* 92–93.

27. I have excluded these eleven states, whose combined population is about two and half million, partly to simplify the analysis here and partly because most of these states, particularly the Caribbean island states, have been continuously democratic since independence and do not generally face the acute challenges of democratic deepening and consolidation that face the posttransition states in Latin America. The two more comparable states are the South American countries of Suriname and Guyana, which account for half the population of this group and

have each experienced recent regime transitions. During 1993, Guyana "made significant headway toward consolidating democratic governance after twenty-eight years of authoritarian rule," but Suriname remains a near democracy, struggling with the legacy of military intervention, armed insurgency, and extensive human rights violations since the return to civilian rule in 1991; Freedom House, *Freedom in the World, 1993–1994,* 289, 519.

28. For a detailed account of the extensive irregularities and institutional bias in Paraguay's May 1993 presidential elections, see Jan Knippers Black, "Almost Free, Almost Fair: Paraguay's Ambiguous Election," *NACLA Report on the Americas* 27 (1993): 26–28.

29. Remmer, "Democratization in Latin America," 93–95.

30. Freedom House, *Freedom in the World, 1993–1994,* 233.

31. Ibid., 163.

32. Remmer, "Democratization in Latin America," 107.

33. Cynthia McClintock, "Peru's Fujimori: A Caudillo Derails Democracy," *Current History* 92 (1993): 113.

34. Ibid., 112.

35. McClintock, "Classifying Regime Types," 28.

36. Freedom House, *Freedom in the World, 1993–1994,* 452–55; McClintock, "Classifying Regime Types," 29.

37. McClintock, "Peru's Fujimori," 113.

38. Ibid, 112–19; Eduardo Ferrero Costa, "Peru's Presidential Coup," *Journal of Democracy* 4 (1993): 28–40; Freedom House, *Freedom in the World, 1992–1993,* 408–11; Human Rights Watch, *World Report, 1992,* 309–20; Human Rights Watch, *World Report, 1993,* 133–39, 142–43. See also David Scott Palmer, chap. 11, this volume.

39. Human Rights Watch, *World Report, 1992,* 309.

40. Francisco Villagrán de León, "Thwarting the Guatemalan Coup," *Journal of Democracy* 4 (1993): 117–24.

41. Freedom House, *Freedom in the World, 1992–1993,* 250–53; Freedom House, *Freedom in the World, 1993–1994,* 281–84; see also Human Rights Watch, *World Report, 1992,* 231–51.

42. Terry Lynn Karl, "The Venezuelan Petro-State and the Crisis of 'Its' Democracy," in *Democracy under Pressure: Politics and Markets in Venezuela,* ed. Jennifer McCoy et al. (New Brunswick: Transaction, 1994); see also Terry Lynn Karl, *The Paradox of Plenty: Oil Booms, Venezuela, and Other Petro-States* (Berkeley: Univ. of California Press, 1995); Moisés Naím, *Paper Tigers and Minotaurs: The Politics of Venezuela's Economic Reforms* (Washington, D.C.: Carnegie Endowment, 1993), esp. chap. 2.

43. Judith Ewell, "Venezuela in Crisis," *Current History* 92 (1993): 121.

44. Ibid., 122. See also Michael Coppedge, "Venezuela's Vulnerable Democracy," *Journal of Democracy* 3 (1992): 32–44.

45. Coppedge, "Venezuela's Vulnerable Democracy," 37; and Michael Coppedge, *Strong Parties and Lame Ducks: Presidential Partyarchy and Factionalism in Venezuela* (Stanford: Stanford Univ. Press, 1994). See also Karl, "Venezuelan Petro-State."

46. Coppedge, *Strong Parties and Lame Ducks,* 163–66.

47. Ewell, "Venezuela in Crisis," 124.

48. Coppedge, *Presidents and Lame Ducks,* 166.

49. Steve C. Ropp, "Things Fall Apart: Panama after Noriega," *Current History* 92 (1993): 105.

50. Hartlyn, "Explaining Crisis-Ridden Elections," 2.

51. Ibid., 5–7.

52. Jonathan Hartlyn, "The Dominican Republic: Contemporary Problems and Challenges," in *Democracy in the Caribbean: Political, Economic, and Social Perspectives,* ed. Jorge I. Dominguez, Robert A. Pastor, and R. DeLisle Worrell (Baltimore: Johns Hopkins Univ. Press, 1993); and Freedom House, *Freedom in the World, 1992–1993,* 207–10.

53. Freedom House, *Freedom in the World, 1993–1994,* 120.

54. Ibid., 104.

55. Ibid., 120; Pepe Eliaschev, "Argentina's War on Journalists," *New York Times,* 22 Sept. 1993.

56. Carlos Eduardo Lins da Silva, "Brazil's Struggle with Democracy," *Current History* 92 (1993): 127.

57. *Economist,* 10 July 1993, 35.

58. Bolivar Lamounier, "Brazil at an Impasse," *Journal of Democracy* 5 (1994): 72.

59. Ibid.

60. Freedom House, *Freedom in the World, 1993–1994,* 164.

61. Weffort, " 'New Democracies,' " 53.

62. In early 1993, right-wing senators blocked bills that would have eliminated the nine appointed seats in the Senate and enabled the president to remove military commanders. By failing in the December 1993 elections to secure a two-thirds majority in the Congress, the Concertación fell short of being able to amend the constitution on its own.

63. See also Felipe Aguero, "Chile: South America's Success Story?" *Current History* 92 (1993): 130–35; *Economist,* 18 Sept. 1993, 48; and Freedom House, *Freedom in the World, 1993–1994,* 196–99.

64. *Economist,* 19 June 1993, 45.

65. Human Rights Watch, *World Report, 1993,* 69.

66. Ibid., 76; *Economist,* 19 June 1993, 45.

67. Human Rights Watch, *World Report, 1993,* 80–81. See ibid., 70–116, for the following six items in this list.

68. Indigenous communities have also been attacked with impunity by miners and loggers in Brazil.

69. Freedom House, *Freedom in the World, 1992–1993,* 104. At its worst, in Guatemala (where "the National Police has effectively been taken over by the army"), this impunity for security forces who violate human rights leaves "murder and intimidation the only reward" for judges, prosecutors, investigators, and human rights monitors "who seek to establish the truth." Human Rights Watch, *World Report, 1993,* 113, 116.

70. Freedom House, *Freedom in the World, 1993–1994,* 284.

71. "A Legacy of Conflict, Confusion," *Los Angeles Times,* 17 Oct. 1993; "Assassinations, Threats of Reprisals Besiege Shaky Salvadoran Peace Process," *Washington Post,* 8 Nov. 1993.

72. Four countries (El Salvador, Panama, Paraguay, and Chile) have improved

since 1987, but most of them came from very low ratings and in the context of a formal transition to democracy.

73. J. Samuel Fitch, "Democracy, Human Rights, and the Armed Forces in Latin America," in *The United States and Latin America in the 1990s: Beyond the Cold War,* ed. Jonathan Hartlyn, Lars Schoultz, and Augusto Varas (Chapel Hill: Univ. of North Carolina Press, 1993), 200.

74. John Higley and Richard Gunther, eds., *Elites and Democratic Consolidation in Latin America and Southern Europe* (Cambridge: Cambridge Univ. Press, 1992); see in particular the introductory and concluding essays by Michael Burton, Gunther, and Higley.

75. A similar conclusion is reached by Michael Coppedge in his recent review of contemporary challenges to governability in nine Latin American countries: "Institutions and Democratic Governance in Latin America" (Aug. 1993), revised version of a paper prepared for the conference, Rethinking Development Theories in Latin America, Institute of Latin American Studies, Univ. of North Carolina, Chapel Hill, 11–13 Mar. 1993.

76. O'Donnell, "Delegative Democracies," 2 (emphasis in the original).

77. Karen L. Remmer, "The Political Impact of Economic Crisis in Latin America in the 1980s," *American Political Science Review* 85 (1991): 777–800; see also Huntington, *Third Wave,* 265–69.

78. See, for example, Huntington, *Third Wave,* 266–67.

79. Juan Carlos Torre, "The Politics of Economic Crisis in Latin America," *Journal of Democracy* 4 (1993): 113; see also Huntington, *Third Wave,* 269–70.

80. Freedom House, *Freedom in the World, 1993–1994,* 164, 237, 428–30, 582.

81. Such institutional decay, which drains constitutional systems of their democratic content and produces escalating political cynicism, apathy, unrepresentativeness, crime, violence, and human rights violations, is anticipated by Stephen Haggard and Robert Kaufman as a likely consequence of prolonged economic crisis. See their chapter, "Economic Adjustment and the Prospects for Democracy," in *The Politics of Economic Adjustment,* ed. Stephan Haggard and Robert Kaufman (Princeton: Princeton Univ. Press, 1992).

82. Juan Linz and Alfred Stepan, "Political Crafting of Democratic Consolidation or Destruction: European and South American Comparisons," in *Democracy in the Americas: Stopping the Pendulum,* ed. Robert A. Pastor (New York: Holmes and Meier, 1989).

83. Ibid., 47.

84. On this point, see also Juan J. Linz, "Legitimacy of Democracy and the Socioeconomic System," in *Comparing Pluralist Democracies: Strains on Legitimacy,* ed. Mattei Dogan (Boulder: Westview, 1988), 65, 92.

85. Torre, "Politics of Economic Crisis," 115.

86. Linz and Stepan, "Political Crafting of Democratic Consolidation," 46–47. For a similar approach, see Huntington, *Third Wave,* 259–60.

87. Seymour Martin Lipset, *Political Man* (Baltimore: Johns Hopkins Univ. Press, 1981), 61–71.

88. Larry Diamond and Juan J. Linz, "Introduction: Politics, Society, and Democracy in Latin America," in Diamond et al., *Democracy in Developing Countries.*

89. Mitchell A. Seligson and Edward N. Muller, "Democratic Stability and Economic Crisis: Costa Rica, 1978–1983," *International Studies Quarterly* 31 (1988): 301–26.

90. Diamond and Linz, "Introduction," 46.

91. O'Donnell, "Delegative Democracy," 4–6; for a much earlier, seminal expression of the relations between political institutionalization and political stability, see Huntington, *Political Order in Changing Societies.*

92. Stephan Haggard and Robert R. Kaufman, "The Political Economy of Inflation and Stabilization in Middle Income Countries," in Haggard and Kaufman, *Politics of Economic Adjustment;* Haggard and Kaufman, "Economic Adjustment and the Prospects for Democracy"; and Michael Coppedge, "Institutions and Democratic Governance in Latin America," 16.

93. Seymour Martin Lipset, "The Social Requisites of Democracy Revisited," 1993 Presidential Address to the American Sociological Association, *American Sociological Review* 59 (1994): 14.

94. Fitch, "Democracy, Human Rights, and the Armed Forces," 188.

95. Jonathan Hartlyn and Arturo Valenzuela, "Democracy in Latin American since 1930," in *The Cambridge History of Latin America,* vol. 6, *Latin America since 1930: Economy, Society, and Politics,* ed. Leslie Bethell (Cambridge: Cambridge Univ. Press, 1994).

96. Daniel H. Levine, "Venezuela: The Nature, Sources, and Future Prospects of Democracy," and Jonathan Hartlyn, "Colombia: The Politics of Violence and Accommodation," both in Diamond et al., *Democracy in Developing Countries: Latin America.*

97. Charles Gillespie and Luis Eduardo Gonzalez, "Uruguay: The Survival of Old and Autonomous Institutions," in Diamond et al., *Democracy in Developing Countries: Latin America;* Charles Gillespie, "The Breakdown of Democracy in Uruguay: Alternative Political Models," Working Paper 143, Latin American Program, Woodrow Wilson Center for International Scholars, Washington, D.C., 1984 (esp. 27–28).

98. Hartlyn, "Colombia," 308–20, 329; Coppedge, "Venezuela's Vulnerable Democracy."

99. Bolivar Lamounier, "Brazil: Inequality against Democracy," in Diamond et al., *Democracy in Developing Countries: Latin America.*

100. Cynthia McClintock, "Peru: Precarious Regimes, Authoritarian and Democratic," in Diamond et al., *Democracy in Developing Countries: Latin America.*

101. Ferrero Costa, "Peru's Presidential Coup."

102. Carlos Waisman, "Argentina: Autarkic Industrialization and Illegitimacy," in Diamond et al., *Democracy in Developing Countries: Latin America.*

103. Diamond and Linz, "Introduction," 23.

104. Coppedge, "Institutions and Democratic Governance in Latin America," 11.

105. Haggard and Kaufman, "Political Economy of Inflation and Stabilization," 279; Haggard and Kaufman, "Economic Adjustment and the Prospects for Democracy," 343. On the politics of trade unions, see Joan M. Nelson, "Poverty, Equity, and the Politics of Adjustment," in Haggard and Kaufman, *Politics of Economic Adjustment.*

106. Haggard and Kaufman, "Political Economy of Inflation and Stabilization," 279–80.

107. Haggard and Kaufman, "Economic Adjustment and the Prospects for Democracy," 345–48.

108. Huntington, *Political Order in Changing Societies,* 13–20.

109. John Peeler, "Elite Settlements and Democratic Consolidation: Colombia, Costa Rica, and Venezuela," in Higley and Gunther, *Elites and Democratic Consolidation;* Larry Diamond, *Political Culture and Democracy in Developing Countries* (Boulder: Lynne Rienner, 1993), 5–6, 427–28.

110. Coppedge, "Institutions and Democratic Governance in Latin America," 7.

111. The reference is to Brazil's Congress but could apply to many other Latin American legislatures. See Freedom House, *Freedom in the World, 1993–1994,* 164.

112. Jonathan Fox, "Latin America's Emerging Local Politics," *Journal of Democracy* 5 (1994): 105–16. See also Diamond and Linz, "Introduction," 30–31.

113. Fox, "Latin America's Emerging Local Politics." See also Lipset, *Political Man.*

114. Brazil already had direct mayoral elections; Fox, "Latin America's Emerging Local Politics."

115. Scott Mainwaring, "Presidentialism, Multipartism, and Democracy," *Comparative Political Studies* 26 (1993): 196–228. See also Arturo Valenzuela, "Latin America: Presidentialism in Crisis," *Journal of Democracy* 4 (1993): 3–16. For the most seminal treatment of the general value of parliamentary over presidential government, see Juan J. Linz, "The Perils of Presidentialism," *Journal of Democracy* 1 (1990): 51–69; and Juan J. Linz, "Presidential or Parliamentary Democracy: Does It Make a Difference?" in *The Failure of Presidential Democracy,* ed. Juan J. Linz and Arturo Valenzuela (Baltimore: Johns Hopkins Univ. Press, 1994).

116. Valenzuela, "Presidentialism in Crisis," 10.

117. Mainwaring, "Presidentialism, Multipartism, and Democracy," 217. Only in Uruguay can the president dissolve Congress in the face of an impasse. Valenzuela, "Presidentialism in Crisis," 9.

118. Linz, "Perils of Presidentialism"; Linz, "Parliamentary or Presidential Democracy"; Valenzuela, "Presidentialism in Crisis."

119. Arturo Valenzuela, "Chile: Origins, Consolidation, and Breakdown of a Democratic Regime," in Diamond et al., *Democracy in Developing Countries: Latin America.*

120. Diamond and Linz, "Introduction," 24–27.

121. Valenzuela, "Presidentialism in Crisis," 7, 8.

122. Ibid., 12–16.

123. Coppedge, *Presidents and Lame Ducks,* 168.

124. Lamounier, "Brazil at an Impasse," 80. As Lamounier notes here, the current system "combines the worst of all worlds: it ends up being individualistic as the Anglo-Saxon single-member district system, but without the latter's requirement that representatives be accountable to geographic constituencies."

125. Ibid., 86.

126. As Coppedge observes, "with this reform, succession struggles would erode presidential leadership at most half of the time." *Presidents and Lame Ducks,* 171.

127. Donald Horowitz, *Coup Theories and Officers' Motives: Sri Lanka in Comparative Perspective* (Princeton: Princeton Univ. Press, 1980).

128. Fitch, "Democracy, Human Rights, and the Armed Forces," 182–87.

129. Raúl Benítez Manaut, "Identity Crisis: The Military in Changing Times," *NACLA Report on the Americas* 27 (1993): 16.

130. Fitch, "Democracy, Human Rights, and the Armed Forces," 190.

131. Presentation by Louis Goodman to the Asia Foundation conference, Democratization in Asia: Meeting the Challenges of the 1990s, Chiang Mai, Thailand, 7–12 Dec. 1992.

132. Alfred Stepian, *Rethinking Military Politics: Brazil and the Southern Cone* (Princeton: Princeton Univ. Press, 1988).

133. In this respect, although some Latin American countries have made progress in certain respects, the overall regional experience compares unfavorably with that in such other third-wave democracies as Spain, Portugal, Greece, and even the Philippines; Huntington, *Third Wave*, 238–51.

134. Fitch, "Democracy, Human Rights, and the Armed Forces," 184.

135. Stepan, *Rethinking Military Politics*, 138–39.

136. This list is much influenced by Huntington's "Guidelines for Democratizers," *Third Wave*, 251–53, but gives more emphasis to sequencing, gradualism, and the crafting of an overall political strategy.

137. Ibid., 251.

138. Improving control over the police is often critical to securing a lasting enhancement of human rights and the rule of law, as well as democratic legitimacy. As Philippe Schmitter argues, "Few things can be more subversive of trust in institutions and legitimacy of the government than the popular perception that 'nothing has changed' at the level of face-to-face contacts between police authorities and the population." See his "Dangers and Dilemmas of Democracy," *Journal of Democracy* 5 (1994): 71.

139. Both quotations are from Julio María Sanguinetti, "Present at the Transition," *Journal of Democracy* 2 (1991): 9; see also Jamal Benomar, "Justice after Transitions," *Journal of Democracy* 4 (1993): 13.

140. Huntington, *Third Wave*, 211–31; the quotation is from 229.

141. Raúl Alfonsín, " 'Never Again' in Argentina," *Journal of Democracy* 4 (1993): 19.

142. Benomar, "Justice after Transitions," 14.

143. Larry Diamond, "Rethinking Civil Society: Toward Consolidation," *Journal of Democracy* 5 (1994): 4–17.

144. Schmitter, "Interests Systems and the Consolidation of Democracies," 160 and passim.

145. Diamond and Linz, "Introduction," 35.

146. Villagrán de León, "Thwarting the Guatemalan Coup," 122–23.

147. I am grateful to Michael Shifter for emphasizing this point to me.

148. María S. Rosa de Martini, "Civil Participation in the Argentine Democratic Process," in *The Democratic Revolution: Struggles for Freedom and Pluralism in the Developing World*, ed. Larry Diamond (New York: Freedom House, 1992); María S. Rosa de Martini and Sofía L. de Pinedo, "Women and Civic Life in Argentina," *Journal of Democracy* 3 (1992): 137–46.

149. Private communication from Michael Shifter, senior program officer for Latin America, National Endowment for Democracy, 19 Nov. 1993.

150. Deidre McFayden, "Invigorating the Public Debate: Popular Media in the Age of Mass Communications," *NACLA Report on Latin America* 27 (1993): 35–37.

151. National Endowment for Democracy, *Annual Report* (Washington, D.C.: NED, 1992 and 1993), 67–78, and 65–76, respectively.

152. Karl, "Venezuelan Petro-State"; Carlos Waisman, "Capitalism, the Market, and Democracy," in Marks and Diamond, *Democracy Reexamined.*

153. Samuel P. Huntington, "What Price Freedom? Democracy and/or Economic Reform," *Harvard International Review* (winter 1992–93): 12.

154. Eduardo Silva, "Capitalist Coalitions, the State, and Neoliberal Economic Restructuring," *World Politics* 45 (1993): 526–59.

155. Haggard and Kaufman, *Politics of Economic Adjustment,* 337–38.

156. Huntington, "What Price Freedom?" 12.

157. Torre, "Politics of Economic Crisis," 111–12.

158. Ibid., 108.

159. See, for example, the essays in Haggard and Kaufman, *Politics of Economic Adjustment;* Thomas R. Callaghy, "Vision and Politics in the Transformation of the Global Political Economy: Lessons from the Second and Third Worlds," in Slater et al., *Global Transformations and the Third World,* 166–70, 239–44, and on Latin America, 197–207.

160. Barbara Geddes, "Challenging the Conventional Wisdom," *Journal of Democracy* 5 (1994), 104–18.

161. Nelson, "Poverty, Equity, and the Politics of Adjustment," 259.

162. Torre, "Politics of Economic Crisis," 113.

163. Haggard and Kaufman, "Introduction," in Haggard and Kaufman, *Politics of Economic Adjustment,* 19–20.

164. Torre, "Politics of Economic Crisis," 113. Even for the paradigmatic case of economic reform under authoritarian rule, this failure "to persuade the population at large of the advantages of reform" left public support for reform quite weak and the process politically vulnerable until near the end of Pinochet's time in office, when the economic benefits of reform finally blossomed. Juan Andres Fontaine, "Economic and Political Transition in Chile, 1970–1990," paper prepared for Hoover Institution/AID, Conference on Economy, Society, and Democracy, Washington, D.C., 5–7 May 1992, 32.

165. Laurence Whitehead, "Democratization and Disinflation: A Comparative Approach," in *Fragile Coalitions: The Politics of Economic Adjustment,* ed. Joan M. Nelson et al. (Washington, D.C.: Overseas Development Council, 1989), 91.

166. Naím, *Paper Tigers and Minotaurs,* 11.

167. Nelson, "Poverty, Equity, and the Politics of Adjustment," 253–58.

168. As argued above, however, such broad, moderate coalitions for reform would be easier to form and especially to maintain in parliamentary systems.

169. Nelson, "Poverty, Equity, and the Politics of Adjustment," 250–58.

170. Even Moisés Naím, the architect of the shock therapy economic reforms of Venezuelan president Carlos Andrés Pérez, faults that government for failing "to build a more effective communication strategy," which, in breaking with the old, centralized style of politics, would have better prepared the public for the changes that were necessary. Naím, *Paper Tigers and Minotaurs,* 141.

171. This is one of the most broadly shared conclusions of scholars writing from a variety of regional and theoretical perspectives. See Larry Diamond and Marc F. Plattner, eds., *Economic Reform and Democracy* (Baltimore: Johns Hopkins Univ. Press, 1995).

172. Whitehead, "Democratization and Disinflation," 92.

173. World Bank, *World Development Report, 1994* (New York: Oxford Univ. Press, 1994), table 30.

174. Inter-American Dialogue, *Convergence and Community,* 43.

175. Ibid., 44.

176. Peter Hakim and Abraham Lowenthal, "Latin America's Fragile Democracies," *Journal of Democracy* 2 (1991): 24.

177. This was one of the most striking common findings across the Latin American case studies in the Democracy in Developing Countries project and was also identified as a matter of concern for the maintenance of democracy in Venezuela and Costa Rica; Diamond and Linz, "Introduction," 40. For a particularly forceful and explicit identification of inequality as a leading obstacle to democratic consolidation, see Lamounier, "Brazil: Inequality against Democracy."

178. Inter-American Dialogue, *Convergence and Community,* 55.

179. Ibid., 42; Hakim and Lowenthal, "Latin America's Fragile Democracies," 25; Diamond and Linz, "Introduction," 38–41.

180. Nelson, "Poverty, Equity, and the Politics of Adjustment," 232.

181. Ibid., 260.

182. Inter-American Dialogue, *Convergence and Community,* 47–53; Nelson, "Poverty, Equity, and the Politics of Adjustment," 239–44.

183. Carol Graham, *Safety Nets, Politics, and the Poor: Transitions to Market Economies* (Washington, D.C.: Brookings, 1994).

184. Nelson, "Poverty, Equity, and the Politics of Adjustment," 260.

185. Fitch, "Democracy, Human Rights, and the Armed Forces," 203 (emphasis in the original).

186. Larry Diamond, "Promoting Democracy," *Foreign Policy* 87 (1992): 25–46.

187. Abraham Lowenthal, ed., *Exporting Democracy: The United States and Latin America* (Baltimore: Johns Hopkins Univ. Press, 1991); Thomas Carothers, *In the Name of Democracy: U.S. Policy toward Latin America in the Reagan Years* (Berkeley: Univ. of California Press, 1991).

188. Lowenthal, *Exporting Democracy,* 263. My recommendations here broadly parallel Lowenthal's approach.

189. Fitch proposes that military aid be conditional not only on decent human rights performance (as evaluated by independent organizations like Amnesty International and the OAS) but also on "certified progress toward greater democratic control" over the military. Fitch, "Democracy, Human Rights, and the Armed Forces," 205.

190. Carothers, *In the Name of Democracy,* 250–52.

191. Fitch, "Democracy, Human Rights, and the Armed Forces," 200–201.

192. Larry Rohter, "NAFTA and the Hemisphere: Latin America Finds Harmony in Convergence," *New York Times,* 21 Nov. 1993.

193. Pastor, *Democracy in the Americas,* xi.

Chapter 4   *The United Nations, Democracy, and the Americas*

1. Samuel P. Huntington, *The Third Wave: Democratization in the Late Twentieth Century* (Norman: Univ. of Oklahoma Press, 1991), chap. 1.

2. See especially Tom J. Farer, "Elections, Democracy, and Human Rights: Toward Union," *Human Rights Quarterly* 11 (1989): 504–21.

3. See also Tina Rosenberg, "Beyond Elections," *Foreign Policy* 84 (1991): 72–91.

4. Huntington, *Third Wave,* 38.

5. Ibid., chap. 6.

6. See especially Zehra F. Arat, *Democracy and Human Rights in Developing Countries* (Boulder: Lynne Rienner, 1991), 129: "A conflict arises if socioeconomic rights draw a declining curve or a constant line while civil and political rights expand over time. This observation, unfortunately, does not allow me to share others' optimistic expectations about the future of democracy in developing countries—expectations that seemed to increase after the wave of democratization in the 1980s. As long as social and economic inequalities persist, developing countries that go through a process of democratization today are doomed to return to some form of authoritarianism."

See also Adamantia Pollis, "Development, Growth, and Human Rights: The Case of Turkey," in *Human Rights and Development,* ed. David P. Forsythe (London: Macmillan, 1989), 237–62. Pollis challenges the argument that civil and political rights have to be suppressed to obtain national economic growth. Rather, she finds that Turkish elites have resorted to repression primarily to suppress demands for socioeconomic rights and socioeconomic distributional policies.

For the same thesis applied to Africa, see Carol Lancaster, "Democracy in Africa," *Foreign Policy* 85 (1991–92): 148–65. For the same thesis applied to Asia, see Ramon H. Myers, "Taiwan: Building toward a Prosperous Democracy," *International Herald Tribune,* 30–31 May 1992.

7. See, for example, Carlos Ayala Corao, "Human Rights in Latin America: A Venezuelan View," in *Human Rights, Development, and Foreign Policy: Canadian Perspectives,* ed. Irving Brecher (Halifax: Institute for Research on Public Policy, 1989), 229–39.

8. Huntington, *Third Wave.*

9. David P. Forsythe, "Human Rights, the United States, and the Organization of American States," *Human Rights Quarterly* 13 (1991): 66–98.

10. See, among others, Lawrence Weschler, *A Miracle, a Universe: Settling Accounts with Torturers* (New York: Viking Penguin, 1990). For an account of some international influence on correcting human rights abuses in Argentina, see Iain Guest, *Behind the Disappearances: Argentina's Dirty War against Human Rights and the United Nations* (Philadelphia: Univ. of Pennsylvania Press, 1990).

11. David P. Forsythe, *The Internationalization of Human Rights* (Lexington: Lexington Books, 1991).

12. Thomas J. Farer, "The United Nations and Human Rights," *Human Rights Quarterly* 9 (1987): 550–86.

13. Jack Donnelly, "International Human Rights: A Regime Analysis," *International Organization* 40 (1986): 599–642.

14. David P. Forsythe, "Human Rights and the United Nations, 1945–1985," *Political Science Quarterly* 100 (1985): 249–67.

15. David P. Forsythe, "Democracy, War, and Covert Action," *Journal of Peace Research* 29 (1992): 385–96.

16. See also Howard Tolley, *The UN Commission on Human Rights* (Boulder: Westview, 1987).

17. See especially Philip Alston, "The Alleged Demise of Political Rights at the UN," *International Organization* 37 (1983): 537–46.

18. While some observers have tried to read a democratic content into the acknowledged right to self-determination, the United Nations, as propelled by state foreign policies, did not. See also Morton H. Halperin et al., *Self-Determination in the New World Order* (Washington, D.C.: Carnegie Endowment, 1992).

19. Theo van Boven, "Human Rights and Development: The UN Experience," in Forsythe, *Human Rights and Development*.

20. S/Res/688.

21. S/Res/794.

22. S/Res/770; S/Res/771.

23. UN, *An Agenda for Peace: Preventive Diplomacy, Peacemaking, and Peacekeeping,* Report of the secretary-general pursuant to the statement adopted by the Summit Meeting of the Security Council on 31 Jan. 1992.

24. A/Res/45-150.

25. A/Res/46-137.

26. A/Res/46-L.8/Rev 1.

27. USUN Press Release 30-(90), 25 Apr. 1990.

28. A/S-18/AC1/L.2 (1990), para. 24.

29. "Seminar of Latin American Experts on 'Human Rights, Democracy, Economic, and Social Development,'" *Human Rights Newsletter* 4 (1992): 7–8.

30. These developments are reviewed by Thomas M. Franck, "The Emerging Right to Democratic Governance," *American Journal of International Law* 86 (1992): 46–91.

31. David Gillies, "Human Rights, Governance, and Democracy: The World Bank's Problem Frontiers," paper prepared for the IPSA Human Rights Conference, Prague, 9–13 June 1992.

32. For increased attention to democracy in U.S. foreign policy, see Larry Diamond, "Promoting Democracy," *Foreign Policy,* 87 (1992): 25–46.

33. See also W. Michael Reisman, "Sovereignty and Human Rights in Contemporary International Law," *American Journal of International Law* 84 (1990): 866–77; and three authors writing under "Agora," *American Journal of International Law* 84 (1990): 494–524.

34. For an overview, see David P. Forsythe, *The Politics of International Law: U.S. Foreign Policy Reconsidered* (Boulder: Lynne Rienner, 1990), chap. 4.

35. See the debate between Tom J. Farer and Anthony D'Amato in "Agora."

36. In addition to ibid., see also Tom J. Farer, "Human Rights in Law's Empire: The Jurisprudence War," *American Journal of International Law* 85 (1991): 117–27; Farer is correct in his observation that states continue to oppose a claimed unilateral right of states to use force abroad for human rights reasons. See further Kelly-Kate S. Pease and David P. Forsythe, "Human Rights, Humanitarian Intervention, and World Politics, *Human Rights Quarterly* 15 (1993): 290–314.

37. "UN Technical Cooperation in the Field of Human Rights: New Challenges and Opportunities," *Human Rights Newsletter* 4 (1991): 1-f.

38. In this section on El Salvador, statements of fact not otherwise attributed are drawn from Terry Lynn Karl, "El Salvador's Negotiated Solution," *Foreign Affairs* 71 (1992): 147–64; and Americas Watch, "El Salvador: Peace and Human Rights," *News from Americas Watch,* 2 Sept. 1992. See also Americas Watch, *El Salvador's Decade of Terror* (New Haven: Yale Univ. Press, 1991).

39. Hugo Caminos and Roberto Vavalle, "New Departures in the Exercise of Inherent Powers by the UN and OAS Secretaries-General: The Central American Situation," *American Journal of International Law* 83 (1989): 395–402.

40. David P. Forsythe, "The UN Secretary-General and Human Rights," in *The Challenging Role of the UN Secretary-General,* ed. L. Gordenker and B. Rivlin (Westport, Conn.: Greenwood, 1993).

41. See, for example, Robert Pastor, "The Latin American Option," *Foreign Policy* 88 (1992): 113.

42. Tim Golden, "General in El Salvador Hints Fight over Purge of Officers," *New York Times,* 5 Nov. 1992. Shirley Christian, "El Salvador Army Purge Violates Peace Accords, UN Chief Says," *New York Times,* 12 Jan. 1993.

43. "El Salvador Finally Removes Military Chiefs," *New York Times,* 2 July 1993.

44. John Tessitore and Susan Woolfson, eds., *Issues before the 47th General Assembly of the United Nations* (Lanham: Univ. Press of America, 1992), 74.

45. The U.S. official commentary on the 1984 elections stresses their shortcomings, while noting in passing that "many foreign observers reported that the balloting appeared to be orderly and honest," U.S. Department of State, *Country Reports on Human Rights Practices for 1984* (Washington, D.C.: GPO, 1985), 622. Two private American observers argue that the elections were flawed but not fraudulent: John B. Oakes, letter to the editor, *New York Times,* 15 Nov. 1984; and Lois Whitman, letter to the editor, *New York Times,* 16 Nov. 1984. Several observers from Western European political parties found the Nicaraguan elections more fair than the 1983 elections in neighboring El Salvador; see *Keesings Contemporary Archives* (London: Longmans, 1984), 33270.

46. Tessitore and Woolfson, eds., *Issues before the 47th General Assembly,* 81–84.

47. Shirley Christian, "Managua Army Chief May Face Trial in 1990 Killing," *New York Times,* 4 July 1992.

48. Extracted from Tessitore and Woolfson, eds., *Issues before the 47th General Assembly,* 77–81.

49. Peter Hakim, "Behind Guatemala's 'Miracle,'" *Christian Science Monitor,* 23 June 1993, 16. See also "Guatemala Journal: An Improbable President's Tall Order," *New York Times,* 17 June 1993.

50. Edmond Mulet, "The Palace Coup That Failed," *New York Times,* 22 June 1993.

51. *UN Chronicle,* June 1991, 26.

52. *UN Chronicle,* Sept. 1991, 24.

53. "Clinton's Haiti Problem: What Price Democracy?" *New York Times,* 7 July 1994.

Chapter 5   *The OAS and the Protection of Democracy*

1. It is debatable whether General Cedras actually led the coup or simply emerged later as its leader. Some observers have suggested that the coup was instigated from within the army rank and file and not from the top of the military hierarchy. See, for example, John M. Goshko, "Proposal for Aristide's Return

Stalls: OAS Efforts Continue after Haiti's Communist Leader Skips Meeting," *Washington Post*, 21 Jan. 1992.

2. "Haiti's Military Assumes Power after Troops Arrest the President," *New York Times*, 1 Oct. 1991. See also Goshko, "Proposal for Aristide's Return Stalls."

3. Compare W. Michael Reisman, who observes that contemporary international law protects "the people's sovereignty rather than the sovereign's sovereignty." See his "Sovereignty and Human Rights in Contemporary International Law," *American Journal of International Law* 84 (1990): 869.

4. Thomas M. Franck, "The Emerging Right to Democratic Governance," *American Journal of International Law* 86 (1992): 50; and Franck, "The United Nations Based Prospects for a New Global Order," *New York University Journal of International Law and Politics* 22 (1990): 601.

5. Ag/Res/1080 XXI-0/91.

6. As of Oct. 1994, only Canada had ratified the Protocol of Washington.

7. Don Podesta, "South America's Trickle-Down Democracy," *Washington Post*, 9 Aug. 1992.

8. Margaret Ball notes in this connection that "to preach democracy without otherwise supporting it was to engage in empty oratory. Self-determination, in an absolute sense, could justify dictatorship—so long as it was popularly based—just as readily as democracy. And nonintervention—again in an absolute sense—could prevent the organization [the OAS] from ever enforcing any decision in the face of member opposition, up to and including decisions the members had previously agreed should be enforced." See Margaret Ball, *The OAS in Transition* (Durham: Duke Univ. Press, 1969), 485. See also Dinah Shelton, "Representative Democracy and Human Rights in the Western Hemisphere," *Human Rights Law Journal* 12 (1991): 353–59.

9. Gonzalo J. Facio, *The Haitian Crisis Is Testing the Democratic Will of the OAS*, Special Report 6 (Washington, D.C.: CIASF, 1992), 2.

10. Inter-American Conference for the Maintenance of Peace, *The International Conferences of American States*, Res/27 Supp 1 (Buenos Aires: IACMP, 1933–40), 160.

11. U.S. Department of State, *U.S. Adherence to Principle Opposing Oppressive Regimes among American Republics*, Bulletin 13 (Washington, D.C.: GPO, 1945), 892. In Latin America, the dangers of excessive reliance on the principle of nonintervention were envisioned several years earlier by Orestes Ferrara y Marino, who, as a member of the Cuban delegation to the Sixth International Conference of American States (Havana, 1928), warned of the risks created by rendering sovereigns completely unaccountable for actions within their own borders. "How much nobility and grandeur there has been in some interventions," he said. "If we declare in absolute terms that intervention is under no circumstances possible, we will be sanctioning all the inhuman acts committed within determined frontiers and, what is worse, we will be avoiding that which is in the hearts of all not to be avoided, the onslaught upon the people's rights of sovereignty and independence, which cynical forces can always trample upon." See C. Neale Ronning, *Law and Politics in Inter-American Diplomacy* (New York: Wiley, 1963), 65–66.

12. Article 12 (2). Article 18 provides that "no State or group of States has the right to intervene, directly or indirectly, for any reason whatsoever, in the internal or external affairs of any other State. The foregoing principle prohibits not only

armed force but also any other form of interference or attempted threat against the personality of the State or against its political, economic, and cultural elements."

13. *Texts Approved by the General Assembly at Its Sixteenth Special Session in Connection with the Amendments to the Charter of the Organization,* Ser/P/AG Doc 11, XVI-E/92 (14 Dec. 1992).

14. Fifth Meeting of Consultation of Ministers of Foreign Affairs, Santiago, Chile, 12–18 Aug. 1959, *Final Act,* Ser/C II.5, 4. The Declaration of Santiago was adopted on the basis of a draft presented by the Brazilian Delegation; see *Actas y Documentos,* Ser/F III.5 (Washington, D.C.: Pan American Union, 1961), Doc 98, *Report of the Chairman of Working Group II.*

15. Fifth Meeting, *Final Act,* 7.

16. Several resolutions are cited by Heraldo Muñoz. See his "The Haitian Crisis Is Testing the Democratic Will of the OAS," 6–8. See also Ball, *OAS in Transition,* 489–97.

17. For example, on 26 June 1954, ten members of the OAS requested that the Meeting of Consultation be convened to consider the danger to the peace and security of the hemisphere and to agree upon measures in view of the "demonstrated intervention of the international communist movement in the Republic of Guatemala." See OAS, *The Inter-American Treaty of Reciprocal Assistance: Applications,* vol. 2, *1948–1959* (Washington, D.C.: OAS, 1973), 165.

18. Eighth Meeting of Consultation of Ministers of Foreign Affairs, Res 3, "Reiteration of the Principles of Nonintervention and Self-Determination," in *Final Act,* OEA Ser/C II.8, 1962, 9. The resolution was adopted by twenty votes. Only Cuba voted against its approval.

19. Robert A. Pastor, *Whirlpool: U.S. Foreign Policy toward Latin America and the Caribbean* (Princeton: Princeton Univ. Press, 1992), 53–54.

20. Res/2, Ser/F II.17, Doc 49/79, Rev 2 (23 June 1979). See also Christina Cerna, "Human Rights in Conflict with the Principle of Non-Intervention: The Case of Nicaragua before the Seventeenth Meeting of Consultation of Ministers of Foreign Affairs," *Derechos Humanos en las Américas* (1984): 93.

21. See Inter-American Commission on Human Rights, *Report on the Situation of Human Rights in Nicaragua,* Ser/L V/II.53 (Washington, D.C.: IACHR, 1981), 2.

22. Several issues with regard to the crisis of Panama were not directly related to the OAS action and, consequently, are not mentioned here. See the following articles in *American Journal of International Law* 84 (1990): Anthony D'Amato, "The Invasion of Panama Was a Lawful Response to Tyranny," 516; Tom J. Farer, "Panama: Beyond the Charter Paradigm," 503; Ved P. Nanda, "The Validity of United States Intervention in Panama under International Law," 494. See also Jennifer Miller, "International Intervention: The United States Intervention of Panama," *Harvard International Law Journal* 31 (1990): 633n.

23. See OAS, Meeting of Consultation of Ministers of Foreign Affairs, *The Serious Crisis of Panama in Its International Context,* Ser/F II.21 Doc 8/89, Rev 2 (17 May 1989).

24. Farer, "Panama: Beyond the Charter Paradigm," 510.

25. Recently, the Chilean representative to the OAS pointed out that "the failure of the OAS in Panama revealed the normative and operational inadequacy of the inter-American system to implement the principles of representative democracy

and democratic solidarity set forth in the Charter." He went on to remark that "the [OAS] General Assembly . . . remedied this inadequacy fairly well when it adopted the Santiago Commitment and the mechanism set out in resolution 1080 on Representative Democracy." See Council for Inter-American Security Foundation 10, *The Haitian Crisis*, Doc CE Carta 27/92 (6 Oct. 1992).

26. Ibid., 512.

27. Laura W. Reed and Carl Kaysen, eds., *Emerging Norms of Justified Intervention* (Cambridge: American Academy of Arts and Sciences, 1993), 137.

28. Heraldo Muñoz, "The Rising Right to Democracy in the Americas," p. 27 of the mimeograph copy that the author made available to us in July 1993. For a more detailed analysis of the Peruvian *autogolpe*, see David Scott Palmer, chap. 11, this volume.

29. OAS, Meeting of Consultation of Ministers of Foreign Affairs, Mre/Res/ 1/92 (13 Apr. 1992).

30. OAS, Meeting of Consultation of Ministers of Foreign Affairs, Mre/Res/ 3/92, corr. 1 (14 Dec. 1992).

31. For a detailed discussion of the Haitian case, see Anthony P. Maingot, chap. 8, this volume.

32. Between Oct. and 16 Dec. 1990, approximately two hundred persons from twenty-six member states were deployed by the OAS in two groups: one as observers and the second as advisers. The UN Observer Group for the Verification of the Elections in Haiti (UNOVEH) consisted of three groups: one for electoral observation, a second for security observation, and a third for administration. See Domingo E. Acevedo, "The Haitian Crisis and the OAS Response: A Test of Effectiveness in Protecting Democracy," in *Enforcing Restraint*, ed. Lori F. Damrosch (New York: Council on Foreign Relations, 1993), 128–29.

33. Howard W. French, "Haitians Overwhelmingly Elect Populist Priest to the Presidency," *New York Times*, 18 Dec. 1990.

34. Howard W. French, "Haiti Leader Faces Task of Controlling Military," *New York Times*, 20 Dec. 1990. See also "Mobilizing Resources for Development: A Retrospect on President Aristide's Economic Strategy for Haiti and His Administration's Record with Aid Donors," *International Policy Update* (1 Apr. 1992).

35. Aristide indeed sought to bypass the National Assembly by refusing to submit to it appointments of Supreme Court judges, cabinet members, and ambassadorial nominations as provided for in the 1987 Constitution. When the National Assembly began to consider a vote of no confidence in Prime Minister René Preval, a mob of "at least two thousand Aristide supporters surrounded the National Assembly on 13 August, roughing up two deputies and threatening to burn others alive" if they moved ahead with the motion against Preval. A senator's home was also attacked by a crowd of Aristide supporters, and a deputy of National Assembly was threatened with the *surplice de Père Lebrun*, or burning alive by a group armed with used tires and a bottle of gasoline (commonly known as "necklacing"). See Howard W. French, "Ex-Backers of Ousted Haitian Say He Alienated His Allies," *New York Times International*, 22 Oct. 1991.

36. Facio, *Haitian Crisis Is Testing The Democratic Will of the OAS*.

37. OAS, CP/Res/567 870/91 (30 Sept. 1991).

38. OAS, Meeting of Consultation of Ministers of Foreign Affairs, Mre/Res 1/91, OEA/Ser F/V.1 (3 Oct. 1991), operative para. 1.

39. OAS, Meeting of Consultation of Ministers of Foreign Affairs, Mre/Res 2/91 (8 Oct. 1991).

40. OAS, Meeting of Consultation of Ministers of Foreign Affairs, Mre/Doc 3/91 (7 Oct. 1991). The Civilian Mission was entrusted with the very difficult task of negotiating with the military and political forces that either participated in or supported President Aristide's deposal, to work out a compromise to facilitate his return to power.

41. See "Countries Ignore Haiti Embargo," *New York Times,* 31 May 1992. The documents, assembled in May 1992 by the GAO, were made available to the author by the office of Senator Edward Kennedy. The United States, which had pushed hardest for the economic embargo, on 4 Feb. 1992 modified its policy when it became clear that U.S. businesses with interests or operations in Haiti would sustain severe losses were the embargo to continue. As a result, the administration announced a number of exemptions (on a case-by-case basis) for the Haitian assembly sector. Under these exemptions, the Treasury Department was authorized to grant licenses to individuals and companies operating in the assembly sector in Haiti, to permit the export of materials manufactured in the United States, the assembly of the finished product in Haiti, and its importation back into the United States. Another explanation given for the decision to modify the policy was that it was necessary to reduce the exodus of Haiti refugees to the United States. Between Oct. 1991 and 1994, more than fifty thousand Haitians fled their country to seek refuge in the United States. The United States established various mechanisms to control the influx of these refugees, including the screening of applications on the sea, establishing temporary centers outside the United States, and intercepting and returning vessels to Haiti.

42. OAS, Meeting of Consultation of Ministers of Foreign Affairs, Mre/Res 3/92 (17 May 1992).

43. See, for example, David W. Dent, "Haiti Could Become a Pawn in U.S. Politics," *Christian Science Monitor,* 3 Mar. 1992, 19; "A Military Force for the Americas," editorial *New York Times,* 24 Mar. 1992; Barbara Crossette, "U.S. Is Discussing an Outside Force to Stabilize Haiti," *New York Times,* 6 June 1992. Robert A. Pastor suggests that "if the OAS succeeds, the next step should be a permanent collective-security mechanism to defend all Western Hemisphere democracies. The OAS needs to make it clear that comparable economic and diplomatic sanctions, and collective military action as a last resort, could be repeated automatically if democracy is toppled, whether in large or small countries, such as Argentina and Guatemala, which have suffered military coups in the past." See "Haiti Is Not Alone," *New York Times,* 4 Oct. 1991. Perhaps a more precise term for this mechanism would be "collective defense," as suggested by, among others, Inter-American Dialogue, *Convergence and Community: The Americas in 1993* (Washington, D.C.: IAD, 1993).

44. OAS, Meeting of Consultation of Ministers of Foreign Affairs, Mre/Res 4/92 (13 Dec. 1992).

45. On 21 Dec., Agence France Press reported that the secretary-general of the OAS had objected to "the involvement of 'other organizations' in the settlement of the Haitian crisis." Reproduced in OAS, Department of Public Information, *Boletín de Noticias,* 22 Dec. 1992, 2. However, in early Jan. 1993 he announced that he had asked Mr. Caputo to serve as his representative as well. The UN initiative

included mediation efforts intended to get both sides (Father Aristide and the de facto government) to agree, in principle, "to end human rights abuses and to start negotiations on issues like de-politicizing the armed forces and rebuilding Haiti's shattered economy." See Steven A. Holmes, "Bush and Clinton Aides Link Policies on Haiti," *New York Times*, 7 Jan. 1993.

46. Howard W. French, "Visiting U.S. General Warns Haiti's Military Chiefs," *New York Times*, 9 Jan. 1993. In mid-January 1993 the U.S. Coast Guard began to deploy large cutters, patrol boats, and at least a dozen aircraft to the international waters north of Haiti to block an expected wave of refugees seeking to reach the United States. The deployment, according to the U.S. officials, was ordered by the outgoing administration in consultation with President-elect Bill Clinton. It was intended, in part at least, to lend credence to Clinton's announcement, on 16 Jan. 1993, that he would continue the Bush policy of returning Haitian boat people, thereby temporarily abandoning a campaign pledge to discontinue the policy of intercepting Haitian boat people on the high seas. See Howard W. French, "Haitians Express Sense of Betrayal," *New York Times*, 17 Jan. 1993. See also Steven A. Holmes, "U.S. Sends Flotilla to Prevent Exodus from Haiti by Sea," *New York Times*, 16 Jan. 1993. For a criticism of Clinton's reversal, see "For Haitians, Cruelty and Hope," editorial, *New York Times*, 16 Jan. 1993.

47. Since 1990, the OAS has also addressed the coup in Suriname in Dec. 1990 (CP/Res 554/90) and the attempted coup in Venezuela in February 1992 (CP/Res 576 887/92).

48. The activities of the UN, the OAS, and the NGOs in establishing, defining, and monitoring free and open elections in independent member states have contributed to the ongoing reevaluation of norms and principles related to sovereignty. See Gregory H. Fox, "The Right to Political Participation in International Law," *Yale Journal of International Law* 17(1992): 539. Franck remarks that "the capacity of the international community to extend legitimacy to national governments, however, depends not only on its capacity to monitor an election . . . but also on the extent to which such international activity has evolved from the ad hoc to the normative: that is, that degree to which the process of legitimation itself has become legitimate." See Thomas M. Franck, "The Emerging Right to Democratic Governance," *American Journal of International Law* 86 (1992): 51.

49. Franck, "Emerging Right to Democratic Governance," 52.

50. Ibid., 81. The monitoring and supervision of elections by international organizations basically ensures that they are free and fair and that the results, as Reisman points out, "serve as evidence of popular sovereignty and become the basis for international endorsement of the elected government." See Reisman, "Sovereignty and Human Rights," 868–69. See also Fox, "Right to Political Participation," 570–95.

51. See Ball, *OAS in Transition*, 495. Also, Inter-American Institute of International Legal Studies, *The Inter-American System: Its Development and Strengthening* (Dobbs Ferry, N.Y.: Oceana, 1966), 60.

52. This view was actually advanced by Michael Reisman, for whom "the most satisfactory solution to this question is the creation of centralized institutions, equipped with decision-making authority and the capacity to make it effective"; see Reisman, "Sovereignty and Human Rights," 85. See also Franck, "Emerging Right to Democratic Governance," 46. Implicit in the suggestion that the enforcement

mechanism should be the task of a multilateral normative regime is the need to determine first what constitutes a legitimate government. Tom Farer notes that during the Reagan administration "the key criterion of human rights performance [was] a government's ability to trace its authority to victory in competitive elections." See Tom Farer, "Elections, Democracy, and Human Rights: Toward Union," *Human Rights Quarterly* 11 (1989): 510.

53. Heraldo Muñoz, "A New OAS for the New Times," in *Latin America in a New World*, ed. Abraham F. Lowenthal and Gregory F. Treverton (Boulder: Westview, 1994), 197, 198.

54. Ibid., 201–2.

55. See Larry Diamond, "Promoting Democracy," *Foreign Policy* 87 (1992): 27.

Chapter 6   NGOs, Democracy, and Human Rights in Latin America

1. For a discussion of transnational issue networks, see Kathryn Sikkink, "Human Rights, Principled Issue Networks, and Sovereignty in Latin America," *International Organization* 47 (1993): 3; Margaret Keck and Kathryn Sikkink, "International Issue Networks in the Environment and Human Rights," paper prepared for the Seventeenth International Congress of the Latin American Studies Association, Los Angeles, 24–27 Sept. 1992. Rather than focusing on a network as a whole, this chapter explores the changing strategies and the impact of nongovernmental actors within the Latin American human rights network.

2. See David Weissbrodt, "The Contributions of International Nongovernmental Organizations to the Protection of Human Rights," in *Human Rights in International Law: Legal and Policy Issues*, ed. Theodor Meron (Oxford: Clarendon, 1984); Henry J. Steiner, *Diverse Partners: Nongovernmental Organizations in the Human Rights Movement* (Cambridge: Human Rights Program and Human Rights Internet, Harvard Law School, 1991); Laurie S. Wiseberg and Harry M. Scoble, "Monitoring Human Rights Violations: The Role of Nongovernmental Organizations," in *Human Rights and American Foreign Policy*, ed. Donald P. Kommers and Gilbert D. Loescher (Notre Dame: Univ. of Notre Dame Press, 1979); Hugo Derech, "Nonprofit Organizations as Opposition to Authoritarian Rule: The Case of Human Rights Organizations in Chile," in *The Nonprofit Sector in International Perspective: Studies in Comparative Culture and Policy*, ed. Estelle James (New York: Oxford Univ. Press, 1989); David Forsythe, *Human Rights and World Politics* (Lincoln: Univ. of Nebraska Press, 1983); Lars Schoultz, *Human Rights and United States Policy toward Latin America* (Princeton: Princeton Univ. Press, 1981).

3. Exceptions include Hugo Frühling, ed., *Derechos humanos y democracia: La contribución de las organizaciones no gubernamentales* (Santiago: Instituto Interamericano de Derechos Humanos, 1991); and Jonathan Fox and Luis Hernández, "Mexico's Difficult Democracy: Grassroots Movements, NGOs, and Local Government," *Alternatives* 17 (1992): 165–208.

4. Margaret Keck, "Sustainable Development and Environmental Politics in Latin America," in *Redefining the State in Latin America*, ed. Colin Bradford Jr.

(Paris: OECD, 1994), 101; Fox and Hernández, "Mexico's Difficult Democracy," 177.

5. This distinction is one of the key differences among NGOs stressed by Frühling, *Derechos Humanos y Democracia,* 19–21.

6. For a detailed analysis of the Argentine human rights movement, see Alison Brysk, *The Politics of Human Rights in Argentina: Protest, Change, and Democratization* (Stanford: Stanford Univ. Press, 1994).

7. Arturo Escobar and Sonia E. Alvarez, "Introduction: Theory and Protest in Latin America Today," in *The Making of Social Movements in Latin America: Identity, Strategy, and Democracy,* ed. Arturo Escobar and Sonia E. Alvarez (Boulder: Westview, 1992), 8.

8. Juan Méndez made the point about the importance of this "dialogue" for the human rights movement at the workshop, Human Rights, Justice, and Society in Latin America, Buenos Aires, 24–25 Oct. 1992.

9. These periods are only approximations, however, and important differences exist from country to country. For example, the human rights movement in Peru, Colombia, and Mexico did not emerge in the 1970s but began to form only in the mid to late 1980s.

10. See Jack Donnelly, *Universal Human Rights in Theory and Practice* (Ithaca: Cornell Univ. Press, 1989), esp. table on 224–25, for a summary of the evolution of human rights regimes. For discussions of the role of NGOs in the building of international action on human rights or in contributing to the adoption and implementation of U.S. human rights policy, see the sources listed in n11.

11. David Weissbrodt and Teresa O'Toole, "The Development of International Human Rights Law," in *The Universal Declaration of Human Rights, 1948–1988: Human Rights, the United Nations, and Amnesty International* (New York: Amnesty International, 1988), 17–22; Forsythe, *Human Rights and World Politics,* 7–10.

12. David P. Forsythe, *Humanitarian Politics: The International Committee of the Red Cross* (Baltimore: Johns Hopkins Univ. Press, 1977); and J. D. Armstrong, "The International Committee of the Red Cross and Political Prisoners," *International Organization* 39 (1985): 615–42; Forsythe, *Human Rights and World Politics,* 7–9.

13. John P. Humphrey, *Human Rights and the United Nations: A Great Adventure* (Dobbs Ferry, N.Y.: Transnational, 1984), 13. Also see U.S. Department of State, *The United Nations Conference on International Organization, San Francisco, California April 25 to June 26, 1945: Selected Documents* (Washington, D.C.: GPO, 1946).

14. Wiseberg and Scoble, "Monitoring Human Rights Violations," 183–84. This was confirmed by interviews with the leaders and staffs of nine key human rights NGOs in the U.S.

15. Kathryn Sikkink, "The Power of Principled Ideas: Human Rights Policies in the United States and Western Europe," in *Ideas and Foreign Policy: Beliefs, Institutions, and Political Change,* ed. Judith Goldstein and Robert O. Keohane (Ithaca: Cornell Univ. Press, 1993).

16. "The Growing Lobby for Human Rights," *Washington Post,* 12 Dec. 1976.

17. Interviews by author with key human rights leaders and activists in the United States.

18. Frühling, *Derechos Humanos y Democracia,* 14.

19. Margaret Keck originated the points about testimony and leverage mentioned in this paragraph, which have been elaborated in greater detail in Margaret Keck and Kathryn Sikkink, "International Issue Networks in the Environment and Human Rights."

20. Interview by author with Michael Posner, executive director, Lawyers Committee for Human Rights, New York, 19 Mar. 1992.

21. These figures were obtained using a relatively restricted definition of human rights (basically rights of the person and civil and political rights) to code organizations listed in the *Yearbook of International Organizations* in 1980 and 1990. The restricted definition of human rights was used to distinguish between human rights organizations and the much larger number of development organizations.

22. Laurie S. Wiseberg and Harry M. Scoble, eds., *Human Rights Directory: Latin America and the Caribbean* (Washington, D.C.: Human Rights Internet, 1990).

23. Based on information from interviews by author with staffs of the three organizations.

24. Laurie S. Wiseberg and Harry M. Scoble, eds., *Human Rights Directory: Latin America, Africa, and Asia* (Washington, D.C.: Human Rights Internet, 1981). Wiseberg and Scoble, *Human Rights Directory: Latin American and the Caribbean.* The definition used by these directories is broader than that used by many human rights groups in Latin America, but the 1981 and 1990 figures show the dramatic growth in the Latin American human rights network and the wide range of groups working on diverse human rights issues throughout the region.

25. David Weissbrodt, "International Law: The Year in Review," in *Proceedings, Eighty-Fourth Annual Meeting, American Society of International Law* (Washington, D.C.: AAIL, 1990), 139. Also see Tamar Jacoby, "The Reagan Turnaround on Human Rights," *Foreign Affairs* 64 (1986): 1066–86.

26. This final point was made by Juan Méndez, director of Americas Watch, at the workshop, Human Rights, Justice, and Society in Latin America, Buenos Aires, 24–25 Oct. 1992.

27. See, for example, Brian H. Smith, "Old Allies, New Enemies: The Catholic Church as Opposition to Military Rule in Chile, 1973–1979," in *Military Rule in Chile: Dictatorship and Oppositions,* ed. J. Samuel Valenzuela and Arturo Valenzuela (Baltimore: Johns Hopkins Univ. Press, 1986), 291.

28. Interviews by author with Peter Bell, New York, 20 Mar. 1992; and William Carmichael, New York, 11 May 1992.

29. Developing countries' NGOs are starting to become more interested in, and more savvy about, the potential role for NGOs at UN human rights meetings. For an article giving practical advice to Latin American NGOs about how to be effective lobbyists at subcommission meetings, see Germán Palacio, "Derechos humanos y trabajo internacional: A propósito de la Subcomisión de las Naciones Unidas para la Prevención de la Discriminación de las Minorías," *El Otro Derecho* 10 (Mar. 1992), 139–58. *Orientation Manual: The U.N. Commission on Human Rights, Its Sub-Commission, and Related Procedures,* prepared by David Weissbrodt and Penny Parker for the Minnesota Advocates for Human Rights and the International Service for Human Rights and designed for first-time NGO participants and observers, offers an overview of the UN human rights machinery and

procedures as well as advice on such practical matters as getting into the UN on your first day and securing credentials.

30. Kenneth Roth, "End of Cold War Opens New Avenues for Advocating Human Rights," *Human Rights Watch Quarterly Newsletter* (winter/spring 1994): 1.

31. Ibid.

32. Interview by author with Charles Reilly, Inter-American Foundation, Washington, D.C., 17 Mar. 1992.

33. One participant at a retreat for NGO activists expressed the resulting sense of isolation: "In the transition period, all these international groups drew back. . . . Then we lost touch with those organizations. That's terrible for us, because there is a kind of central decision that, when a country starts a new process, there is no longer any need for international action and support." Steiner, *Diverse Partners,* 51.

34. Aryeh Neier, "El Salvador Work Shaped the Human Rights Movement," *Human Rights Watch Quarterly Newsletter* (winter 1992): 3.

35. See, for example, Americas Watch, *Human Rights in Mexico: A Policy of Impunity* (New York: Human Rights Watch, 1990); Amnesty International, *Mexico: Torture with Impunity* (New York: Amnesty International USA, 1991). Americas Watch, *Prison Conditions in Brazil* (New York: Human Rights Watch, 1989); Americas Watch, *The Struggle for Land in Brazil: Rural Violence Continues* (New York: Human Rights Watch, 1992).

36. Amnesty International, "Twentieth International Council Meeting: Report and Decisions," Yokohama, 31 Aug.–7 Sept. 1991.

37. Roth, "End of the Cold War Opens New Avenues for Advocating Human Rights," 8.

38. The Inter-American Institute for Human Rights, based in Costa Rica, has been offering classes and training sessions for human rights leaders and activists since it was established in 1980. The International Human Rights Internship Program arranges internships and training opportunities for human rights activists in both the North and the South.

39. I am indebted for some of these ideas to comments by Marcelo Cavarozzi, Catalina Smulovitz, and Carlos Acuña in response to a presentation of a study at CEDES in Buenos Aires.

40. See Lisa Martin and Kathryn Sikkink, "U.S. Policy and Human Rights in Argentina and Guatemala, 1973–1980," in *Double-Edged Diplomacy,* ed. Peter Evans et al. (Berkeley: Univ. of California Press, 1993); and Kathryn Sikkink, "The Effectiveness of U.S. Human Rights Policy: Argentina, Guatemala, and Uruguay," paper prepared for the Meeting of the International Political Science Association, Buenos Aires, 21–25 July 1991.

41. This argument is reinforced by the two-level game negotiation theory proposed by Robert Putnam, who argues that international pressure may enable government leaders to shift the balance of power in their domestic game in favor of a policy they desire but feel powerless to implement. Robert Putnam, "Diplomacy and Domestic Politics: The Logic of Two-Level Games," *International Organization* 42 (1988): 457.

42. Guillermo O'Donnell and Philippe Schmitter, *Transitions from Authoritarian Rule: Tentative Conclusions about Uncertain Democracies* (Baltimore: Johns Hopkins Univ. Press, 1986), 19.

Notes to Pages 158–161

43. Americas Watch, *Human Rights in Mexico.*

44. This argument is developed further in Sikkink, "Human Rights, Principled Issue Networks, and Sovereignty in Latin America."

45. According to Denise Dresser, "foremost among the priorities of Salinas's foreign policy is the avoidance of diplomatic conflicts that might sabotage Mexico's shared economic interests with the U.S." See her "Mr. Salinas Goes to Washington: Mexican Lobbying in the United States," Paper 62, conference, Crossing National Borders: Invasion or Involvement, Columbia University, 6 Dec. 1991, 5. Also see Ellen L. Lutz, "Human Rights in Mexico: Cause for Continuing Concern," *Current History* 92 (Feb. 1993).

46. Interview by author with Rachel Neild, staff associate, Washington Office on Latin America, Washington, D.C., 11 Aug. 1992.

47. The two networks included European-Guatemalan solidarity organizations and the Copenhagen Initiative for Central America (CIFCA), made up of fifteen large European NGOs working on Central America. Interview by author with Eric Oostrijk, HIVOS, 4 Nov. 1993, The Hague.

48. "Guatemala's Countercoup: A Military About-Face," *New York Times,* 3 June 1993.

49. Forsythe, *Human Rights and World Politics,* 210, and Schoultz, *Human Rights and U.S. Policy toward Latin America,* 373, both stress the importance of NGOs in contributing to the adoption and maintenance of U.S. human rights policy. A number of human rights activists and policymakers also cite this as one of the main successes of the human rights movement. Interviews by author with Kenneth Roth, New York, 11 May 1992; Margo Picken, New York, 20 Mar. 1992; and Donald Fraser, Minneapolis, 18 Mar. 1991.

50. Interview with Posner.

51. Alexander Wendt stresses that sovereignty exists "only in virtue of certain intersubjective understandings and expectations," which in turn constitute a particular kind of state. He argues that sovereignty norms are now so taken for granted that "it is easy to overlook the extent to which they are both presupposed by an ongoing artifact of practice." See his "Anarchy Is What States Make of It: The Social Construction of Power Politics," *International Organization* 46 (1992): 412–13.

52. Interview with Posner.

53. Iain Guest, *Behind the Disappearances: Argentina's Dirty War against Human Rights and the United Nations* (Philadelphia: Univ. of Pennsylvania Press, 1990), 182–83.

Chapter 7   *The International Donor Community*

This chapter draws heavily on Joan Nelson and Stephanie Eglinton, *Encouraging Democracy: What Role for Conditioned Aid?* Policy Essay 4 (Washington, D.C.: Overseas Development Council, 1992; and Nelson and Eglinton, *Global Goals, Contentious Means: Issues of Multiple Conditionality,* Policy Essay 10 (Washington, D.C.: Overseas Development Council, 1993).

1. For reviews of the evidence, see Stephan Haggard and Robert Kaufman, "The Politics of Stabilization and Structural Adjustment," in *Developing Country Debt and Economic Performance,* vol. 1, ed. Jeffrey D. Sachs (Chicago: Univ. of Chicago

Press, 1989), 232 ff.; Karen Remmer, "The Politics of Economic Stabilization: IMF Standby Programs in Latin America, 1954–1984," *Comparative Politics* 19 (1986): 1–25; Adam Przeworski and Fernando Limongi, "Political Regimes and Economic Growth," *Journal of Economic Perspectives* 7 (1993): 51–69.

2. Since the end of the Cold War, both bilateral and multilateral donors are increasingly willing to address another (once taboo) issue: the high levels of military expenditures and influence in many recipient countries. The IMF has begun to collect data on defense spending as part of its regular public expenditure reviews. The World Bank and several bilateral donors are encouraging reductions in military spending during consultations with recipients and have supported demobilization efforts in countries such as Nicaragua and Uganda. These efforts are vital to the consolidation of democracy in developing countries. See Nicole Ball, *Pressing for Peace: Can Aid Induce Reform?* Policy Essay 6 (Washington, D.C.: Overseas Development Council, 1992).

3. Prepared statement by Lawrence Summers, undersecretary for international affairs, U.S. Department of Treasury, Hearing before the Subcommittee on International Development, Finance, Trade, and Monetary Policy of the Committee on Banking, Finance, and Urban Affairs of the U.S. House of Representatives, 5 May 1993, app. 69.

4. U.S. Agency for International Development, "Democracy and Governance," USAID, Washington, D.C., November 1991.

5. In June 1993 the House of Representatives unexpectedly voted not to authorize funding for the National Endowment for Democracy. The Senate later restored funding, but the incident illustrates how the flush of enthusiasm for promoting democracy has receded since 1989.

6. Section 502B and Section 116 of the Foreign Assistant Act of 1961. See Center for International Policy, International Policy Reports, "Military Aid Law" and "Economic Aid Law," Washington, D.C., 1991.

7. Suspending loans to bad political performers is not a matter determined by World Bank staff but must be approved by the governing board, which represents both rich and poor member nations.

8. Of international financial institutions, only the European Bank for Reconstruction and Development (EBRD) has overtly political objectives. The EBRD was created in 1990 to help finance Eastern Europe's economic and political transitions. Its charter is precedent setting in that it is committed to "multiparty democracy, pluralism, and market economies" as conditions for assistance.

9. For a more detailed discussion, see World Bank, *Governance and Development* (Washington, D.C.: World Bank, 1992).

10. For a lucid and concise discussion of governance issues, see Carol Lancaster, "Governance and Development: The Views from Washington," *IDS Bulletin* 24 (1993): 9–15.

11. See, for instance, David Gillies, "Human Rights, Democracy, and Good Governance: Stretching the World Bank's Policy Frontiers," International Centre for Human Rights and Democratic Development, Montreal, June 1992.

12. See Richard Feinberg and Delia M. Boylan, *Modular Multilateralism: North-South Economic Relations in the 1990s,* Policy Essay 1 (Washington, D.C.: Overseas Development Council, 1991), 40.

13. For data, see United Nations, *World Economic Survey* (New York: UN, 1993), table A-27.

14. Organizations for Economic Cooperation and Development, *DAC Orientations on Participatory Development and Good Governance* (Paris: OECD, 1993), paras. 4, 9.

15. For a further discussion, see Moisés Naím, "Latin America: Post-Adjustment Blues," *Foreign Policy* 92 (1993).

Chapter 8   *Haiti*

I wish to thank David Nicholls for his incisive comments on a draft of this chapter.

1. Arguably, the first democratic election was won by Francois Duvalier in 1957; it was never internationally certified.

2. Precisely because the issue is far from settled, the American Academy of Arts and Sciences has launched a major study of the way the traditional prerogatives of national sovereignty have been subordinated to new norms emphasising common humanity. See Laura W. Reed and Carl Kaysen, eds., *Emerging Norms of Justified Intervention* (Cambridge: American Academy of Arts and Sciences, 1993). On the trend toward an emphasis on democracy as exemplified through free and fair elections, see David P. Forsythe, chap. 4, this volume.

3. See Viron P. Vaky and Heraldo Muñoz, *The Future of the Organization of American States* (New York: Twentieth Century Fund, 1993), 42, 83–84.

4. David P. Forsythe, "Human Rights, the United States, and the Organization of American States," *Human Rights Quarterly* 13 (1991): 66.

5. *New York Times,* 17 Mar. 1993.

6. From an early version of David Forsythe's chapter, this volume (chap. 4). A similar argument is made by Tom J. Farer, "The OAS at the Crossroads: Human Rights," *Iowa Law Review* 72 (1987): 405–13.

7. Ludwell Lee Montague, *Haiti and the United States, 1714–1938* (Durham: Duke Univ. Press, 1940), 210–11. Haitian anthropologist Rémy Bastien notes that opponents of the U.S. occupation emphasized the political aspects of the occupation, wrongly minimizing the economic ones. This concern is repeated by noted Haiti scholar David Nicholls, in a personal communication (13 July 1993). Whatever the U.S. economic designs might have been, even Bastien admits that there were few economic benefits to be had, and U.S. concerns soon departed. See Remy Bastien, "Haiti: clases y perjuicios de color," *Aportes* 9 (1968): 5–25.

8. J. C. Dorsainvil, *Manuel d'histoire d'Haiti* (Port-au-Prince, 1924), 289.

9. Montague, *Haiti and the United States,* 212.

10. Ibid., 215.

11. Cited in Arthur C. Millspaugh, *Haiti under American Control, 1915–1930* (Boston: World Peace Foundation, 1931), 96n.

12. See David Healy, *Gunboat Diplomacy in the Wilson Era: The U.S. Navy in Haiti, 1915–1916* (Madison: Univ. of Wisconsin Press, 1976), 210.

13. See J. Michael Dash, *Literature and Ideology in Haiti, 1915–1961* (Totowa, N.J.: Barnes and Nobel, 1981).

14. David Nicholls, *From Dessalines to Duvalier* (London: Cambridge Univ. Press, 1979), 142.

15. Hans Schmidt, *The United States Occupation of Haiti, 1915–1934* (New Brunswick: Rutgers Univ. Press, 1971), 7.

16. Ibid., 102–3.

17. See Inaugural Address, 7 Feb. 1991, reprinted in National Democratic Institute for International Affairs, *The 1990 Elections in Haiti* (Washington, D.C.: NDIIA, 1991), 108–20.

18. Testimony of Lt. Col. A. S. Williams, *Inquiry into Occupation and Administration of Haiti and Santo Domingo.* Hearings, Select Committee on Haiti and Santo Domingo, U.S. Senate, 67 Cong. (Washington, D.C.: GPO, 1922), 497.

19. Ramón Barceló, "Changements techniques et paupérisation dans les campagnes; dix ans d'agriculture en Amérique latine," *Amérique latine* 14 (Apr.–June 1983): 14.

20. Paul Moral, *Le paysan haïtien* (Paris: G. P. Maisonneuve et LaRose, 1961), 189–207; George Anglada, *L'espace haïtien* (Montreal: Editions des Alizes, 1981), 107–8; Pierre-Jacques Roca, "Agriculture et dépendence: la paysannerie haitiénne dans l'impasse," *Amérique Latine* 21 (1985): 12–16.

21. W. A. Lewis, "Economic Development with Unlimited Supplies of Labour," Manchester School of Economics and Social Studies, May 1954.

22. Alain Rocourt is quoted in Richard M. Morse, ed., *Haiti's Future: Views of Twelve Haitian Leaders* (Washington, D.C.: Woodrow Wilson Center Press, 1988), 73–78.

23. See ibid., 36.

24. Jean-Bertrand Aristide, *In the Parish of the Poor: Writings from Haiti,* ed. and trans. Amy Wilentz (New York: Orbis, 1990), 15.

25. Amy Wilentz, *The Rainy Season: Haiti since Duvalier* (New York: Simon and Schuster, 1989).

26. Amy Wilentz, in *New York Newsday,* 14 May 1990.

27. See Gregorio Selser, "Haiti: El drama permanente de su pueblo. Entrevista al sacerdote Jean-Bertrand Aristide," *El Caribe contemporáneo* (Mexico) 22 (Jan.–July 1991): 41–63.

28. *Haiti 1990: Quelle démocratie* (Port-au-Prince: Haiti Solidarité Internationale, 1990).

29. Puebla Institute, *Haiti: Looking Forward to Elections: An Interim Report* (Washington, D.C.: Puebla Institute, 1990), 7–8.

30. Reprinted in Paul Dejean, *Dans la tourmente* (New York: Bohiyo Enterprises, 1990), 199.

31. Don Bohning, *Miami Herald,* 26 Nov. 1990.

32. Amy Wilentz, "Foreword," in Aristide, *In the Parish of the Poor.*

33. *Haiti Insight,* Oct. 1991.

34. Inaugural Address, reprinted in NDIIA, *1990 Elections in Haiti.*

35. Christophe Wargny, "Introduction," in Jean-Bertrand Aristide, *Aristide: An Autobiography* (New York: Orbis, 1993), 11.

36. See Don Bohning, *Miami Herald,* 2 May 1991.

37. Ibid.

38. Howard French, *New York Times,* 4 Aug. 1991.

39. "Business Risks in the Americas," *Miami Herald,* Special Report, 22 Apr. 1991.

40. See the monumental bibliography compiled by Michel S. Laguerre, ed., *The Complete Haitiana: A Bibliographic Guide to the Scholarly Literature, 1900–1980* (New York: Kraus International Publications, 1982).

41. See James Leyburn, *The Haitian People* (New Haven: Yale Univ. Press, 1941); Mats Lundahl, *Peasants and Poverty: A Study of Haiti* (New York: St. Martin's, 1979); Robert Heinl and Nancy Heinl, *Written in Blood* (Boston: Houghton Mifflin, 1978); Alain Tournier, *Quand la Nation demande des comptes* (Port-au-Prince: Impr. Le Natal, 1989).

42. Emmanuel Edouard, *Essai sur la politique intérieure d'Haiti* (Paris, 1890), 42, 99–100 passim.

43. Melville J. Herskovits, *Life in a Haitian Valley* (New York: Knopf, 1937), 297.

44. Ibid., 299.

45. Aristide, *Aristide: An Autobiography,* 32.

46. Robert Rotberg, *Haiti: The Politics of Squalor* (Boston: Houghton Mifflin, 1971), 17–19.

47. Lawrence E. Harrison, "The Cultural Roots of Haitian Underdevelopment," in *Small Country Development and International Labor Flows,* ed. Anthony P. Maingot (Boulder: Westview, 1991); Rémy Bastien, "Vodoun and Politics in Haiti," in *Religion and Politics in Haiti,* ed. Rémy Bastien and Harold Courlander (Washington, D.C.: Institute for Cross-Cultural Research, 1966).

48. Artistide, *Aristide: An Autobiography,* 168.

49. This and the following passages are taken from ibid.

50. Aristide, quoted in Amy Wilentz, *Rainy Season,* 276.

51. The meeting took place in Miami under the sponsorship of Florida International University's Latin American and Caribbean Center, 22–24 July 1993. I moderated the discussion on public sector/private sector collaboration. This section is drawn from the notes from that meeting.

52. The patriotic sentiments were made evident when, unexpectedly during the third day of meetings, all participants spontaneously stood up and sang the Haitian national anthem.

53. While not a new phenomenon, it is believed that, with the chaos that followed the fall of Jean-Claude Duvalier in 1986, Colombian mafias spread their tentacles deep into the commercial and military elites of the island. See U.S. Senate, *Drugs, Law Enforcement, and Foreign Policy,* Committee on Foreign Relations, U.S. Senate, 100 Cong., 2 Sess. (Washington, D.C.: GPO, 1988.)

54. I recommended this option in A. P. Maingot, *Grasping the Nettle: A "National Liberation" Option for Haiti,* Agenda Paper 6, March (Miami: North-South Center).

55. "Haiti and Beyond," *Miami Herald,* 1 Mar. 1992.

56. Vaky and Muñoz, *Future of the Organization of American States,* 83.

57. See UN Development Program, *Human Development Report, 1993* (New York: Oxford Univ. Press, 1993).

Chapter 9   *El Salvador*

1. UN, *Information Notes,* May update (New York: Department of Peace Keeping Operations and Field Operations, 1994), table showing growth of field operations, 1989–93. Costs for UN peacekeeping operations have more than tripled, from about $1 billion to $4 billion, a figure that does not cover humanitarian programs.

2. In Angola and Nicaragua, for example, the comparatively weak international commitment to overseeing the peace process is held partly to blame for the resurgence of violence that occurred in both countries. It is extremely difficult at present to find sources of support in war-torn Sudan, Afghanistan, and Burundi.

3. These terms are taken from a forthcoming book, *Nurturing Peace: Why Peace Settlements Succeed or Fail,* in which Fen Hampson illustrates the importance of third parties in a number of cases, including that of El Salvador.

4. Comisión Economica para América Latina y el Caribe, *La Economía salvadoreña en el proceso de consolidación de la paz,* LC/Mex/R.414/Rev 1 (29 June 1993) (Mexico City: CEPAL, 1993), 3.

5. The group—named for its meeting place in Panama—presented the Contadora Act for Peace and Cooperation in June 1986, which was signed by the Central American presidents.

6. Esquipulas refers to the meeting place in Guatemala. Esquipulas II linked regional peace to development. With respect to the large numbers of uprooted people throughout the region, the regional governments called on the UNHCR and the UNDP to launch a regional humanitarian initiative in the five Central American countries, Belize, and Mexico. The resulting initiative—a conference on Central American refugees, CIREFCA—was aimed specifically at encouraging regional dialogue and reconciliation and at mobilizing funds for programs to benefit the hundreds of thousands who had been uprooted by war.

7. Christopher C. Coleman, "The Salvadoran Peace Process: A Preliminary Inquiry," Report 173 (Norwegian Institute of International Affairs, Dec. 1993), 15; Jorge G. Castañeda, *Utopia Unarmed: The Latin American Left after the Cold War* (New York: Knopf, 1993), 102.

8. In September, the UN was asked by both sides to observe peace talks between them, but the talks came to nothing.

9. S. Neil MacFarlane and Thomas G. Weiss, *The United Nations Regional Organizations and Human Security: Building Theory in Central America,* Report 1994-2, Regional Responsibilities and the United Nations System (Providence: Academic Council on the United Nations System, Brown University, 1994), 34–35.

10. See Terry Lynn Karl, "Salvador's Negotiated Revolution," *Foreign Affairs* 71 (1992): 147–64. Also of interest is David Holiday and William Stanley, "Building the Peace: Preliminary Lessons from El Salvador," *Journal of International Affairs* 46 (1993); Gerardo L. Munck, "Beyond Electionism in El Salvador: Conflict Resolution through Negotiated Compromise," *Third World Quarterly* 14 (1993): 75–93; Coleman, "The Salvadoran Peace Process"; Alvaro de Soto and Graciana del Castillo, "Obstacles to Peacebuilding," *Foreign Policy* 94 (1994): 69–83.

11. Iqbal Riza, a Pakistani, had recently participated in implementing the Nicaraguan cease-fire. In 1993 he was replaced by former Colombian foreign minister, Augusto Ramírez Ocampo. He, in turn, was replaced in 1994 by a Dutch national, Enrique Her Host. On 20 May 1991, the Security Council passed Resolution 693 establishing ONUSAL as an integrated peacekeeping operation to monitor all agreements reached through the negotiation process.

12. The FMLN had insisted for years on incorporation into the national armed forces. Facing steadfast resistance on this point from the military, they compromised on the plan for the new police force.

13. Toward the end of the peace negotiations, the United States began to actively support the process.

14. The ONUSAL role is elaborated in Cynthia Arnson, *Peace and Human Rights: Successes and Shortcomings of the United Nations Observer Mission in El Salvador*, vol. 4 (New York: Americas Watch, 1992), 8; and in Holiday and Stanley, "Building the Peace."

15. Phillipe Texier was followed by Peruvian jurist Diego Garcia Sayan.

16. The military division was reduced precipitously in Dec. 1992, after demobilization and the completion of the cease-fire process. As of the end of 1993, the police force numbered 279.

17. Interviews by author with members of the ONUSAL Human Rights Division.

18. UN Dept. of Public Information, "El Salvador Agreements: The Path to Peace," 85.

19. UNDP, "Report on UNDP Activities and Coordination Related to the Peace Process in El Salvador," 29 Apr. 1993; UNDP, "Introduction," *Launching New Protagonists in Salvadoran Agriculture: The Agricultural Training Programme for Ex-Combatants of the FMLN* (San Salvador: UNDP, 1993).

20. UN S/23999, 26 May 1992, 6–8; interviews by author with ONUSAL and UNDP officials. While not included in planning for the academy, the FMLN was party to deliberations concerning the National Civilian Police itself, through the Police Subcommission of COPAZ.

21. UNDP, "Annual Report of the Resident Coordinator for El Salvador," UNDP, San Salvador, 4. The program for middle-level FMLN officers is evaluated critically in Kevin Murray et al., *Rescuing Reconstruction: The Debate on Post-War Economic Recovery in El Salvador* (Cambridge, Mass.: Hemispheric Initiatives, 1994), 35–42.

22. It is regrettable that FAO resources and technical advice in agrarian sector programs were not more widely used. Lacking the independent funds that other agencies had, the FAO received only a small amount of the funding donors provided to the UNDP.

23. The United States continued to exert major influence on the Salvadoran process following the war, but the fact that for more than a year there was no U.S. ambassador in El Salvador reduced overall U.S. visibility.

24. Somalia seems to be the most dramatic case of poor relations. In Mozambique, as well, interagency cooperation has been difficult to achieve. In Cambodia, although relations were positive on the whole, UNTAC tended to marginalize agencies not operating under its authority.

25. The coordinator was a former official of the UNHCR, with experience directing operations of refugee camps, so the initial estimates of needs in these sectors were based on refugee camp experiences. The former combatants, however, insisted on considerably superior caloric intake and living conditions.

26. UNDP, "Report on UNDP Activities and Coordination Related to the Peace Process in El Salvador."

27. See Jack Spence and George Vickers, *El Salvador Elections 1994: Toward a Level Playing Field?* (Washington, D.C.: Hemispheric Initiatives, 1994).

28. With Swedish, Danish, and U.S. funding, the UNHCR and the Salvadoran Institute of Municipal Development materially supported municipal offices, re-

stored civil registries destroyed during the war using records preserved in the Supreme Electoral Tribunal, and promoted popular participation through community-level workers and NGOs.

29. One of the tasks to which ONUSAL devoted much effort was restoring public administration, i.e., working out agreements between municipalities and mayors that would allow the latter to return to the communities that had ousted them during the war. The documentation process helped to encourage dialogue in some of these places and to garner public appreciation for those mayors who devoted themselves to documenting, without trying to enrich themselves thereby. Not all shared such a public-spirited attitude.

30. The Salvadoran armed forces were to concentrate forces in sixty-two locations, while the FMLN located some 8,500 armed men and women in fifteen assembly points. The former was to reduce its numbers by about half and the latter to demobilize in five stages, destroying arms at each stage.

31. The issues involved in delaying demobilization are detailed in S/23999 (26 May 1992), para. 15. To break the deadlock, the secretary-general on 13 Oct. presented a new land transfer proposal, which was accepted by both sides.

32. In May 1993, after the FMLN had demobilized and supposedly surrendered its arms, a large cache of hidden FMLN armaments exploded in Nicaragua. Although both ONUSAL and the government were aware that the FMLN had not accounted for all arms, as they were supposed to do, ONUSAL had verified the disarming of the FMLN. The event produced tensions all around but did not undermine the process. Upon the revelation, the FMLN destroyed this and other hidden arms caches.

33. In addition to the United States, Norway and Spain have funded the Training Academy. Donors contend that the PNC is the responsibility of the Salvadoran government.

34. UN S/1994/561 (11 May 1994), 11.

35. The problems associated with the PNC are discussed in William Stanley, "Risking Failure: The Problems and Promise of the New Civilian Police in El Salvador" (Washington, D.C.: Hemispheric Initiatives, 1993). The issue is discussed in the periodic reports of ONUSAL operations published by the UN Security Council. See particularly S/26790 (23 Nov. 1993).

36. UN, "Report of the Joint Group for the Investigation of Illegal Armed Groups with Political Motivation in El Salvador" (28 July 1994). An early, informal translation and summary was produced by the Center for Democracy in the Americas.

37. For a broader review of human rights, see Cynthia Arnson, *El Salvador, Darkening Horizons: Human Rights on the Eve of the March 1994 Elections,* vol. 6 (New York: Americas Watch), 1; UNCHR, E/CN.4 1884/11, "Informe del Experto Independiente, Prof. Pedro Nikken sobre la evolucion de los derechos humanos en El Salvador. . . ," 1994; ONUSAL, Report 9, Nov. 1994.

38. These experts were from the UN Electoral Division in New York and from the San José–based private organization CAPEL, funded by USAID.

39. In a few communities of northern Morazan and Chalatenango, where the left was believed to dominate, 60–70 percent of registrants did not receive voting cards.

40. UN S/26790 (23 Nov. 1993), 12.

41. According to U.S. State Department sources, by Feb. 1995 about 17,900 beneficiaries had received land.

42. S/1994/1000, Report of the secretary-general on the UN Observer Mission in El Salvador (26 Aug. 1994), 6.

43. The land program is described in detail in UNDP, "Launching New Protagonists in Salvadoran Agriculture"; the reports of the secretary-general describe progress and setbacks in the program.

44. For a comprehensive evaluation of national reconstruction efforts in El Salvador, see Murray et al., *Rescuing Reconstruction.*

45. The Social Investment Fund, FIS, supported by the Inter-American Development Bank, was evenhanded in its funding, but the amounts were small. The secretariat's strategies and leadership were established as an outgrowth of a previously existing wartime entity, the Commission for the Reconstruction of Areas (CONARA). Financed by the United States, CONARA offered public works projects to municipalities in war zones, with funds sometimes channeled through deposed mayors. CONARA essentially was a counterinsurgency strategy.

46. S/1994/561 (11 May 1994), 21.

47. This was the position taken by the IBRD representative at the Consultative Group meeting for El Salvador in Paris, 1 Apr. 1993. He applauded the government's structural adjustment policies, urging donors to fill in the consequent gaps on social spending.

48. This argument is most forcefully made in Alvaro de Soto and Graciana del Castillo, "Obstacles to Peacebuilding," *Foreign Affairs* 94 (1994): 69–83.

49. The demobilization was not as large as it appears on paper. During the negotiations, the Salvadoran government substantially overestimated the number of troops under arms, hence its reduction by about half was actually much less than that.

Chapter 10   *Chile*

1. See Eugenio Lahera, *Influencias externas sobre el desarrollo político de Chile entre 1930 y 1970,* Contribuciones 22 (Santiago: FLACSO, 1983).

2. Larry Diamond and Juan J. Linz, "Introduction: Politics, Society, and Democracy in Latin America," in *Democracy in Developing Countries: Latin America,* ed. Larry Diamond, Juan J. Linz, and Seymour Martin Lipset (Boulder: Lynne Rienner, 1989), 1–58.

3. Arturo Valenzuela, "Chile: Origins, Consolidation, and Breakdown of a Democratic Regime," in Diamond, Linz, and Lipset, *Democracy in Developing Countries.*

4. Diamond and Linz, "Introduction," 8.

5. Before that, the democratic development also had some blemishes. For example, it seems difficult to imagine the survival of an almost feudal institution, the *inquilinaje* (a serflike relationship that had existed in the Chilean countryside since the seventeenth century) within a highly developed democratic system. The *inquilinaje* was finally abolished in the mid-1960s, at the time of the agrarian reform.

6. Atilio Borón, *La evolución del régimen electoral y sus efectos en la representación de los intereses populares: el caso de Chile,* Estudios de ELACP 24 (Santiago:

ELACP, 1971). See also Timothy R. Scully, *Los partidos de centro y la evolución política chilena* (Santiago: CIEPLAN, 1992).

7. For different perspectives regarding the role of foreign actors during this crucial period, see Joaquín Fermandois, *Chile y el mundo, 1970–1973: La política exterior del gobierno de la Unidad Popular y el sistema internacional* (Santiago: Ediciones Universidad Católica de Chile, 1985); Clodomiro Almeyda, *La política internacional del gobierno de la Unidad Popular,* Avances de Investigación 23 (Mexico: Centro de Estudios Latinoamericanos, UMAM, 1977). Documents regarding U.S. intervention can be found in the Senate hearings about covert action by the CIA and the activities of ITT.

8. If political events after 1983 are analyzed, the defeat of Pinochet in a fair election (at the plebiscites of 1978 and 1980, which were both won by the military regime, considerable fraud seems to have taken place) is not so surprising. The economic crisis of 1982 led to massive social protests, and in the following years an increasingly credible political coalition formed, which included all opposition parties in the center and on the left of the political spectrum, except the Communist Party (which advocated armed struggle among its political strategies). This coalition, even if it had to accept the political rules set by Pinochet, became a real government alternative and was able to break the myth of the military's political omnipotence.

9. Alan Angell and Benny Pollack, "The Chilean Elections of 1989 and the Politics of the Transition to Democracy," mimeo.

10. See Brian Loveman, "*¿Misión Cumplida?* Civil Military Relations and the Chilean Political Transition," *Journal of Interamerican Studies and World Affairs* 33 (1991): 35–74.

11. Concertación de Partidos por la Democracia, *Bases programáticas de la Concertación de Partidos por la Democracia* (Santiago: Concertación de Partidos, 1989).

12. A symbol of the difficulty of getting through any kind of reform is the fact that 11 Sept. (the anniversary of the 1973 military coup) is still a national holiday, although at every legislative session since 1990 the government coalition has presentation bills to abolish the holiday.

13. Concertación de Partidos por la Democracia, *Un gobierno para los nuevos tiempos, Bases programáticas de la Segundo Gobierno de la Concertación* (Santiago: Concertación de Partidos, 1993).

14. On the legitimacy of the influence of foreign actors, see Manuel A. Garretón, "Límites y dilemas de la influencia externa," in *Estados Unidos y Chile hacia 1987, Serie Política Exterior y Relaciones Internacionales,* ed. Edgardo Boeninger et al. (Santiago: FLACSO, 1987); for precise definitions of the different forms of intervention (soft, hard, and forcible), see Fernando R. Tesón, chap. 2, this volume.

15. For an interesting discussion of the political, historical, and legal issues involved, see the collection of essays in Laura W. Reed and Carl Kaysen, eds., *Emerging Norms of Justified Intervention* (Cambridge, Mass.: American Academy of Arts and Sciences, 1993).

16. A good description of this period can be found in Heraldo Muñoz and Carlos Portales, *Una amistad esquiva: Las relaciones de Estados Unidos y Chile* (Santiago: Pehuén, 1987); and in Heraldo Muñoz, "Chile: The Limits of 'Success,'" in *Exporting Democracy: The United States and Latin America,* ed. Abraham F. Lowenthal (Baltimore: Johns Hopkins Univ. Press, 1991).

17. Alicia Frohmann, "U.S.-Chile Relations: The Perspective from Chile," in *Chile: Ten Years and Beyond* (Washington, D.C.: Washington Office on Latin America, 1983).

18. Muñoz, "Limits of 'Success,'" 165.

19. Thomas Carothers, "The Reagan Years: The 1980s," in Lowenthal, *Exporting Democracy,* 109; see also, by the same author, *In the Name of Democracy: U.S. Policy toward Latin America in the Reagan Years* (Berkeley: Univ. of California Press, 1991).

20. For an account of the National Endowment's activities, see Josephine Buckley McNeill, *La cara cambiante de la hegemonía: el Fondo Nacional por la Democracia,* Cono Sur 9 (Santiago: FLACSO, 1990).

21. Carothers, "Reagan Years," 110.

22. For an interesting account of the 1988 plebiscite, see Pamela Constable and Arturo Valenzuela, "The Chilean Plebiscite: Defeat of a Dictator," *Current History* 88 (1989): 536.

23. Carlos Portales, *Los factores externos y el régimen autoritario: evolución e impacto de las relaciones internacionales de Chile en el proceso de transición a la democracia,* Documento de Trabajo 419 (Santiago: FLACSO, 1989).

24. This has been argued persuasively by Jeffrey M. Puryear, *Building Democracy: Foreign Donors and Chile,* Conference Paper 57 (New York: National Resource Center for Latin American and Caribbean Studies, Columbia University–New York University, 1992). See also the chapter on funding agencies and the generation of usable knowledge, in Alicia Frohmann, "¿Para qué estudiar la pobreza? Objetivos y apropiación instrumental de la investigación social sobre pobreza", in G. Briones et al., *Usos de la investigación social* (Santiago de Chile: FLACSO, 1993).

25. This argument is developed by Richard Feinberg, "Think Tanks in Democratic Chile," *North-South Magazine* (Feb.–Mar. 1992).

Chapter 11 *Peru*

1. This phenomenon has been the subject of a number of important studies. All define Latin America, as does the author, as the twenty independent Spanish-, Portuguese-, and French-speaking countries of the Western Hemisphere. See particularly Guillermo O'Donnell, Phillippe C. Schmitter, and Laurence Whitehead, eds., *Transitions from Authoritarian Rule: Comparative Perspectives* (Baltimore: Johns Hopkins Univ. Press, 1986); Larry Diamond, Juan J. Linz, and Seymour Martin Lipset, eds., *Democracy in Developing Countries: Latin America,* vol. 4 (Boulder: Lynne Rienner, 1989); and Karen Remmer, "The Political Economy of Elections in Latin America, 1980–1991," *American Political Science Review* 87 (1993): 393–407.

2. Many scholars define Mexico as authoritarian, albeit civilian and electoral, because of the dominance of a single party since 1930, now called the Partido Revolucionario Institucional (PRI). See, for example, the table, "Democratization since 1975," in Ernst B. Haas, "Beware the Slippery Slope: Notes toward the Definition of Justifiable Intervention," in *Emerging Norms of Justified Intervention,* ed. Laura W. Reed and Carl Kaysen (Cambridge: Committee on International

Security Studies, American Academy of Arts and Sciences, 1993), app. 82–84. Mexico is listed, circa 1992, as, "an authoritarian state committed to liberalization," 82–83. "The Appendix was compiled partly from information provided by area specialists," 87 n24. Colombia, Costa Rica, and Venezuela are the only Latin American countries listed in the table as "states with a relatively unbroken record of peaceful change of government by democratic means before and since 1975," 82–83.

3. Panama's democracy was instituted in Dec. 1989. For a detailed analysis, see Steve C. Ropp, "Panama: The United States Invasion and Its Aftermath," *Current History* 90 (1991): 113–16 ff.

4. I use the definition of *coup* as in Arthur S. Banks, *Cross-Polity Time-Series Data* (Cambridge: MIT Press, 1971), Segment 1, Field e: "a successful extra constitutional or forced change in the top governmental elite and/or its effective control of the nation's power structure." For a complete listing of Latin American coups by country and decade, 1810–1980, see David Scott Palmer, "The Military in Latin America," in *Latin America: Perspectives on a Region,* ed. Jack W. Hopkins (New York: Holmes and Meier, 1985), table 2.

5. Palmer, "Military in Latin America," table 2.

6. Data is from David Scott Palmer, *Peru: The Authoritarian Tradition* (New York: Praeger, 1980), fig. 3.1; and Palmer, "Military in Latin America," table 2.

7. Samuel P. Huntington, "Political Development and Political Decay," *World Politics* 17 (1965): 388.

8. This dynamic is a central component of the framework developed by Karl Deutsch, "Social Mobilization and Political Development," (1961). It is closely related to Huntington's concept of political modernization, in "Political Development."

9. Lars Shoultz, *Human Rights and United States Policy toward Latin America* (Princeton: Princeton Univ. Press, 1981).

10. Carlos Valenzuela, "Evaluación de Helsinki y Belgrado en la política internacional de derechos humanos," in *Derechos humanos y relaciones internacionales,* ed. Walter Sánchez (Santiago: Instituto de Estudios Internacionales, 1979).

11. Lars Schoultz, "The Carter Administration and Human Rights in Latin America," in *Human Rights and Basic Needs in the Americas,* ed. Margaret E. Crahan (Washington, D.C.: Georgetown Univ. Press, 1982).

12. Schoultz, *Human Rights and United States Policy,* 74–88.

13. Bryce Wood, "Human Rights and the Inter-American System," in *The Future of the Inter-American System,* ed. Tom J. Farer (New York: Praeger, 1979); Louis B. Sohn, "The Improvement of the United Nations Machinery on Human Rights," in Sánchez, *Derechos humanos.*

14. Manfred Mols, "The Latin American Connection," in *West German Foreign Policy: Dilemmas and Directions,* ed. Peter H. Merkl (Chicago: Univ. of Chicago Press, 1982). Also, Eusebio Mujal-León, "Rei(g)ning in Spain," *Foreign Policy* 51 (1983): 108.

15. Karen L. Remmer, *Military Rule in Latin America* (Boston: Unwin Hyman, 1989), 191–204. Also, Palmer, "Military in Latin America," 270–71.

16. Among others, see Alain Rouquié, *The Military and the State in Latin America,* trans. Paul E. Sigmund (Berkeley: Univ. of California Press, 1987), esp. 342–405.

17. A wide-ranging set of essays on the problem may be found in Robert A. Pastor, ed., *Latin America's Debt Crisis* (Boulder: Lynne Rienner, 1987).

18. Each Latin American case was different but with similar denouements resulting in elected civilian governments. Peru had multiple riots, a national strike, and a violent confrontation between police and army units in 1976 and 1977. Argentina witnessed virtually total popular revulsion after the Malvinas/Falklands invasion failure in 1982. Chile's 1988 referendum produced a no-vote majority against extending the Pinochet regime. Uruguay had a similar experience in 1985, voting against the military's proposed authoritarian constitution. In each case, the military soon moved to extricate itself from politics. For details, see country case chapters in Diamond, Linz, and Lipset, *Latin America*.

19. Remmer, *Military Rule;* Rouquié, *Military and the State;* Larry Diamond and Juan Linz, "Introduction: Politics, Society, and Democracy in Latin America," in Diamond, Linz, and Lipset, *Latin America*, 31–35.

20. Contrasting perspectives are offered by Constantine Menges, *Inside the National Security Council: The True Story of the Making and Unmaking of Reagan's Foreign Policy* (New York: Simon and Schuster, 1988); and Thomas Carothers, *In the Name of Democracy: United States Policy toward Latin America in the Reagan Years* (Berkeley: Univ. of California Press, 1991).

21. This was especially true for Uruguay, Chile, and Peru at the time of extrication and for Argentina during the course of the Alfonsín government. See case studies in Louis Goodman, Johanna Mendelson, and Juan Rial, eds., *The Military and Democracy: The Future of Civil-Military Relations in Latin America* (Lexington, Mass.: Lexington Books, 1990).

22. For the Contadora process, see Bruce Bagley, ed., *Contadora and the Diplomacy of Peace in Central America*, vol. 2, *The Contadora Process*, SAIS Papers in Latin American Studies (Boulder: Westview, 1987). For an overview of the peace accords process, see Latin American Studies Association, Commission on Compliance with the Central American Peace Accord, *Final Report: Extraordinary Opportunities . . . and New Risks* (Pittsburgh: LASA, 1988).

23. For example, James M. Malloy, *Authoritarianism and Corporation in Latin America* (Pittsburgh: Univ. of Pittsburgh Press, 1977); David Collier, ed., *The New Authoritarianism in Latin America* (Princeton: Princeton Univ. Press, 1979); Glen Caudill Dealy, *The Public Man* (Amherst: Univ. of Massachusetts Press, 1977).

24. Diamond and Linz, "Introduction," 19; Palmer, "Military in Latin America," 262–66, and figs. 1 and 2, 264 and 265.

25. Diamond and Linz, "Introduction," 49–50. Page numbers in the list refer to ibid.

26. This critical element is explicitly tied to Huntington's institutionalization criteria: *substantive coherence* about policy, organization, and discipline; *complexity* of internal structure by function, local, and national organization; *autonomy* vis-à-vis individual leaders, the state, or social interests, and *adaptability* to changing circumstances.

27. Indicators include the capacity to maintain public order and rule of law, the expansion for welfare and economic production and regulation where representative institutions are well established, and the mechanisms for effective delivery of resources to the periphery (ibid., 27, 29, 30).

28. Such development explicitly includes an "autonomous, pluralistic, vigorous, and democratic" mass media.

29. Diamond and Linz see this as more important than a high level of socioeconomic development, presumably because such steady growth provides more jobs, which makes people better off, thus providing government with increased tax revenues for the services and infrastructure needed and demanded by the people.

30. This is analogous to Karl Deutch's concept of social mobilization, as elaborated in "Social Mobilization and Political Development." It is distinct from his key component 2 (elites making room for political expression of new popular interests), because it concerns society rather than the polity and the terms by which new social groups became politically incorporated.

31. Various studies of Latin American politics make, and elaborate upon, this point. See, for example, the collection of essays in Howard J. Wiarda, ed., *Politics and Social Change in Latin America: The Distinct Tradition,* 2d rev. ed. (Amherst: Univ. of Massachusetts Press, 1982).

32. Edward P. Lanning, *Peru before the Incas* (Englewood Cliffs, N.J.: Prentice-Hall, 1967); C. H. Haring, *The Spanish Empire in America* (New York: Harcourt, Brace, and World, 1963).

33. Richard Graham, *Independence in Latin America* (New York: Knopf, 1975), 43–45.

34. Heraclio Bonilla et al., *La independencia en el Perú* (Lima: Instituto de Estudios Peruanos, 1972). Diamond and Linz reach a different conclusion; see their "Introduction," 6.

35. Palmer, *Peru,* table 3.1. Diamond and Linz's analysis does not take into consideration the dramatic differences between the various parts of the Spanish New World in colonial settlement, control, and administration.

36. Palmer, *Peru,* 24–33. See the comparable conclusion of Diamond and Linz, "Introduction," 8, on somewhat different grounds.

37. Palmer, *Peru,* 26, 33; Diamond and Linz, "Introduction," 6.

38. See, among others, Cynthia McClintock, "Peru: Precarious Regimes, Authoritarianism and Democratic," in Diamond, Linz, and Lipset, *Latin America,* esp. 340–52.

39. Banks, *Cross-Polity Time-Series Data,* as updated and presented in Palmer, "Military," table 2.

40. As Diamond and Linz's analysis concludes, "Introduction," 5 and 11. However, as they would surely agree, it is useful to provide the more distal elements relevant to framing the context within which the political system developed—and which may well continue to set the parameters of the politically possible even 170 years later. By way of comparative illustration, consider the degree to which the British colonial experience in North America—governmental structures, legal system, and so forth—has affected to the present the political context, culture, and dynamics of the United States. Yet this has occurred in the aftermath of a colonial experience that was only half as long as that of most of Spanish and Portuguese America.

41. The notion of antipolitics was originally used to characterize military rule and referred to the view that the military—with its superior discipline, hierarchy, and respect for order—can accomplish modernization, economic development, and political stability more effectively than civilian politicians, who are charac-

terized by bungling, ineptitude, and corruption. Brian Loveman and Thomas M. Davies Jr., eds., *The Politics of Anti-Politics: The Military in Latin America* (Lincoln: Univ. of Nebraska Press, 1978), 3–5. The context for President Fujimori's *autogolpe,* with the full support of the Peruvian military, demonstrates how easily antipolitics can be transferred to a civilian actor.

42. David Werlich, *Peru: A Short History* (Carbondale: Southern Illinois Univ. Press, 1978), 95–98, 106–17.

43. José Clavero, *El tesoro del Perú* (Lima: Torres Aguirre, 1896), 51; cited in Ernesto Yepes del Castillo, *Perú, 1820–1920: Un siglo de desarrollo capitalista* (Lima: Instituto de Estudios Peruanos, 1972), 130 n4.

44. Palmer, *Peru,* tables 3.6 and 4.1.

45. Rory Miller, "The Making of the Grace Contract: British Bondholders and the Peruvian Government, 1885–1890," *Journal of Latin American Studies* 8 (1976): 73–100.

46. Steve Stein, *Populism in Peru* (Madison: Univ. of Wisconsin Press, 1980), 40–44.

47. Carol Graham, *Peru's APRA: Parties, Politics, and the Elusive Quest for Democracy* (Boulder: Lynne Rienner, 1992), 23–38.

48. Víctor Villanueva, *El militarismo en el Perú* (Lima: T. Scheuch, 1962); and Jorge Rodríguez Beruff, *Los militares y el poder* (Lima: Mosca Azul, 1983).

49. Henry A. Dietz and David Scott Palmer, "Citizen Participation and Innovative Military Corporatism in Peru," and Sandra L. Woy, "Infrastructure of Participation in Peru: SINAMOS," both in *Political Participation in Latin America,* ed. John A. Booth and Mitchell A. Seligson, vol. 1, *Citizen and State* (New York: Holmes and Meier, 1978).

50. Daniel M. Schydlowsky and Juan Wicht, "The Anatomy of an Economic Failure," in *The Peruvian Experiment Reconsidered,* ed. Cynthia McClintock and Abraham F. Lowenthal (Princeton: Princeton Univ. Press, 1983).

51. Guillermo Rochabrún Silva, "Crisis, Democracy, and the Left in Peru," *Latin American Perspectives* 15 (1988): 77–96.

52. For the progress and vicissitudes of Peruvian politics during the 1980s and early 1990s, see the almost annual accounts and analyses in *Current History,* issues on Latin America or South America in Feb. or Mar., by various scholars, including David Werlich, Cynthia McClintock, and myself.

53. See David P. Werlich, "Fujimori and the 'Disaster' in Peru," *Current History* 90 (1991): 61–64ff.

54. For an overview and assessment of the Belaúnde government, see James D. Rudolph, *Peru: The Evolution of a Crisis* (Westport: Praeger, 1992), chap. 5. A valuable study of the formation and operation of the Shining Path during the first half of the Belaúnde government is Gustavo Gorriti Ellenbogen, *Sendero: Historia de la guerra milenaria en el Perú I* (Lima: Editorial Apoyo, 1990).

55. Two excellent overviews of APRA and the García government are Graham, *Peru's APRA;* and John Crabtree, *Peru under García: An Opportunity Lost* (Pittsburgh: Univ. of Pittsburgh Press, 1992). A detailed critique of García's economic policies is Daniel Schydlowsky, "La debacle peruana: ¿Dinámica económica o causas políticas?" *Apuntes* (Lima) 25 (1989): 3–25.

56. Details of the *autogolpe* may be found in Cynthia McClintock, "Peru's Fujimori: A Caudillo Derails Democracy," *Current History* 92 (1993): 112–19.

57. For a detailed presentation and analysis of political violence data, see David Scott Palmer, "The Revolutionary Terrorism of Peru's Shining Path," in *Terrorism in Context,* ed. Martha Crenshaw (College Station: Pennsylvania State Univ. Press, 1994), passim and tables 1 and 2.

58. Giovanna Peñaflor G., "Y el ganador es . . . ," *Quehacer* (Lima) 80 (1992): 30–37.

59. In 1993, newspaper accounts indicate that the Shining Path assassinated about thirteen mayors and candidates and that about a hundred others resigned. "Bombs, Killings Rock Peru on Eve of Elections," *Boston Globe,* 29 Jan. 1993. In the run-up to the 1989 municipal elections, however, over a hundred political authorities were assassinated and about 400 of Peru's almost 1,800 elected mayorships were vacant due to resignations. Piedad Pareja Pflücker and Eric Torres Montes, *Municipios y Terrorismo: Impacto de la violencia subversiva en los gobiernos locales* (Lima: Centro de Estudios Peruanos, 1989). Also Palmer, "Revolutionary Terrorism," n34.

60. Manuel Córdova, "El 'voto útil' y la política inútil," *Quehacer* 81 (1993): 4–7.

61. Ayacucho's voting record for the four municipal elections 1980–89 provides clear indications of the connection between violence and voting. The following are in percentages:

Election year	Did not vote	Blank ballots	Spoiled ballots
1980	52	6	10
1983	75	4	9
1986	29	5	10
1989	85	4	6

The 1980 elections were held in the first year that illiterates could vote, so a high total of nonvoting and invalid ballots was to be expected; 1983 was a peak year of military and police repression in Ayacucho; 1989 marked a period of intense Shining Path activity; in 1986 violence had receded notably in the region, and substantial return migration occurred. Data from Fernando Tuesta Soldevilla, *Perú político en cifras* (Lima: Fundación Friedrich Ebert, 1987); and Richard Webb and Graciela Fernández Baca de Valdez, *Anuario Estadístico: Perú en números, 1991* (Lima: Cuánto S.A., 1991), 1021.

62. Carol Graham, "Government and Politics," in *Peru: A Country Study,* ed. Rex Hudson (Washington, D.C.: Federal Research Division, Library of Congress, 1994).

63. José Mariá Salcedo, "Grupo Propuesta: Sí hay alternativas," *Quehacer* 79 (1992): 16–19.

64. Fujimori's political approach is an example of Guillermo O'Donnell's "delegative democracy" formulation, by which elected Latin American presidents often interpret their mandate as a charge to bypass institutions like party, congress, and bureaucracy. Jorge Heine, "¿Hacia una democracia delegativa? Una entrevista a Guillermo O'Donnell," *LASA Forum* 23 (1992): 7–9.

65. Córdova, "El voto útil," 7.

66. Carol Graham, "The APRA Government and the Urban Poor: The PAIT Programme in Lima's Pueblos Jóvenes," *Journal of Latin American Studies* 23 (1991): 91–130; and Susan C. Stokes, "Politics and Latin America's Urban Poor:

Reflections from a Lima Shantytown," *Latin American Research Review* 26 (1991): 75–101.

67. Hernando de Soto, *El otro sendero* (Lima: Instituto Libertad y Democracia, 1987).

68. These and other issues are elaborated in Reed and Kaysen, *Emerging Norms of Justified Intervention*. See, particularly, Robert A. Pastor, "Forward to the Beginning: Widening the Scope for Collective Global Actions."

69. Until the 1930s, unilateral intervention in a country unable to pay its foreign debts—whether Latin American or other—was commonly undertaken and acquiesced to under international law, even as Latin American governments pursued the nonintervention principle with the Drago and Calvo doctrines. The Latin American debt crisis of the 1980s, however, was treated differently. From an initial U.S. position, à la Calvin Coolidge, of "They hired the money, didn't they?" the view slowly shifted to one much more sympathetic with debt reduction and forgiveness. Negotiations under the Brady Plan, during the Bush administration, produced substantial debt relief for Mexico, Costa Rica, Venezuela, and Argentina between 1990 and 1992, including forgiveness of 15–40 percent of private bank loans. At least part of the motivation for such relief stemmed from the fear that democratic processes could be undermined by the economic problems related to the heavy foreign debt burden. See the historical overview in Marc Trachtenberg, "Intervention in Historical Perspective," in Reed and Kaysen, *Emerging Norms*.

70. Most international human rights organizations emphasize *government* human rights abuses in their reports, which is appropriate. Governments should be held accountable for the enforcement of their countries' own laws and the protection of their own citizens. Peru's situation has been sufficiently distinctive, however, with the systematic violence committed by guerrillas, especially the Shining Path, to warrant more attention than that normally devoted to the problem by such organizations as Amnesty International, Americas Watch, and the Washington Office on Latin America.

To illustrate, Americas Watch April 1993 report, *Human Rights in Peru One Year after Fujimori's Coup,* devotes just over two pages of a fifty-page presentation to "violations of the laws of war by insurgents." The rest focuses on the abuses, manipulations, and limitations of the Peruvian government. The almost eighteen pages devoted to the "politicization of justice" is a particularly valuable contribution, but the report as a whole does not give sufficient context to help the reader fully appreciate the particularly difficult circumstances under which the government was operating.

Since 1980, most of the 22,633 incidents through June 1993 were committed by the guerrillas. In the period Jan.–June 1993, for example, one study shows that there were 793 incidents (up 32 percent over the same period of 1992), of which 705, or 89 percent, were attributed to the Shining Path or the MRTA. Deaths due to political violence for the same period totaled 1,106 (down about a third from the 1992 rate), of which 609, or 55 percent could be traced to the Shining Path (549) or the MRTA (60). *PeruPaz* (Instituto Constitución y Sociedad) 2, (1993): 8–9, 20–21. Also see Martin J. Scurrah, "La política de la no-política: Los derechos humanos y la democracia en el Perú," paper prepared for the Latin American Studies Association Meeting, Los Angeles, 24–27 Sept. 1992; and Angela Cornell and

Kenneth Roberts, "Democracy, Counterinsurgency, and Human Rights: The Case of Peru," *Human Rights Quarterly* 12 (1990): 529–53.

71. The dramatic revelation of a 15 Sept. 1993 letter from Guzmán to Fujimori suing for peace negotiations, although rejected out of hand by the government, could give domestic and international organizations an opening to begin efforts to get the Shining Path and the government to work toward some definitive resolution of the violence. Paul Lewis, "President of Peru Says He Is Confident of Defeating Guerrilla Group," *New York Times*, 2 Oct. 1993.

72. Palmer, *Peru*, tables 4.3 and 4.4.

73. Shane Hunt, "Peru: The Current Economic Situation in Long-Term Perspective," Sept. 1993 (North-South Center, Univ. of Miami).

74. Palmer, *Peru*, table 5.1 shows a 64.3 percent decline in Peru's national government revenues per capita between 1929 and 1933.

75. Richard Goodwin, "Letter from Peru," *New Yorker*, 17 May 1969.

76. Abraham Lowenthal, ed., *The Peruvian Experiment* (Princeton: Princeton Univ. Press, 1975).

77. Schydlowsky and Wicht, "Anatomy of an Economic Failure."

78. David Scott Palmer, "United States–Peru Relations in the 1990s: Asymmetry and Its Consequences," in *Latin America and Caribbean Contemporary Record, 1989–1990,* ed. Eduardo Gamarra and James Malloy (New York: Holmes and Meier, 1994), 9.

79. For details, see Domingo Acevedo and Claudio Grossman, chap. 5, this volume. Also, Eduardo Ferrero Costa, ed., *Proceso de retorno a la institucionalidad democrática en el Perú* (Lima: CEPEI, 1992), for analysis and official statements and documents from 5 Apr. through 1 Sept. 1992.

80. See the scathing reports by Americas Watch, including *Human Rights in Peru One Year after Fujimori's Coup* (New York: Americas Watch, 1993); and "Peru: Anatomy of a Cover-Up: The Disappearances at La Cantuta," *Americas Watch* 5 (1993).

81. Telephone interviews by the author with Coletta Youngers of the Washington Office on Latin America, 24 Nov. 1993; and with Juan Méndez of Americas Watch, 15 Dec. 1993. For a comprehensive overview of U.S. policy, see Kenneth Roberts and Mark Peceny, "Human Rights and United States Policy toward Peru," in *The Peruvian Labyrinth,* ed. Maxwell Cameron and Philip Mauceri (forthcoming).

82. Robert Goldman, a distinguished international lawyer and member of a commission of international jurists team sent to study Peru's judicial system and prepare a report, summarized in scathing terms the team's findings at a Washington, D.C., conference on Peru, 12 Nov. 1993. The final report, *Informe de la Comisión de Juristas Internacionales Sobre la Administración de Justicia en el Perú,* released 30 Nov. 1993 (Washington, D.C.: International Joint Commission, 1993), was also harshly critical of the Peruvian legal process as reorganized after the *autogolpe.*

83. This fact is reflected in periodic news updates in *PERUNEWSLETTER,* prepared and disseminated by the Embassy of Peru, Washington, D.C., starting in 1993.

84. The first opinion polls taken after the 5 Apr. 1992 *autogolpe* show levels of support for President Fujimori's action in metropolitan Lima of 71–88 percent. Ferrero Costa, *Proceso de retorno,* 140–44.

Chapter 13 *External Pressures and Domestic Constraints*

1. Piero Gleijeses, "Perspectives of a Regime Transformation in Guatemala," in *Political Change in Central America: Internal and External Dimensions,* ed. Wolf Grabendorff, Heinrich-W. Krumwiede, and Jörg Todt (Boulder: Westview, 1984), 137.

2. For an insightful analysis of the dynamic between multilateralism and democracy in Latin America, see Robert B. Andersen, "Democratic Crises, Regional Responses: The OAS and Democracy since 1991," paper prepared for the annual meeting of the American Political Science Association, Washington, D.C., 2–5 Sept. 1993.

Chapter 14 *Cuba in the International Community in the 1990s*

1. José Luis Rodríguez, "La economía cubana en 1986–1989," *Economía y Desarrollo* 20 (1990): 26–43; Julio Carranza, "Cuba: los retos de la economía," *Cuadernos de Nuestra América* 9 (1992): 131–58.

2. For a particularly potent example, see Carlos Aldana's address to Cuba's National Assembly, held 26–27 Dec. 1991; at the time, Aldana was Communist Party secretary for ideology and one of the top-ranking members of the party's Political Bureau. *Granma Weekly Review,* 1 Jan. 1992.

3. For the importance of formal adherence to norms, even as lip service, see Kathryn Sikkink, "Human Rights, Principled Issue Networks, and Sovereignty in Latin America," *International Organization* 47 (1993): 412–15.

4. See discussion in Samuel P. Huntington, *The Third Wave: Democratization in the Late Twentieth Century* (Norman: Univ. of Oklahoma Press, 1991), 6–7.

5. Adam Przeworski, "Some Problems in the Study of the Transition to Democracy," in *Transitions from Authoritarian Rule: Comparative Perspectives,* ed. Guillermo O'Donnell, Philippe C. Schmitter, and Laurence Whitehead (Baltimore: Johns Hopkins Univ. Press, 1986), 59.

6. For elaboration of many of these points by Cuban social scientists, see Haroldo Dilla, "Democracia y poder revolucionario en Cuba," and Fernando Martínez, "Transición socialista y democracia: el caso cubano," both in *Cuadernos de Nuestra América* 4 (1987): 55–75 and 76–115, respectively.

7. Darío L. Machado, "¿Cuál es nuestro clima socio-político?" *El militante comunista* (1990): 6.

8. This section has benefited greatly from Michael Krinsky and David Golove, *United States Economic Measures against Cuba: Proceedings in the United Nations and International Law Issues* (Northampton, Mass.: Aletheia, 1993).

9. A lesser-known dimension of the Cuban Democracy Act (approved as Title XVII of the National Defense Authorization Act for fiscal year 1993) is its encouragement and authorization of the executive branch to lift those aspects of the trade embargo that would foster communications between the United States and Cuba, such as telephones and direct mail. For the act's authorization of certain flexibility within the trade embargo, see Section 1705.

10. UN, A/47/L.20/Rev.1 (23 Nov. 1992), adopted as General Assembly Resolution 19 (XLVII).

11. See UN Special Rapporteur, "Human Rights in Cuba," *Interim Report,* A/47/625 and Corr. 1 (19 Nov. 1992); and the General Assembly's Resolution, AC.3/47/L.70 (2 Dec. 1992).

12. UN Special Rapporteur, "Human Rights in Cuba," 21–22.

13. *Granma Weekly Review,* 3 Nov. 1991, 9.

14. Press coverage of the medical emergency and of the incidents of violence attributable to Cuban border guards is well summarized in the periodical *CubaINFO* 5 (1993), various issues.

15. Jorge I. Domínguez, "Cooperating with the Enemy? U.S. Immigration Policies toward Cuba," in *Western Hemisphere Immigration and United States Foreign Policy,* ed. Christopher Mitchell (University Park: Pennsylvania State Univ. Press), 31–88.

16. J. D. Richardson, ed., A *Compilation of the Messages and Papers of the Presidents* (Washington, D.C., 1898), 10:139 and ff.

17. For the Christopher statement, see Office of the Spokesman, *Remarks by Dr. Clifton R. Wharton, Jr., Deputy Secretary of State, on Behalf of Secretary of State Warren Christopher to the Council of the Americas* (Washington, D.C.: U.S. Department of State, 1993).

18. The information in this and the next paragraph comes from interviews by author with U.S. and Cuban government officials, 1993.

19. María Luisa Martínez Sierra, *Vida política de mi patria: cuaderno de trabajo* (Havana: Editorial Pueblo y Educación, 1981), 88.

20. *Granma Weekly Review,* 28 Dec. 1980, 13.

21. Martínez Sierra, *Vida política de mi patria,* 84.

Chapter 15   *Treading Lightly and without a Stick*

1. Enrique Krauze, *Caras de la historia* (Mexico City: Joaquin Mortiz, 1983), 52.

2. David Ronfeldt and Caesar Sereseres, "The Management of U.S.-Mexico Interdependence: Drift toward Failure?" in *Mexican-U.S. Relations: Conflict and Convergence,* ed. Carlos Vázquez and Manuel García y Griego (Berkeley: Univ. of California Press, 1983).

3. Terry Karl, "Democratization around the Globe: Its Opportunities and Risks," in *World Security: Trends and Challenges at Century's End,* ed. Michael T. Klare and Dan Thomas (London: St. Martin's, 1993).

4. Ibid.

5. For an analysis of how pressures from the international system and civil society can contribute to political change within the state, see Alison Brysk, "From Above and Below: Social Movements, the International System, and Human Rights in Argentina," *Comparative Political Studies* 26 (1993): 259–85.

6. For a description of forms of indirect support that can strengthen democratic institutions in Latin America, see Abraham F. Lowenthal, "The United States and Latin American Democracy: Learning from History," in *Exporting Democracy: The United States and Latin America, Themes and Issues,* ed. Abraham F. Lowenthal (Baltimore: Johns Hopkins Univ. Press, 1991).

7. See Kathryn Sikkink "Human Rights, Principled Issue Networks, and Sovereignty in Latin America," *International Organization* 47 (1993): 411–41.

8. Ibid.

9. Roger Bartra, "Revolutionary Nationalism and National Security in Mexico," in *Mexico in Search of Security*, ed. Bruce Michael Bagley and Sergio Aguayo Quezada (New Brunswick, N.J.: Transaction, 1993), 147.

10. Lorenzo Meyer, "Mexico: The Exception and the Rule," in Lowenthal, *Exporting Democracy.*

11. Nora Lustig, *Mexico: The Remaking of an Economy* (Washington, D.C.: Brookings, 1993).

12. Manuel Pastor and Carol Wise, "The Origins and Sustainability of Mexico's Free Trade Policy," *International Organization* 48 (1994): 459–89.

13. Jorge Chabat, "Mexico's Foreign Policy in 1990: Electoral Sovereignty and Integration with the United States," *Journal of Interamerican Studies and World Affairs* 3(1991):4.

14. Sidney Weintraub and M. Delal Baer, "The Interplay between Economic and Political Opening: The Sequence in Mexico," *Washington Quarterly* 15 (1992): 187–200; Luis Rubio, "Economía y Democracia."

15. President Salinas spelled out this contention on numerous occasions. Challenging the assertion that he fostered "perestroika without glasnost," he told one interviewer:

> Freedoms of what you call the glasnost kind have existed for decades in Mexico. What hasn't existed is the freedom of productive activity, because the government owned so many enterprises. So actually, we have been more rapidly transforming the economic structure while striving along many paths of reform on the political side. But let me tell you something. When you are introducing such a strong economic reform, you must make sure that you build the political consensus around it. If you are at the same time introducing additional drastic political reform, you may end up with no reform at all. And we want to have reform, not a disintegrated country . . . as we move along the path toward consolidating our economic reforms, political reform will continue to evolve in Mexico.

Cited in Peter Smith, "The Political Impact of Free Trade on Mexico," *Journal of Interamerican Studies and World Affairs* 34 (1992): 1–25.

16. Liberalization is not the same as democratization. Liberalization may not necessarily lead to democratization. For a discussion of the distinction between the two concepts, see Alfred Stepan, "Introduction," in *Democratizing Brazil,* ed. Alfred Stepan (Baltimore: Johns Hopkins Univ. Press, 1991); and Terry Lynn Karl, "Dilemmas of Democratization in Latin America," *Comparative Politics* 23 (Oct. 1990): 1–21.

17. See Lucy Conger, *Human Rights in Mexico, 1982–1993*, Americas Watch Report (New Haven: Yale Univ. Press, forthcoming); and Ellen L. Lutz, "Human Rights in Mexico: Cause for Continuing Concern," *Current History* (Feb. 1993): 78–82.

18. Lorenzo Meyer, "El lomite neoliberal," *Nexos* 163 (July 1991): 34.

19. U.S. lack of concern with Mexico's protracted transition to democracy fit with a historic pattern, interrupted only by a brief interlude in the mid-1980s, during the Reagan period. From the Reagan perspective, the perceived weakness of the Mexican government provided an opportunity to encourage its definitive transformation, by encouraging a bipartisan political arrangement. By supporting polit-

ical reform that favored the right-wing PAN, Washington could serve its own interests, for the PAN's views coincided with the Reagan line regarding economic policy and Central America. See Chabat, "Mexico's Foreign Policy," 10.

20. Ibid., 9.

21. Ibid., 7–9.

22. Cited in "Economic and Political Change in Mexico: In Sequence or out of Sync?" *North South Focus on Mexico,* June 1992.

23. Interview by author with Fernando Solana, former minister of foreign affairs, Mexico City, 4 Dec. 1993.

24. "Quinto Informe Presidencial," *La Jornada,* 2 Nov. 1993.

25. Chabat, "Mexico's Foreign Policy," 12.

26. Ibid., 11–12.

27. Jorge Chabat, "Mexico: So Close to the United States, So Far from Latin America," *Current History* (Feb. 1993): 55–58.

28. Mexico's reluctance to support a multilateral stance regarding the promotion and protection of democracy in Latin America came into clear contradiction with its diplomatic activism south of the Suchiate. Under Salínas, Mexico developed an active political leadership in the region. Mexico sponsored new Latin American forums (the Group of Three and the Iberoamerican Summit), subregional initiatives, bilateral free trade zones, and bilateral cooperation agreements.

29. The term "modernizing authoritarian" was coined by historian Lorenzo Meyer.

30. For an analysis of the roots of the Chiapas uprising, see Luis Hernández Navarro, "La nueva guerra maya," *Enfoque,* 9 Jan. 1994.

31. Julio Moguel, "Salinas' Failed War on Poverty," *NACLA Report of the Americas* (July 1994): 38–41.

32. See Sikkink, "Human Rights."

33. Sikkink defines issue networks as a set of organizations bound by shared values and dense exchanges of information and services working across borders. See ibid. The diverse entities that make up the international human rights network include parts of international organizations at both the international and regional levels (international human rights NGOs, domestic human rights NGOs, and private foundations).

34. Margaret Keck and Kathryn Sikkink, "International Issue Networks in the Environment and Human Rights," paper prepared for the Seventeenth International Congress of the Latin American Studies Association, 24–27, Los Angeles, Sept. 1992.

35. See David Ronfeldt and Cathryn L. Thorup, "North America in the Era of Citizen Networks: State, Society, and Security," paper prepared for RAND and the Ford Foundation, Aug. 1993.

36. The potential impact of cross-border coalitions on U.S.-Mexico relations is discussed in Cathryn Thorup, "La democratización y la agenda bilateral," *Nexos* 162, June 1991. Thorup defines "cross-border coalitions" as informal and formal joint activities by nongovernmental groups across national boundaries. See also Cathryn L. Thorup, "The Politics of Free Trade and the Dynamics of Cross-Border Coalitions in U.S.-Mexican Relations," *Columbia Journal of World Business* 26 (1991).

37. Sikkink, "Human Rights."

38. Ibid., 431.

39. Interview by author with Sergio Aguayo, Mexico City, 13 Oct. 1993.

40. Sikkink, "Human Rights," 431–32.

41. The idea of an independent electoral observation was conceived by the Mexican Human Rights Academy, whose president had participated with the Carter team in the observation of the Haitian elections in 1990. The academy's report on elections in San Luis Potosí was published in *La Jornada,* Aug. 1991.

42. Interview by author with MariClaire Acosta, Mexico City, 4 Oct. 1993.

43. Sikkink and Keck, "International Issue Networks," 9.

44. For an analysis of the emergence of incipient forms of citizenship, see Jonathan Fox, "The Difficult Transition from Clientelism to Citizenship: Lessons from Mexico," *World Politics* (spring 1994).

45. Brysk, "From Above and Below," 264.

46. Interview by author with Adolfo Aguilar Zínser, spokesman for the Cuauhtémoc Cárdenas campaign, Mexico City, 4 Oct. 1993.

47. See "The Recent Presidential Elections in Mexico," transcript of remarks by Sergio Aguayo, cofounder of the Civic Alliance, at the National Endowment for Democracy breakfast discussion, Washington, D.C., 7 Oct. 1994.

48. Civic Alliance/Observation '94, "The Quality of the Election Day Process, August 21, 1994," 19 Sept. 1994.

49. For an analysis of the effects of transnational linkage on the power of domestic organizations, see Brysk, "From Above and Below," 262.

50. Ibid., 262–63.

51. Carter Center, "Electoral Reform in Mexico, Final Report," Emory Univ., Atlanta, Georgia, Nov. 1993.

52. Sallie Hughes, "Carter Center Credits Salinas with Reforms, but More Are Needed," *El Financiero International,* 25–31 Oct. 1993.

53. Until 1992 most NED grants were channeled to Mexican business organizations that promoted free market economics and advocated economic liberalization. NED also sponsored grants to train journalists in free market economics and to help them place their economic policy op-ed pieces in Mexican newspapers. See "NED in Mexico: Issues and Challenges," *NED Backgrounder* 2 (1993).

54. The organizations receiving NED grants for their election-related activities since 1982 are the Council for Democracy (Consejo para la Democracia), the Convergence of Civic Organizations for Democracy (Convergencia de Organizaciones Civiles por la Democracia), and the Civic Front of San Luis Potosí (Frente Cívico Potosino); ibid., 3.

55. Between 1985 and 1992, NED alotted $1,227,897 to programs in Mexico, a minor sum compared to the $12,600,438 doled out to the Nicaraguan opposition in 1990 alone. See Lilia Bermúdez and Mauricio Dardin, "El COFIPE, la NED, y el financiamiento externo," *Perfil de la Jornada,* 22 Nov. 1993.

56. *The 1994 Mexican Election: A Question of Credibility* (Washington D.C.: Washington Office on Latin America and Academia Mexicana de Derechos Humanos, 1994).

57. Alison Brysk, *The Politics of Human Rights in Argentina: Protest, Change, and Democratization* (Stanford: Stanford Univ. Press, 1995); and Brysk, "From Above and Below," 273–80.

58. Ibid.

59. Lutz, "Human Rights in Mexico."

60. Sikkink, "Human Rights."

61. See "The Missing Reform in Mexico," *New York Times,* 26 Aug. 1991; and "Salinas' Opportunity," *Wall Street Journal,* 29 Aug. 1991.

62. Interview by author with Tim Golden, Mexico Bureau chief, New York Times, Mexico City, 6 Oct. 1993.

63. Interview by author with historian and political columnist Lorenzo Meyer, Mexico City, 30 Sept. 1993.

64. Interview by author with political columnist Raymundo Riva Palacio, Mexico City, 5 Oct. 1993.

65. "Salinas al Wall Street Journal: permitire el PRI verificación externa del padrón electoral," *La Jornada,* 23 Nov. 1993.

66. See, for example, Anne Marie Mergier, "Democracia, justicia y derechos humanos, reclama a México el parlamento europeo," *Proceso,* 31 Jan. 1994; "The Other Mexico," *New York Times,* 7 Jan. 1994; Carlos Puig, "Despliegue a la pobreza de Chiapas y a los dramas de la guerra, en prensa, radio y television de los Estados Unidos," *Proceso,* 10 Jan. 1994; "The Clash in Mexico," *Economist,* 22–28 Jan. 1994.

67. See, for example, "Segundo Comunicado de Organizaciones Sociales Sobre el Conflicto en Chiapas," which was signed by fifteen organizations, including the Mexican Academy for Human Rights, the Convergence of Civic Organizations for Democracy, and the Mexican Commission for Defense and Promotion of Human Rights.

68. "Comunicado del Comité Clandestino Revolucionario," 4.

69. Jared Kotler, "The Clinton Administration and the Mexican Election," Washington Office on Latin America, Washington, D.C., Nov. 1994, 2.

70. According to Clinton administration figures, more than 1.4 million in U.S. government funds were provided for "election-related" activities in fiscal year 1994. See ibid., 7.

71. The 1994 electoral reforms established for the first time the right of Mexican citizens to participate as election observers and allowed the presence of foreign nationals as "invited foreign visitors." Of these visitors, 775 traveled to Mexico to observe the 1994 presidential election.

72. Lowenthal, "United States and Latin American Democracy."

73. Sikkink, "Human Rights," 437.

74. As the Washington Office on Latin America has argued, the amount of public funding these organizations provided (approximately $1.42 million in 1994) was relatively small compared to U.S. contributions to other electoral processes. Also, the connections between funding decisions and U.S. policy were almost nonexistent. Ties between the NED and Mexican observer groups were established years ago and without any explicit approval from Congress or the executive. See WOLA, *1994 Mexican Election,* 34.

75. NED, *Backgrounder,* 5.

76. Jack Donnelly, "Human Rights, Humanitarian Intervention, and American Foreign Policy," *Journal of International Affairs* 37 (1983): 311–28.

77. I borrow this point from Ronfeldt and Thorup, "North America in the Era of Citizen Networks."

78. According to Jeff Puryear, these strategies had a significant impact on the

Chilean transition. See his "Building Democracy: Foreign Donors and Chile," paper prepared for the conference, Crossing National Borders: Invasion or Involvement? New York, 6 Dec. 1991.

79. For a comparative analysis of the potential democratizing role of the media, see Thomas E. Skidmore, ed., *Television, Politics, and the Transition to Democracy in Latin America* (Baltimore: Johns Hopkins Univ. Press, 1993). For a discussion of the role of the media in Mexico's political transition, see Alonso Lujambio, "Elites politícas y cultura política: Democratización vía televisiva," *Enfoque,* 12 Dec. 1993; and Raymundo Riva Palacio, "The Media and Democracy," *El Financiero International,* 1–7 Nov. 1993.

80. The political impact of globalization is discussed in David Held, "Democracy and Globalization," *Alternatives* 16 (1991): 201–8.

Notes on Contributors

DOMINGO E. ACEVEDO is principal legal advisor to the Inter-American Commission on Human Rights and adjunct professor of law at the Washington College of Law, American University. He is a former member of the Executive Council of the American Society of International Law and is currently a member of the Advisory Board of *International Legal Materials*. He is also a member of the Advisory Board of the *American University Journal of International Law and Policy*.

Dr. Acevedo is the author of many articles on specific issues in international law, published in books and specialized journals. He received his Ph.D. in international law from the University of Cambridge.

LARRY DIAMOND is a senior research fellow at the Hoover Institution, Stanford University; coeditor of the *Journal of Democracy;* and codirector of the National Endowment for Democracy's International Forum for Democratic Studies. He is coeditor with Juan J. Linz and Seymour Martin Lipset of the four-volume series *Democracy in Developing Countries*, and, with Marc F. Plattner, of *The Global Resurgence of Democracy* and *Nationalism, Ethnic Conflict, and Democracy*. He has written extensively on problems of democratic development and international policies to promote democracy in Africa and throughout the developing world. He is now completing a collection of his essays entitled *Developing Democracy*.

JORGE I. DOMÍNGUEZ is a founding member and senior fellow at the Inter-American Dialogue and Frank G. Thomson Professor of Government at Harvard University. A past president of the Latin American Studies Association and member of the Council on Foreign Relations, he is a member of the editorial boards of *Mexican Studies, Cuban Studies, Political Science Quarterly,* and the *Journal of Inter-American Studies and World Affairs*. Dr. Dominguez is author, editor, and coauthor of more than a dozen books, including *Essays on Mexico, Central and South America: Scholarly Debates from the 1950s to the 1990s* (seven volumes, 1994); *Democracy in the Caribbean* (1993); *To Make a World Safe for Revolution: Cuba's Foreign Policy* (1989); and *Mexico's Political Economy: Challenges at Home and Abroad* (1982).

DENISE DRESSER is professor of political science at the Autonomous Technological Institute of Mexico (ITAM). She has been visiting senior fellow at the Inter-American Dialogue and has consulted for the United Nations Development Program and the United Nations Economic Commission on Latin America and the Caribbean. Dr. Dresser has done postdoctoral work at the Center for U.S.-Mexican Studies, University of California—San Diego, and at the Center of International Studies, University of Southern California. Her recent publications include "Five

Scenarios for Mexico," *Journal of Democracy* (July 1994); "Embellishment, Empowerment, or Euthanasia of the PRI? Neoliberalism and Party Reform in Mexico," in K. Middlebrook, J. Molinar, and M. Cook, eds., *The Politics of Economic Restructuring in Mexico* (forthcoming); and *Neopopulist Solutions to Neoliberal Problems: Mexico's National Solidarity Program* (1991). She is on the advisory board of *Este País*. Dr. Dresser received her Ph.D. from Princeton University.

STEPHANIE J. EGLINTON recently received a master's degree from the Terry Sanford Institute of Public Policy at Duke University and is now serving as a Jacob K. Javits Fellow in the U.S. Senate. As a research assistant at the Overseas Development Council from 1991 to 1993, she coauthored, with Joan Nelson, *Encouraging Democracy: What Role for Conditioned Aid?* (1992) and *Global Goals, Contentious Means: Issues of Multiple Conditionality* (1993). Ms. Eglinton, who holds a degree in international relations from Tufts University, has worked for the U.S. House of Representative and has traveled and studied in Latin America.

PATRICIA WEISS FAGEN is research director of the Challenge of Rebuilding War-Torn Societies, a project of the United Nations Research Institute for Social Development and the Graduate Institute of International Studies, in Geneva. She is on leave from the United Nations High Commissioner for Refugees, where her most recent post was chief of mission in El Salvador. Dr. Weiss Fagen has been a visiting scholar at the School for International Service of the American University, professor of history at San Jose State University, senior research associate at the Refugee Policy Group, and consultant to the Center for International Policy and the Inter-American Commission for Human Rights of the OAS. She served on the Executive Committee of the Latin American Studies Association and on the Executive Committee and Board of Directors of Amnesty International, USA, where she was vice chair of the board in 1985. Dr. Weiss Fagen's publications include *Fear at the Edge: State Terror and Resistance in Latin America* (coeditor and author, 1992); *Central Americans in Mexico and the United States* (with Sergio Aguayo, 1989); *Exiles and Citizens, Spanish Republicans in Mexico* (1973); and *Chilean Universities: Problems of Autonomy and Dependence* (1973).

TOM FARER is professor, Grazier Fellow, and director of the Joint Degree Program in Law and International Relations at the American University in Washington, D.C., former president of the Inter-American Commission on Human Rights of the Organization of American States, and former president of the University of New Mexico. He has taught law at Columbia, Rutgers, MIT, Harvard, and Tulane; and international relations and American foreign policy at Princeton and Johns Hopkins; he has participated in the Salzburg Seminars as a member of their faculty. He has been a senior fellow of the Carnegie Endowment and the Council on Foreign Relations and special assistant to the general counsel of the Department of Defense and to the assistant secretary of state for inter-American affairs. He is chair of the United States–Azerbaijan Council and serves on the boards of Americas Watch, the International League for Human Rights, and the International Human Rights Law Group.

Tom Farer is author and editor of ten books and monographs on international law and international relations. His numerous articles have appeared in such journals as *Foreign Affairs, Foreign Policy,* the *New York Review of Books,* the *London Review of Books,* and the *Law Review* of both Harvard and Columbia; his shorter pieces have appeared in the *New York Times,* the *Washington Post,* the *Los Angeles Times,* and *Newsweek.*

DAVID P. FORSYTHE is professor and chair of the Department of Political Science at the University of Nebraska, Lincoln. He was a visiting professor at the Graduate Institute of International Studies in Geneva, Switzerland, and has held postdoctoral fellowships at Princeton and Yale. He is a vice president of the International Studies Association. Among his recent books are *The United Nations and Changing World Politics* (coauthor, 1994); *Human Rights in the New Europe* (editor, 1994); and *Human Rights and Peace* (1993). Recent articles have appeared in *Political Studies, Global Governance, Ethics and International Affairs,* and *Journal of Peace Research.*

ALICIA FROHMANN is Research Professor at the Latin American Faculty for the Social Sciences (FLACSO—Chile). She is a historian and has done extensive research on inter-American political relations and economic integration. She is editor of FLACSO's international studies publications *Cono Sur,* has taught political science at the University of Chile, and has served as vice president of the Chilean Association for Political Science. Her book *Puentes sobre la Turbulencia,* about the multilateral initiatives of the Contadora and the Rio Group, was published in 1990. She has also written extensively about regional, subregional, and hemispheric trade liberalization. Her most recent writings include *U.S.-Chile Free Trade* (with A. Butelmann); *Labor and the U.S.-Chile FTA; Chile: External Actors in the Transition to Democracy;* and *The Multilateral Diplomacy of the Rio Group.*

CLAUDIO GROSSMAN is professor and dean of graduate studies at the Washington College of Law, the American University in Washington, D.C. Currently an R. Geraldson Scholar for International and Humanitarian Law, Dr. Grossman prior to his appointment in the United States in 1993 taught in The Netherlands and Chile. He was elected to serve as a member of the Inter-American Commission on Human Rights by the General Assembly of the OAS in 1994. Dr. Grossman is also a Board Member of the Permanent Council of the Inter-American Institute, is General Rapporteur of the Inter-American Bar Association and has served as observer, adviser, and rapporteur on numerous international legal and human rights missions. His most recent publications include *Manual de derecho internacional público* (coauthor, 1994); "El régimen hemisférico sobre situaciones de emergencia," in *Estudios Básicos de Derechos Humanos* I (1994); "Inter-American System and Asylum," in *American University Journal of International Law and Policy* (1994); and "Disappearences in Honduras: The Need for Direct Victim Representation in Human Rights Litigation," in *Hastings International and Comparative Law Review* (1992). Dr. Grossman received his doctorate in the science of law from the University of Amsterdam in 1990.

ANITA ISAACS is associate professor of political science at Haverford College in Pennsylvania and previously taught at Oxford University and New York University. She has served as program officer for the Ford Foundation and as a consultant to the

Canadian International Development Research Centre (IDRC). Her publications include *The Politics of Military Rule and Transition in Ecuador* (1993); "Ecuador," in *Oxford Companion to World Politics* (1993); and "Problems of Democratic Consolidation in Eduador," *Bulletin of Latin American Research* (1991). Dr. Isaacs holds a Ph.D. in politics from Oxford University.

ANTHONY P. MAINGOT is a professor of sociology at Florida International University, Miami, and has held positions at Yale University and the University of the West Indies, Trinidad. Born in Trinidad, Dr. Maingot was a member of the Constitutional Reform Commission of Trinidad, was President of the Caribbean Studies Association, and has held one-year visiting appointments at the Institute of Developing Economies, Tokyo, Japan, and the RAND Corporation, Santa Monica, California. His most recent books include *Small Country Development and International Labor Flows: Experiences in the Caribbean* (1991); and *The United States and the Caribbean: Challenges of an Asymmetrical Relationship* (1994). He is coauthor of *A Short History of the West Indies* (now in a fourth edition) and founding editor of *Hemisphere,* a magazine of Latin American and Caribbean Studies.

JOAN M. NELSON is a senior associate of the Overseas Development Council and consults for the World Bank, AID, and the IMF. Her work at ODC during the past several years has focused on the politics of economic stabilization and adjustment; on interactions between market-oriented economic reforms and democratization in Eastern Europe and Latin America; and on the uses and limits of conditioned aid as a means to promote noneconomic as well as economic reforms. Dr. Nelson has taught at MIT, the Johns Hopkins School of Advanced International Studies, and the Woodrow Wilson School at Princeton. Among her publications are *Aid, Influence, and Foreign Policy* (1968); *No Easy Choice: Political Participation in Developing Countries* (with Sam Huntington, 1976); *Access to Power: Politics and the Urban Poor* (1979); *Economic Crisis and Policy Choice* (editor and contributor, 1990); *Encouraging Democracy: What Role for Conditioned Aid?* (1992); and *Intricate Links: Democratization and Market Reforms in Latin America and Eastern Europe* (editor and contributor, 1994).

DAVID SCOTT PALMER is professor of international relations and political science at Boston University and founding director of its Latin American Studies Program. Formerly he served as chair of Latin American and Caribbean Studies and associate dean for programs at the State Department's Foreign Service Institute, where he received the department's Meritorious Honor Award. A past president of the Inter-American Council of Washington, D.C., and of the New England Council on Latin American Studies, Dr. Palmer has taught at several colleges and universities, including the University of Huamanga (Ayacucho) and the Catholic University (Lima), in Peru, and in the United States at Bowdoin, the School of Advanced International Studies of Johns Hopkins, Princeton, George Washington, and Georgetown. His published work includes studies of authoritarianism and democracy in Latin America, U.S.–Latin American relations, and Peruvian politics, of which his most recent book (as editor and contributor) is *Shining Path of Peru* (1992, revised and updated second edition, 1994).

KAREN L. REMMER is professor of political science at the University of New Mexico and associate editor of the *Latin American Research Review*. Her publications include two books, *Military Rule in Latin America* (1989), and *Party Competition and Public Policy* (1984), as well as a series of scholarly articles on Latin American politics. Dr. Remmer's current research focuses on the political economy of stabilization and adjustment in Latin America. Her publications on this topic include two recent articles in the *American Political Science Review:* "The Political Economy of Elections in Latin America, 1980–1991," and "Economic Crisis and Elections in Latin America, 1982–1990."

KATHRYN A. SIKKINK is associate professor of political science at the University of Minnesota. She received her doctorate from Columbia University. Her published works include *Ideas and Institutions: Developmentalist Policy Making in Brazil and Argentina* (1991); "Human Rights, Principled Issue Networks, and Sovereignty in Latin America," in *International Organization* (1993); "The Origins and Continuity of Human Rights Policies in the United States and Western Europe," in *Ideas and Foreign Policy,* edited by Judith Goldstein and Robert Keohane (1993); and "U.S. Policy and Human Rights in Argentina and Guatemala, 1973–1980," in *Double-Edged Diplomacy: International Bargaining and Domestic Politics*, edited by Peter Evans and others (1993).

FERNANDO R. TESÓN is visiting professor of law at Cornell University School of Law in Ithaca, New York, and professor of law at Arizona State University. He has been a visiting professor at the University of California; Hastings College of Law, San Francisco; University College, London; Indiana University; and the University of San Diego; and associate professor of international law at the University of Buenos Aires and the University of La Plata, Argentina. As a career diplomat in the Argentine Foreign Service, Dr. Tesón served as a member of the Argentine delegation to the Malvinas (Falkland) negotiations and as second secretary of the Argentine Embassy in Brussels. He received his Doctor of Juridical Science degree from Northwestern University School of Law in Chicago. Dr. Tesón's publications include *Humanitarian Intervention: An Inquiry into Law and Morality* (1988); "The Kantian Theory of International Law," *Columbia Law Review* (1992); and "International Obligation and the Theory of Hypothetical Consent," *Yale Journal of International Law* (1990).

Index

Bazin, Marc, 142, 201
Belaúnde Terry, Fernando, 265, 266, 269, 272
Belizaire, Dejean, 203
Bolivia, 61, 258; economic reform in, 95–96, 103; external actors and, 94, 101, 172; income distribution in, 99; party system in, 59, 80
Bosnia, 114, 213
Boutros-Ghali, Boutros, 114, 121
Brazil: amnesty in, 71, 91; and Central America, 216; democracy in, 62, 68–70, 72, 73, 74, 76, 77, 83, 85; economic reform in, 94, 186; electoral system in, 86; and Haiti, 128; human rights in, 72, 73, 155, 159–60; income distribution in, 99; media in, 93; party system in, 59, 77, 80, 82, 86
Büchi, Hernán, 243, 244
Bush, George: and Chile, 253, 254; and Cuba, 311–12; and El Salvador, 118, 121; and Haiti, 144; and Mexico, 320, 321; and Nicaragua, 124, 125; and Panama, 139
business: in Chile and the transition, 242, 249, 254; in Guatemala, 20, 127; and human rights lobbies in the U.S., 167; in Latin America, and effectiveness of external pressure, 22, 290–91; U.S., and Haiti, 191–92, 369n41; U.S., and Unidad Popular government in Chile, 238

Caldera, Rafael, 66
Calderón Sol, Armando, 122
Camacho, Manuel, 334
Cambio, 90, 265, 266
Cambodia, 117, 213–14, 223
Canada, 23–24, 103, 158, 175, 227
Caputo, Dante, 128, 144
Cárdenas, Cuauhtémoc, 333
Cardoso, Fernando Henrique, 69
Caribbean, 5, 16, 17, 61, 73, 304
Caribbean Basin Initiative, 20
Carpio, Ramiro de León, 20–21, 127, 165
Carpizo, Jorge, 334
Carter, Jimmy: and Haiti, 48, 129, 132; and Nicaragua, 12, 125
Carter administration, 137, 155, 250–51
Carter Center, 103, 329–30
Castro, Fidel, 310–11, 314
Castro, Raúl, 308

Catholic Church: in Chile, 159, 254–55; in Guatemala, 126, 127
Cedras, General Raoul, 132
Center for Legal and Social Studies (CELS, Argentina), 152
Central American peace initiatives, 12, 119, 123–24, 185, 216–17, 260–61, 279. See also names of specific initiatives
Cerezo, Vinicio, 21, 164
Chamorro, Violeta, 76, 124, 125
Chiapas, 317, 323, 324–25, 333–35
Chile: amnesty, 71, 91, 246–47; business in, 242, 249, 254; Catholic Church in, 159, 254–55; constitutional reform in, 243–44, 245–46; decentralization in, 84, 94, 245; democracy in, 70–71, 77, 239–41, 263, 291–92; economic reform in, 95, 96, 103; effectiveness of external actors reviewed, 290; electoral system in, 244–45; external actors and the Aylwin government, 253–55; external actors and the transition to democracy, in, 248–53, 278; external actors and the UP government in, 238, 240–41; human rights NGOs under Pinochet, 154, 155, 158, 161, 162; human rights under democracy, 159, 246–47, 254; income distribution in, 99; internationalization of the economy, 242, 249–50, 254; judicial reform in, 246–47; military in, 70–71, 87, 108, 243, 247–48, 253–54; 1988 plebiscite, 242, 252–53, 256, 278; parties in, 59, 77, 79, 81, 252, 254; presidentialism in, 85; think tanks in, 255, 256; U.S. policy towards the dictatorship, 250–52
China, 16, 166
Christian Democratic party (Chile), 239, 240, 243, 251
Christopher, Warren, 312
Church-based rights groups, 155, 157, 159, 167
CIREFCA (conference on Central American refugees), 217, 218, 233–34
Civic Alliance (Mexico), 329, 330, 336
civil society, 21–22, 91–94, 183. See also non-governmental organizations
Clinton, Bill: and Chile, 254; and Cuba, 311, 312; democracy and human rights, 25, 170; and Haiti, 16, 48,

416

Library of Congress Cataloging-in-Publication Data

Beyond sovereignty : collectively defending democracy in the
Americas / Tom Farer, editor.
    p.   cm. — (An Inter-American Dialogue book)
Includes bibliographical references and index.
ISBN 0-8018-5165-3 (hardcover : alk. paper).
— ISBN 0-8018-5166-1 (pbk. : alk. paper)
1. Sovereignty.   2. Democracy.   3. Latin America—Politics and
government.   4. International agencies—Latin America.   I. Farer,
Tom J.   II. Series.
JX4041.B487   1996
320.98′09′049—dc20   95-23782